RESPECTABLE RADICALS

A History of the National Council of Women of Australia 1896–2006

MARIAN QUARTLY AND JUDITH SMART

Published by Monash University Publishing
in conjunction with the National Council of Women of Australia
2015

© Copyright 2015 Marian Quartly and Judith Smart
All rights reserved. Apart from any uses permitted by Australia's Copyright Act 1968, no part of this book may be reproduced by any process without prior written permission from the copyright owners. Inquiries should be directed to Monash University Publishing.
Published by Monash University Publishing in conjunction with the National Council of Women of Australia

Monash University Publishing
Matheson Library and Information Services Building
40 Exhibition Walk
Monash University
Clayton, Victoria 3800, Australia
www.publishing.monash.edu

Monash University Publishing brings to the world publications which advance the best traditions of humane and enlightened thought.

Monash University Publishing titles pass through a rigorous process of independent peer review.

www.publishing.monash.edu/books/rr-9781922235947.html

Design: Les Thomas

Front cover image: Members of the NCWA with Dame Maria Ogilvie Gordon in Melbourne in January 1938. From the Brookes collection, National Library of Australia. Back cover image: NCWA conference delegates 1988. From the NCWA collection.

National Library of Australia Cataloguing-in-Publication entry:	
Creator:	Quartly, Marian, author.
Title:	Respectable radicals : a history of the National Council of Women of Australia 1896 - 2006 / Marian Quartly, Judith Smart.
ISBN:	9781922235947 (paperback)
Series:	Australian history.
Subjects:	National Council of Women of Australia--History. Feminism--Australia--History. Women--Australia--Social conditions. Australia--Social conditions--20th century
Other Creators/Contributors:	Smart, Judith, 1950- author.
Dewey number:	305.420994

Printed in Australia by Griffin Press an Accredited ISO AS/NZS 14001:2004 Environmental Management System printer.

The paper this book is printed on is certified against the Forest Stewardship Council ® Standards. Griffin Press holds FSC chain of custody certification SGS-COC-005088. FSC promotes environmentally responsible, socially beneficial and economically viable management of the world's forests.

CONTENTS

About the Authors vii
Foreword viii
Acknowledgements x
Disclaimer xi
List of Abbreviations xii

INTRODUCTION   1

PART ONE: Creating Common Cause 1896–1931   23
  1. Towards National Organisation 25
  2. Home and Family Enter the Body Politic 53
  3. A Growing Commitment to Rights and Equality 90
  4. Developing International Identity 106

PART TWO: NCWA Takes Shape 1931–1950   129
  5. Organisational Challenges and Achievements 132
  6. Home and Society 151
  7. Rights, Equality and International Affairs 193

PART THREE: The Golden Years 1950–1970   245
  8. Organisational Developments 251
  9. Women, Home and Family 267
  10. Women in the Workforce 283
  11. Australia and the World 309

PART FOUR: Remaking the National Councils 1970–2006   341
  12. The Years of Rapid Change 1970–1975 349
  13. A Decade for Women? 1976–1985 379
  14. The New Face of the National Council 1986–2006 419

Afterword 470
Appendix: Donors to this Project 472
Select Bibliography 474
Index 489

*This book is dedicated to all members
of the National Council of Women of Australia,
past, present and future.*

ABOUT THE AUTHORS

Marian Quartly holds the position of Professor Emerita at Monash University's School of Philosophical, Historical and International Studies. Her long-term research concern is the history of family in late twentieth-century Australia. She has recently completed two large co-operative projects: a history of Australian adoption, and a history of the National Council of Women of Australia.

Judith Smart is Principal Fellow at the University of Melbourne and Adjunct Professor at RMIT University. She has published on Australian women's organisations in the first half of the twentieth century, as well as on women and political protest, women and religion, and the social history of the home front during World War I. She is co-editor, with Shurlee Swain, of *The Encyclopedia of Women and Leadership in Twentieth-Century Australia*, a reference tool available online at http://www.womenaustralia.info/leaders/index.htm, and has co-authored, with Marian Quartly and Jan Hipgrave, *Stirrers with Style: Presidents of the National Council of Women of Australia and its Predecessors*, available online at https://web.esrc.unimelb.edu.au/AWAPt/exhib/ncwa/index.html.

FOREWORD

by Annette M Lourigan JP
Vice President NCW Queensland

When I first received the web link to *Stirrers with Style*, my head went off in several directions. Thinking there must be a spoon exhibition on, or cocktail stirrers, I spent a little time reminiscing over Fluffy Ducks and Blue Lagoons. I was wrong on both counts. The stirrers on the web were the Presidents of NCWA and this book *Respectable Radicals* tells their story.

I did not know that, in amongst the pages, I would find moments that personally affected me as I started to see that these stirrers, these respectable radicals, had been hugely influential in my own life, women like my own mother, who have allowed myself and many others to stand on their shoulders and walk on the many paths they illuminated for us.

In amongst the pages one finds passionate agitators and advocates who fought for the rights of women and children who they more than likely would never meet. The accounts of these poised and strong women are not just the history of NCWA, they are the history of Australia. These women changed the course of politics, altered the attitudes of many and are part of the reason that we live in one of the best countries of the world. They did not just ensure that women could work; they made sure that we could have careers. They were not just focused on ensuring that girls could go to school; they ensured that we could have an education. Without their dedication women would still be fighting for equal rights in divorce proceedings today. These women were not meek and they walked their talk, often under difficult and challenging conditions. They saw to the implementation of safe, nurturing child care. They gained longer shopping hours for us and a grandparents' carer benefit. Traditionally they came from conservative backgrounds,

FOREWORD

though it did not stop them from firmly debating about the need for women in government at all levels, local, state and federal.

It is an emotional read. It is hard not to get caught up in their activism, their strength and their passion. So you are all respectable radicals and stirrers with style. All of you have confronted the thoughts of others, you have all stood up for what you believe and have made this country and the world a better place. If we were a collection of spoons, some of us would be silver, some tarnished, some plastic and there are a couple of cocktail sticks in the mix, but all collected together you can and have achieved real results in this country. We thank you.

ACKNOWLEDGEMENTS

Respectable Radicals would not exist without the people and organisations named below. At the 2003 National Triennial Meeting of the National Council of Women of Australia in Perth, Western Australia, the motion was put by Janet Galley OAM of Victoria that, to mark the 75th anniversary of the national body, the history of the National Council of Women of Australia should be researched and published. In 2008 we received an Australian Research Council Linkage Grant (LP088371) auspiced by the University of Melbourne to carry out this project, in partnership with historians Judith Smart and Marian Quartly. We wish to thank our research assistant, Jan Hipgrave, and all the archives and libraries of Australia, both state and national, whose documents clarified our research. Our authors interviewed many past and present members of the National Council of Women across Australia, and we are grateful for their time, memories and hospitality. Our thanks also go to Nikki Henningham and Helen Morgan of the Australian Women's Archive Project at Melbourne University for their assistance in mounting the online exhibition *Stirrers with Style,* which showcases the lives of the presidents of NCWA. Sincere thanks to Nathan Hollier and his staff at Monash University Publishing for their advice and great patience. Most importantly of all, we wish to thank our generous donors, both large and small, who enabled us to achieve what at times seemed to be impossible. Your names are recorded with great gratitude as an appendix here, and this publication, with your help, is a tangible tribute to all the women of Australia.

The NCWA History Steering Committee: Adjunct Professor Judith Smart of RMIT University and University of Melbourne, Professor Emerita Marian Quartly of Monash University, Janet Galley OAM, Sylvia Gelman MBE AM, Leonie Christopherson AM DSJ (Chair).

DISCLAIMER

Our thanks to those who have given us permission to reproduce copyright material in this book. Every effort has been made to contact the copyright holders of text and photographs. The editors and publishers apologise in those cases where this has proved impossible.

LIST OF ABBREVIATIONS

AAUN	Australian Association of the United Nations
ABC	Australian Broadcasting Commission
ACT	Australian Capital Territory
ACTU	Australian Council of Trade Unions
ADAB	Australian Development Assistance Bureau
ADB	Australian Dictionary of Biography
AFUW	Australian Federation of University Women
AFWS	Australian Federation of Women's Societies
AFWV	Australian Federation of Women Voters
AIDS	Acquired Immune Deficiency Syndrome
ALC	Australian Group of the Liaison Committee of Women's International Organisations
ANCUN	Australian National Council of the United Nations
ANCW	Australian National Council of Women
ASIO	Australian Security and Intelligence Organisation
AWC	Australian Women's Coalition
AWCC	Australian Women's Co-operating Committee
AWNL	Australian Women's National League
AWR	Australian Women's Register
BA	Bachelor of Arts
CAPOW	Coalition of Participating Organisations of Women
CBE	Commander of the Order of the British Empire
CEDAW	Convention on the Elimination of All Forms of Discrimination Against Women
CIAC	Commonwealth Immigration Advisory Council
CPD	Commonwealth Parliamentary Debates
CSW	Commission on the Status of Women
CTI	Coalition (Tasmania) Inc.
CWA	Country Women's Association
CYSS	Community Youth Support Scheme
ECAFE	Economic Commission for Asia and the Far East
ECOSOC	UN Economic and Social Council
ESCAP	Economic and Social Commission for Asia and the Pacific

LIST OF ABBREVIATIONS

FCNCWA	Federal Council National Councils of Women of Australia
IAW	International Alliance of Women
ICW	International Council of Women
ICW-CIF	International Council of Women—Conseil International des Femmes
IFRWH	International Federation for Research in Women's History
ILC	Liaison Committee of Women's International Organisations
ILO	International Labour Organization
IWSA	International Woman Suffrage Alliance
IWY	International Women's Year
IYF	International Year of Family
KOWANI	Kongres Wanita Indonesia
LINC	Learning and Information Network Centre Tasmania
LNU	League of Nations Union
MA	Master of Arts
MBE	Member of the Order of the British Empire
MLC	Methodist Ladies' College
NAA	National Archives of Australia
NAC IWY	National Advisory Committee for International Women's Year
NATWAC	National Women's Advisory Council
NCW	National Council of Women
NCWA	National Council of Women of Australia
NCWACT	National Council of Women of Australian Capital Territory
NCWL	National Council of Women Launceston
NCWNSW	National Council of Women of New South Wales
NCWNT	National Council of Women of Northern Territory
NCWQ	National Council of Women of Queensland
NCWSA	National Council of Women of South Australia
NCWT	National Council of Women Tasmania
NCWV	National Council of Women of Victoria
NCWWA	National Council of Women of Western Australia
NGO	Non-government Organisation
NHMRC	National Health and Medical Research Council
NLA	National Library of Australia
NRC	National Referendum Council
NWAC	National Women's Advisory Council

NWCC	National Women's Consultative Council
OBE	Order of the British Empire
OSW	Office of the Status of Women
PLC	Presbyterian Ladies' College
PPA	Past Pupils' Association
PNG	Papua New Guinea
RMIT	Royal Melbourne Institute of Technology
SIP	Sisterhood of International Peace
SLNSW	State Library New South Wales
SLQ	State Library Queensland
SLSA	State Library South Australia
SLV	State Library Victoria
SLWA	State Library Western Australia
SPELD	Dyslexia and Specific Learning Difficulties Association
SWC	Status of Women Commission
TAFE	Technical and Further Education
TAHO	Tasmanian Archive and Heritage Office
UAW	Union of Australian Women
UNAA	United Nations Association of Australia
UNDP	United Nations Development Program
UNESCO	United Nations Educational, Scientific and Cultural Organisation
UN	United Nations
USL	Universal Service League
VSCC	Victorian Society for Crippled Children
VWF	Victorian Women's Federation
VWGA	Victorian Women Graduates Association
WCTU	Woman's Christian Temperance Union
WEB	Women's Employment Board
WEL	Women's Electoral Lobby
WIDF	Women's International Democratic Federation
WILPF	Women's International League for Peace and Freedom
WPA	Women's Political Association
WWWW	Women Who Want to be Women
YWCA	Young Women's Christian Association

INTRODUCTION

Margaret Windeyer was not yet thirty when she called together representatives of as many New South Wales women's organisations as she could identify. The resulting meeting, on 26 June 1896, was attended by more than two hundred women. On the stage with Windeyer in the Sydney Town Hall that day were all the main leaders of the suffrage and ladies' philanthropic societies of New South Wales (NSW).[1] This gathering marked the formation of the first National Council of Women (NCW) in Australia. From that time until the 1970s, NCWs were the principal means by which representative women in Australia could come together, exchange views, learn from each other and often speak publicly with one voice. Windeyer, under the influence of her mother, Lady Mary Windeyer, had become a committed suffragist early in her life, and was introduced to the council idea when, as a commissioner for NSW to the Chicago World Exhibition in 1893, she sought out leaders of American women's organisations and attended the landmark World's Congress of Representative Women, representing NSW on its advisory council. She was the only delegate from the Australian colonies, though South Australia's Catherine Spence was also in attendance.[2]

The broad council concept was the brainchild of two of these American women leaders, suffragist Susan B. Anthony and fellow activist May Wright Sewall. Six years earlier, in June 1887, Anthony

---

1   Numbers noted in minutes of the first council meeting. NCWNSW Council Minutes, 26 August 1896, Box MLK03009, MS3739, NCWNSW Papers, State Library of New South Wales (SLNSW).
2   Heather Radi, 'Windeyer, Margaret (1866–1939)', *Australian Dictionary of Biography* (*ADB*), http://adb.anu.edu.au/biography/windeyer-margaret-margy-1058; Susan Eade (Magarey), 'Spence, Catherine Helen (1825–1910)', *ADB*, http://adb.anu.edu.au/biography/spence-catherine-helen-4627; Anna Garlin Spencer, *The Council Idea: A Chronicle of its Prophets and a Tribute to May Wright Sewall: Architect of its Form and Builder of its Method of Work*, New Brunswick NJ, Heidingsfeld Press, 1930, pp. 29–30.

had issued an international call to 'all women of light and learning, to all associations of women in trades, professions and reforms, as well as to those advocating political rights',[3] to come together on 25 March 1888 at a conference hosted by the National Woman Suffrage Association in Washington DC to celebrate the fortieth anniversary of the Women's Rights Convention held at Seneca Falls in 1848. The ideal, to form an international women's movement that went beyond political rights and reflected all the interests of women engaged in public work, was summed up by Sewall as the 'Council Idea'. Because the council was conceived as an umbrella structure, existing women's groups of all kinds could gather under its canopy at national and international levels to discuss matters of common interest, to gather information and to learn from each other in order to promote peace and general wellbeing.[4] Thus the gathering in 1888 saw the birth of both the International Council of Women and the first National Council of Women, appropriately in the United States.

In the following years, Sewall elaborated on the 'Council Idea' as having five key objects: the opportunity for women from different branches of work and organisations to become acquainted; the growth of reciprocal sympathy through realisation that their different areas of work were convergent; the correlation of the spiritual imperatives underpinning their varied work; the exercise of this spiritual influence on public opinion in the interest of progress; and the cultivation of humanitarian, moral, social and political ideals rather than territorial identity as the basis of both nationalism and internationalism.[5] She chaired the committee of organisation of the 1893 congress, in which Margaret Windeyer participated, and at which speeches were given by over 300 women from 27 countries. The largest and most representative gathering of women yet held anywhere in the world, the congress also

---

3 Leila Rupp, *Worlds of Women: The Making of an International Women's Movement*, Princeton, Princeton University Press, 1997, p. 15.
4 Leen Van Molle and Eliane Gubin (eds), *Women Changing the World: A History of the International Council of Women*, Brussels, Éditions Racine, 2005, p. 16.
5 Spencer, *The Council Idea*, pp. 17–18.

INTRODUCTION

provided the forum for planning the structure and further development of ICW, which Sewall in her closing address envisaged as evolving into a 'permanent international parliament of women'.[6] In these ideals—what she termed 'new internationalism'—we can see both the beginnings of a feminist transnational sensibility and a vision of collaborative governance that distinguished this 'first and most successful of the international women's organizations' from the combative and competitive internationalism that dominated contemporary political discourse and relations between nations. Sewall envisaged the 'Council Idea' not only as a permanent forum 'where all the great questions that concern humanity shall be discussed from the woman's point of view' but also as a means of fostering, in historian Karen Offen's words, 'human harmony and spiritual one-ness that could mute class and ethnic boundaries'.[7]

The council movement, like feminism of all kinds, was a product of late nineteenth-century western modernity, and it similarly promoted education and scientific thought as instruments for breaking down difference and division worldwide—among women as well as between men and women. It was also part of a broader internationalist spirit that spread through the western world in an attempt to counter the strident nationalism of the era. We can see some parallels with ICW in the emergence of the Hague peace congresses, the Student Christian Movement, and the World's Woman's Christian Temperance Union, not to mention the Socialist International, around the same time. However, National Councils of Women, while undoubtedly part of this modernity, also emphasised traditional values associated with motherhood and the domestic sphere, though their maternalism was given a new scientific gloss and cast as a rationale for political engagement. The major early constituent women's organisations in Europe, America and other

---

6   Spencer, *The Council Idea*, pp. 23–34.
7   Karen Offen, 'Overcoming Hierarchies through Internationalism—The Council Idea: May Wright Sewall's Objectives for the International Council of Women (1888–1904)', paper presented at IFRWH/CISH Conference, Amsterdam, August 2010. The quotation from Sewall also comes from this paper.

western countries were predominantly philanthropic, premised on Christian conviction and the belief that women had a duty to bring their special qualities of compassion and nurture—their mother-love—into the public sphere where, as citizens, they would 'raise the tone of society and tend to a higher ideal of life'.[8] It was this selflessness, moralism and stress on the spiritual that women of most persuasions—radical feminists included—felt was the essence of their difference from men, and the source of their unitary and unique mission in society as women.[9] It is inseparable from the modernist impulse guiding the formation of ICW and the National Councils of Women it spawned in Australia, as elsewhere.

The two founding objectives of ICW dedicated the organisation to 'unity of thought, sympathy and purpose' among women 'of all classes, parties and creeds' and, importantly, to the 'the application of the Golden Rule to society, custom and law' in the interests of, as the preamble to the constitution put it, 'the highest good of the family and the State'. All the Australian councils included variations on these words in their own constitutional preambles. But ICW also recognised from the beginning that, if the first goal ('unity of thought, sympathy and purpose') was to be achieved, the limits of council control over affiliates must be defined and its political engagement circumscribed. Thus ICW included in its constitution a statement of policy, followed with only minor variations of wording by all affiliated councils. The version in the Victorian council's constitution agreed to in 1904 was:

> This Council is organised in the interest of no one propaganda, nor can it ally itself to any political or sectarian party, nor does it claim any power over its members except that of sympathy and

---

[8] *Court*, October 1894.
[9] Judith Smart, 'Modernity and Motherheartedness: Spirituality and Religious Meaning in Australian Women's Suffrage and Citizenship Movements, 1890s–1920s', in Ian Fletcher, L. Nym Mayhall and Philippa Levine (eds), *Women's Suffrage in the British Empire: Citizenship, Nation and Race*, New York, Routledge, 2000, pp. 51–67.

suggestion. Therefore no society willing to become affiliated with it shall render itself liable to be interfered with in respect to its complete organic unity, independence, or methods of work, beyond compliance with the terms of this constitution.[10]

This policy has remained central to the operations of the council movement,[11] But proscription of sectarian, ideological and party political advocacy by councils did not mean they were non-political. Insofar as they have engaged in lobbying governments and international bodies such as the Hague Peace Conferences, the League of Nations, the United Nations and the International Labour Organization, as well as intervening locally in royal commissions, committees of enquiry and court hearings, and working to change public opinion on a variety of issues, the councils have behaved in overtly political ways from the outset. They always justified such action as being in pursuit of the 'highest good of the family and the State' whose interests they regarded as indivisible. American historian Kathleen McCarthy argues that the work of organisations such as the National Councils of Women was politically significant because it created parallel structures for women's engagement in public work outside the spheres dominated by men; provided sources for recruitment, socialisation, training and advancement of women into public roles; and created sites in which women could reshape public policies and popular attitudes concerning gender, class, domesticity and race.[12]

---

10 Taken from NCWV Constitution, Article III—Policy, agreed to on 30 March 1904, NCWV Papers, State Library of Victoria (SLV) (classification pending). The version given by Ada Norris in *Champions of the Impossible: A History of the National Council of Women of Victoria, 1902–1977*, Melbourne, Hawthorn Press, 1978, p. 9, has some minor differences of wording.
11 For example, the NCWV constitution of March 2002, in Article 4, Policy: 'The Council is broadly based non party political and non sectarian, bringing together a wide range of community interests. Therefore, an organisation willing to become affiliated with Council shall remain to all intents and purposed autonomous beyond compliance with the terms of this Constitution'.
12 Kathleen D. McCarthy, 'Parallel Power Structures: Women and the Voluntary Sphere', in Kathleen D. McCarthy (ed.), *Lady Bountiful Revisited: Women, Philanthropy and Power*, New Brunswick and London, Rutgers University Press, 1990, pp. 1–31.

Ishbel Hamilton-Gordon, Marchioness of Aberdeen and Temair, and wife of the governor-general of Canada, was an enthusiastic supporter of the council idea and the moving force behind the Canadian NCW founded in May 1893, the second after the United States. A woman of liberal and reformist sympathies, she accepted the ICW presidency at the first formal meeting of the organisation on 19 May 1893 and started work on what became known as the first quinquennial conference, scheduled to take place in London five years later.[13] Aberdeen was a strategic choice, broadening the leadership beyond the United States and suffragist politics, and providing the organisation with a figurehead whose status and contacts extended throughout the British Empire. She thus provided the type of leadership needed for the council movement to expand beyond circles of existing feminist activism, her stated aim being 'in every country … to include in our councils the women of conservative views and those who are termed old-fashioned workers, as well as those who belong to the more progressive party'.[14] Two European vice-presidents were appointed (from Finland and France), while Sewall continued her educational and promotional activities as vice-president at large. As part of the preparation for the London conference, representative women from many countries were appointed honorary vice-presidents and encouraged to form national councils in the intervening period.[15] Margaret Windeyer was the first Australian to take up this challenge but, given that the Australian colonies had not yet federated, her formative work was confined to New South Wales.

---

13 The periodic ICW conferences were called 'quinquennials' because they took place every five years, though there were executive meetings in between. During the 1930s, full ICW conferences were held more frequently, and after World War II they became triennial.
14 Extract from Aberdeen's presidential speech at the 1899 quinquennial, quoted in *Advertiser*, 12 September 1902, p. 3.
15 Offen, 'Overcoming Hierarchies'.

INTRODUCTION

Detailed preparation went into the planning of the NSW council through the latter part of 1895 and the first months of 1896.[16] As the day approached, the youthful Windeyer felt some trepidation. A fellow suffragist and the first principal of Women's College at the University of Sydney, Louisa Macdonald, wrote that she had spent an hour and a half working with 'Margie' on her speech the day before and, in the event, it was 'very good'. Lady Hampden, wife of the colony's governor, agreed to preside, which she did 'amiably but without much ability',[17] confessing that she 'she did not know exactly what the objects of the Council were' but that she had 'much pleasure in calling on Miss Windeyer to explain them'.[18] Windeyer did so lucidly and succinctly, elaborating on the origins of ICW before focusing on the advantages of collective action to 'establish solidarity of sentiment and purpose among women' and give their endeavours 'increased moral force'. In putting 'the wisdom and experience of each at the service of all, it would unite all societies of women, that with a mighty aggregate of power they might move in directions upon which all could agree'.

Macdonald moved the resolution to form the council, speaking of its significance in Australian national terms, though Federation was still over four years away, and stressing its advantages as a means to broaden outlook, mitigate narrowness, spread common ideas and provide information, thus becoming 'a permanent body of advice and guidance in all that pertains to women's work'.[19] Among others providing support that day were prominent suffragists Rose Scott and Maybanke Wolstenholme. Though only six societies affiliated immediately, this had

---

16 See provisional committee minutes 17 November 1895 – 13 June 1896, NCWNSW Minute Book 1895–1904, Box MLK03009, MS3739, NCWNSW Papers, SLNSW.
17 Letter Louisa Macdonald to Miss Grove, 27 June 1896, Box MLK03009, MS3739, NCWNSW Papers, SLNSW.
18 *Sydney Morning Herald*, 27 June 1896.
19 'The National Council of Women of N.S.W', pamphlet describing the inaugural meeting, in NCWNSW Minute Book 1895–1904, Box MLK03009, MS3739, NCWNSW Papers, SLNSW.

risen to 11 within months and continued to grow steadily to reach 39 in the early years of the Great War.[20]

The NSW council was not the first in Australasia. It was pipped by the New Zealand NCW, which had held its first meeting just two months earlier, on 13 April 1896. Both Kate Sheppard (a leading figure in the Woman's Christian Temperance Union (WCTU) and suffrage movement) and Anna Stout (suffragist and wife of former prime minister Sir Robert Stout) had been approached by ICW's foreign corresponding secretary, Eva McLaren, to take up the baton. While McLaren thought Stout's élite status and credentials qualified her to become the first president, and it was Stout who explained in detail the origins and purpose of the council movement to those gathered at the first meeting, the women present preferred Sheppard to lead them. Though NCW New Zealand was initially a broadly representative body, Sheppard's election indicated the dominance of the more radical sections of the women's movement. Over the following years, the press increasingly painted NCWNZ as unrepresentative of New Zealand women, and divisions soon became apparent; by 1902, the number of affiliated societies was only six, down from a peak of sixteen in 1898, and by 1906 it had collapsed.[21]. Meanwhile the movement across the Tasman was flourishing, having taken off outside NSW and spread to the colony of Tasmania and then to the other states after Federation in 1901. In all cases, the press was supportive and gave the council movement extensive coverage, perhaps because of the largely upper class nature of its early leadership.

The initiative for the other Australian councils mostly came from outside their respective colonies or states, though local women were very

---

20 Martha Sear, *The National Council of Women of NSW: A Chronology 1896–1996*, Sydney, NCWNSW, 1996, unpaginated.

21 See Dorothy Page, *The National Council of Women: A Centennial History*, Auckland and Wellington, Auckland University Press and Bridget Williams Books, with the National Council of Women of New Zealand, 1996, pp. 14–46; Roberta Nicholls, 'The Collapse of the Early Council of Women of New Zealand, 1896–1906', *New Zealand Journal of History*, 27 (2), 1993, pp. 157–72.

Emily Dobson
President Australian Delegation 1906–1921

Emily Dobson was the leading figure among the Australian National Councils of Women until 1924, having helped found four of the state councils. Through her willingness and financial ability to travel, she maintained contact with the International Council of Women as president of the Australian delegation from 1906 to 1921. Without her contribution and commitment, it is unlikely that the Australian NCWs would have flourished here and in the wider world.

Dobson was born in 1834 at Port Arthur, Tasmania. She had no formal schooling, being tutored at home by her father. She married Henry Dobson in 1868 and her prominence in public welfare coincided with her husband's early parliamentary career.

The 1890s depression encouraged charitable activity for middle-class women, who helped provide assistance for the poor and destitute. Dobson was one of the first publicly active Tasmanian women; she was interested in some women's rights, though not in others such as suffrage. She played a leadership role in the Tasmanian community for over 40 years and was influential in more than 20 philanthropic, child welfare and women's organisations.

In 1891, Dobson became secretary of the Women's Sanitary Association (later the Women's Health Association of which she was vice-president), founded to combat the typhoid epidemic that was raging through Hobart at the time, worsening the effects of economic depression. From 1892 to 1895, Mrs Dobson's Relief Restaurant Committee ran a soup kitchen that supplied up to 1,000 meals a day. When the unemployment crisis lessened, the committee initiated the Association for Improvement of Dwellings of the Working Classes.

Throughout her life Dobson championed the cause of women and internationalism. In 1899 she became vice-president of the newly formed Tasmanian National Council of Women and its president from 1904 to 1934. She attended the first major conference of the International Council of Women in London in1899 and then attended almost every executive and quinquennial conference until 1932 when she made her 33rd visit overseas. She was elected ICW vice-president in 1914 and made an honorary life vice-president in 1924.

Widely respected, Dobson was known as 'Hobart's Grand Old Lady'. She died there in 1934. She was inducted into the Tasmanian Honour Roll of Women in 2005 for service to the community. She would have been proud to know that, 169 years after her birth, at the other end of Australia, her great granddaughter, Naomi Wilson, was inaugural president of the Cairns branch of the National Council of Women in Far North Queensland.

Explore further resources about Emily Dobson in the Australian Women's Register.

willing to be engaged. Lady Aberdeen, given her status and experience in matters vice regal, was able to make direct approaches to governors' wives in the colonies of the British Empire, including Australia. Thus the early years of the council movement in Australia were dominated by women of the social and political élite, though concerted efforts were made to bring in representatives of all women's organisations. Outside vice-regal circles, leaders were drawn from the wives and daughters of landowners, politicians and businessmen, these groups being the nearest Australia could come to an aristocracy; during their frequent visits 'Home' to London, these women moved in the same circles as those who led Britain's NCW. Moreover their wealth enabled them to travel and act as delegates to the conferences of ICW. Emily Dobson, founder, long-term leader and patron of NCW Tasmania, and wife of a former premier, made over thirty overseas trips and attended nearly every ICW quinquennial and executive meeting between 1899 and 1925.[22]

Before World War I, the respective state governors' wives nearly always accepted the position of president, even if in some cases their role was tokenistic. In NSW, for example, Margaret Windeyer, after taking the first steps to form the council, accepted the relatively humble position of corresponding secretary, making way for Lady Hampden as president. And Lady Aberdeen, for her part, observed protocol, sending 'a cordial letter' of congratulations to Windeyer on the formation of the council through Lady Hampden.[23] Early in 1897, Windeyer resigned as corresponding secretary on her departure for Europe, where she joined Aberdeen and the ICW executive in planning the first quinquennial.[24] She did not return to live permanently in Australia till 1901; thereafter she retained an interest in NCWNSW but did not again hold elected

---

22 'Emily Dobson', *Stirrers with Style! Presidents of the National Council of Women of Australia and Its Predecessors*, http://www.womenaustralia.info/exhib/ncwa/presidents-09.html.
23 NCWNSW Council Minutes, 26 August 1896, Box MLK03009, MS3739, NCWNSW Papers, SLNSW.
24 NCWNSW Council Minutes, 11 February 1897, 21 October 1897, Box MLK03009, MS3739, NCWNSW Papers, SLNSW.

INTRODUCTION

office. The council had grown in strength and confidence during her absence and no longer depended on her input, though it honoured her as its founder.

The first of the other Australian colonies to take up the cause was Tasmania. Again the initiative came from Government House, where the chief justice was acting as administrator in the absence of the governor. It was his wife, Emily Dodds, who, in response to a request from Lady Aberdeen, called a meeting of representative women's organisations at the Hobart Town Hall on 12 May 1899 after some weeks of preparation in both Launceston and Hobart. Meetings in both cities passed resolutions to form a Tasmanian council in order 'To promote greater unity of thought, sympathy, and purpose between women workers of all classes, parties and creeds' and 'To further the application of the Golden Rule to society, custom, and law'. Like Margaret Windeyer three years earlier, Emily Dodds 'laid before the [Hobart] meeting a short history of the formation of the International Council of Women'. She explained that the council movement was not only 'instrumental in breaking down prejudice' but also 'collected and spread correct information about women's work' and, by encouraging 'interchange of views and personal touch with other workers', 'prevented the overlapping and multiplication of organisations for kindred causes'.[25] Lady Gormanston, wife of the governor, was chosen as president but it was Emily Dobson, one of the committee members, who was to become the dominant figure both in the Tasmanian council and in the Australian council movement generally for the next quarter of a century and more. The founding of the Tasmanian council was just in time for its appointed local representative—Mrs Dobson—to set sail for the first ICW quinquennial conference in London.[26]

Held in London from 28 June to 4 July 1899, the ICW congress was attended by thousands of women, among them representatives of NSW,

---

25   *Mercury*, 13 May 1899, p. 1.
26   *Mercury*, 13 May 1899, p. 1

Victoria and South Australia as well as Tasmania. Victoria's leading suffragist, Annette Bear-Crawford, travelled to England specifically in order to attend the conference but tragically died of pneumonia before it began. The leading lady of Victorian society and philanthropic endeavour, Janet Lady Clarke, was also in London at the time and was asked to attend the ICW conference in Bear-Crawford's stead. Charged by Lady Aberdeen and the new ICW president, May Wright Sewall, to form a Victorian council on her return, Clarke seems to have procrastinated until pushed into action by the Tasmanian vice presidents, Emily Dobson and Lady Alice Braddon. These two stalwarts travelled to Melbourne late in 1901 to persuade Lady Clarke to call interested representatives of women's organisations together. Janet Clarke gave her 'sympathy and support', and made her home 'Cliveden' available for a meeting to form the Victorian council on 22 November. After Mrs Dobson and Lady Braddon had explained the purposes of the council movement, the WCTU's Victorian president, Margaret McLean, moved formation of a state NCW.[27] A second meeting, chaired by Lady Braddon, took place on 28 November, when further information was provided about ICW by both Dobson and the former NSW state secretary, Mrs Aronson.

As in the other states, a preparatory committee was formed, leading suffragist Vida Goldstein suggesting that its secretary provide all the woman's organisations with a copy of the rules of ICW and request them to appoint delegates to a meeting early in the new year. Meanwhile, Goldstein advertised the advantages of the movement in her paper, the *Australian Woman's Sphere*, and strongly urged 'every society of women to join the Council'. So too did the *Sun: An Illustrated Journal for the Home and Society*, edited by suffragists Evelyn Gough and Catherine Hay Thompson.[28] The official foundation meeting on 11 March 1902, again held at 'Cliveden', saw representatives of eighteen disparate women's

---

27 *Australian Woman's Sphere*, December 1901, pp. 130–1; Kate Gray, 'The Acceptable Face of Feminism: The National Council of Women of Victoria 1902–18', MA thesis, University of Melbourne, 1988, pp. 34–5.
28 *Australian Woman's Sphere*, December 1901, p. 131; Gray, 'Acceptable Face', p. 35.

INTRODUCTION

organisations agree to affiliate.[29] Janet Clarke became the first president but, within a year, the precedent of NSW and Tasmania was taken up and the governor's wife, Lady Caroline Clarke, was asked to assume this role.[30] Problems could have arisen when a competing organisation with links to the labour movement, the Victorian Women's Federation, was set up in November 1902. The following year saw protracted but ultimately unsuccessful negotiations between the two bodies, a proposal for union finally being rejected by NCWV in March 1904.[31] About half of VWF's affiliates were already members of the council and, in the ensuing years, as NCWV expanded, the federation faded away.

The South Australian council, in its first incarnation, was also founded in 1902. Lady Sarah Cockburn, a suffragist and the wife of a former premier, had represented South Australian women at the ICW quinquennial in London three years earlier, where she was appointed honorary NCWSA vice-president and deputed by Sewall to take up the cause in her home state. Given that she was now permanently domiciled in London, she was unable to do so, and turned to fellow South Australian suffragist Elizabeth Nicholls, who was visiting London in 1900. Nicholls, president of the Australian WCTU as well as former and subsequent president of South Australia's WCTU, was well connected and well equipped to launch the SA council but her WCTU work prevented her from doing so immediately, though she made contact with Emily Dobson in Tasmania to seek advice. Finally, with the co-operation of the venerable but still influential Catherine Spence and the support of Rose Birks, another South Australian suffragist and newly elected president of SA YWCA, NCWSA was launched on 24 September 1902.

As in the other states, vice-regal support was sought and gained, and Lady Katharine Way, wife of the chief justice and lieutenant governor,

---

29 Gray, 'Acceptable Face', pp. 35–6.
30 Norris, *Champions*, p. 13.
31 NCWV Executive Minutes, 9 March 1904, NCWV Papers, SLV (classification pending).

took the chair and was elected president, Spence and Birks, along with Lady Cockburn from afar, becoming vice presidents. It was a promising start, with 'a large and representative gathering' that included ten leading women's societies.[32] But the SA council failed to thrive. Catherine Spence resigned in 1906 because of its leaders' 'apparent disinclination to touch "live" subjects'[33] and, by 1907, the number of affiliated societies had shrunk to seven, all of them religious and/or philanthropic. The more political organisations had left, as had the WCTU, and, of the three founders, only Rose Birks remained active. It was she who protested at the annual meeting in 1907, perhaps rather too adamantly, that 'some people considered that the National Council of Women was a dead thing. This was far from the case, however'. 'Next year they hoped to carry out a more active year's work.' Secretary Louise Anderson, while admitting the lack of 'works brought to a definite conclusion', denied that this was in any way a 'confession of failure', explaining that it had been a year of 'preparation for the hard work that the council hopes to accomplish during the ensuing year'.[34] The hard work did not happen.

The organisation limped on into 1909, Lady Cockburn agreeing to represent them at an ICW planning meeting in Geneva in 1908, and its president, Lady Holder, continuing as delegate for the council on other groups such as the Anti-gambling League in 1909. But there are no indications in the press of active public engagement and no further reports of meetings.[35] Though the council was still listed as an Australian affiliate in the transactions of the Toronto quinquennial in 1909, it did not submit a report of its activities or appoint a delegate, and it is not listed among the Australian affiliates in the 1911–12 ICW report. NCWSA's demise seems to have been, as with the New Zealand

---

32 *Register*, 25 September 1902, p. 3.
33 Catherine Spence, *An Autobiography*, Adelaide, W.K. Thomas, 1910, cited in Barbara J. Pitt, 'The History of the National Council of Women in South Australia 1902–1980', typescript, Adelaide, NCWSA, 1986, p. 4.
34 *Advertiser*, 4 December 1907, p. 7; *Register*, 4 December 1907, p. 9.
35 *Advertiser*, 2 October 1908, p. 11; 17 August 1909, p. 9.

council, a result of failure to retain the broad support of representative women's organisations, though in South Australia's case it was the more radical wing that departed and, as in New Zealand, generational loss also played a part. In both cases, failure to influence government policy on matters of significance undoubtedly discouraged enthusiasm and effort.[36]

Though South Australian women's organisations continued to co-operate on a range of issues, it was not until March 1920, when 24 societies gathered to consider how to deal with the immigration of British war service women, that the idea of rekindling the council was born. A further meeting in April agreed to establish a council rather than an interim organisation to deal with the immediate problem before them and, on 7 May, delegates from 27 societies resolved that 'The National Council be formed or reformed'. This was just in time for NCWSA to send a representative, Mrs J.P. Morice, to the first post-war ICW quinquennial meeting in Norway in September 1920.[37] The New Zealand council also re-formed on a more representative basis in 1918, this time establishing branches throughout the nation and tempering its radicalism in the interests of inclusion and stability.[38]

The remaining Australian states all had councils by the outbreak of the Great War. The origins of the Queensland council can be traced back to 1903 and the influence of key members in the other Australian councils. The first contact was with Louisa Bevan, a founding member and vice-president of NCWV, who addressed the Queensland WCTU about the council idea in July.[39] The second was Rose Scott, who was asked to explain how NSW's council worked to an informal gathering of leading women in Brisbane in October. The result was the formation

---

36   Page, *National Council of Women*, pp. 44–6.
37   Pitt, 'History of the National Council of Women in South Australia', pp. 5–6.
38   Pitt, 'History of the National Council of Women in South Australia', p. 4; Page, *National Council of Women*, pp. 54–6.
39   Niel Gunson, 'Bevan, Louisa Jane', *ADB*, http://adb.anu.edu.au/biography/bevan-louisa-jane-5632.

of a provisional committee, which worked towards a public meeting on 9 October 1905 at which Emily Dobson spoke on 'The Aim and Scope of National Councils'. NCWQ dates its foundation from this occasion, when a resolution was passed to form the council and 21 societies signified their intention to join. The two-year planning period resulted in a strong, active and well-organised council from its inception. Like its Australian predecessors, the Queensland council sought and gained vice-regal patronage—from Lady Frances Chelmsford, wife of the state governor, third Baron Chelmsford. The Queensland council's first president was Catherine Bell, wife of the state minister for lands, J.T. Bell. Office bearers included leading women of the day such as Christina Corrie, a founder of the Queensland Women's Electoral League, and Annie Carvosso and Agnes Williams, prominent figures in the WCTU. NCWQ quickly sought and gained ICW affiliation, formed standing committees, sent representatives to the Geneva executive meeting in 1908 and appointed delegates to the 1909 quinquennial in Toronto, though in the event they were 'prevented from coming'.[40]

The last state to form a council was Western Australia. In this case, the governor's wife, Lady Edeline Strickland, had had experience working with NCW in Tasmania when her husband was governor there from 1904 to 1909, and became the 'driving force' behind the council's formation. She instigated the inaugural meeting of representatives from thirteen societies on 5 January 1911 at Government House, having failed to persuade the Women's Service Guild to take up the running, and then 'very kindly consented' to be the first president.[41] As in the

---

40 *The First Fifty Years in the History of the National Council of Women of Queensland*, Brisbane, NCWQ, 1959, pp. 9–13, 29; *Brisbane Courier*, 10 October 1905, p. 3; Countess of Aberdeen (ed.), *Report of Transactions of the Fourth Quinquennial Meeting Held at Toronto, Canada, June 1909: With Which Are Incorporated the Reports of the National Councils and of International Standing Committees for 1908–1909*, London, Constable, 1910, p. 22.

41 Noreen Sher, *'The Spirit Lives On': A History of the National Council of Women of Western Australia, 1911–1999*, Perth, NCWWA, 1999, p. 1; *Western Mail*, 14 January 1911, p. 45.

other states, those at the first meeting included leading women workers and activists. Among them were Australia's first woman member of parliament in 1921, Edith Cowan (successor to Lady Strickland as NCWWA president in 1913), Bessie Rischbieth (later founder of the Australian Federation of Women Voters (AFWV)), Ettie Hooton (best known afterwards as a Labor Party activist), Ethel Joyner (another later AFWV leader), and Lady Gwenyfred James (first president of the Women's Service Guild 1909–14, then NCWWA vice president in 1911 and president in 1924).[42] Modelling its constitution broadly on that of the Victorian council, NCWWA held its first general meeting on 21 April and, by the end of the first year of operation, seventeen organisations were affiliated. The WA council also quickly affiliated with ICW, sending a representative to an executive meeting in Stockholm soon after its foundation in 1911, and establishing standing committees during 1912.[43]

By this stage, the International Council of Women had pledged itself to a number of specific causes, most of which were furthered by standing committees that were replicated to a greater or lesser extent in the various National Councils of Women. Broadly, there were eight such causes by 1911: international peace and arbitration; opposition to the 'white slave traffic' and support for the principle of equal moral standards for both sexes; woman suffrage in all countries with representative governments; advocacy on laws concerning the legal position and general welfare of women; improvement of public health; education; protection of emigrants and immigrants, especially women and children; and inclusion of women on all authorities and bodies dealing with public work.[44] Work on these issues and discussion of problems arising provided topics for exchange of views and information

---

42 *Western Mail*, 14 January 1911, p. 45.
43 Sher, *'The Spirit Lives On'*, pp. 1–5.
44 These issues were listed in a long article on the council movement by 'Adrienne' in the *Western Mail*, 21 January 1911, p. 39, published in the wake of the formation of NCWWA.

between the Australian councils and eventually afforded a rationale for federation that went beyond the mechanics of ICW representation. National identity in the Australian council movement was thus ironically more a result of international activism than a contributing factor to it.

The six Australian state councils finally came together to form the National Council of Women of Australia in 1931,[45] though it was a tortuous journey towards federation. Despite their adopted designation as 'national', the links between their leaders, and considerable efforts made to attend each others' annual meetings to confer, the councils in the early years formed only token and minimalist national links for the purpose of their relations with the ICW and were mostly disinclined to create a permanent national body for dealing with Australian matters. This reflected the low priority given to national issues in most of the women's groups that were affiliated to state NCWs. Their preoccupations in the pre–World War I years were provincial and local, and it is not surprising that the councils' understanding of women's responsibility as citizens was similarly locally defined. The causes to which ICW pledged itself facilitated the growth of national identity among delegates to the Australian councils as they took them up and recognised their common concerns.

Two more councils affiliated to NCWA after it was formed. The NCWs of the Australian Capital Territory and the Northern Territory were partly a product of the federal body's work. The ACT council, formed in 1939, drew on the experience of Victorians Ivy Brookes and May Couchman, both of whom were influential figures in NCWA.[46] Their involvement also reflected the importance of Melbourne in the early years of the ACT's history, given that it had been the national

---

45 At its foundation, the name it took was National Council of Women of Australia (NCWA), but it became known generally as the Australian National Council of Women (ANCW) in the following decades before it officially returned to being NCWA in 1970.

46 Freda Stephenson, *Capital Women: A History of the Work of the National Council of Women (ACT) in Canberra 1939–1979*, Canberra, Highland Press for NCWACT, 1992, p. 5.

INTRODUCTION

capital until 1927. The Northern Territory council did not come into being until 1964 and disbanded at the end of the 1980s. This in turn owed its formation to members of the ACT council, wives of bureaucrats temporarily transferred from Canberra, and its existence was continually threatened and eventually doomed by the loss of its leaders to the whims of the Australian public service.

The formation of state councils and their gradual move towards federal organisation not only marks the beginnings of a national and an international common cause among organised women in Australia, it also constitutes the beginning of mainstream feminism in this country. We have deliberately used the term 'mainstream' to describe the work of the national councils rather than alternatives such as 'conservative'. In general, we can observe that the councils opted at first for a style of activism that drew mainly on existing women's philanthropic and educational organisations, and on ideals of individual responsibility informed by nineteenth-century moral and religious values. These increasingly came to be inflected with, then dominated by, the language of liberal rights and equality, and modern twentieth-century progressivist notions of scientific rationality and efficiency, reflecting the growing influence of professional women in council leadership circles. This trend was accentuated by the federation of the councils in 1925 and the creation of NCWA as a peak body in 1931.

In the succinct words of 1920s Queensland president Zina Cumbrae-Stewart, NCW was an 'organization which brings together for discussion, the forming of public opinion, the workers who are doing the practical work of social education and improvement'.[47] Though it included radicals among its affiliates, the feminist face it presented emphasised information, education and co-operation rather than activism, agitation and opposition. This irritated some of the early constituent societies, leading them to create their own national bodies

---

47 'Presidential Address', *National Council of Women of Queensland Annual Report 1930/1931*, p. 7.

and to affiliate with rival international organisations, especially the International Woman Suffrage Alliance (IWSA) (itself a breakaway from ICW in 1904)[48] and the Women's International League for Peace and Freedom (WILPF) (in effect a wartime breakaway from IWSA in 1915).[49] But few of these more radical groups actually left the Australian councils, recognising the value of working within the mainstream movement as well as independently. Internationally, too, ICW, IWSA and WILPF co-operated and lobbied together through a joint standing committee, then a 'Liaison Committee', from the mid-1920s onwards, and these were replicated in Australia soon after.

By the 1970s, NCWA was said to represent well over a million women nation-wide through the affiliates of its constituent state councils—a much larger number than any other national coalitions or unaffiliated associations of women. Before then as well as since, it consistently espoused and lobbied for the causes on the agenda of liberal feminism. In most cases, the councils did not themselves initiate schemes for extensive or radical reform and sometimes they lagged behind. Sometimes some of their own affiliates independently took the lead, and sometimes—especially in more recent decades—the initiative came from external groups. Generally the NCWs followed rather than led, and advocated working within the system rather than undermining it. The council movement's crucial role and major achievement lay in making broadly feminist ideas seem safe, relatively uncontroversial and acceptable to large numbers of ordinary Australian women.

Not that achieving consensus was easy. There have been periods of grave disharmony, both between the councils and internally. Divisions occurred in Western Australia during World War I, the late 1920s and early 1930s, and in Victoria during World War I, and a continuing

---

48   This became the International Alliance of Women for Suffrage and Equal Citizenship in the late 1920s, then the International Alliance of Women: Equal Rights–Equal Responsibilities in 1946.
49   Rupp, *Worlds of Women*, details the origins and growth of all three up to World War II.

INTRODUCTION

tension between Launceston and Hobart boiled over in the 1990s in Tasmania. And state councils have often been divided when particularly sensitive issues were raised at national conferences. But despite the challenges, Australia's council movement has survived and for long periods it has thrived. NCWA and the state councils retained their peak status among Australian women's organisations until well into the 1970s and still have a significant voice in state and federal forums, though no longer claiming to represent or speak for a majority of women's associations at any of these levels. Internationally, ICW engaged with League of Nations bodies during the 1920s and 30s and today holds general consultative status with the United Nations Economic and Social Council, the highest accreditation an NGO can achieve. Through its ICW affiliation and its participation in world and regional conferences and seminars, NCWA is still the strongest non-government organisational channel through which Australian women can speak and be heard internationally.

For all these reasons it is important that the history of NCWA be written. Only by making public and accessible its activities, the obstacles and problems it has faced, its achievements and its failings, can the extent of women's activism in this country be appreciated and understood.

The organisation of this book is both chronological and thematic. It is divided into four periods: 1896–1931; 1931–50; 1950–70; 1970–2006. The first period, 1896–1931, traces the emergence of national organisation, interests and identity. The second, 1931–50, examines the consolidation of NCWA in the face of internal and external challenges and disruptions arising from the Great Depression and World War II. The post-war decades 1950–70 are analysed as the peak of council expansion and influence. And the final period, 1970–2006, is framed as one of adjustment to difference and division among women, and of discovering new ways of working in a political and cultural context where active citizenship itself seems to be challenged by the decline of voluntary association. Within each of these periods, we discuss organisational challenges, and NCWA's concerns and activities with regard to home and family, rights and equality, and international and world affairs. The idea is to link the local, national and international in the structure of the book, as NCWA itself does by sitting 'between state and world'. The way we have arranged and emphasised these themes in each period varies, and the balance of the narrative reflects our interpretation of the key events and foci of the councils' collective work in those years. We do not expect all our readers or actors in the events described to agree with our views and the ways we have told NCWA's story, but we hope this book will provide a good starting point for further research and discussion, and the telling of alternative stories.

PART ONE
CREATING COMMON CAUSE
1896–1931

Although the National Council of Women of Australia did not formally come into being until 1931, it was preceded by interstate conferences from as early as 1902, by agreements on federation for purposes of financial and representation arrangements with the International Council of Women dating from 1906, and by a federal council formed in 1924–25. The process was slow and tentative, and it took nearly three decades for the state councils to create a permanent national body after the first interstate meeting. This delay seems to have been unique to Australia, for comparable countries with a federal structure such as the USA and Canada formed nationwide councils from the beginning. Why did it take so long in Australia and what were the obstacles that stood in the way?

This section will first endeavour to answer those questions in a chapter tracing the stages of development of the national organisation, including the contributions of the women who worked towards it and the sources of resistance. It will then examine the growth of common interests and policy considerations among the state councils that, over three decades, came to provide the basis for converting expedient co-operation into genuinely national common cause and interest. The process by which this occurred will be discussed in three chapters, dealing first with home, family and social reform, then with the growing interest in rights and equality, and finally with the ongoing concern about national security and peace, and recognition of the benefits of international co-operation for expanding the rights of women.

Chapter 1

TOWARDS NATIONAL ORGANISATION

The emergence of separate and autonomous National Councils of Women in each of the Australian states created an anomaly for the International Council of Women. As historian Susan Zimmermann has written, from its inception 'ICW was built strictly and exclusively on [the] idea that the national constituted the international'. It saw 'the international as a multiplication of the national', even if it had difficulty in deciding precisely what a national unit was. The preferred model was clearly the independent nation-state, with which the council movement's first-generation leaders were most familiar, but the actual reality ICW had to deal with was more complex. It included multinational empires, such as the Habsburg Empire, and colonial empires like that of Britain. A new settler nation like the Australian Commonwealth could also create problems, made up as it was of former semi-independent colonies. Nevertheless, ICW's direction was clear from 1904, when it established a committee 'to define philosophically and historically what is a nation as a basis for just action on the part of the International Council'.[1] The result was, in Zimmermann's words, that

> With its politics of building the international on the national, the international women's movement contributed to, and in many cases actively promoted, the country-wide organization of

---

1   Berlin 1904, 'ICW Resolutions', http://www.ncwcanada.com/ncwc2/wp-content/uploads/2014/02/ICW-CIF_Resolutions1.pdf, p. 3.

women's associations that had hitherto barely existed, promoting a trend of nationalization through internationalization.²

Few seemed to realise at the time that this would serve to weaken the early transnational ideals of founder May Wright Sewall. It was a pragmatic solution to a difficult problem and was rarely questioned after the fourth quinquennial in Toronto in 1909, when an advisory board to recommend on applications for affiliation 'from countries forming new Councils' was formalised.³

Lady Aberdeen had begun lobbying for federation of present and future Australian national councils from the formation of the Commonwealth in 1901, and it was the Australian issue that triggered general ICW debate about the most equitable way to represent national entities at international council meetings. The New South Wales and Tasmanian councils had been able to affiliate individually since, at the time of their formation, they represented separate self-governing colonies within the British Empire, but Australian Federation created a different context for the affiliation of the councils formed after 1901, as well as making the separate status of the first two councils anachronistic.

There was as yet no imagined Australian community among the women who founded the first councils; their identities were defined instead by provincial loyalties and the 'crimson thread of kinship' tying them to the British Empire.⁴ Still, some could see that some kind of federal arrangement would soon be necessary. At the first annual congress of the Tasmanian council in April 1901, just three months

---

2   Susan Zimmermann, 'The Challenge of Multinational Empire for the International Women's Movement: The Hapsburg Monarchy and the Development of Feminist Inter/national Politics', *Journal of Women's History*, 17 (2), 2005, pp. 87–117.

3   Toronto 1909, 'ICW Resolutions', at http://www.ncwcanada.com/ncwc2/wp-content/uploads/2014/02/ICW-CIF_Resolutions1.pdf, p. 3.

4   Imperial identity was supported by family connections to different parts of the Empire through the armed forces, the civil service and business, as well as by racial assumptions, history and sentiment. On the strength of these ties, see Angela Woollacott, *To Try Her Fortune in London: Australian Women, Colonialism and Modernity*, New York et al., Oxford University Press, 2001, pp. 164–71.

after the nation was formed, Lady Alice Braddon moved that 'in the opinion of this meeting it is desirable that councils of the different States of the Australian Commonwealth should be formed in a Federal Council provided that their representation on the International Council does not suffer thereby'—a significant proviso in the light of things to come. It was agreed that, if two other states concurred in this proposal, representatives of all councils should come together to 'form a scheme for the federation of the councils'.[5]

By the time the Victorian council had formed the following year, pressure was mounting in ICW. NCW leaders in the United States were adamant that the combined Australian representation at these congresses be limited to the three votes allowed to other national delegations. On her return from the United States in 1902, Vida Goldstein told the NSW executive that ICW president May Wright Sewall was planning to travel to Australia the following year to help form a federal council.[6] The visit did not eventuate in 1903, and, in the meantime, the newly formed South Australian council was granted ICW affiliation. In December 1903, the NSW executive appointed a subcommittee to draw up a 'basis for union'. It only went so far as to recommend a mechanism for each state to participate in selecting three national delegates to future ICW quinquennial conferences.[7] In Victoria, the state president, governor's wife Lady Caroline Clarke, was contacted by Lady Aberdeen early in 1904 to warn of growing ICW concern and to request the total Australian delegation to the impending Berlin conference be limited to three. This met an aggressive response, the Victorian executive 'pointing out that so long as each Australian Council is on the same financial basis as those of the U.S.A. & Canada then voting power should be on

---

5   *Mercury*, 27 April 1901, p. 4.
6   NCWNSW Executive Minutes, 20 August 1902, Box MLK03009, MS3739, NCWNSW Papers, State Library of New South Wales (SLNSW).
7   NCWNSW Executive Minutes, 9 December 1903, 8 April 1904, Box MLK03009, MS3739, NCWNSW Papers, SLNSW.

a similar basis'.⁸ But NCWV's resolution to this effect was rescinded when Emily Dobson advised that it was unwise and 'prejudicial' to their long-term interests, given Lady Aberdeen's commitment to closer union and the likelihood she would be the next ICW president.⁹

Dobson had begun to campaign on the issue by early 1904, seeking middle ground. 'We, of Australia, have a very important decision to make at the quinquennial in Berlin', she told the Tasmanian council: 'It is if the States shall federate and accept a diminished voting power'. Like the NSW council, she baulked at union and suggested a compromise on representation to be put to ICW. While recognising the injustice of six Australian councils potentially being able to command eighteen votes if all were affiliated separately, she nevertheless believed there was a case for more than the three votes Canada and the US and the different European member countries had accepted.¹⁰ Though Canada and the United States were of comparable size and also had separate state or provincial councils, as in Australia, they had both started with strong unified national councils, the constituent branches having been largely formed from the centre. The nations in both cases were older and their problems of identity and communication were thus less severe. Emily Dobson argued that, for the time being, each of the Australian councils should be allowed one vote, this more liberal representation recognising 'the size of [our] territory and the difficulties of transit quite inferior to that of the other nations'.¹¹

The Australian councils did not come to an agreement on this issue in time for the 1904 quinquennial and were taken to task by the American delegates. Reporting to the Victorians on her return from

---

8   NCWV Executive Minutes, 18 March 1904, State Library of Victoria (SLV) (classification pending).
9   NCWV Executive Minutes, 24 March 1904, SLV (classification pending). Aberdeen resumed the presidency in 1904 after May Wright Sewall had completed one term from 1899–1904 and decided to step down.
10 *Mercury*, 12 February 1904, p. 6.
11 *Mercury*, 12 February 1904, p. 6.

Berlin, Dobson explained that although she had persuaded ICW that affiliation of each state council should be 'recognised as valid' for the moment, she had in return for this concession undertaken to ensure they would 'confer with a view to federation or to determining some scheme' before the next quinquennial planned for Toronto in 1909.[12] It would take another two years for the Australian councils to devise a formula for representation that was acceptable to them all.

The difficulties were first fully aired at an interstate conference in Melbourne in October 1905.[13] Victoria was in favour of national union; New South Wales proposed limited co-operation for the sole purpose of representation at ICW.[14] After 'long and exhaustive discussion upon the advisability of complete federation at the present time', five resolutions to be taken back to state councils were passed: that they would federate 'only for purposes of finance and representation until after the next quinquennial'; that each council would have two delegates only; that the delegates would 'elect one of themselves to be president', who would also represent them all on ICW executive; that ICW be requested to alter the constitution so affiliation fees would be proportionate to representation; and that the conference would reconvene in Hobart in March 1906 to receive state council responses. Delegates were divided over a further resolution hoping 'this temporary arrangement' would be 'only the preliminary to a larger federation of the national councils of Australia', the two original councils opposing, while Victoria, South Australia and the new Queensland council voted in favour.[15]

---

12 NCWV Council Minutes, Annual Meeting, 28 October 1904, SLV (classification pending).
13 For preparations for the Melbourne conference, see *Argus*, 29 October 1904, p. 23; *Mercury*, 18 March 1905, p. 6.
14 NCWNSW Executive Minutes, 14 September 1905, Box MLK03009, MS3739, NCWNSW Papers, SLNSW.
15 *Mercury*, 20 November 1905, p. 7; see also report of letter to NCWNSW executive from Dobson explaining that Victoria, SA and Queensland were in favour of union but that she had, as a proxy NSW delegate as well as a Tasmanian representative,

Over the following months, Dobson and the NSW council lobbied the newer councils. The reconvened meeting in Hobart in February 1906 agreed on the substance of the resolutions passed in Melbourne but, significantly, the clause relating to the election of a president saw the role limited to 'the time being (i.e. during the quinquennial meetings)', and a resolution expressing hope for a 'larger federation' was defeated, Victoria now being the only state to vote for it.[16] We can speculate on the reasons for the opposition of NSW and Tasmania to a 'larger federation' at this time. Both saw it as 'impracticable' because of 'great distance' and poor physical communication services, agreeing that 'the time was not yet ripe'. Dobson argued further that it would be 'folly' to commit themselves before the report of the ICW 'Committee considering the composition of a National Council is received'.[17] This last reason hints at fears that Tasmania (and Dobson) would lose status and influence at ICW in a unified national council inevitably dominated by NSW and Victoria. Given its foundational role and location in the 'mother state', the motives of the NSW council are harder to understand. Rose Scott, like Emily Dobson, may have been reluctant to lose the status and intimacy with ICW leaders revealed in her correspondence. And the evident pride of the NSW council in its seniority as the first Australian council may indicate unwillingness to see its status submerged in a federation, especially since Melbourne was now the national capital and Victoria's council was in a good position to claim a leading role in any unified organisation. NCWV was already the largest of the councils. But, whatever the practical, political or personal reasons for rejecting closer union, they clearly outweighed national sentiment and identity at this time.

---

    pushed the NSW resolution for limited federation at the Melbourne conference. NCWNSW Executive Minutes, 17 November 1905, Box MLK03009, MS3739, NCWNSW Papers, SLNSW.

16   *Mercury*, 15 February 1906, p. 5.

17   NCWNSW Executive Minutes, 14 September 1905 (adjourned), 20 October 1905, 17 November 1905, Box MLK03009, MS3739, NCWNSW Papers, SLNSW.

Under the arrangements agreed on in Hobart, the Australian councils would jointly pay the full affiliation fee to ICW and, for purposes of ICW conference representation, they would form a single delegation with an Australian president appointed from among them. However, they would each retain separate affiliation, reporting to and corresponding with ICW individually.[18] This compromise was accepted as a special case at the Geneva meeting in 1908, then by the 4th ICW quinquennial at Toronto in June 1909, on Dobson's grounds that distance and differences in legislation and social policy between the states made further steps towards federation impossible at this stage. An Australian delegation of six attended under Dobson's presidency and was later congratulated by re-elected president Lady Aberdeen for the new arrangements.[19] They were sufficiently buoyed and confident in their ability to co-operate to invite ICW to hold its next quinquennial in Australia, though the offer was declined in favour of Italy.[20]

International pressure continued to drive national co-operation. A special meeting for Australian and Canadian council members was held in London in the summer of 1911 when many were visiting for the coronation of George V.[21] As a result of encouragement received there, the Australian councils convened what they termed the 'first Interstate Congress of the National Council of Women' a year later, in July 1912, in Sydney. All five councils were represented for the first time.[22]

---

18   Ada Norris, *Champions of the Impossible: A History of the National Council of Women of Victoria, 1902–1977*, Melbourne, Hawthorn Press, 1978, p. 66.
19   The six delegates listed were all from Tasmania and Victoria, it being noted in the transactions that: 'The delegates from New South Wales and Queensland were prevented from coming'. See Countess of Aberdeen (ed.), *Report of Transactions of the Fourth Quinquennial Meeting Held at Toronto, Canada, June 1909: With Which Are Incorporated the Reports of the National Councils and of International Standing Committees for 1908–1909*, London, Constable, 1910, pp. 22, 134. See also Norris, *Champions*, p. 66; *Argus*, 23 October 1909, p. 18; NCWV, *Report for 1910*, p. 7.
20   NCWV, *Report for 1908–9*, p. 6.
21   Countess of Aberdeen (ed.), *International Council of Women Report of the Quinquennial Meetings Rome 1914*, Karlsruhe, G. Braunsche Hofbuchdruckerie und Verlag, p. 52.
22   Western Australia was the fifth state, South Australia having by now disbanded.

NCWNSW president, governor's wife Lady Frances Chelmsford, made what was effectively an appeal for national unity and co-ordination, especially 'the need of uniformity of method and better organisation ... There must be a bond of union between those who were working so keenly for the welfare of women in the different States', if they were to be 'truly representative of the women of Australia'.[23] At the present time, they were lagging behind the rest of the international council, and were 'so far from the other centres that they had to a certain extent to carve out their own career', but this could be assisted by closer co-operation between the states:

> On the question of uniformity they should remember that, though they had five national councils in Australia, yet in the international council they spoke with only one voice, so they should work together as one. It would be well to have the same constitution for all the State councils.[24]

Chelmsford was supported by the governor general's wife, Lady Gertrude Denman, who spoke of her contact with Lady Aberdeen concerning the need for Australia's councils to take on more international work. She also pointed out that 'A great deal of the work done by the council was in moulding public opinion' and that 'It was much easier to do this if all the councils in all the States were working on the same lines'. To counteract the problem of distance, she recommended regular interstate conferences before the annual meetings of the state councils: 'It was very important that the national councils of Australia should work together'.[25] The 1912 Sydney conference was reported at the 1914 quinquennial in Rome as

---

23 *Advertiser*, 31 July 1912, p. 11; *Argus*, 31 July 1912, p. 6, *Sydney Morning Herald*, 31 July 1912, p. 10.
24 *Sydney Morning Herald*, 31 July 1912, p. 10.
25 *Sydney Morning Herald*, 31 July 1912, p. 10, *Advertiser*, 31 July 1912, p. 11; *Argus*, 31 July 1912, p. 6. Representation of WA was a major achievement, given that it took six days to travel from Perth to Sydney at this time. Rail linkage between the state capitals was not complete until the east–west transcontinental railway joining WA to the eastern states was finished in 1917. Rail travel remained complicated by different state gauges necessitating time-consuming changes.

a significant step towards the 'union of the women of the Australian Commonwealth'.[26] In this light, ICW also decided that the Australian president for the conference should in future be elected by the Australian councils rather than the delegates.[27] However, the 1912 conference had made no decision about a uniform constitution. While Victoria's Alison Pymm claimed her state's constitution should serve as a model, her colleague, Dr Edith Barrett, commented more realistically that getting all councils to agree would be 'almost impossible'.[28]

For all the viceregal pressure for national organisation, the effect of the 1909 ICW compromise on Australian representation was to reinforce provincialism over national interests. Lady Denman deplored the situation at the Victorian state conference held a few months after the 1912 interstate meeting; rather than each state working 'alone in so many directions', she said, 'the National Councils in each state should come into closer touch, and should all simultaneously take up one big public matter'.[29] But, even without formal co-operation, the link with ICW did serve to encourage common cause at state level. In addition to joint representation at ICW conferences—led in 1914 by Emily Dobson[30]—ICW affiliation encouraged the state organisations to form action committees parallel to those of ICW to which they forwarded regular reports, thus learning to work within a common framework. Initially there were four such ICW committees: Laws Affecting Domestic Relations of Women (soon renamed Laws and Legal Position of Women); Finance; Press; and Peace and Arbitration. After the 1904 Berlin quinquennial, two more committees—Suffrage and Rights of Citizenship, and White Slave Traffic and Equal Moral Standard (soon renamed Equal Moral Standard and Traffic in Women)—were added,

---

26 Aberdeen (ed.), *Report of the Quinquennial Meetings Rome 1914*, p. 55.
27 Resolution XXXV—Alteration in terms of affiliation of the Australian Councils, in Aberdeen (ed.), *Report of the Quinquennial Meetings Rome 1914*, p. 34.
28 *Sydney Morning Herald*, 2 August 1912, p. 7; *Advertiser*, 31 July 1912, p. 11.
29 *Argus*, 20 November 1912, p. 5.
30 Aberdeen (ed.), *Report of the Quinquennial Meetings Rome 1914*, pp. 460–1.

and from 1909 there were another three—Education; Emigration and Immigration; and Public Health. The Rome quinquennial in 1914 supplemented these with a committee on Trades and Professions.[31] Each of the Australian councils implemented enough of the 'standing committee' system to channel their work into common patterns, at the same time fostering their politicisation and initiating a self-consciously national direction.

This politicisation, however, could also work against a national focus. It was promoted by the affiliation to the councils of women's organisations formed to educate women as political citizens. While societies emerging from the suffrage campaigns tended to be self-consciously 'non-party', dedicated to representing the interests of all women, later affiliates were committed to the support of particular political parties. Vida Goldstein's Women's Political Association in Victoria, Rose Scott's Women's Political and Education League in New South Wales, and Western Australia's Women's Service Guild were among the early non-party affiliates but were small. The political interest groups with the biggest memberships were those formed to support conservative parties—the Women's Liberal League in New South Wales and, largest of all, the Australian Women's National League (AWNL) in Victoria.[32] Labor Party women's organisations were precluded by party rules from joining the NCW in most states. As a result political discourse in the councils was increasingly dominated by conservative views, especially in

---

31 Leila Rupp, *Worlds of Women: The Making of an International Women's Movement*, Princeton, Princeton University Press, 1997, p. 22; Catherine Jacques and Sylvia Lefebvre, 'The Working Methods of the ICW: From its Creation to the Second World War', in Eliane Gubin and Leen Van Molle (eds), *Women Changing the World: A History of the International Council of Women*, Brussels, Éditions Racine, 2005, pp. 95–102.

32 The AWNL claimed 52,000 members by 1914. It affiliated with NCWV in 1910. See Judith Smart, 'Eva Hughes: Militant Conservative', in Marilyn Lake and Farley Kelly (eds), *Double Time: Women in Victoria—150 Years*, Melbourne, Penguin, 1985, pp. 179–89. See also Marian Quartly, 'Defending "the purity of home life" against Socialism: The Founding Years of the Australian Women's National League', *Australian Journal of Politics and History*, 50 (2), 2004, pp. 178–93.

Victoria, where the AWNL exercised considerable weight.³³ Delegates from these groups were generally suspicious of central political authority, regarding it as 'socialistic'. Such women tended to defend states rights even as the national government was developing policy and legislation in the sphere of social reform and acquiring greater economic and industrial powers. They brought this suspicion of federal power to discussions about greater unity between the state councils.

The outbreak of the Great War in August 1914 stalled any momentum towards more systematic national co-operation. Between this time and the Kristiania quinquennial in 1920, there were no ICW congresses, and meetings and reports of the international standing committees were suspended until the end of hostilities.³⁴ Lady Aberdeen thought it best 'if the women of every country do what appears to them to be their duty as citizens of their countries'.³⁵ Thus 'all regular communication between the International Council and the National Councils stopped for six years, leading to a "loosening of the ties of common work within the international body"'.³⁶ The loss of regular international contact and an upsurge of imperial loyalty among the councils' leaders narrowed the outlook of the NCWs in Australia, as did the all-encompassing obsession with the war effort. Red Cross comforts and fund-raising work took over from the activities of the standing committees, which were mostly disbanded during the war years.

The war also gave rise to serious conflicts within state councils, especially in Victoria and Western Australia, where pacifist members

---

33 See especially Kate Gray, 'The Acceptable Face of Feminism: The National Council of Women of Victoria, 1902–18', MA thesis, University of Melbourne, 1988, pp. 101–03. Even before the AWNL affiliated, many of its leaders represented other organisations at NCW and continued to do so afterwards.

34 Maria Ogilvie Gordon, 'The International Council of Women (1888–1938)', *International Council of Women Bulletin*, No. 10, June 1938 (Jubilee Edition), p. 78.

35 Letter cited in NCWNSW Executive Minutes, 25 March 1915, Box MLK 03009, MS3739, NCWNSW Papers, SLNSW.

36 Quotations from Ishbel Aberdeen to Gertrud Bäumer [German], April 1915, HLA, 84–330(8), LB; Anna Backer, 'Annual Report of the Corresponding Secretary', *ICW Annual Report*, 1920–22. Both cited in Rupp, *Worlds of Women*, p. 26.

and delegates resigned or were expelled, and, in the case of WA, three organisations that had helped found the council disaffiliated. By 1916, most of Australia's NCWs had to varying degrees become mouthpieces for pro-war political conservatism and patriotism.[37] This patriotism was largely Empire focused, as demonstrated by the Victorian council's letter to the prime minister in May 'congratulating him' not only on his electoral victory over the Labor Party, but 'on the fact that Australia had proved her loyalty to the Empire'.[38] Yet the idea of nation—militarised though it was—developed alongside the old imperial identity, encouraged in part by the nation-wide organisation of Red Cross activities, with the governor-general's wife, Lady Helen Munro Ferguson, efficiently if not always harmoniously co-ordinating the efforts of the state governors' wives.[39] The fact, too, that many council leaders had sons fighting and dying in the Australian armed services added to a growing national sensibility and pride.

The Queensland council, perhaps the least affected by internal wartime differences, took the initiative early in 1916 to call for a 'properly constituted interstate Congress'. As a result, representatives from the Tasmanian, New South Wales, Victorian and Queensland councils met in Melbourne in November and formed an interim interstate committee, though Emily Dobson had argued that 'the present time was unsuitable'.[40] But, as NSW's Edith Fry commented, 'We must be national before we could be international' and interstate organisation

---

37 See, for example, Judith Smart, 'Women Waging War: The National Council of Women of Victoria 1914–1920', *Victorian Historical Journal*, 85 (1), 2015, pp. 61–82.
38 NCWV Executive Minutes, 8 May 1917, SLV (classification pending).
39 Melanie Oppenheimer, '"The Best P.M. for the Empire in War"?: Lady Helen Munro Ferguson and the Australian Red Cross, 1914–1920', *Australian Historical Studies*, 33 (119), 2002, pp. 108–24.
40 NCWQ Executive Minutes, 28 February 1916, Box 16045, 7266 NCWQ Minute Books, NCWQ Papers, State Library of Queensland (SLQ); NCWNSW Executive Minutes, 30 March 1916, 2 May 1916, 19 September 1916, 2 November 1916, 16 November 1916, Box MLK03009, MS3739, NCWNSW Papers, SLNSW; NCWV Executive Minutes, 12 November 1916, 13 March 1917, 20 March 1917, 17 April 1917, 12 May 1917, 18 May 1917, NCWV Papers, SLV (classification pending). WA's Mrs Bennett had reiterated the suggestion for a national president or secretary

would, in Queensland's Freda Bage's words, 'help to keep the various States in touch with each other's work and objects'.[41] In May 1917, a follow-up conference, also in Melbourne, confirmed the interstate committee and established its aims and objectives. It was resolved that there be two interstate conferences in the quinquennial period (one before and one after the ICW conference); that an interstate committee be formed to carry out conference resolutions and co-ordinate state council work; that the committee should comprise the president and secretary of the host state and all the other state council presidents; that the committee's power of initiative be limited to suggesting matters for federal action though it could be empowered by individual state councils to act for them; that conferences take place in the different states in order of their affiliation to ICW; that voting delegates be limited to state presidents and two others from each state; and that subjects for discussion must be submitted to the interstate committee six months before conference.[42] Victoria's Lillias Skene took on the work of interstate committee secretary.

The gathering planned for Sydney in May 1918 to ratify these decisions was postponed, most likely in consequence of the disruptive effects in late 1917 of major strikes in Sydney and women-led food riots in Melbourne, and political upheaval over conscription. As NSW's Ruby Board commented, it was doubtful 'if in these times any would be interested' in meeting and it was 'therefore better to postpone it than to have a fiasco'.[43] The meeting finally took place in Sydney in October

---

and/or a national newspaper early in 1915 but nothing came of it (letter referred to in NCWQ Council Minutes, 14 May 1915, Box 16045, 7266 NCWQ Minute Books, NCWQ Papers, SLQ).

41 NCWNSW Executive Minutes, 26 April 1917, Minute Book Executive 1917–21, Box MLK 03009, MS3739, NCWNSW Papers, SLNSW; *Argus*, 22 November 1916, p. 13.

42 NCWNSW Executive Minutes, 7 June 1917, 4 October 1917 (typed copy of resolutions appended), Box MLK 03009, MS3739, NCWNSW Papers, SLNSW.

43 NCWNSW Executive Minutes, 6 December 1917, Box MLK 03009, MS3739, NCWNSW Papers, SLNSW. The other states took some time to respond but, by May 1918, Victoria, Western Australian and Queensland had all agreed.

1919, nearly a year after the end of the war. Tasmania's Emily Dobson again claimed that it was unnecessary though she made the effort to attend.[44] Minor changes to the constitution of the interstate committee were referred to state councils for approval, but the main focus was on issues of common interest and preparation for the first post-war ICW quinquennial at Kristiania in September 1920 for which, as NSW's Rose Scott put it, the committee would 'provide machinery for united action'.[45]

In accordance with the 1917 agreement, a post-quinquennial conference took place in Hobart in January 1922, where, according to newspaper reports, the constitution as amended in 1919 was confirmed, with the addition of new rules for selecting ICW delegates to include representatives from the reconstituted South Australian council (re-formed in 1920). The Hobart conference marked the first gathering of delegates from all six states. It was chaired by Lady Rachel Forster, wife of the new governor general, who, like Lady Denman before the war, stressed the need for councils to unite 'for consultation and concerted action'; 'such union [was] necessary in the case of a young country like the growing Commonwealth', if they expected 'Australian opinion to count in the counsels of the world'. 'Only by effective union, too', she added, 'could they achieve the unification of the laws of the Australian States affecting women and children, and such questions [as] marriage and employment'.[46] She claimed a personal interest in the issue, for she had been president of the Kent branch of Britain's national council and, through her contacts with Lady Aberdeen, had become familiar with the anomalous position of the Australian councils.[47] The interstate

---

44   NCWNSW Executive Minutes, 17 July 1919, Box MLK 03009, MS3739, NCWNSW Papers, SLNSW.

45   Marchioness of Aberdeen and Temair (ed.), *Report on Quinquennial Meeting, Kristiania 1920*, Aberdeen, Rosemont Publishing, 1921, p. 288.

46   *Mercury*, 19 January 1922, p. 5.

47   See her address to the Victorian council in NCWV Council Minutes, 29 September 1921, NCWV Papers, SLV (classification pending), and to the NCWQ in NCWQ Council Minutes, 10 August 1921, Box 16045, 7266 NCWQ Minute Books,

committee was a step in the right direction but in her view it was only an interim measure. What was needed was a permanent federal body.

The need for an enduring national organisation was indeed becoming more urgent. Other women's organisations were taking the initiative, following the much earlier example of the WCTU and the Young Women's Christian Association (YWCA). Western Australia's Bessie Rischbieth was working to bring together the more progressive feminist organisations in Australia for the purpose of affiliation with ICW's radical offshoot, the International Woman Suffrage Alliance (IWSA).[48] Openly critical of the NCWs and impatient with their reluctance to federate as well as their slow and cumbersome processes of decision-making, Rischbieth targeted particular women at the triennial national conference of the WCTU in Perth in 1918 to form an interstate committee. Following the next WCTU conference in Melbourne in 1921, Rischbieth formed the Australian Federation of Women's Societies (AFWS) in order, as she said, to take women's organisation in Australia beyond 'the colonial stage of development'.[49]

The national councils also faced the anomalous situation that several of their affiliated organisations had by 1923 formed national bodies; among them, in addition to the WCTU, the YWCA and the AFWS, were the Australian Federation of University Women and the Housewives' Associations. With the support of Lady Forster, a concrete proposal to federate the NCWs was now put forward by Victorian vice-president Eleanor Glencross, also the first president of the Federated Housewives' Associations of Australia.[50] At a meeting of NCWV on

---

NCWQ Papers, SLQ.

48 Vida Goldstein's Women's Political Association had been affiliated but was disbanded in 1919, leaving a vacuum in Australian representation.

49 Lake, *Getting Equal*, p. 157; Bessie Rischbieth, 'AFWV: An Impression of Twenty-seven Years Activity for Equal Citizenship in the Australian Commonwealth', 2004/5/3022, MS2004, Rischbieth Papers, National Library of Australia (NLA). WCTU triennial conferences were the only forums at which large numbers of women regularly met nationwide.

50 On the Housewives' Associations, see Judith Smart, 'The Politics of Consumption: The Housewives' Associations in Southeastern Australia before 1950', *Journal*

22 March 1923, her arguments were cogent and pragmatic: 'she was convinced of the necessity of forming an Australian Council', given that 'several of the affiliated organisations already had Federal Associations ... As a Council we are weakened as a force if we have not a strong federated body'. She moved:

> That the delegates and associates of the National Council of Women strongly recommend that the next Interstate Conference adopt a scheme whereby a Federal body be formed, drawn from the various States' Councils with the object of enhancing the power of Councils in dealing with matters of Australian concern.

The resolution was 'carried absolutely unanimously'.[51] Victorians then began to proselytise in the other states. After Mary Bage's address in August to NCWQ's annual general meeting, the Queensland council agreed that its incoming executive should formulate a resolution for federation of the national councils of Australia.[52] NCWQ then wrote to the NSW and SA councils urging the formation of an Australian National Council of Women. Victoria also wrote in similar vein to NCWSA, and Lady Forster let her views be known to the other councils.[53]

From Tasmania, Emily Dobson made a bid to stymie proceedings. Victoria's resolution, she wrote, was 'ultra vires as the Australian Council was formed and its affiliation accepted by the I.C.W. in consequence of

---

of Women's History, 18 (3), 2006, pp. 13–39, and 'A Mission to the Home: The Housewives' Association, the Woman's Christian Temperance Union and Protestant Christianity, 1920–40', *Australian Feminist Studies*, 13 (28), 1998, pp. 215–34.

51 Meredith Foley, 'Glencross, Eleanor (1876–1950)', *Australian Dictionary of Biography* (*ADB*), http://adb.anu.edu.au/biography/glencross-eleanor-6402/text10943; Book 7, NCWV, 'Foundation Australian NCW', p. 1, loose material, NCWV Papers, SLV (classification pending).

52 NCWQ Council Minutes, Annual General Meeting, 1 and 2 August 1923, Box 16045, 7266 NCWQ Minute Books, NCWQ Papers, SLQ.

53 NCWNSW Executive Minutes, 6 September 1923, Box MLK 03009, MS3739, NCWNSW Papers, SLNSW; NCWSA Council Minutes, 11 September 1923, 11 October 1923, SRG297, NCWSA Papers, State Library of South Australia (SLSA).

a resolution uniformly voted by the Australian Councils' back in 1906. Her solution was to revise the rules governing what she held to be the ICW-recognised body in order to strengthen the office of Australian president (which she regarded as her own) by directing through it the international channels of communication and influence currently enjoyed by the individual councils. Purely Australian matters could be dealt with by the existing interstate committee, with 'the President and Secretary of the Hostess-State of each Conference' continuing in those roles 'until the next Interstate Conference'.[54]

The issue of a permanent federal body was the first business of the interstate conference that opened in Melbourne on 21 October 1924. All states were well represented, and Lady Forster agreed to chair proceedings. Again Dobson protested that an Australian council was already in existence in the form still recognised by ICW, but the Victorians had responses prepared.

> What we are proposing ... is really an Interstate Council, which will have nothing to do with the I.C.W. If we choose to have an Interstate Conference or an Australian Council merely for the sake of certain questions which concern Australia only, I do not see what that has to do with the I.C.W.

The resolution finally carried simply read: 'That a Federal Council be formed from the State National Councils of Women of Australia'.[55] The remaining four days of the conference saw the formulation of a constitution that preserved the existing agreement for state ICW representation and finance but gave the new body responsibility for 'internal questions which concern the Commonwealth as a whole' and 'such other matters as may be referred to it by any State Councils'.

---

54 NCWV, 'Foundation Australian NCW', pp. 4 and 8, loose material, NCWV Papers, SLV (classification pending); reference to a letter on this matter from Dobson to NCWSA can also be seen in NCWSA Council Minutes, 23 October 1923, SRG297, NCWSA Papers, SLSA.

55 NCWs of Australia, Minutes of Interstate Conference, October 1924, Box 12, MS7583, NCWA Papers, NLA.

Lillias Skene
FCNCWA President 1924–1927

Lillias Skene played a leading role in the creation of the federal body representing all the Australian National Councils of Women in 1924. Born in rural Victoria in 1867, she was educated locally at Alexandra College. She married in 1888 and had four children. A series of economic difficulties forced them to give up the land and the family settled in Melbourne in 1910.

Like many progressive reformers of the time, Skene worked to improve the living conditions of the poor, especially women and children. She represented the Guild of Play on the National Council of Women of Victoria until the 1920s. Her first paper to the council in 1908, 'A City Milk Supply', contributed to the foundation of the Lady Talbot Milk Institute to supply fresh milk to babies and to educate their mothers on appropriate feeding methods. Skene represented NCW Victoria at a conference called to establish baby health clinics in Melbourne, and played a leading part in the council's campaign against prostitution and venereal disease.

During the war Skene worked with other leading members of NCW Victoria to exclude from the council the delegates of organisations with pacifist or socialist sympathies. She helped found the British (Australian) Red Cross in 1914, and remained dedicated to Red Cross work after the war, serving as outreach officer in 1939 and as chair of the Home Hospital Committee from 1943. In 1919, she was appointed honorary secretary of the Women's Hospital Committee, a position she held for 30 years.

Skene became president of NCW Victoria in 1924. On Victoria's initiative, a preliminary Federal Council of the National Councils of Women of Australia was established that year with Skene as its foundation president; its aim was to provide one truly national voice both for Australia and for the outside world. After consolidating the national body, Skene continued to contribute to council work until the late 1940s.

Skene was appointed MBE in 1919 for her patriotic work during the Great War. She was one of Victoria's first 7 women justices of the peace in 1927; in the same year she was appointed to the Victorian Nursing Board and in 1929 to the State Relief Committee. According to the *Australasian*, she was 'entitled to first place in a gallery of those women who are leaders of their sex in the public life of the Commonwealth'. She died in 1957.

Explore further resources about Lillias Skene in the Australian Women's Register.

The Federal Council of the National Councils of Women of Australia (FCNCWA) would meet annually, would comprise the president, secretary and four other delegates from each state, and would elect its own office-bearers each year, no president to hold office for more than five consecutive years. In addition, two conferences would be held in each quinquennial period.[56] The conference baulked at taking the further step to ICW affiliation in place of the separate states, despite Lady Forster's clear preference for the new body to assume international representative responsibilities. As Lillias Skene, first FCNCWA president, confessed: 'We are rather afraid that if this Council deals with international affairs as well as Australian, we will lose our separate autonomy and our direct touch with the International, and simply become provincial Councils'.[57]

Dobson's insistence that she, and she alone, held the ICW-recognised title of Australian president, and that the president of the federal council could not therefore also hold the title, led to an acrimonious correspondence between Dobson, Victoria's Alice Michaelis (elected secretary of the new FCNCWA in 1924) and Lady Forster, and to a refusal by Dobson to hand over correspondence relating to the next quinquennial conference arrangements. After three months of mutual recrimination and constitutional argument, Michaelis, having carefully researched ICW resolutions on the subject since 1906, composed two admirably clear letters—one to Emily Dobson and the other to Lady Aberdeen. In the former, dated 5 February 1925, she wrote:

> In all of these resolutions it states distinctly that the president is appointed to represent Australia at the I.C.W. meetings only, not for the Quinquennial period ... There has not been nor is there an Australian National Council, merely a federation for purposes only of finance and representation at I.C.W. meetings.

---

56 NCWs of Australia, Minutes of Interstate Conference, October 1924, Box 12, and 'Constitution of the Federal Council of the National Council of Women of Australia', Box 12, MS7583, NCWA Papers, NLA.

57 NCWs of Australia, Minutes of Interstate Conference, October 1924, Box 12, MS7583, NCWA Papers, NLA.

The new federal council was not in any case seeking ICW affiliation, she continued, and while 'Its president's office is a permanent one for Australia … that president is not ex officio the president of a delegation unless elected by the State Councils'.[58] To Lady Aberdeen, a month later, she was more forthright, reiterating the results of her research but also explaining that

> Mrs Dobson considers that an Australian National Council was formed in 1906, and that the Australian President appointed to a Quinquennial Delegation is appointed for the full quinquennial period, she, therefore maintains that as President elected for the last Quinquennial meeting she acts until the next at Washington.

Michaelis then pointed out that ICW reports up until the most recent one had made no mention of an Australian president. It was her belief that it was only 'now included in consequence of the letter heading used by Mrs. Dobson, without the knowledge of the State Councils, since the proposal of the formation of the Federal Council'. Previously Dobson had written on letterhead as president of NCW Tasmania, according to Michaelis, but 'now she uses paper headed "National Council of Women of Australia, Commonwealth President, Mrs. Henry Dobson", and I would ask you to have this matter corrected in any subsequent publication'. In a slightly more placatory tone, she explained that

> Mrs. Dobson had been re-elected over and over again as President of the various delegations, which has obscured her true position both to her and us. It was not until the formation of the Federal Council that we realised Mrs. Dobson's assumption.

To reassure Lady Aberdeen that she was not writing without authority, she noted that the previous day's federal council executive meeting, presided over by Lady Forster, had given its 'full agreement with the views

---

58 Alice Michaelis, Hon. Sec. FCNCWA, to Mrs Dobson, 5 February 1925, in folder, 'Reports on Interstate Conference 1924–1925 and Interstate Correspondence 1926–1927', Miscellaneous NCWQ Papers (in temporary possession of the authors).

expressed in this letter'. She then requested all future correspondence regarding ICW meetings be sent to her as 'Federal Secretary'.[59]

As the body co-ordinating the state councils, FCNCWA was determined to assert its right to arrange for the election of the leader of the next ICW delegation. Though Dobson had announced her intention to step down as Australian president and ICW vice-president at the next quinquennial meeting, the new federal executive was unwilling to concede her any right in the interim to continue using the title Australian or Commonwealth president. In the period between the 1924 interstate conference and the first conference of the federal council in September 1925, an Australian delegation led by NSW's Ruby Board attended the ICW quinquennial congress in Washington. Emily Dobson was present and was appointed an honorary life vice-president of ICW. But she clearly regarded Board's elevation as president of the Australian delegation as a slight, and continued to dispute the validity of FCNCWA. The Melbourne conference in September 1925 saw her last serious effort to block the trajectory towards a national organisation and identity for the NCWs. Its defeat marked the waning of Emily Dobson's earlier unquestioned pre-eminence, as another generation of women, made confident by the war years and subsequent organisational experience, dared to challenge her tutelary position and expertise.

Dobson first questioned the minutes of the 1924 conference, and then challenged the delegation's report of the ICW Board of Officers meeting in Washington, where the constitution of FCNCWA was provisionally accepted. Then, after the Melbourne conference confirmed the establishment of the federal council in the form agreed to the previous year, Dobson proposed a series of constitutional amendments aimed at keeping power in the hands of the states and rendering

---

59   Alice Michaelis, Hon. Sec. FCNCWA, to Lady Aberdeen, 5 March 1925, in folder, 'Reports on Interstate Conference …', Miscellaneous NCWQ Papers (in temporary possession of the authors).

FCNCWA redundant. They all failed.[60] When the president moved to welcome the honour that Dobson's ICW life vice-presidency conferred on Australian councils as a whole, Dobson responded with a long statement, which by agreement was not recorded in the minutes. Miss Board 'expressed regret' about Dobson's statement and hastened to move: 'That we place on record the very sincere admiration we have for Mrs. Dobson and thanks for all the work and long service she had given to Australia'. The meeting also immediately agreed to make provision in FCNCWA's constitution for the award of honorary life vice-presidencies to those who have 'given special service to the whole of the Australian Councils', but significantly 'without the right to vote'. The first such award went, not surprisingly, to Emily Dobson, who recovered her dignity sufficiently to thank the council 'for the honour conferred'.[61]

It was an appropriate gesture from the new national body. Despite her resistance to change and the diminution of her power, Emily Dobson had made an unparalleled contribution to the development of the early council movement in Australia. Without her willingness to travel and devote her time and talents to the organisations, it is unlikely that they would have survived, let alone maintained links with ICW and each other, before the 1920s.[62]

Over the ensuing two years, the federal council worked hard to demonstrate its efficacy, and, in her presidential addresses at the annual meetings in 1926 and 1927, Lillias Skene emphasised the achievements.[63] Her recommendation in 1926 that the interstate

---

60   First Annual Meeting of FCNCWA, 22–26 September 1925, Melbourne, Box 12, MS7583, NCWA Papers, NLA.

61   First Annual Meeting of FCNCWA, 22–26 September 1925, Melbourne, Box 12, MS7583, NCWA Papers, NLA.

62   'Emily Dobson', *Stirrers with Style! Presidents of the National Council of Women of Australia and Its Predecessors*, http://www.womenaustralia.info/exhib/ncwa/presidents-09.html.

63   'Lillias Skene', *Stirrers with Style! Presidents of the National Council of Women of Australia and Its Predecessors*, http://www.womenaustralia.info/exhib/ncwa/presidents-26.html.

conferences be absorbed into the annual meetings of FCNCWA was accepted without controversy and constituted a further step to closer union. But the pressure that finally transformed the federal council into a national body that also spoke for the councils internationally came primarily from outside.

In 1925, ICW had taken steps to form what came to be known as the Joint Standing Committee of the Women's International Organisations, mainly 'to push for the appointment of women to the League of Nations'.[64] This was not discussed by the federal council in Australia until after the national general secretary of YWCA took the initiative in February 1928 of informally calling together representatives of the five national organisations of women with international affiliations[65] to deal with representation of Australian women at the imminent Pan Pacific Women's Conference. In July, the provisional standing committee (including FCNCWA representatives) went ahead with the selection of delegates and appointed AFWV president Bessie Rischbieth as leader. At the federal council meeting in Sydney in July, the new president, NSW's Mildred Muscio,[66] reported these events and assured states' council representatives that she had made it clear that:

> the National Councils of Women must decide for themselves at their annual Federal meeting whether they wished the Joint Standing Committee to continue, and unless they did so, it could not have any official status as far as they were concerned.[67]

The ensuing discussion revealed confusion and anxiety for it was obvious that the prestige and pre-eminence of the councils was under

---

64 Rupp, *Worlds of Women*, p. 37.
65 Australian Federation of University Women, Australian Federation of Women Voters, Australian National YWCA, Australian WCTU, and the Federal Council of the NCWs of Australia.
66 'Mildred Muscio', *Stirrers with Style! Presidents of the National Council of Women of Australia and Its Predecessors*, http://www.womenaustralia.info/exhib/ncwa/presidents-21.html.
67 FCNCWA Conference Minutes, July 1928, Box 12, MS7583, NCWA Papers, NLA.

Mildred Muscio
FCNCWA President 1927–1931

Mildred Muscio was the second president of the Federal Council of the National Councils of Women of Australia (FCNCWA). Her leadership was the crucial factor in the creation of the National Council of Women of Australia, which in 1931 succeeded the FNCWA and became the single channel for Australian representation at the International Council of Women.

Born in 1882 at Copeland, NSW, she was educated at Sydney Girls' High School and the University of Sydney, graduating with BA Honours in 1901 and MA in 1905. She worked as a teacher while completing her studies and was principal of the Brighton College for Girls, Manly, from 1906 to 1912. Muscio travelled to England, and while living there married Bernard Muscio, philosopher and industrial psychologist, of Cambridge University, and attended the first congress of the International Federation of University Women in London in 1920.

Returning to Australia in 1922 on her husband's appointment to the University of Sydney, she helped establish the university women's movement in this country. She was president of the Sydney Women Graduates' Association from 1923 to 1926, and the Sydney University Women's Union from 1927 to 1928. She became an executive member of the Sydney University Settlement, helped found the Institute of Industrial Psychology, and lectured in psychology for the University Extension Board.

Muscio's association with the National Council of Women of NSW began in 1922 when she was invited to organise the Good Film League, of which she became vice-president. She joined the council's executive as press secretary in 1924 and was its president from 1927 to 1938. With a fine intellect and more progressive than her predecessors, Muscio also had the gift of persuasion, and used it to overcome fears of change and loss of autonomy among state council delegates to the FCNCWA conference in 1929. After the NCWA formally came into being in July 1931, she acted as caretaker president until elections could be held in October that year.

She was a member of many other organisations, such as the Lyceum Club and the Australian Red Cross Society. In 1927 she served on the Commonwealth royal commission into child endowment, and submitted a minority report with John Curtin calling for means-tested endowment for the third and subsequent children. In 1937 she served as Australia's alternate delegate to the League of Nations.

Muscio was appointed an Officer of the Order of the British Empire (OBE) in 1938. She died in 1964. She is remembered for her powers of persuasion, her organising abilities, and her sympathetic spirit.

Explore further resources about Mildred Muscio in the Australian Women's Register.

threat. Most felt that joining the joint standing committee would signal a concession of power to the other organisations but agreed that some links were necessary, preferably, as Victorian president Eleanor Glencross suggested, by 'giving Internationally affiliated bodies representation on the Federal Council' where they would operate under the aegis of the NCWs.[68] But events overtook them once more.

On her return to Australia in November, Rischbieth convened a conference of the same five organisations to formalise the joint standing committee and establish a permanent body, the Australian Women's Co-operating Committee of Federal Organisations. This would have power to recommend the names of Australian women qualified for service on the committees and commissions of the League of Nations, ensure election of nominees to represent Australia at important international conferences, and receive correspondence from abroad 'in which action of Australian women as a national entity may be sought'.[69] The NCWs were left scrambling to catch up without losing face, especially since the co-operating committee was modelled on the international Joint Standing Committee established by ICW, to which the Australian councils had turned a blind eye. To add insult to injury, it was pointed out that there were problems in admitting the FCNCWA to full membership of the co-operating committee since it did not have international affiliation to ICW in its own right, that connection still residing with the state councils. For the time being, the federal council decided to adopt observer status on both the co-operating and Pan Pacific committees, but the underlying problem had to be resolved.

At the 1929 FCNCWA conference in September in Perth, the Queensland and NSW councils took the lead, Queensland moving for the establishment of an Australian council having international affiliation. Most of the delegates expressed a conservative distaste for

---

68   FCNCWA Conference Minutes, July 1928, Box 12, MS7583, NCWA Papers, NLA.
69   Reported in *White Ribbon Signal*, 8 July 1929, p. 103.

'concentration of power' as well as a predilection for 'no change' and 'staying our hand'. Even the report of an interview with Lady Aberdeen, 'who expressed the keenest desire that an Australian Council should be formed', failed to impress. Then the president, NSW's Mildred Muscio, vacated the chair, taking control of the argument for a national council and dealing briskly with all the traditional sources of opposition and fear. Differences between the states were exaggerated; indeed '[w]e are on the whole more homogeneous, our laws more similar than in other country of comparable size'. 'Progressive improvements' in communications had made the problem of distance and expense of travel irrelevant. The state councils would continue to be the building blocks of the national organisation and 'would suffer no loss of importance, or prestige, or identity'. '[W]e have to make up our minds to come into line with the rest of the world' and do more as Australians—'Australia is becoming one unit'. But, although this appeal to national identity now had some resonance, the clinching argument came from Muscio's New South Wales colleague and federal council secretary, Evelyn Tildesley, who resorted to traditional imperial loyalties: 'Are we going to ... embarrass an International President, who is a British woman and finds it difficult to meet foreign criticism of Councils within the Empire?' Tildesley also drove home the necessity for national organisation by frankly acknowledging that 'the real danger is not finance or centralised control, but [the] Joint Standing Committee. The next Pan-Pacific Conference over, the Australian Co-operating Committee will go on and evolve to a super-N.C.W. unless we have something else to offer'. The resolution finally passed approved 'the principle of one N.C.W. for Australia' and instructed the federal executive to prepare a draft constitution to be finalised at the next annual meeting.[70]

The last conference of the federal council took place in Hobart in January 1931, where a constitution 'designed to make the minimum of

---

70   FCNCWA Conference Minutes, September 1929, Box 12, MS7583, NCWA Papers, NLA.

alteration in the existing constitution' was approved, and the name of the new body—the National Council of Women of Australia (NCWA)—unanimously endorsed.[71] The key change to the constitution was the addition of a new first object, which read 'to be the link between the State Councils of Women of Australia and the International Council of Women'. But in order to assert itself as at least equal in status to the Australian Co-operating Committee, the council added to the voting membership of the new body 'The President or her proxy of each women's organisation having international affiliation with the State Councils in each State of the Commonwealth'.[72]

The first meeting of the new NCWA executive was held in Melbourne in October. New officers were elected, Lady Aberdeen's acknowledgement of the new constitution was received, and a strategy was discussed to deal with Western Australia's decision not to join the national body.[73] That was to consume much energy over the following months and delayed the holding of the first national conference for over a year.

Bringing the Australian national councils together in a permanent federal body that spoke with a single and united voice at national and international levels had been a long and difficult process, driven at least as much by external pressure (both Australian and international) as by a sense of common purpose. Though the NCWs were able to imagine

---

71 FCNCWA Conference Minutes, January 1931, Box 12, NCWA Papers, NLA. National Council of Women of Australia was the official title of the organisation, which Ivy Brookes changed to Australian National Council of Women (ANCW) in 1950. In 1971, the original title was officially restored.
72 FCNCWA Conference Minutes, January 1931, Box 12, MS7583, NCWA Papers, NLA.
73 Executive Committee NCWA, Melbourne, 13–14 October 1931, Box 12, MS7583, NCWA Papers, NLA.

a national identity by the 1920s, its development had been retarded by an entrenched commitment to states rights and loyalties. Personal and political rivalries and competition for national and international influence arising from an expansion and diversification of the women's movement forced the councils finally to reach an accommodation. Nevertheless, without a developing sense of nation-wide collective purpose arising from a common social reform agenda based on commitment to home and family, national organisation would have lacked a solid foundation. It is to the evolution of this sense of common social and moral purpose that we now turn.

Chapter 2

HOME AND FAMILY ENTER THE BODY POLITIC

Organisational imperatives were not the major reason for communication between Australia's national councils, nor the principal rationale for interstate meetings in the period before a permanent national structure emerged.[1] The main topics discussed were those relating to home and family. The first meeting of interstate representatives seems to have been the Tasmanian conference of January 1902, when Dr Mary Booth from NSW and Dr Mary Stone and Mrs Evelyn Gough from Victoria spoke on the teaching of physiology to girls and on domestic and factory labour.[2] Topics like these, together with more general issues of family welfare and women's citizenship, were stalwarts of interstate council meetings over the following decades.

Historians identify the dominant concern of women working for women in the early twentieth century as 'maternal feminism'—a feminism focusing mainly on the welfare of home and family. This holds true for all the women involved with the early councils, whether they were philanthropists, reformers, suffragists, political conservatives, or among the small coterie of professional women entering NCW ranks.

---

1   Evelyn Gough in Victoria and Rose Scott in NSW were particularly active correspondents. See Kate Gray, 'The Acceptable Face of Feminism: The National Council of Women of Victoria, 1902–18', MA thesis, University of Melbourne, 1988, p. 42.
2   *Mercury*, 7 January 1902, p. 4. Note that NCWV had not yet been formed at this stage, but Gough and Stone were to become key figures in its early years.

The focus of action for feminists of this kind can be summed up as protection, education, health and morals, all essential and interconnected elements of the discourse of philanthropy and rescue that persisted into early twentieth-century Australian ideals of progressivist reform and social liberalism.[3]

Rarely did the councils conceive problems in terms of political economy and class and only occasionally did they identify them as questions of social justice. Although scientific evidence gradually became more important in their arguments, with qualified experts gaining greater prominence among office-bearers and advisers, the councils still mostly saw their work as ameliorative and gave no support to programs of structural change to society as a whole. They did, however, gradually come to espouse a more individualist rights-based feminism alongside the dominant maternalism in the interwar and post-World War II years.

Maternal feminism was the key justification in council circles for women's entry into public life. Tasmanian president in 1901, Lady Dodds, quoted ICW's Lady Aberdeen as saying: 'We hold fast to the belief that woman's first duty must be her home ... and that by its home life every country will stand or fall'.[4] The preambles of the various Australian council constitutions all invoked the belief that:

> the best good of our homes and State will ... be advanced by our greater unity of thought, sympathy and purpose, and that an organised movement of women will best conserve the highest good of the family and the State.[5]

---

[3] On maternal feminism see Karen Offen, 'Defining Feminism: A Comparative Historical Approach', *Signs*, 14 (Autumn), 1988, pp. 119–57. On progressivism in Australia, see Michael Roe, *Nine Australian Progressives: Vitalism in Bourgeois Social Thought 1890–1960*, Brisbane, University of Queensland Press Scholars' Library, 1984; and on social liberalism, see Marian Sawer, *The Ethical State? Social Liberalism in Australia*, Melbourne, Melbourne University Press, 2003.

[4] *Mercury*, 26 April 1901, p. 4.

[5] Taken from NCWNSW Constitution, dated 27 February 1903.

Towards the end of the period dealt with in this chapter, Mildred Muscio, newly elected NSW president and soon to be federal council president, wrote:

> there is no real opposition between women's interests inside the home and her interests outside the home. She must go outside the home in order to be efficient within it; and it is because of her real and important experience within the home that woman ought to go outside to take place in public affairs.[6]

Muscio clearly recognised the change modern professional and scientific approaches had brought to this work, a process of reorientation and rationalisation historical sociologist Kerreen Reiger has termed the 'disenchantment of the home'.[7] As Muscio observed, 'the woman who now faces these domestic problems is not the woman who faced them half a century ago: she brings education, science, logic and experience of the outside world to aid her'. She recognised too that domestic problems 'have become national problems', and, in dealing with them, 'No gulf separates the interests of the professional woman from those of the non-professional woman'. 'Now the chief business of Parliaments is the business of the homes of the people … Industry, economics, politics, laws are only our own experience written larger'.[8]

Doctors, lawyers, teachers and university women in the NCWs played a key role in this development. In effect, the women's movement had conducted a successful assault on the masculinist preoccupations of the public sphere, though women had not achieved the power necessary to create real change. The councils came increasingly to identify gendered inequality in the distribution of power as the major factor blocking the development and implementation of public policy—as it still is today.

---

6   'Presidential Address', NCWNSW, *Biennial Reports for 1926–1928*, pp. 3 and 4.
7   After Max Weber. See Kerreen Reiger, *The Disenchantment of the Home: Modernizing the Australian Family 1880–1940*, Melbourne, Oxford University Press, 1985.
8   'Presidential Address', NCWNSW, *Biennial Reports for 1926–1928*, pp. 3 and 4.

Protecting Women and Children

Marilyn Lake describes the first three decades of twentieth-century women's activism in Australia as an attempt 'to reconcile [a] maternalist mission of protection with a feminist emphasis on the independence due to full citizens'.[9] Protection was the initial inspiration. It was a keystone of philanthropy, conceived ideally as a paternal/maternal relationship of generous benefactor and grateful recipient. This was an inherently unequal relationship justified by lady philanthropists as Christian compassion and social duty rather than desire for power or tangible benefit. It was, nevertheless, one of the few ways women could exercise power outside the home, albeit primarily over other women and children.

In the essentialist understanding of maternal feminists, mother love, the nearest human beings could come to comprehending and mirroring the love of God,[10] endowed women with the spiritual qualities necessary to 'build up our young nation upon all that is righteous'. This was the essence of women's difference from men and the basis of the claims for women's citizenship made by women leaders in the post-suffrage years. In Rose Scott's opinion, the future of the nation would be assured by 'the individual consciences of its women'.[11] This rationale for public or civic motherhood, rooted in Christian conviction, was most evident in women's long-standing attempts to protect the welfare of infants and children, especially those defined as neglected or destitute.

Work among children and babies marked the origins of middle-class women's philanthropic activity in the Australian colonies. Its early forms were institutional—orphanages, industrial schools and

---

9   Marilyn Lake, 'A History of Feminism in Australia', in Barbara Caine (ed.), *Australian Feminism: A Companion*, Melbourne, Oxford University Press, 1998, p. 134. This accords with Karen Offen's distinction between relational and individual feminism and the gradual strengthening of the latter.

10 Sarah Lewis quoted in Jane Rendall, *The Origins of Modern Feminism: Women in Britain, France and the United States*, Basingstoke, Macmillan, p. 75.

11 *Australian Woman's Sphere*, 5 December 1903. See also Judith Allen, *Rose Scott: Vision and Revision in Feminism*, Melbourne, Oxford University Press, 1994, chapter 3, for a full discussion of Scott's arguments.

reformatories—and protection, education and reform were inextricably intertwined elements of what was seen as rescue work. In the second half of the nineteenth century, the involvement of the state in regulating this activity expanded, and policy took shape through legislation and regimes of inspection and supervision. While women did not make the laws, they did exert influence on policy and its operation through the press and public meetings, and through the voluntary labour they undertook on behalf of the state and charity organisations.

Australian pre-war reformers, as in Britain and America, attached central importance to the health, wellbeing and training of the young as the key to social order, good citizenship, national strength and racial efficiency. A commentator noted the 'The present day is said to be "an age of child worship"' but suggested this arose from 'fears of a child famine'.[12] Anxiety about the declining birth rate in the early twentieth century was common to many nations. It was most cogently expressed in Australia in the 1904 report of the exclusively male NSW royal commission into the birth rate, which concluded that a selfish preoccupation with material prosperity underpinned a readiness among middle-class women to use artificial means of contraception.[13] The commissioners and middle-class women themselves were also concerned with the high infant mortality rate among the working classes and the quality of the rising generation in the cities. Governments and reformers alike saw the solution in elevating standards of mothering and working-class family life, and in extending regulation, inspection and surveillance, rather than dealing with the underlying problem of poverty. Gradually women asserted their claims to professional expertise in this area and NCWs, on taking these issues up, accelerated the process without challenging the overall direction of policy. Within this framework, they chalked up some notable achievements.

---

12   W.T. Rhodes, Chairman, Interstate Congress of Workers in the Field of Dependent Children, Adelaide, May 1909, p. 6.
13   Neville Hicks, *'This Sin and Scandal': Australia's Population Debate, 1891–1911*, Canberra, ANU Press, 1978.

The women who came together at interstate Woman's Christian Temperance Union (WCTU), then NCW, meetings in the 1890s and the early twentieth century quickly recognised common problems and the inadequacy of existing legislation and institutions. Their mutual activism was encouraged by ICW requests to all national councils for information about legislation 'concerning women and children in their respective countries'.[14] In Australia, an interstate Congress of Workers Among Dependent Children held in Adelaide in May 1909 had as one of its principal objectives uniformity of policy throughout the Australian Commonwealth. Delegates to the Adelaide conference included women belonging to the Queensland and Victorian NCWs, as well as Catherine Spence, a long-term child-welfare worker and founder of the by-then defunct SA council. Ideas from this gathering were taken back to the state councils and informed work that had proceeded largely independently until that time. Child and infant welfare thus became matters of national concern from 1909, and were given encouragement and international context by ICW resolutions and calls for action.

By the end of the nineteenth century most of the Australian colonies had adopted the system of 'boarding out', under which children removed from homes considered 'unsuitable' were fostered by 'the families of the respectable poor' rather than being consigned to residential industrial schools and other institutions.[15] Though women did not control the schemes, supervision was largely assigned to voluntary local 'ladies' committees', whose members were deputed to visit and report on the homes to which the children were assigned. Though boarding out seemed more humane than the institutional alternatives and the lady visitors were mostly compassionate, the scheme was bedevilled by

---

14   London 1899 and Toronto 1909, 'ICW Resolutions', http://www.ncwcanada.com/ncwc2/wp-content/uploads/2014/02/ICW-CIF_Resolutions1.pdf, pp. 17, 113.

15   Margaret Barbalet, *Far from a Low Gutter Girl: The Forgotten World of State Wards: South Australia 1887–1940*, Melbourne, Oxford University Press, 1983, pp. 190–6; Nell Musgrove, *The Scars Remain: A Long History of Forgotten Australians and Children's Institutions*, Melbourne, Australian Scholarly Publishing, 2013, chap. 2; Interstate Congress of Workers in the Field of Dependent Children, p. 111.

problems of abuse and exploitation of the children. Legislative regulation and voluntary inspection were weak and these issues were among those taken up by the emerging NCWs.

A humane extension of the boarding-out system allowed children under state protection to be fostered by their own mothers. The colony of Victoria had led the way in 1880 in experimenting with returning state children to 'deserving' mothers with secure accommodation, and making foster payments to them.[16] NSW legislated custody and payment to widowed or deserted mothers from 1896, Queensland was boarding some children out to their mothers by 1908–09, and, in South Australia, the practice was extended beyond a limited probation system just before World War I.[17] Children boarded out to their mothers or on probation in their own families were thus subjected to supervision and inspection just like other foster families, an area of immediate interest to women in the NCWs.

Three of the outstanding early Australian feminists—Catherine Spence, Vida Goldstein and Rose Scott—all founding members of their respective colonial and state councils, were among the loudest voices in the campaign for child and infant welfare reform. Spence helped inaugurate the boarding-out system, and she was also a key figure in the organisation of the 1909 congress on neglected children in Adelaide.[18] Goldstein fought for control and inspection by 'properly qualified women' and was commissioned by the new Commonwealth government

---

16   The scheme was suspended but re-instated in 1890, and, by 1914, more children were boarded out to their own mothers than to foster mothers, though this practice was not recognised in law until 1919.

17   Donella Jaggs, *Neglected and Criminal: Foundations of Child Welfare Legislation in Victoria*, Melbourne, Phillip Institute of Technology, 1986, pp. 109–12; Brian Dickey, *No Charity There: A Short History of Social Welfare in Australia*, Sydney, Allen & Unwin, 1987, p. 86; Barbalet, *Far from a Low Gutter* Girl, pp. 200–02; Interstate Congress of Workers in the Field of Dependent Children, p. 111.

18   Barbalet shows inaccuracies and exaggerations in Spence's account, *State Child in Australia*. Its interstate and international impact was mentioned in the published report of the 1909 Interstate Congress of Workers in the Field of Dependent Children, p. 6.

to report on developments in the field of child welfare while overseas in 1902; she too attended and spoke at the 1909 congress, representing Victoria.[19] And Scott took the leading role in the campaigns for state children's and infant protection legislation in NSW during 1902–03, resulting in the acts of 1903 and 1904.[20] In Queensland, Agnes Williams was a key figure in NCWQ's agitation to extend the system of payment to natural mothers fostering their own children, and she led the campaign in Brisbane to establish a State Children's Council to oversee issues relating to neglected children.[21]

Labor Party and socialist women took up the idea of paying mothers to mother, successfully persuading Prime Minister Andrew Fisher in 1912 to introduce a maternity allowance of £5 for every mother giving birth, married or unmarried. A once-off payment that was equal to five weeks average wages for a working woman, it was justified as recognition of the rights of citizen-mothers and their service to the nation and as a means of reducing infant mortality by providing for a woman's needs in childbirth. Labour and socialist women saw it as only the first instalment of full endowment of motherhood. Since citizenship was racially defined in the early Commonwealth, the allowance excluded Aboriginal and Asiatic women. Many in the NCWs were at first ambivalent about the so-called 'baby bonus' as endorsing immorality and undermining individual responsibility but none, except radical feminist Vida Goldstein, objected to the racial exclusions.[22]

---

19   Janette Bomford, *That Dangerous and Persuasive Woman: Vida Goldstein*, Melbourne, Melbourne University Press, 1993, pp. 32, 33; Shurlee Swain, '"The Supervision of ... Babies Is Woman's Work, And Cannot Be Rightly Done By Men": Victorian Women's Organisations and Female Child Welfare Inspectors 1890–1915', *Victorian Historical Journal*, 79 (2), 2008, p. 317.

20   Allen, *Rose Scott*, p. 190; NCWNSW Council Minutes, 18 November 1902, and Special Executive Minutes, 2 October 1903, Box MLK03009, MS3739, NCWNSW Papers, State Library of New South Wales (SLNSW).

21   NCWQ Council Minutes, 19 March 1909, 6 and 21 August 1909, 10 September 1909, 6 December 1909, Box 16045, 7266 NCWQ Minute Books, NCWQ Papers, State Library of Queensland (SLQ).

22   Marilyn Lake, 'State Socialism for Australian Mothers: Andrew Fisher's Radical Maternalism in its International and Local Contexts', *Labour History*, 102, May

The focus of all these women was largely on white children in the industrial suburbs of the major cities. None of them talked about protection of Aboriginal infants and children, and issues relating to Indigenous child removal were only occasionally referred to by the Australian councils before the 1920s. It was in the 1920s that child rescue took on an international dimension, and ICW recommended its member councils to co-operate with the Save the Children Fund national committees in their respective countries in preparing a Children's Charter suitable to their particular needs.[23] At the 1926 FCNCW conference, president Lillias Skene reminded all the Australian councils of the charter and their 'incumbency to carry [it] into effect' in their states.[24] From this would grow a new notion of children as bearers of rights as well as subjects of protection, but it was welfare and protection—from physical and moral dangers—that continued to dominate the Australian councils' thinking.

In dealing with infant welfare issues, the early national councils focused particularly on the need for qualified women inspectors, preferably nurses, and on education of mothers. In putting forward their case for women inspectors, the councils argued in Spence's words that 'the supervision of homes and food and care for babies is women's work and cannot be rightly done by men'. Some interpreted this in traditionally moral terms. Brisbane's Sister Mary Gloriana of the Anglican Sisterhood wrote a paper on 'Rescue Work' for the first NCWNSW congress in 1904, arguing that a 'low standard of morals', and homes 'devoid of love and religion' were the root cause of neglect among children and that the only safeguard lay in 'proper information'

1912, pp. 55–70.

23   Executive, Copenhagen 1924, 'ICW Resolutions', http://www.ncwcanada.com/ncwc2/wp-content/uploads/2014/02/ICW-CIF_Resolutions1.pdf, p. 18; NCWV, *Report for 1926*, p. 9.

24   NCWV, *Report for 1926*, p. 18.

imparted to children by their mothers.²⁵ But we also see a movement beyond female philanthropy in Goldstein's insistence on paid women inspectors, on professional qualifications and on 'more scientific methods of treating the whole neglected children's question' rather than what she, perhaps unfairly, called the 'dilettante' interests of 'ladies' committees'.²⁶ In Queensland, NCW campaigned against a proposed state foundling hospital in 1916—small homes where mother and baby could be cared for together by a professional nurse were, council members argued, more likely to increase the survival rate of such infants.²⁷

While women's organisations and the councils were soon successful in having paid women inspectors appointed in most states, those appointed by governments to supervise boarded-out children and infants were not always professionally qualified. Nurses asserted their expertise for inspection of foster homes but their claims were not widely acknowledged. Victoria's first woman visiting officer, appointed in 1905, had been a district visitor for the Melbourne Ladies' Benevolent Society, precisely one of those 'dilettantes' Goldstein had warned against. While her appointment, and the creation two years later of a fully female inspectorate for boarded-out babies, signified a victory for payment of work previously seen as purely philanthropic,²⁸ Victoria's NCW was not satisfied and declared its intent to continue working for the appointment of 'only trained nurses as inspectors … and of medical women as chief inspectors and superintendents' with the long-term aim of 'a Department officered by women for the protection of boarded-out children'.²⁹

---

25 First Congress NCWNSW Minutes, 14 October 1904, Box MLK03009, MS3739, NCWNSW Papers, SLNSW.
26 *Australian Woman's Sphere*, October 1901, cited in Swain, '"The Supervision of … Babies"', pp. 316–17. Swain also defends the work of many of the women on the 'ladies' committees'.
27 NCWQ Council Minutes, 10 March 1916, Box 16045, 7266 NCWQ Minute Books, NCWQ Papers, SLQ.
28 Swain, '"The Supervision of … Babies"', pp. 320–3.
29 Quoted in Gray, 'Acceptable Face', p. 76.

Supporting Mothers

Closely related to the issue of boarding out neglected children was the problem of maintenance of mothers who no longer had breadwinners to support themselves and their children. While state-funded boarding out of children to their mothers recognised this problem, the support was primarily directed to widows; though deserted and single mothers were not excluded, they were more likely to fail the tests for respectability and secure accommodation. National councils were wary of giving this system unqualified support because they believed on moral grounds that deserting fathers and fathers of illegitimate children should be made accountable by law. Common law inherited from England and existing colonial and state legislation included provisions for extracting payments from these men, but the laws were almost impossible to enforce.[30] In early twentieth-century NSW, the council fought successfully for the passage of a stronger act to enable an unmarried pregnant woman to sue the father of her child for prenatal expenses and maintenance for herself and the child (Infant Protection Act 1904), but there is no evidence that it was effective or much used by the predominantly poor and powerless women who found themselves in these circumstances.[31]

The pursuit of deserting husbands was stymied in all states by unequal marriage laws, stipulating among other things a married woman's dependent domicile, which meant that her legally defined place of residence, whether state or nation, followed that of her husband. Federation should have helped but did not. The problem was that marriage laws were controlled by the states and this made it easy for men to escape their obligations by fleeing interstate. Even though, from 1901, the Commonwealth Constitution empowered the federal government to legislate on marriage and divorce, and on parental rights and custody related to marital causes, no government took up the challenge until

---

30   Jaggs, *Neglected and Criminal*, p. 108.
31   Judith Allen, 'Rose Scott (1847–1925)', *Australian Dictionary of Biography* (*ADB*), http://adb.anu.edu.au/biography/scott-rose-8370/text14689.

1959.³² The existence of six different sets of law and jurisdictions made enforcement across state borders of court orders regarding maintenance extremely difficult and expensive for both the women concerned and the authorities.

In September 1910, the NSW council decided to give priority to the issues of family maintenance, issuing questionnaires to parliamentary candidates on the subject, and, during 1911 and 1912, Queensland's NCW also took up the issue.³³ After ICW's executive in September 1911 passed a resolution concerning failure to pay maintenance,³⁴ the interstate meeting of the Australian councils in Sydney in 1912 recommended 'national councils in each state to carefully consider the question of deserting husbands and fathers'.³⁵ In New South Wales, Rose Scott argued for both a uniform federal marriage law and ongoing pressure on the state government for family maintenance legislation. The need for a co-ordinated response is also evident in Queensland's motion of August 1913 'That this Council in conjunction with the National Councils in other States use every effort to secure legislation to make deserting husbands & fathers support their wives and children'.³⁶ These concerns were reinforced by the injunction of ICW at its last conference before going into recess on the outbreak of World War I to work for legal provision of maintenance, together with international agreements

---

32 Section 51 xxi and xxii.
33 NCWNSW Council Minutes, 10 September 1910, 3 November 1911, Box MLK 03009, MS3739, NCWNSW Papers, SLNSW; NCWQ Council Minutes, 30 August 1911, 28 August 1912, 7 December 1912, Box 16045, 7266 NCWQ Minute Books, NCWQ Papers, SLQ.
34 Executive, Stockholm, 1911, 'ICW Resolutions', http://www.ncwcanada.com/ncwc2/wp-content/uploads/2014/02/ICW-CIF_Resolutions1.pdf, p. 114.
35 *Sydney Morning Herald*, 31 July 1912, p. 10.
36 NCWQ Council Minutes, 9 August 1913, Box 16045, 7266 NCWQ Minute Books, NCWQ Papers, SLQ; NCWNSW Council Minutes, 3 August 1911, 3 October 1912 and 31 August 1916, Box MLK 03009, MS3739, NCWNSW Papers, SLNSW. Scott was state convenor of NCWNSW's laws committee.

to 'protect the legal rights of women and children especially with regard to deserted wives and children'.[37]

In the post-war years, effective domicile and maintenance legislation remained high on the agendas of both the Australian councils and ICW,[38] and the laws standing committees in the states played a major role in maintaining a high profile for this and other legal disabilities suffered by women. The growing influence of women lawyers in council ranks was evident on these standing committees and at annual conferences by the 1920s, as more states admitted women to practice. The councils had some success in getting state governments to pass stronger laws to deal with maintenance owed by husbands fleeing interstate,[39] but maintenance orders remained all but useless where men were determined to evade them. Thus state-financed schemes such as boarding out children to their mothers were unavoidable. But they were also inadequate. Not only did they require the mother to be respectable and living in secure accommodation, the funds they provided were calculated on the number of children and allowed nothing for the mother herself. Widows' pensions in NSW (1926) and Victoria (1937) eased the situation for some but not for the deserted wives or unmarried mothers,

---

37   Executive, Stockholm, 1911, and Conference, Rome, 1914, 'ICW Resolutions', http://www.ncwcanada.com/ncwc2/wp-content/uploads/2014/02/ICW-CIF_Resolutions1.pdf, pp. 114–15.

38   Indeed the ICW resolution of 1924 enjoined national councils to study the text of laws relating to desertion in their countries and recommend modifications or amendments necessary. See Executive, Copenhagen, 1924, 'ICW Resolutions', http://www.ncwcanada.com/ncwc2/wp-content/uploads/2014/02/ICW-CIF_Resolutions1.pdf, p. 116. They also asked the League of Nations through its Codification of International Law committee to study the question of 'desertion of the family' and, later, to draw up a Convention to enforce the payment of alimony, including sanctions against debtors. See Executive, Geneva, 1927, 'ICW Resolutions', http://www.ncwcanada.com/ncwc2/wp-content/uploads/2014/02/ICW-CIF_Resolutions1.pdf, pp. 116–17.

39   NCWNSW, *Biennial Reports for 1919–1920*, p. 5, referred to the passage of the Interstate Destitute Persons Relief Act to enable a 'deserted wife to obtain payment under a Maintenance Order, made against her husband who has deserted to another State'.

many of whom had to give their children into state or authorised agency care or put them up for adoption.[40]

The inadequacies of these schemes, together with the stimulus provided by a growing market for babies and the rising survival rates of illegitimate infants in orphanages, saw adoption become 'a leading topic of reform in child welfare circles' during and after the Great War.[41] Up until 1926, there was no provision for legal adoption in English law, and most Australian states followed English precedent into the 1920s. This held that natural parents' rights and responsibilities towards their children were inalienable, though it did not prevent de facto adoption practices through both private informal agreements and quasi-adoption arrangements by state and voluntary organisations as a cheaper alternative to boarding out. Pressure to provide legal certainty for all parties grew in the first two decades of the new century, and National Councils of Women were key players, sometimes taking the initiative, as in South Australia, of suggesting legislative models to the government.[42] Most of the Australian states passed legislation legalising and supervising adoption during the 1920s. But the terms and conditions of adoption in each state varied and, once again, the problem arose of the law of one state not being recognised in another. The NSW council brought this to the attention of the other councils, recommending at the 1925 federal conference in Melbourne that they inquire 'into the procedure

---

40 Jaggs, *Neglected and Criminal*, pp. 115–16.
41 Jaggs, *Neglected and Criminal*, p. 125. Shurlee Swain's research in contemporary newspapers has uncovered widespread advertising for infants in the late nineteenth and early twentieth centuries. Swain also notes the rising survival rates in institutions (though it was still poor) in *Single Mothers and their Children: Disposal, Punishment and Survival in Australia*, Cambridge, Cambridge University Press, 1995, pp. 106–07. Contemporary writers also noted the rise in demand as a result of the deaths of large numbers of young men in the war. See R. Lowenstern, 'The Adoption of Children', *Australian Law Journal*, 1 (11), 1928, pp. 328–31.
42 NCWSA Minutes, 16 September 1924, 12 February 1925, SRG297, NCWSA Papers, State Library of South Australia (SLSA).

of the different Australian states' in the hope that 'some uniformity be arrived at'.[43]

By 1926 Victoria was the only state without legal adoption, and, during the following year, the executive of NCWV worked with the Children's Welfare Association and the Children's Welfare Department to ensure a proposed bill reflected the 'best features' of the British, New Zealand and other states' legislation.[44] They also circulated a questionnaire to all parliamentary candidates.[45] NCWV argued that, following South Australian precedent, adoption should be decided in a court 'composed of a special magistrate and two justices of the peace, one of whom must be a woman',[46] and they won their point.[47] The councils pursued uniformity through the Commonwealth royal commission into the constitution of 1927–29, Joyce Cocks from the NSW council laws committee arguing that 'reasons similar to those which make it desirable that there should be an Australian law of marriage are strong arguments in favour of the Commonwealth having power to legislate with respect to adoption and legitimation'.[48] In supporting one adoption law for the whole of Australia they were in accord with much of the legal profession, which also argued the case to the royal commission, albeit without success.[49]

The fact that promotion of secure legal adoption of infants was never premised on the interests or needs of the predominantly unmarried mothers went unrecognised by the councils, which largely endorsed

---

43   FCNCWA Conference Minutes, November 1925, Box 11, MS7583, NCWA Papers, National Library of Australia (NLA).
44   *Argus*, 31 August 1927, p. 22. The NCWV meeting was told that discussions had been going on for some months. See also Jaggs, *Neglected and Criminal*, pp. 126–7.
45   Ada Norris, *Champions of the Impossible: A History of the National Council of Women of Victoria 1902–1977*, Melbourne, Hawthorn Press, 1978, p. 56.
46   *Argus*, 25 May 1928, inserted in NCWV Minute Book 1928–33, NCWV Papers, State Library of Victoria (SLV) (classification pending); see Lowenstern, 'The Adoption of Children', on South Australia.
47   Jaggs, *Neglected and Criminal*, p. 128.
48   Royal Commission on the Constitution, 1927–29, Minutes of Evidence. p. 1183.
49   Lowenstern, 'The Adoption of Children', pp. 328–31.

contemporary rhetoric about the advantages to these women of secrecy, a new start and a secure future for their babies. Recent scholarship has shown that the adoptive parents, the emerging profession of social work and the state were the real beneficiaries, and the children themselves were largely objects of exchange despite claims that their interests were the primary concern.[50] Beliefs about the benefits of adoption were, however, sincerely held and there was very little contemporary criticism at any level of society before the 1970s. In seeing adoption as humane and progressive, the councils were in accord with the dominant discourses of modern social reform in the interwar period.

There remained the entrenched problem of a married woman's risk of being reduced to penury, along with her children, through no fault of her own. The councils began to consider how economic self-sufficiency for married women, deserted or not, might be achieved and, by the 1920s their concern to protect women and children was fostering a more radical consideration of the advantages of independence. As early as 1901, Rose Scott had made a radical plea for marriage as 'a partnership between equals economically' and the 'right' of a wife to 'a fair share of her husband's earnings', to be met with the response that she had overlooked 'the element of love' that justified 'cheerfully accept[ing] burdens and dependence on that account'.[51] But support for independent economic security for wives grew in the following two decades and, at the post-war ICW conference in Kristiania in 1920, delegates resolved that a wife 'should be legally entitled to a certain just proportion of her husband's income'.[52] After this matter was first raised at the Hobart interstate conference in 1922, the Australian state delegates took it back to their own councils for consideration.

---

50   Marian Quartly, Shurlee Swain and Denise Cuthbert, *The Market in Babies: Stories of Australian Adoption*, Melbourne, Monash University Publishing, 2013, chapters 3 and 4.
51   NSWNCW Council Minutes, 25 June 1901, Box MLK03009, MS3739, NCWNSW Papers, SLNSW; *Daily Telegraph*, 26 June 1901.
52   Krisitiania, 1920, 'ICW Resolutions', http://www.ncwcanada.com/ncwc2/wp-content/uploads/2014/02/ICW-CIF_Resolutions1.pdf, p. 115.

In the meantime, in March 1923, the Victorian council organised a nation-wide conference of 120 women's organisations in Melbourne, the largest conference of women held in Australia to that point, to provide input to the federal government's proposed reconsideration of the maternity allowance introduced in 1912. Medical women in the councils were increasingly taking the position that the money would be more efficiently deployed in funding ante- and post-natal services, but those at the conference, including a majority of council delegates, voted overwhelmingly to retain the allowance. However, councils also recognised that the bonus, popular as it was, did not provide the regular economic support many wives and mothers needed.[53] By 1925, the Victorians were prepared to support the suggestion of basic wage royal commissioner A.B. Piddington for an ongoing system of motherhood endowment paid to women by the state and funded through changes to the arbitrated family wage.[54] They took the proposal to the second conference of the new Federal Council of National Councils of Women of Australia in 1926, which resolved 'That the N.C.'sW. of Australia approve of the principle of family endowment by a re-adjustment of the method of payment of wages' so as 'to ensure the mother receiving her share'.[55] Rose Scott's early stance was thus vindicated, but she had died the year before.

Mildred Muscio, federal council president from 1928–31, was appointed to the Commonwealth royal commission set up in 1927 to consider a national scheme of endowment. The proposal foundered on

---

53 Lake, *Getting Equal*, pp. 77–9. Only NCWSA actually opposed the resolution to retain the allowance in its existing form.
54 See, for example, resolution passed by NCWV in June 1925, in NCWV, *Report for 1925*, p. 4. Piddington addressed the council on his proposal on 12 May. See NCWV Council Minutes, 12 May 1925, NCWV Papers, SLV (classification pending).
55 FCNCWA Conference Minutes, July 1926, Box 12, MS7583, NCWA Papers, NLA. The rationale came from Victoria's Cecilia Downing (proxy for WA). SA voted against the resolution, its delegates upholding the traditional values of thrift and industry and opposing any measure that would sap these virtues, raise taxes and weaken the duty of men to provide for their families. See also *Argus*, 24 July 1926, p. 26; 26 July 1926, p. 22.

the broad consensus among the male commissioners that dividing the family wage and 'treating the wife as a separate economic unit on the pay-roll of the state' would destroy 'family life as we know it'.[56] Former Queensland NCW president Irene Longman presented the case for just such an independent income for every mother for her 'services to the State'. Muscio formed an unlikely alliance with Labor's John Curtin to present a minority report in support of means-tested endowment for third and subsequent children. Like the women in the Labor Party, she was forced to back down on any reduction to the family or breadwinner's wage, which was based on the needs of parents and two children.[57] She saw this compromise as the best chance of achieving a modicum of economic justice for the most needy women. Child endowment on this basis would at least give the poorest mothers some independent maintenance that was not reliant on what father or husband deigned or was forced to hand out. But, in taking this position, Curtin and Muscio had to couch their arguments less in terms of a wife's independence than 'in the interests of children as national assets'. Their scheme would still preserve the family wage as the property of the husband.[58] But it was not to be. The Commonwealth government endorsed the majority report's opposition to any proposal for endowment. While a non-wage-related scheme operated in NSW from 1927, it was 1941 before a federal scheme of child endowment paid directly to mothers came into operation. Thus the issue of maintenance remained important to all the national councils for practical as well as those moral reasons arising from a conviction that deserting husbands and fathers must be held accountable for their wrong-doing.

---

56 Lake, *Getting Equal*, pp. 103–09.
57 John Murphy, *A Decent Provision: Australian Welfare Policy, 1870–1949*, Farnham, Ashgate, 2011, pp. 138–49; Marilyn Lake, 'The Independence of Women and the Brotherhood of Man: Debates in the Labour Movement over Equal Pay and Motherhoood Endowment in the 1920s', *Labour History*, 63, November 1992, pp. 1–24.
58 Murphy, *A Decent Provision*, pp. 138–49.

Women, Children and the Criminal Law

Determination to humanise the operation of the criminal law and protect children and vulnerable women from its harshest effects were early concerns of the NCWs, well before the admission of women in significant numbers to the legal profession. A major early battle was for separate children's courts with specially assigned magistrates and appointment of women probation officers. The councils also fought for women police and women justices of the peace.

As in Britain, the Australian colonies in the nineteenth century had no specific laws for juvenile offenders, who were therefore subject to the same laws and courts as adults. Gradually provision was made in all jurisdictions for dealing with children summarily and committing them to industrial and reformatory schools rather than mainstream gaols. Child welfare reformers began agitating for separate courts for children from the 1880s, not on the grounds of rights and civil liberties but rather as an instrument of moral reform, social order and diversion from a life of crime.[59] South Australia established a separate court in 1895 before a national council was formed, though women reformers in the WCTU among others were key figures in its establishment. The first decade of the twentieth century saw dedicated courts established in Tasmania and NSW (1905), Victoria (1906) and Western Australia (1907), the councils playing a key role in the first three and women who helped found NCWWA four years later, notably Edith Cowan, taking a leading part in the West.[60] Queensland's council began lobbying for a court in 1907 and continued to do so through the 1920s but without success.[61]

---

59 See especially Jaggs, *Neglected and Criminal*, pp. 90–3.
60 Annette Davis, 'Infant Mortality and Child-saving: The Campaign of Women's Organizations in Western Australia 1900–1922', in Penelope Hetherington (ed.), *Childhood and Society in Western Australia*, Perth, UWA Press with Centre for WA History, 1988, pp. 161–73, Musgrove, *The Scars Remain*, p. 43.
61 *The First Fifty Years in the History of the National Council of Women of Queensland*, Brisbane, NCWQ, c. 1960, p. 12; NCWQ Council Minutes, 13 July 1923, Box 16045, 7266 NCWQ Minute Books, NCWQ Papers, SLQ.

In Victoria, pressure came initially from the WCTU, assisted by the press and feminist journalists Vida Goldstein and Alice Henry. In 1904, after hearing a paper 'A Children's Court of Justice' by Miss Henry, the recently formed NCWV joined in a deputation to the attorney general,[62] but it was the success of the movement in NSW in 1905 that fired up their campaign a year later. The government capitulated reluctantly to this pressure with a hastily drawn-up and inadequate bill that it was forced to revise extensively after the council mobilised child welfare workers. The legislation provided for supervised probation and special magistrates with specialised knowledge, but retained the normal rules on admissibility of evidence, together with custodial sentences and other adult punishments. Nevertheless, it was an early victory for council political pressure in the interests of protecting and moulding children. And members worked assiduously for its effective operation. Two-thirds of the first 58 voluntary probation officers appointed in 1907 were women, most affiliated to NCWV through the WCTU.[63] By the late 1920s, women justices of the peace in most states were also presiding in the children's courts.[64] The councils pursued this concern with juvenile justice at a federal level, resolving unanimously in 1928 that all states 'should work for the establishment of Remand Homes for juvenile and other youthful offenders, apart from gaol'.[65]

The related issues of women police and women justices of the peace were initially understood in the familiar terms of protection but, by the 1920s, the campaign for female JPs and for extension of the powers of women police was also being couched in the language of equality. Women police were at first envisioned primarily as moral guardians of women and children in public places. The first women police were

---

62 Norris, *Champions*, pp. 17, 18. Henry also spoke on the subject to the Tasmanian annual conference in 1905. *Mercury*, 17 March 1905, p. 6.
63 Jaggs, *Neglected and Criminal*, pp. 95–104.
64 NCWV, *Report for 1927*, p. 9.
65 FCNCWA Conference Minutes, July 1928, Box 12, MS7583, NCWA Papers, NLA.

appointed in South Australia in 1915 as a result of pressure from the Women's Non-Party Political Association, later an affiliate of the revived South Australian council. National councils in the other states were the major force in lobbying for women police, NSW achieving success a little after South Australia in 1915, Western Australia and Victoria in 1917, Tasmania the following year, and Queensland in 1931. The first appointees had no powers of arrest, but that changed gradually from the mid-1920s as women in the councils and other organisations began to lobby about equality in employment. Federal council thus resolved in 1926 that policewomen be appointed 'on the same basis as policemen'.[66] This trend was also evident in an interstate conference resolution for the right of women to sit on juries,[67] and in the fight for women justices of the peace. The last state to provide for women JPs was Victoria, where the enabling act, introduced by long-time supporter of women's rights, Maurice Blackburn, was significantly titled the Women's Qualifications Act (1926), and was aimed more broadly at removing discrimination against women in public affairs and the professions.[68] Six of the first seven Victorian JPs appointed in 1927 were members of NCWV.[69]

Educating the Mothers of the Race

Making society the larger home envisaged by women activists required a new understanding of the relationship between individuals and the state that went beyond protection and paternalism without completely eschewing them. It was an understanding that had at its core concerns for the survival of race and nation.

Protection of children at known risk was only one step towards the ideal domestic order envisioned by philanthropic and progressivist

---

66 NCWV, *Report for 1926*, p. 21.
67 NCWV, *Report for 1924*, p. 13.
68 Susan Blackburn Abeyasekere, 'Blackburn, Maurice McCrae (1880–1944)', *ADB*, http://adb.anu.edu.au/biography/blackburn-maurice-mccrae-5258/text8861.
69 NCWV, *Report for 1927*, p. 7.

women in Australia's NCWs. For the infant mortality rate to decline and the physique of the population to improve, it was necessary to educate the mothers of the race. While poor housing and poverty were acknowledged as problems, reformers put greater faith in training women in habits of cleanliness, healthy food preparation and infant care. From their earliest years, the councils called on the expertise of the first generation of women doctors and professionalised nurses. In addressing the NSW council in August 1903 on 'Women's Work in Social and Sanitary Science', Dr Kate Hogg argued that the necessary work of reforming home life and children's health could and should be carried out by women trained in sanitary science who understood 'the awful waste of infant life through improper feeding', a major factor in 'producing racial degeneration'.[70] Similar arguments were mounted by women in the Australian Health Society, an affiliate of the NCW in Victoria.[71]

Privately run schools for mothers appeared in Sydney in 1908, in both Melbourne and Adelaide in 1909, and, after South Australia's leading woman doctor Helen Mayo spoke to the Queensland council, Brisbane established one in 1913. NCW women Alice Rawson in Sydney and Cecilia Downing in Melbourne played leading roles in establishing these schools, where lectures were delivered by doctors and nurses on household hygiene and caring for infants, and babies were weighed and checked. Beginning as projects directed towards enlightening working-class mothers, they developed during the next two decades into government-supported baby clinics with a more universal application. NCW activism was behind this process with NSW leading the way in 1914, and Victoria following suit in 1917. A combined AWNL–NCWV initiative, Baby Week, held in the Melbourne Town Hall in April 1918, led to the formation of the Victorian Baby Health Centres

---

70 NCWNSW Minutes, 21 August 1903, Box MLK03009, MS3739, NCWNSW Papers, SLNSW.
71 Reiger, *Disenchantment*, p. 43; NCWV *Annual Report 1907–08*.

Association in June/July. Baby Health Centres began to spread through the suburbs, forty having been established in the state by 1922.[72] Dr Vera Scantlebury Brown, the first director of the infant welfare section in the Health Department in 1926, was the first convenor of NCWV's child welfare standing committee in 1927.[73]

Domestic science also had to be brought to the current generation. Kindergartens should teach children basic hygiene and inculcate it in their mothers too, for: 'Children make the nation and are missionaries in themselves'.[74] At the other end of the educational spectrum, the councils waged a campaign for colleges of domestic science and chairs in domestic science at university level, to train teachers appropriately but also to give professional women greater power in the state education departments. Encouraged by the lobbying and support of NCWV, among others, Victoria's College of Domestic Economy opened in 1906. In 1913 the council established a committee to raise funds for its extension, but the demand for places was so high that by 1915 delegates unanimously voted to urge government action. Over a decade later a bequest finally placed the college on a firm footing, as the Emily McPherson College.[75] The NSW council was also pushing for a training college from 1907, but deputations to and promises by successive governments came to nothing.[76] In Western Australia, NCW agitated unsuccessfully for a Bachelor of Domestic Science course at the new University of Western

---

72 *Woman*, XI, 1, 1 March 1918; XI, 7, 1 September 1918; *Argus*, 28 March 1918; Reiger, *Disenchantment*, pp. 130–8; Heather Sheard, 'Victoria's Baby Health Centres: A History 1917–1950', MEd, University of Melbourne, 2005, pp. 39–50.

73 Kate Campbell, 'Scantlebury Brown, Vera (1889–1946)', *ADB*, http://adb.anu.edu.au/biography/scantlebury-brown-vera-8350/text14491; NCWV, *Report for 1927*, p. 3.

74 NCWNSW Council Minutes, 18 November 1898, Box MLK03009, MS3739 NCWNSW Papers, SLNSW.

75 NCWV Executive Minutes, 8 August 1913, NCWV Papers, SLV (classification pending); *Argus*, 26 March 1915, p. 8; Reiger, *Disenchantment*, pp. 59–60. The Emily McPherson College opened in 1927.

76 NCWNSW Council Minutes, 22 March 1907, and Special Executive Minutes, 4 April 1907, Box MLK03009, MS3739, NCWNSW Papers, SLNSW.

Australia in 1913.[77] NCWSA, on the urging of Agnes Goode, a main driver of the Housewives' Association there, also pushed for a college during the 1920s.[78] The bulk of council activity, however, was directed to the issue of domestic science education in schools.

A motive here was the perennial need of middle and upper class women for domestic servants. As early as January 1902, a council congress in Hobart discussed a business scheme for training girls in domestic service proposed by Emily Dobson—one that would finance itself by 'selling the products'.[79] The shortage of servants, or 'home help', remained a key factor in council discussions over the following three decades. This carried over into consideration of working conditions and ways of improving the status of domestic service, even, in the case of Western Australia, to the point of co-operating with Labor women in a deputation in 1919 urging amendment to the Arbitration Act to cover domestic workers.[80] Council leaders from the outset were largely in accord with contemporary experts who believed domestic education was a necessary part of the process by which the Australian home—working-class and middle-class—was to become a modern and efficient workplace.[81]

Other council leaders feared that compulsory domestic science classes would limit the academic options of female students. As early as 1897–98, the NSW council balked at compulsion, advocating instead measures to make lessons in domestic science available to 'the class that needed it most' by increasing the numbers of domestic science centres

---

77 See NCWWA Council Minutes, 29 January and 28 February 1913, MS1389A, NCWWA Papers, State Library of Western Australia (SLWA).
78 Suzanne Edgar, 'Goode, Agnes Knight (1872–1947)', *ADB*, http://adb.anu.edu.au/biography/goode-agnes-knight-6421/text10981.
79 Gray, 'Acceptable Face', p. 92; *Mercury*, 7 January 1902, p. 4.
80 NCWWA Council Minutes, 6 December 1918, 28 March 1919, 16 May 1919, MS1389A, NCWWA Papers, SLWA.
81 Reiger, *Disenchantment*, pp. 56–64.

in public schools.⁸² Compulsion was debated in the Victorian council in June 1914, where teacher delegate and Women's Political Association member Clara Weekes argued that current domestic science classes began at far too early an age. Most delegates did not believe that compulsory training would prevent girls achieving success in other subjects, and gave it in-principle support.⁸³ The *Age*, in recording council's discussions, also reported that 'the trend of public opinion is in favor, if not of compulsory domestic training, at any rate of providing every girl with facilities for getting that training'.⁸⁴ Further discussion followed in 1915 and again 1916, when a resolution moved by Weekes opposing compulsory training before the age of fourteen was agreed to. At the same time, NCWV resolved that the school leaving age should be raised to fifteen and 'more adequate ... technical education of girls and women' provided.⁸⁵

After the war most councils again took up the question of domestic science⁸⁶ and, in 1924, the NSW council proposed to the interstate conference in Melbourne that all NCWs 'urge upon their Governments and educational authorities the need for including in the education of every girl an organised course in home-training to be given at whatever time appears most suitable in the primary or secondary stage'.⁸⁷ An Australian resolution to this effect was sent to the 1925 ICW quinquennial in Washington and, to the immense gratification of the NSW Education Committee, resulted in a recommendation to all

---

82 See resolutions and discussion in NSW Council Minutes, 26 May 1897, 4 November 1897, 23 March 1898, 27 May 1898, 18 November 1898, Box MLK03009, MS3739, NCWNSW Papers, SLNSW.
83 Gray, 'Acceptable Face', pp. 88–90.
84 *Age*, 1 July 1914. The impact of American efficiency ideas such as Taylorism is evident in the newspaper's view that the education of the female child should aim to increase 'the efficiency of the home in its function of a domestic workshop'.
85 *Argus*, 26 March 1915, p. 8; 23 June 1916, p. 8; NCWV Council Minutes, 24 February 1916, NCWV Papers, SLV (classification pending).
86 See for example, NCWNSW *Biennial Reports for 1919–1920*, p. 9.
87 NCWNSW *Biennial Reports for 1923–1924*, p. 16.

affiliated councils that they demand 'a scientific study of conditions and practice in the whole field of domestic science and of home-making' in their countries, and that 'research and teaching in this field ... should be added to the already existing departments of the Universities'.[88]

Organised play, central to the New Education philosophy, was also part of the education agenda of the national councils and they were significant participants in the playgrounds movement that emerged in Australian capital cities from the first decade of the twentieth century onwards. In Victoria, the council contributed a much-admired model playground to the 1907 Women's Work Exhibition, and agitation for supervised playgrounds, especially in the inner city suburbs, was an ongoing feature of most councils' work. The federal council considered the issue in 1926 and passed a resolution for 'adequate Playgrounds to be set apart for supervised recreation for all ages in all States'.[89]

With the growing demand for experts in all these fields of social reform, doctors and lawyers were welcomed into council circles but, by the 1920s, NCW leaders were also recognising that wider avenues of education for women were needed if their claims to be represented on government boards and committees of enquiry were to be taken seriously. University-trained women in science, philosophy, psychology, history, industrial hygiene and other fields entered the councils' ranks and women graduates' associations emerged and affiliated in most states in 1920–21. Outside the universities the councils pushed for reform of nursing and midwifery (obstetric nursing) training and for new areas of specialisation like mothercraft nursing, and, in the post-war years, they began to agitate for reform of traditional university courses such as medicine, and to work with university specialists for new programs such as vocational education and, most of all, social work.

---

88   It was they said, 'identical with what this Council has for some years now hoped to see realised'. NCWNSW *Biennial Reports for 1924–1926*, pp. 12–13.
89   NCWV, *Report for 1926*, p. 22.

In medicine, in light of rising maternal mortality figures, the councils agitated for expanded programs in obstetrics. In Melbourne, advocacy from NCWV was a factor in the Wilson Trust's donation for the appointment of a director of obstetrics by the university in 1925.[90] In Sydney, the council was 'instrumental in having lectures given on the subject' and achieved success in having a chair of obstetrics established at the university after deputations were organised to the minister and the university senate.[91] And the federal council, for its part, resolved in 1929 to request the Commonwealth government to subsidise all the state governments to establish and maintain a chair of obstetrics in each university.[92] But perhaps of most significance in terms of the niche careers the national councils helped carve out for women in child welfare, probation and supervision of foster homes was the work of the NSW council in the late 1920s to get a social work program established at Sydney University. A resolution passed at FCNCWA's conference in Adelaide in 1927 had recommended that the state councils 'promote the establishment of classes in social science'. The NSW council immediately established a subcommittee comprising the president and the convenors of the education and health standing committees, along with representatives of the YWCA, the University Settlement and women involved in industrial welfare. Together they forged an alliance with sympathetic men at the university to form a Board of Social Studies and Training in 1928, and were instrumental in shaping curriculum and practice for training social workers before the university formally instituted a social work program in 1940. The pattern was similar in Victoria and South Australia.[93]

---

90 NCWV, *Report for 1925*, p. 15
91 NCWNSW, *Biennial Reports for 1924–1926*, p. 5.
92 NCWV, *Report for 1929*, p. 15.
93 NCWNSW, *Biennial Reports for 1926–1928*, p. 17; Shurlee Swain, 'Social Work', in Judith Smart and Shurlee Swain (eds), *The Encyclopedia of Women and Leadership in Twentieth-Century Australia*, http://www.womenaustralia.info/leaders/biogs/WLE0636b.htm.

Morality in 'Modern' Guise

The main preoccupations of ICW's standing committee on public health in this period overlapped with those of the standing committee on equal moral standards; they were alcohol, venereal diseases, and, by the late 1920s, 'dangerous drugs'.[94] These were also the key areas of concern in the Australian councils, alongside a growing fear of the corrosive impact of films. Alarm about the effects of alcohol consumption and the increased incidence of venereal disease on the health and future of the nation were evident during the first decade of the councils' existence but reached a peak during the war years. Concern about cinema began in the war years and became more dominant in the interwar period.

Temperance reformers at first attributed dysfunctional drinking to weakness of will, and proposed as a solution self-discipline or self-control, but, by the time the national councils were formed, they had also come to support medical and psychological intervention, and selective state regulation and enforcement. Doctrinaire moral attitudes and Christian values remained fundamental to the movement but by 1914 it was also characterised by the secular and progressivist ideals of scientific organisation, rational teaching and debate, and modern methods of propaganda and publicity. Thus the war-time anti-drink campaigns were couched largely in terms of national efficiency, and, even when linked with sexual licence and venereal disease, the focus remained on civil and military effectiveness.

The Woman's Christian Temperance Union led the campaign for dry canteens in army camps, dry troopships and early closing of hotels after outbreaks of drunken violence among soldiers in the streets of Melbourne and at Liverpool in Sydney. But they were supported by most women's organisations and the National Councils of Women threw their weight behind the campaign. During February and March of 1915, the Rev. Dr J. Laurence Rentoul, a leading Presbyterian

---

94 'ICW Resolutions', http://www.ncwcanada.com/ncwc2/wp-content/uploads/2014/02/ICW-CIF_Resolutions1.pdf. pp. 69–71.

minister in Melbourne and chaplain general in the First AIF, asserted that recruits at Broadmeadows were being seduced from their duty not only by the 'liquor evil' but by the adjacent 'camp of the harpies'.[95]

This linking of drink, soldiers' health and sexual morality was a powerful means of manipulating public emotions. The April meeting of NCWV was addressed by Dr Harvey Sutton on the 'mental and physical weakening' effects of alcohol, one of 'our real enemies', and passed a series of resolutions. Prefacing the first was a statement of concern about 'the grave danger to the whole of the British Empire and to womanhood arising from indulgence in alcohol'. The following motions urged prompt government action to limit the hours of sale of alcohol, to ban sales in cafés, and to close hotels at 6pm, and called on all affiliates 'to follow the noble example of His Majesty by themselves at once abstaining from and discouraging the use of alcohol in their households'.[96] A week later, the council participated in a deputation to the premier. Standing for 'many thousands of women', the deputation argued for early closing of hotel bars in the interests of 'military efficiency' and the 'general public interest during this time of stress'.[97] The Intoxicating Liquor (Temporary Restriction) Act—to close hotels before 9am and after 9.30pm—was passed in July 1915.[98]

In February 1916, soldiers' riots in Sydney caused NSW's Premier Holman to promise a referendum on early closing, resulting in an overwhelming victory for six o'clock in June. The campaign was led there by Caroline David, a leading light in NCWNSW, who corresponded with Victoria's council about the methods used. NCWV in the meantime passed resolutions urging the federal defence minister to close all hotels in the vicinity of military camps and demanding the immediate introduction of six o'clock closing across the state. South Australia had

---

95 *Argus*, 27 February 1915, p. 19.
96 NCWV Minutes, 22 April 1915, NCWV Papers, SLV (classification pending); *Argus*, 24 April 1915, p. 20.
97 *Argus*, 1 May 1915, p. 16.
98 *Victorian Government Statutes*, 1915; *Victorian Year Book*, 1914–15, p. 457.

already voted for six o'clock closing in a referendum held in March. Tasmania followed suit in April, after a campaign in which the national council was prominent.[99] The Victorian government shillyshallied on the issue, announcing a popular referendum then abandoning it because of the impending conscription plebiscite. NCWV was prominent in the Citizens' National Executive formed to lobby parliamentarians, and in August the council inaugurated a Women's National Movement to publicise the issues among ordinary citizens.[100] Six o'clock closing was finally achieved in Victoria in December 1916 by act of parliament.[101] All four states that had introduced six o'clock closing had the support of the national councils when it was made it permanent in the wake of the war.

March 1915 saw the return of the first troops from overseas, many of them suffering from venereal disease. Sent at once to Langwarrin in Victoria, originally a camp for prisoners of war, they were initially herded behind barbed wire in appalling accommodation.[102] In October, Melbourne was alarmed by the news that 85 of them had escaped and that 60 of them were still at large.[103]

NCW concern about the venereal diseases predated the war. In Victoria, debate in the medical profession about policy towards syphilis and gonorrhoea was sparked by publicity at the 1908 Australasian Medical Congress about their extent in patients at the Melbourne

---

99 *Argus*, 4 March 1916, p. 19; 19 July 1916, p. 10; NCWV Minutes, 23 March 1916, NCWV Papers, SLV (classification pending). Caroline (Cara) David was married to Tannatt Willliam Edgeworth David, renowned geologist and Antarctic explorer.
100 *Argus*, 8 July 1916, p. 20; 12 September 1916, p. 6.
101 NCWV Minutes, 27 July 1916, NCWV Papers, SLV (classification pending); *Argus*, 8 September 1916, p. 6; 12 September 1916, p. 6; Judith Smart, 'The Pattern of Liquor Legislation in Victoria, 1906–1919 with Particular Reference to the Impact of World War I', BA Hons thesis, Monash University, 1971, chap. III.
102 A.G.H. Butler, *The Australian Army Services in the War of 1914–18*, vol. III, Canberra, Australian War Memorial, 1943, p. 175
103 *Woman Voter*, 28 October 1915, p. 2. The figures vary. In state parliament the number of escapers mentioned was 60 and those still not recaptured, 19. *Victorian Parliamentary Debates*, vol. 141, Legislative Assembly, 26 October 1915, p. 2967.

Hospital.[104] In 1910, a trial system of notification of suspected cases of syphilis showed that 3167 patients had indications of the disease.[105] Aware of the political power of moral opposition to any regulation, the government enlisted the co-operation of the Council of Churches and the National Council of Women in a public education campaign to support compulsory notification and treatment.[106]. In 1914, NCWV also agreed to join the Australian Natives Association and members of the medical profession in their efforts to 'mitigate ... the spread of venereal disease' by circulating information brochures prepared by the Board of Health. While not eschewing traditional moral judgements about the sinfulness of extra-marital sex, the national councils in Victoria and elsewhere looked to government regulation and medical science for immediate solutions to the venereal diseases problem.[107]

The spectre of infected soldiers triggered government action across Australia. The Western Australian government passed an act that included compulsory—though anonymous—notification and mandatory treatment. It also contained a system of reporting those suspected of having venereal disease and punishing those who knowingly infected others. The New South Wales Labor government took a different approach and established a voluntary venereal clinic in Sydney in January 1915. A Commonwealth committee of inquiry into the causes of death and invalidity also issued its recommendations about venereal diseases in 1916, giving alarmist statistics about the incidence of syphilis and gonorrhoea. The committee suggested the Western Australian legislation as a model for all states and promised to subsidise them

---

104 Cited in Department of Trade and Customs, Committee Concerning Causes of Death and Invalidity in the Commonwealth, 'Report on Venereal Diseases', *Commonwealth of Australia Parliamentary Papers*, 1914–15–16, vol. 5, p. 114 (Report pagination, p. 4).
105 *Truth*, 4 September 1909, p. 5; 8 July 1911, p. 6; 5 August 1911, p. 3.
106 *Truth*, 26 August 1911, p. 3; 30 September 1911, p. 5.
107 NCWV Executive Minutes, 7 April and 8 May 1914, NCWV Papers, SLV (classification pending).

if they followed suit.[108] A bill designed on the recommended lines was introduced into Victorian parliament in August 1916 and passed in December.[109]

The vast majority of the medical profession believed that coercive legislation with compulsory treatment and detention was the only way the spread of venereal disease could be halted, and that the moral arguments distracted people from the main problem. The women's movement was not so sure. In Western Australia, the national council divided over the issue and the three largest affiliates—the Women's Service Guild led by Bessie Rischbieth, the WCTU, and the Women's Labour Social Club—eventually withdrew in opposition to the majority view, which favoured regulation.[110] In Victoria, most women's groups, led by NCWV, supported regulation; even the WCTU, previously staunchly anti-regulation, was at best ambivalent. In May, NCWV agreed to consider a motion urging state legislation on the lines of the Western Australian Act, and executive member and Australian Women's National League president Eva Hughes moved that 'medical women' rather than 'medical men' be invited to speak at the meeting called to consider it, 'as we have perfect confidence in them'.[111] Meetings in June and July canvassed an array of views. The July meeting heard Dr Roberta Jull from the Western Australian council, who assured them that the act treated men and women equally. The resolution was passed in the face of objections from those, like Clara Weekes, who remained convinced that the bill would victimise young women in order

---

108 Department of Trade and Customs, Committee Concerning Causes of Death and Invalidity in the Commonwealth, 'Report on Venereal Diseases', *passim*.

109 Between 1916 and 1920, all the other states followed suit in putting such legislation on the books, though NSW and South Australia were more reluctant than the others to take punitive measures; in fact, the South Australian legislation was not proclaimed.

110 Noreen Sher, *The Spirit Lives On: A History of the National Council of Women of Western Australia 1911–1999*, Perth, NCWWA, 1999, chap. 1.

111 NCWV Minutes, 25 May 1916, NCWV Papers, SLV (classification pending).

to protect soldiers, despite its apparent gender neutrality.[112] The radical feminists of the Women's Political Association were the measure's principal opponents in Victoria, arguing that to use law and regulation was to deal with symptoms not causes. Compulsory notification and what amounted to regulation of prostitutes detained and controlled the wrong section of the population. It was in their view a revival of contagious diseases measures long opposed by women's organisations. But this social feminist position on the venereal diseases problem was a very isolated one in 1916.[113]

The Western Australian act and the 1916 and 1918 Victorian legislation constituted a victory for the dominance and power of the medical profession, including the women doctors treated as expert advisors by the national councils.[114] The onset of war had given a fillip to both the temperance movement and to the agitation for regulations controlling the spread of venereal disease. Morally coercive laws to control venereal diseases, like temperance measures, could be easily justified in terms of patriotic sacrifice and national efficiency, especially by women who were unable to fight and had to prove their citizenship in other ways.[115] Both issues remained important in council discussions during the postwar decade but were largely dealt with at state level. As broadly representative umbrella organisations, the councils were wary of taking a position on prohibition, war-time controls being the limit of what they judged to be acceptable to their membership. The 1929 federal

---

112 NCWV Minutes, 18 July and 31 August 1916, NCWV Papers, SLV (classification pending).
113 Judith Smart, 'Feminists, Labour Women and Venereal Disease in Early Twentieth Century Melbourne', *Australian Feminist Studies*, 15, 1992, pp. 25–40.
114 Victoria's amending act of 1918 'tightened up' the earlier act. Measures for arresting those escaping from treatment and for stronger discipline in places of detention were added, and it was made mandatory for doctors to inform the parents or guardians of intending marriage partners if one or other of them was suffering from a venereal disease.
115 Judith Smart, 'Sex, the State and the "Scarlet Scourge": Gender, Citizenship and Venereal Diseases Regulation in Australia during the Great War', *Women's History Review*, 7 (1), 1998, pp. 5–36.

conference resolved in favour of 'scientific education in Temperance' but emphasised that this did not mean advocacy of prohibition. This was reinforced by a similar resolution at the 1931 conference where ICW policy was cited in support of the view that temperance education meant education in the 'temperate use of alcohol'.[116]

The enormous growth in popularity of the moving picture—cinema—was the dominant cultural and moral preoccupation of the national councils in conference during the 1920s and the 1930s. Discussion of film took off during the war years, when the major focus was 'the moral and social welfare of the community' and a demand for censorship. NCWV, for example, participated in a deputation of 'religious and educational institutions' to the chief secretary in June 1916 to present a resolution calling for 'legislation for the control of picture films and picture theatres by a board of censors'.[117] A further deputation of Victorian women's organisations in 1918 elicited a sympathetic response from the chief secretary, who promised to strengthen controls over the production and distribution of films and was supportive of 'a mother' on the censorship board.[118] Censorship boards were also established in other states and, from 1917, a federal body, under the Customs Act, examined all films entering the country.[119]

Although moral concerns, together with a distaste for popular culture and the dominance of Hollywood, remained dominant themes during the 1920s, leading members of NCWNSW, notably Evelyn and Beatrice Tildesley and Mildred Muscio, came to a more complex appreciation of the educational possibilities and cultural value of film. As historian Jill Matthews has commented, 'Mildred Muscio, professional psychologist and committee-woman extraordinaire, President of the NSW National

---

116 FCNCW Conference Minutes, July 1929, and January 1931, Box 12, MS7583, NCWA Papers, NLA.
117 *Argus*, 1 June 1916, p. 5.
118 *Argus*, 31 October 1918, p. 4.
119 Jill Julius Matthews, *Dance Hall and Picture Palace: Sydney's Romance with Modernity*, Sydney, Currency Press, 2005, p. 220.

Council of Women for over a decade ... also went to the pictures'. In 1922, at the behest of NCWNSW, Muscio helped form the Better Film League (later the Good Film League). Its aims were unambiguous—better and more educational films, and greater influence of women in film censorship.[120] The national distribution of moving pictures made their regulation and censorship an issue for the federal council of the NCWs. Though delegates initially favoured a combination of state and federal censorship, they were moving towards a single federal board by 1926, when a resolution was passed agreeing 'that comprehensive powers should be given by Act of Parliament to the Federal Board of Censors ... to regulate all films, posters and advertisments'. But whatever the mix of state and federal authorities preferred, they consistently pushed for women to be appointed as censors.[121]

The focus, as with so much of council debate and activism in this period, was at once traditionally moralistic as well as progressivist. NCW leaders, typically of the cultural elite, were concerned by what they saw as the vulgar excesses of popular culture epitomised by the American movie monopoly. Their aim was protection—particularly of children and the vulnerable 'modern girl'—against the potential for exploitation and corruption they saw in the industry's unlimited expansion and in the condition of venues where films were shown.[122] They aimed too to protect the Britishness of Australian culture against vulgar Hollywood commercialism. But the progressivist reformers among them also emphasised the possibilities for education and uplift that the new media promised. The tension was apparent at the 1926 federal conference when 'a spirited discussion ensued' following an address by the president of the Motion Picture Distributors of Australia advocating the benefits of film and outlining 'precautions' already taken by the industry against 'harmful or objectionable pictures being shown in Australia'. Muscio

---

120 Matthews, *Dance Hall*, pp. 195, 210–11.
121 FCNCW Conference Minutes, July 1926, Box 12, MS7583, NCWA Papers, NLA.
122 Matthews, *Dance Hall*, pp. 201–17.

diplomatically defended the reforms that had occurred while agreeing that 'violence' and 'indecency' should always be condemned.[123] Some tension was also evident in the submissions of NCW members, most of whom also belonged to the Good Film League in Sydney, to the 1927 royal commission into the moving picture industry. Their main concern was moral but they were also concerned about the aesthetic influence of Hollywood and the Americanisation of language.[124]

Councils were now also beginning to see the potential of film as 'the easiest and most effectual way' to convey information, the NSW council recommending to the 1927 federal conference that the Commonwealth government be urged to establish 'a library of general and specialised Health films' for loan to the states.[125] And in 1930, the Victorian council expressed support for instructional films in schools as well as the inclusion of 'at least one educational film' in the children's sessions at local picture theatres. They also 'viewed with satisfaction the establishment of the Children's Cinema Council' in 1931, an organisation aiming to create 'a taste for good films, suitable for the clean entertainment and instruction of the young'. They nevertheless continued to advocate censorship to ensure the 'moral tone' of commercial films.[126] The fall-back position for the councils was always regulation and censorship, and they were pleased when one of their own, former Victorian president Eleanor Glencross, was the first woman appointed to the federal Censorship Board in 1928.[127]

---

123 FCNCW Conference, July 1926, Box 12, MS7583, NCWA Papers, NLA; Matthews, *Dance Hall*, p. 217.
124 Matthews, *Dance Hall*, pp. 225–6.
125 NCWNSW, *Biennial Reports for 1926–1928*, pp. 14, 19.
126 NCWV, *Report for 1930*, p. 5; Helen Gillan, *A Brief History of the National Council of Women of Victoria, 1902–1945*, Melbourne, Spectator, 1945, pp. 37–8; NCWV, *Resolutions Passed by the Council for the Year Ended October 31st 1931*, p. 3.
127 NCWV, *Report for 1929*, p. 4.

HOME AND FAMILY ENTER THE BODY POLITIC

Throughout the three decades leading to the establishment of the National Council of Women of Australia, 'the fundamental interests of the home and family' underpinned, then provided the glue for a sense of common purpose among the national councils throughout the Australian states. Without their shared concerns for the welfare of women and children there would have been no lasting rationale for the formation of a national organisation. Arguments for a national body were further strengthened by the councils' growing commitment to the principle of gender equality, and to national and international action to achieve this. It is to this that the next chapter is devoted.

Chapter 3

A GROWING COMMITMENT TO RIGHTS AND EQUALITY

Although protection of women and children and promotion of the home were the primary drivers of social reform activism in Australia's National Councils of Women during their first three decades, a concern for rights and equality as congruent with these objectives is also evident from the earliest years. It became stronger as the state councils moved towards federal organisation. This concern was broadly focused but three issues predominated: political equality and full citizen rights; equal pay and equal access to all spheres and levels of employment; and equal marriage and divorce laws.

Political Equality

As we have seen, the International Council of Women was set up to be inclusive of the range of women's public work rather than focusing on political rights. Nevertheless, women's suffrage was a matter of discussion from the beginning. While ICW never conceived of such rights as its primary purpose, it did resolve at the Berlin quinquennial in 1904 to form a standing committee to fight for suffrage and citizenship rights. But the various councils in different states and nations were free to choose how much or little energy they devoted to this cause.[1] Those who chose to make it their main focus formed an alternative international

---

1   See Leila Rupp, *Worlds of Women: The Making of an International Women's Movement*, Princeton, Princeton University Press, 1997, p. 22.

organisation, the International Woman Suffrage Alliance (IWSA). In Australia, Vida Goldstein's Women's Political Association and, later, Bessie Rischbieth's Australian Federation of Women Voters (AFWV) both affiliated with IWSA.[2] This did not preclude cross affiliation with the national councils, however, and although tensions between AFWV and the NCWs rose and fell, the two groups concurred and co-operated on a number of important issues.

Only three of the Australian councils had come into being before the women in their area of jurisdiction had achieved the right to vote—New South Wales (1896), Tasmania (1899) and Victoria (1902). Prominent members of the NSW council were active suffragists, but they are on record only once as using the council as a forum for their overtly political work. On 29 November 1900, on Rose Scott's motion, NCWNSW agreed to 'respectfully urge the government to use further means to secure the enfranchisement of the women of N.S.W.' in the wake of the Legislative Council's rejection of a government bill. No further mention was made of the subject until after the state suffrage was achieved (1902).[3] There are no Tasmanian NCW records for the period before 1905 but the extant sources in the press do not indicate that the council was involved in the campaign, and the husbands of the two leaders, Emily Dobson and Alice Braddon, were staunch public opponents of women's suffrage.[4] Dobson herself could say quite openly as late as 1907 that, though she was now in favour of women having

---

[2] It changed its name to the International Alliance of Women for Suffrage and Equal Citizenship in the late 1920s and then to the International Alliance of Women (IAW) in 1946.

[3] NCWNSW Council Minutes, 29 November 1900, Box MLK03009, MS3739, NCWNSW Papers, State Library of New South Wales (SLNSW). In 1904, NCWNSW was even sceptical about the wisdom of supporting suffrage as an issue for discussion at the ICW quinquennial conference that year, in view of the potential for damaging conflict between the various nations' representatives (8 April 1904). On the fate of the NSW bill of November 1900, see Audrey Oldfield, *Woman Suffrage in Australia: A Gift or a Struggle*, Cambridge, Cambridge University Press, 1992, pp. 90–1.

[4] NCWT Executive Minutes, 25 March 1907, NS325/1/8, NCWT Papers, Tasmanian Archive and Heritage Office (TAHO), LINC Tasmania.

access to the vote 'on the grounds of justice', she and her executive must 'disapprove of universal suffrage for either sex'.

Only in Victoria was the position of the council on this fundamental issue of political rights for women of any real significance. Given that the 35 constituent organisations that formed NCWV in 1902–03[5] varied in their views from opposition through indifference to passionate support, the question had to be delicately handled in council. Suffragists such as Vida Goldstein, Evelyn Gough and Louisa Bevan were early members of the executive but seem not to have used the council as a platform for their views, given ICW's lack of support before mid-1904. Although veteran suffragist Annie Lowe was one of Victoria's first vice-presidents and gave a lecture at the first annual congress in October 1903 on 'The History of the Suffrage', she had disappeared from the executive and list of delegates by early 1904, and suffrage is barely mentioned in council records or accounts of meetings for the next two years.[6] The Victorian council's entry into the last stages of the struggle for the vote was, then, gradual and tentative, and its involvement was generally low key.

In the last stages of the campaign, NCWV threw its support behind the movement. Urged by ICW suffrage convenor, American Anna Howard Shaw, council formed a suffrage committee in mid-1906, which organised a deputation to the premier in November. It included representatives from the WCTU, the Women's Political Association and the United Council of Suffrage Societies, and was led by lawyer, journalist, suffragist and council member Stella Allan.[7] The following September, NCWV sent two of its leading members, Evelyn Gough and Dr Mary Page Stone, to make further representations, and the premier promised to give them a reply within a fortnight. He finally

---

5   NCWV, *Annual Report 1902–03*.
6   NCWV Council Minute Books, 1903–05, NCWV Papers, State Library of Victoria (SLV) (classification pending).
7   Farley Kelly, 'The Woman Question in Melbourne 1880–1914', PhD thesis, Monash University, 1982, p. 387; Oldfield, *Woman Suffrage*, p. 167; Patricia Keep, 'Allan, Stella May (1871–1962)', *Australian Dictionary of Biography* (*ADB*), http://adb.anu.edu.au/biography/allan-stella-may-4998/text8307.

capitulated to the women's demands in early October. Though there is ongoing debate as to what changed his mind, we believe that NCWV intervention was significant. The fact that a coalition of more than thirty women's organisations was now prepared to give public support to the suffrage put paid to the claim that the majority of Victorian women were not interested in this fundamental right of citizenship.

The decades that followed saw the state councils demanding legislation that established the principle of women's equal legal status. In 1918 the NSW council achieved the passage of an act that gave women the right to be elected to all levels of government, to be appointed as judges and magistrates and justices of the peace, and to be admitted to the bar.[8] South Australia women already had the right to stand for state parliament but the passage of the Sex Disqualification (Removal) Act in 1921 provided the additional right for women to practise as public notaries and justices of the peace.[9] In Western Australia, NCW's Edith Cowan, elected to parliament in 1921, was responsible for the Women's Legal Status Act of 1923, which opened legal and other professions to women in that state.[10] The Federal Council of the National Councils of Women of Australia (FCNCWA), on the motion of the Victorian delegates, threw its weight behind this strategy in 1926, unanimously resolving: 'That all State Councils not yet enjoying the privilege should urge their Governments to introduce a bill providing for the equal legal status of women'.[11] Though they had early been admitted to the bar and belatedly conceded the right to stand for state parliament (1923), Victorian women were at this stage the only ones not eligible to become justices of the peace, as we have seen. That right was finally won with

---

8   NCWNSW, *Biennial Reports for 1919–1920*, p. 4.
9   Helen Jones, *In Her Own Name: A History of Women in South Australia from 1836*, Adelaide, Wakefield Press, revised ed. 1994, pp. 342–3.
10 Margaret Brown, 'Cowan, Edith Dircksey (1861–1932)', *ADB*, http://adb.anu.edu.au/biography/cowan-edith-dircksey-5791/text9823.
11 FCNCWA Conference Minutes, September 1925, Box 12, MS7583, NCWA Papers, National Library of Australia (NLA).

the passage of a broadly focused piece of legislation, the Women's Qualification Act 1926.[12]

Equal Pay for Equal Work

Equal pay for equal work was on the agenda at the 1899 ICW congress in London, though no vote was taken on the subject. Radical members brought the issue to the Australian councils very early, but leaders were reluctant to take it up before members and affiliates were ready. Again the issue was the preservation of the family and women's role as wives and mothers, seen by some as threatened by the economic independence equal pay would make possible. As early as November 1896, two resolutions in support of equal pay for equal work were read to the NCWNSW executive, with the suggestion they be put to the next council meeting, but it was decided instead to ask council members to write papers on the subject so members might be given a chance to consider all the issues involved. On further reflection, however, the executive later agreed that 'the time had not arrived for its discussion' and 'to put it aside for the present'.[13] In Victoria, a paper on the subject was given at the first annual conference in 1903 by Stella Allan.[14] From 1909, the Victorian council made tentative steps towards support for equal pay, though less as a matter of principle than as one of justice for a particular group of respectable middle-class women—teachers.[15] When Vida Goldstein requested state councils to put the issue to candidates in the 1909 federal election, the Queensland council agreed and undertook

---

12   Ada Norris, *Champions of the Impossible: A History of the National Council of Women of Victoria, 1902–1977*, Melbourne, Hawthorn Press, 1978, pp. 46, 48, 52, 54; Susan Blackburn Abeyasekare, 'Blackburn, Maurice McCrae (1880–1944)', *ADB*, http://adb.anu.edu.au/biography/blackburn-maurice-mccrae-5258/text8861.
13   NCWNSW Executive Minutes, 12 November 1896; 20 November 1896, Box MLK03009, MS3739, NCWNSW Papers, SLNSW.
14   Norris, *Champions*, p. 14.
15   Evelyn Gough, 'Report National Council of Women', presented to ICW Toronto quinquennial meeting, 1909, NCWV Papers, SLV (classification pending). Gough was NCWV international secretary.

to explain it to affiliates. But this was still a step too far for NSW council leaders, the president and senior vice-president persuading the executive to defer consideration of the issue.[16]

Before and during the Great War, the councils moved slowly towards endorsing the general principle of equal pay for equal work. In Victoria, employers appealed successfully in March 1913 to overthrow a judgement awarding equal pay to commercial clerks, and women across the political spectrum mounted a campaign to have the original determination restored.[17] When Victoria's Women's Political Association, Lady Teachers' Association and People's Liberal Party women called a rally demanding equal pay legislation in July 1913, NCWV did not itself participate though the initiators were affiliates of the council.[18] The Victorian council executive did, however, appoint a representative to work with the equal pay movement[19] and, a year later, NCWV was represented at a meeting in the Athenaeum Hall called to discuss the specific refusal of the government to remedy the position of women teachers. The gathering supported a motion demanding equal pay for equal work across the board as 'fair play'.[20] The momentum of the movement as a whole was lost in the war years, though the NSW and Queensland councils passed resolutions in 1915 in support of equal pay for women taking men's positions. When in 1918 Victoria's women teachers revived their campaign for at least four-fifths of the male rate, council passed a resolution of support and asked all affiliated societies to send individual resolutions to the premier.[21] In 1921, NCWV extended

---

16 NCWQ Executive Minutes, 7 June and 5 July 1909, Box 16045, 7266 NCWQ Minute Books, NCWQ Papers, State Library of Queensland (SLQ); NCWNSW Executive Minutes, 3 June 1909; 1 July 1909, Box MLK03009, MS3739, NCWNSW Papers, SLNSW.
17 *Journal of Commerce*, vol. LX, no. 755, 5 August 1914, p. 142.
18 *Argus*, 1 August 1913, p. 8.
19 Mrs Alison Pymm. See NCWV Executive Minutes, 8 July 1913, NCWV Papers, SLV (classification pending).
20 *Age*, 3 July 1914, p. 11.
21 NCWQ Executive Minutes, 30 August 1915, Box 16045, 7266 NCWQ Minute Books, NCWQ Papers, SLQ; Martha Sear, *The National Council of Women of NSW:*

their campaign beyond teachers and joined a deputation to the premier urging equal pay for equal work in the public service.²²

In taking these positions, the Australian councils were ahead of ICW, which did no more than discuss conditions and pay of women workers and only established its Standing Committee on Trades and Professions and Employment at the Rome conference of 1914. Signs of a more political approach were halted by war and the cessation of meetings and standing committee activities.²³ In the immediate post-war years ICW policy moved quickly, and was soon in advance of the Australian councils. Following the principle accepted in Article 427 of the Treaty of Versailles 'that men and women should receive equal remuneration for work of equal value', an executive meeting at the Hague in 1922 affirmed 'the principle of "equal pay for equal work" which signifies that payment be not influenced by the sex of the worker'. This resolution was strengthened at the full ICW meeting in Washington in 1925 to read support for 'the principle of "Equal pay for Equal work" which signifies that wages should be established on the basis of the occupation and not on the basis of sex'.²⁴

By this time, Australian women's organisations had come to link economic independence of women in marriage to the equal pay question. As we have seen, Australian councils' arguments for child endowment were premised on modification of the basis of wage fixation by substituting an individual-based wage award for the existing family-based one, with additional separate state-provided endowment

---

A Chronology 1896–1996, Sydney, NCWNSW, 1996; NCWV Council Minutes, 24 July and 22 August 1918, NCWV Papers, SLV (classification pending).

22 Norris, *Champions*, p. 41.
23 Catherine Jacques and Sylvie Lefebvre, 'The Working Methods of the ICW: From its Creation to the Second World War', in Eliane Gubin and Leen Van Molle (eds), *Women Changing the World: A History of the International Council of Women*, Brussels, Éditions Racine, 2005, pp. 101–04.
24 The Hague 1922, Washington 1925, 'ICW Resolutions', http://www.ncwcanada.com/ncwc2/wp-content/uploads/2014/02/ICW-CIF_Resolutions1.pdf, p. 176.

A GROWING COMMITMENT TO RIGHTS AND EQUALITY

of mothers as well as children.[25] There could be no grounds in this view for awarding men higher wages than women doing the same work, and, in line with ICW, the Australian councils came to argue that sex should play no part in determining any pay rates.[26] Support for this principle was a significant step for Australia's NCWs, since most remained committed to the ideal of maternalist citizenship, which assumed different roles and responsibilities for men and women and different needs. The issues raised by ICW were discussed at an interstate conference in 1922 and referred back to the state councils.[27] Four years later, at the 1926 FCNCWA conference, delegates indicated how far they had progressed in the intervening period, resolving 'to oppose the professional inequality of women, and demand for them equal opportunities and rights within the various employments', including 'equal pay for equal work, which signifies that wages should be established on the basis of the occupation and not on the basis of the sex'.[28] When the issue arose again in 1929 in relation to women teachers, some noted that governments did not get full returns for their costs in training women, but a resolution confirming support for a specific ICW policy of equality of pay and opportunity in all spheres of education was nevertheless carried without dissent.[29] There was, however, no direct reference as yet to the right of married women to equal employment opportunities and remuneration.

---

25 See Marilyn Lake, 'The Independence of Women and the Brotherhood of Man: Debates in the Labour Movement over Equal Pay and Motherhoood Endowment in the 1920s', *Labour History*, 63, November 1992, pp. 1–24.
26 See also Penelope Johnson, 'Gender, Class and Work: The Council of Action for Equal Pay Campaign in Australia during World War II', *Labour History*, 50, May 1986, especially pp. 134–7.
27 For example, NCWQ Council Minutes, 13 October 1922, Box 16045, 7266 NCWQ Minute Books, NCWQ Papers, SLQ.
28 FCNCWA Conference Minutes, July 1926, Box 12, MS7583, NCWA Papers, NLA.
29 FCNCWA Conference Minutes, September 1929, Box 12, MS7583, NCWA Papers, NLA.

Equality in Marriage

By the 1920s, the national councils had come to see uniform federal marriage and divorce law as the most effective way of tackling the problem of maintenance. The federal council passed increasingly detailed resolutions calling for uniformity in 1925, 1926 and 1927, and support for a federal law was presented to the royal commission into the Commonwealth Constitution by the Queensland council in 1927.[30] That economic considerations remained centrally important in council consideration of uniform laws is evident in the decision of the 1928 federal conference not only to reaffirm the necessity for federal legislation,[31] but also to tackle the issue of the 'economic independence of wives' directly in that context. Two years earlier, the laws committee of the NSW council had concluded that current policy treated the family as an attachment to a man who is a wage earner.

> They are his belongings, called ... "dependents." What we wish to see recognised is the woman's share in the national income as apart from any wage or salary earned by the father of the children. The children are the mother's share in the production of the country's wealth. Properly speaking she is not a dependent, but a producer of wealth of the first importance.[32]

South Australia's Agnes Goode had also told the 1926 federal council that 'marriage would be placed on an infinitely better level if it were possible to make both parties economically independent'.[33] Though a proposal for funding endowment by readjustment of wage-setting procedures was one path being followed, some believed that mandated

---

30   FCNCWA Conference Minutes, September 1925 and July 1926, Box 12, MS7583, NCWA Papers, NLA; NCWQ, *Annual Report 1927/28*, p. 24.
31   FCNCWA Conference Minutes, July 1928, Box 12, MS7583, NCWA Papers, NLA.
32   NCWNSW, *Biennial Reports 1924–26*, p. 22. Lawyer Sibyl Morrison was the author of this report. She and Mary Jamieson Williams, WCTU and AFWV activist, chaired the laws standing committee in this period.
33   *Argus*, 29 July 1926, p. 20.

economic equality in marriage law would have more certainty. In 1928, the state councils were asked to consider a model already in place—the Swedish marriage law, which decreed an equal economic partnership between husband and wife—with a view to the principle being 'embodied in our Federal marriage law'.[34] Councils took this seriously and, in 1929, the federal secretary agreed to have translations of the law made and distributed.[35]

What they were offered by the federal government was considerably less than uniformity, let alone 'a law providing for shared income'. Prime Minister Bruce suggested a cheaper and less radical alternative to a new uniform federal marriage law, one that simply provided for an Australian domicile, and, in 1929, the councils reluctantly accepted this in the context of the current serious economic downturn. Without a uniform national law, domicile would remain a 'burning' problem unless tackled nationally and its resolution would at least make enforcement of state maintenance orders easier.[36] But even this modicum of reform failed to eventuate. Bruce lost government and his seat at the subsequent election, and the economic crisis visited on the nation by the Great Depression made default in maintenance payments and desertion seem less important to subsequent governments than other causes of family destitution such as unemployment. The issue remained unresolved before the creation of the National Council of Women of Australia but it was one that helped bring the councils together on a unified national basis in 1931.

Another focus for the councils' laws standing committees was the need to protect women and children from destitution arising from the right of a married man to 'bequeath all his property to strangers … and

---

34   Reported in NCWQ, *Annual Report 1927/28*, pp. 25, 26.
35   FCNCWA Conference Minutes, September 1929, Box 12, MS7583, NCWA Papers, NLA.
36   FCNCWA Conference Minutes, September 1929, Box 12, MS7583, NCWA Papers, NLA.

to leave his wife and children absolutely penniless'.[37] They were equally concerned about his power to assign guardianship of his children away from their mother on his death. Awareness of these and associated issues was reinforced by ICW, which in 1914 resolved that 'the law should give equal rights to father and mother in all respects with regard to their children'.[38] State standing committees on law and the legal position of women kept the issue of these and other legal disabilities alive. The NSW council was able to report progress in 1915/16 with the passage of two pieces of state legislation women had been asking for since before NCWNSW was formed. These acts made it possible for the state to interfere with any will leaving the wife and children of the testator without adequate support, and made the mother the legal guardian of her children on the death of their father unless the courts judged her unsuitable.[39] But a major loophole soon became apparent. Because the latter act did not actually make women and men equal guardians of their children, living fathers could still remove children from their mothers at will.

Again an initial concern for protection of wives and children quickly metamorphosed into support for equality between spouses. By the early 1920s, the NSW council laws committee was once more formulating suggestions for amendment to the legislation.[40] Meanwhile, the Queensland council's attention had been drawn by a guest speaker to the absolute rights of custody of men and, in the West, NCWWA organised a deputation to the premier requesting equal guardianship legislation,

---

37 Address by Victoria's (and Australia's) first woman lawyer, Flos Greig, to NCWV annual conference, *Argus*, 26 October 1905. See also topics listed for interstate conference by NSW in NCWNSW Council Minutes, 6 July 1911, Box MLK03009, MS3739, NCWNSW Papers, SLNSW.
38 Rome 1914, 'ICW Resolutions', http://www.ncwcanada.com/ncwc2/wp-content/uploads/2014/02/ICW-CIF_Resolutions1.pdf, p. 17.
39 NCWNSW, *Biennial Reports for 1915–1916*, p. 5.
40 NCWNSW, *Biennial Reports for 1921–1922*, p. 7.

A GROWING COMMITMENT TO RIGHTS AND EQUALITY

and, after a somewhat discourteous reception, took to lobbying MPs.[41] In South Australia, Agnes Goode told the council executive in June 1924 that the father had all legal rights even over the unborn child, and council discussed the subject of equal guardianship on a number of occasions over the following year.[42] Queensland's laws committee, after being directed to make the issue a focus of their work, reported that 'the law does not accord [the mother] any rights regarding her children', and proposed that equal guardianship of children be added to the agenda of the interstate conference in Melbourne in October 1924.[43] The NSW council, in light of the well-publicised case of actress Emilie Polini being refused custody of her daughter, also asked the Melbourne conference to support equal guardianship by both parents of minor children.[44]

Delegates quickly recognised the need for this to be tackled as a national issue and resolved not only that the 'principle of equal guardianship be applied to all legislation dealing with the powers, rights and duties of parents in respect of the custody and control of children' but also asked the states 'to endeavour to get uniformity and improvement of laws relating to this question'.[45] It remained a matter of unifying concern throughout the decade, the federal council resolving again in 1929 that 'those states where the mother is not legally recognised as equal with the father in the guardianship of their children urge upon the Governments to amend the law so as to achieve this equality'.[46] As with maintenance and adoption, the councils were concerned that equal

---

41 NCWQ Council Minutes, 13 April 1917, Box 16045, 7266 NCWQ Minute Books, NCWQ Papers, SLQ; *West Australian*, 30 December 1919; 16 March 1920; NCWWA Council Minutes, 26 March 1920, 3 December 1920, MS1389A, NCWWA Papers, State Library of Western Australia (SLWA).
42 NCWSA Council and Executive Minutes, 1924–25, SRG297, NCWSA Papers, State Library of South Australia (SLSA).
43 NCWQ Council Minutes, 27 March 1922, 29 May 1922, 15 July 1923, 15 October 1923, Box 16045, 7266 NCWQ Minute Books, NCWQ Papers, SLQ.
44 NCWNSW, *Biennial Reports for 1923–1924*, p. 5.
45 NCWV, *Report for 1924*, p. 12.
46 FCNCWA Conference Minutes, September 1929, Box 12, MS7583, NCWA Papers, NLA.

guardianship status in one state might not be recognised in the others. A uniform marriage law had the potential to redress the problem, if it also provided for equality. While, as historian Heather Radi has pointed out, this focus on equality could not solve the problem of courts making judgements against mothers on moral and behavioural grounds, its embodiment in law was, as the councils recognised, a necessary condition for recognition of a woman's parental rights.[47]

Of all the possible remedies for women's inequality within marriage, the establishment of uniform grounds for divorce was the matter with the greatest potential to divide the national councils in Australia. From the earliest period, the mainstream women's movement was more concerned to preserve marriage than to consider its dissolution. The stigma attached to divorce and fears that easier access would only bring hardship to women and children were widespread. While many members of Australia's NCWs supported Australia's first woman MP, Edith Cowan, in her opposition to any measures that could make divorce easier,[48] there were radical feminists in both ICW and the Australian councils who stood opposed on principle to the unequal legal status of men and women within marriage, including unequal grounds for divorce.[49] If equality resulted in more divorces, that was regrettable, but not a reason to oppose reform. Council leaders had to steer a path between these views. One tactic was to focus on the protective purpose of reform proposals; another was to call on the expertise of women lawyers.

---

[47] Heather Radi, 'Whose Child? Custody of Children in NSW 1854–1934', in Judy Mackinolty and Heather Radi (eds), *In Pursuit of Justice: Australian Women and the Law 1788–1979*, Sydney, Hale & Iremonger, 1979, pp. 119–30.

[48] Edith Cowan (later president of NCWWA) wrote to Rose Scott of the NSW council that she would vote against Federation of the Australian colonies on these grounds alone. Cited in Judith Allen, *Rose Scott: Vision and Revision in Feminism*, Melbourne, Oxford University Press, 1994, p. 148.

[49] Countess of Aberdeen (ed.), *Report of Transactions of the Fourth Quinquennial Meeting Held at Toronto, Canada, June 1909: With Which Are Incorporated the Reports of the National Councils and of International Standing Committees for 1908–1909*, London, Constable, 1910, pp. 279–95.

A GROWING COMMITMENT TO RIGHTS AND EQUALITY

After the Great War, the increasing numbers of women lawyers graduating and practising, at least in the eastern states, provided a large pool of experts able and willing to advise the national councils on the anomalies of divorce law. From this time, they typically headed the councils' standing committees on laws and the legal position of women and thus also acted as conduits with ICW. By the mid-1920s, legal advocates of divorce reform in the councils, such as NSW's Sibyl Morrison, were speaking the modern language of equal rights rather than protection at federal conferences. Victoria's Joan Rosanove similarly told Victorian women that marriage should be based on 'the idea of partnership and equality', rather than the husband's ownership of the wife. 'Whilst not dealing with the question of whether divorce is a good or bad institution ... there is a set of rules by which a man can divorce his wife, and another set for a woman.'[50] A uniform equal federal marriage and divorce law, these women lawyers argued, was the most effective way of tackling this problem and, given the councils' growing commitment to gender equality, this seemed less confronting than in previous years.

The South Australian council passed a resolution of support for such legislation in November 1924 and the following June agreed to send it on to the first federal council conference.[51] As we have seen, the federal council supported uniformity in principle in 1925 and 1926, and, in 1927, support for a federal law was presented to the royal commission into the Commonwealth Constitution by the Queensland council.[52] The federal council conference of that year agreed that the state

---

50 FCNCWA Conference Minutes, July 1926, Box 12, MS7583, NCWA Papers, NLA; Norris, *Champions*, pp. 67–9; *Housewife*, 5 November 1929, p. 4; Joan M. O'Brien, 'Morrison, Sibyl Enid (1895–1961)', *ADB*, http://adb.anu.edu.au/biography/morrison-sibyl-enid-7664/text13407; Barbara Falk, 'Rosanove, Joan Mavis (1896–1974)', *ADB*, http://adb.anu.edu.au/biography/rosanove-joan-mavis-11560/text20631.
51 NCWSA Council Minutes, 15 November 1924, 2 June 1925, SRG297, NCWSA Papers, SLSA.
52 FCNCWA Conference Minutes, September 1925, and Brisbane, July 1926, Box 12, MS7583, NCWA Papers, NLA; NCWQ, *Annual Report 1927/28*, p. 24.

councils would 'make further endeavours to obtain exact information on desirable amendments to the laws in each State with the object of embodying them in one Federal Act'.[53] Another resolution passed in 1928 produced an initial expression of willingness by Prime Minister Bruce to hear concrete proposals, especially after the state premiers also threw their weight behind the cause,[54] but, with the onset of depression, the Commonwealth government backed away from major change and nothing had been achieved by the time the NCWA came into being in 1931.

In pursuing equal and uniform federal divorce legislation and retaining the support of state councils and their affiliates, NCWA leaders consistently assured members that their actions did not mean support for divorce as such. Their coupling of the matter with the domicile and maintenance issues and the principle of legal equality points to the motivation of many women reformers and the point on which radicals and conservatives could agree: the need to relieve the problems of women whose marriages had irretrievably broken down.

By the time the Australian national councils had federated for national purposes and then taken the further step of forming a national body responsible for communicating with the International Council of Women, the language of rights and equality had become an accepted part of their regular discourse. It did not replace their main preoccupation with family welfare, but, alongside the change of approach to philanthropic reform brought about by the progressivist incorporation of scientific frames of reference and professional expertise, the notions

---

53 Report of conference in *Argus*, 17 September 1927, p. 40.
54 FCNCW Conference Minutes, July1928, and September 1929, Box 12, MS7583, NCWA Papers, NLA.

of rights and equality gave a feminist ballast to the primary focus on maternalism, and the emphasis on citizenship gave the councils' work a political edge. This trend was reinforced by a rising international engagement and awareness of developments outside Australia fostered first by limited but growing pre-war peace activism, then by the challenges of the war years, and, after the war, by the involvement of ICW in League of Nations debates and issues concerning women and children. Along with other women's alliances, the council movement worked to encourage a national and international culture of peace and negotiation in the post-war decade. The last chapter in this section is devoted to these influences on the Australian councils as they moved towards a permanent national organisation.

Chapter 4

DEVELOPING INTERNATIONAL IDENTITY

The Australian council movement helped build local awareness and engagement with women's reform activism in other parts of the world through its links with the International Council of Women (ICW) and, after the Great War, with the League of Nations and other international women's alliances. The main areas of focus before the formation of the National Council of Women of Australia (NCWA) were peace and arbitration, war and patriotism, the problem of nationality for married women, and League of Nations representation and anti-war work. The end of the first post-war decade also saw preliminary steps in the federal council towards engagement with women's activities in the Pacific region, a theme taken up in more detail in the next section of this book.

Peace and Arbitration

The origins of the International Council of Women and the council movement as a whole coincided with those of the world peace movement. Only in the late nineteenth century did peace societies emerge and only at the very end of the century did the word 'pacifism' come into use. The arms race of the two decades before World War I was the main force behind the peace movement. Three streams were evident: pacifist, liberal/humanitarian, and socialist. Women were active in most of the groups that emerged, taking a leading role in many as well as promoting peace ideals in their own organisations. For a significant proportion of pacifist and liberal women, peace was a central principle of the ideal Christian social order to which they aspired. The societies that met in a series of international peace congresses after 1889 could agree, if not on pure or absolute pacifist principles, at least on a pragmatic and rational liberal internationalism. This aimed to gain acceptance for a set of rules and procedures that would provide international security without force through means such as tribunals, third-party mediators, neutrality treaties and arbitration. The ideas generated by these peace activists gave rise to the official Hague conferences of 1899 and 1907, and the latter saw the first attempt at an international court. Socialist peace activists worked through their own international gatherings.[1]

One of the key women in the American and international peace movement from the 1880s until her death was ICW founder and president from 1899 to 1904, May Wright Sewell. And peace was one of the earliest considerations of ICW. Before the 1899 quinquennial meeting, the question arose, in the words of the first president, Lady Ishbel Aberdeen,

> as to whether it would be in harmony with the Constitution, which forbade identification with any one propaganda, to place on the Agenda of the International Council Plenary Meeting in London, 1899, a resolution pledging the I.C.W. to the promotion of Peace through Arbitration.[2]

All the councils agreed that consideration of the subject was entirely appropriate and, indeed, that 'the claims of World Peace' should be seen 'as the best possible illustration of the Golden Rule, and as transcending all other needs for the progress and happiness of mankind'. Canada proposed the resolution, passed 'unanimously with enthusiasm' at a special meeting during the ensuing London quinquennial: 'That

---

1 See Carolyn Rasmussen, *The Lesser Evil? Opposition to War and Fascism in Australia 1920–1941*, Melbourne, History Department, University of Melbourne, 1992, Introduction.
2 Ishbel Aberdeen and Temair, 'How the I.C.W. Accepted the Principle of International Arbitration', *ICW Bulletin*, 10, June 1938 (Jubilee edition), p. 74.

the International Council of Women do take steps in every country to further and advance by every means in their power the movement towards International Arbitration'.[3]

Since the first Hague peace conference was meeting at the same time, 'a message was despatched immediately' to participants 'with the assurance of the earnest support of their efforts by the women of the World'. ICW thereafter held that it was 'the first International Women's Association to identify itself with the Peace movement'.[4] Whether or not this was true, the Standing Committee for Peace and Arbitration was certainly the first of ICW's committees for special subjects, and most existing and subsequently affiliated national councils formed their own local peace standing committees. ICW itself was unable to sustain the early commitment to arbitration, for the recommendations of its standing committee were thwarted by dissent among some of the constituent councils. The Toronto quinquennial in 1909 'dropped or modified' resolutions of support for the Hague conference and for decrease in armaments, confining itself instead to endorsing less controversial recommendations for engaging in local peace congresses, forming study groups on alternatives to war, and promoting annual peace days. These activities and the promotion of new school textbooks emphasising peace and arbitration remained important in the work of the international council and many of its affiliates,[5] though the Great War temporarily redirected the energies of most councils, including those in Australia.

It took some time for peace committees to establish firm roots in the Australian councils. In Victoria, Vida Goldstein proposed the

---

3   London 1899, 'ICW Resolutions', http://www.ncwcanada.com/ncwc2/wp-content/uploads/2014/02/ICW-CIF_Resolutions1.pdf, p. 85.
4   Aberdeen, 'How the I.C.W. Accepted the Principle of International Arbitration', p. 74.
5   See Catherine Jacques and Sylvie Lefebvre, 'From Pacifism to Humanitarian Action', in Eliane Gubin and Leen Van Molle (eds), *Women Changing the World: A History of the International Council of Women*, Brussels, Éditions Racine, 2005, chap. VII, pp. 171–94; also Toronto 1909, 'ICW Resolutions', http://www.ncwcanada.com/ncwc2/wp-content/uploads/2014/02/ICW-CIF_Resolutions1.pdf, p. 86.

formation of the Peace and Arbitration Committee after the constitution providing for standing committees had been passed in March 1904. Jessie Strong, wife of the Reverend Charles Strong, the founder of the Melbourne Peace Society, was appointed convenor, but NCWV's Peace and Arbitration Committee made no identifiable contribution to the annual reports and seems to have met rarely in the early years. Strong most likely subsumed the committee's work in that of the Peace Society. In New South Wales, Rose Scott assumed the leading role in council peace work as international secretary but also as president of the Sydney Peace Society. The pattern was repeated elsewhere. In its report to ICW in 1910–11, the Tasmanian council, like NCWNSW, expressed some interest in peace work but nominated little activity except through the medium of the local peace society, and Queensland's council reported 'sympathy' but 'no peace department'. The Victorian report to ICW made no direct reference to peace work at all.[6]

The immediate pre-war years saw increased interest in peace work in the Australian councils but much of it continued to be indirect. As Rose Scott reported to NCWNSW in 1913/14:

> I regret to say that so far all the educational work done in New South Wales for the cause of Peace and Arbitration has been done, not by our National Council of Women, but by the Peace Society of New South Wales.[7]

In Victoria more initiatives now came from within. There was an address to council on the Hague Tribunal in 1909, and in June 1912 members listened to a lecture by local pacifist the Reverend Leyton Richards on Norman Angell's book about the futility of war, *The Great Illusion*.[8] Then,

---

6   ICW, *Second Annual Report of 5th Quinquennial Period 1910–11*, Report from Standing Committees—Peace and Arbitration, pp. 94–5.
7   NCWNSW, *Biennial Reports for 1913–1914*, p. 5.
8   NCWV Council Minutes, 27 June 1912, NCWV Papers, State Library of Victoria (SLV) (classification pending). Richards, an Englishman later involved in Britain's wartime peace movement, was minister at the Collins Street Independent Church 1911–13.

in March 1914, leading international peace activist and president of the World Peace Foundation, David Starr Jordan, spoke to the council on 'Womanhood and War'. Starr Jordan's view that 'A nation in arms could not remain a nation of democracy'[9] prefigured many of the arguments in which members of NCWV were embroiled only a year later.

War, Patriotism and Internal Division

Once war broke out in August 1914, peace activism declined and was barely tolerated in most NCW circles by 1916. This was most evident in Victoria, where it disappeared entirely under the influence of the powerful and very pro-Empire Australian Women's National League (AWNL), affiliated since 1910. With no ICW congresses between the Rome quinquennial in 1914 and Kristiania in 1920, meetings and reports of the international standing committees, including peace and arbitration, were suspended until the end of the war, and Lady Aberdeen instructed national councils to do what they felt to be necessary in their national contexts.[10]

While the NSW council expressed 'profound sympathy' for the international president's 'sad position' and Scott was trying to keep channels of communication open,[11] the Victorian council showed little willingness to continue international contacts or peace talk. Within the first few weeks of the war, NCWV issued a curt response to the Peace Society's request for co-operation that 'it was not within the province of the Council'.[12] Peace and international arbitration work was now regarded as disloyal. In 1915 Jessie Strong, who had helped form the Sisterhood of International Peace (SIP) for education and discussion

---

9   *Argus*, 21 March 1914, p. 21.
10 Maria Ogilvie Gordon, 'The International Council of Women (1888–1938)', *International Council of Women Bulletin*, 10, June 1938 (Jubilee Edition), p. 78.
11 NCWNSW Council Minutes, 6 August 1914, Box MLK03009, MS3739, NCWNSW Papers, State Library of NSW (SLNSW).
12 NCWV Council Minutes, 25 September 1914, NCWV Papers, SLV (classification pending).

purposes, felt compelled to resign from NCWV after the council decided not to accede to her request that the peace standing committee be revived, instead decreeing that the question of peace should not be discussed at all. Jessie Strong was a founding member of the Victorian council and its much-respected senior vice president, so her resignation could not be taken lightly. Although requested to reconsider, Mrs Strong declared that this censorship of open discussion was intolerable. Her decision, she said, reflected her 'growing dissatisfaction at the way the business of the Council was conducted ... and the underhand tactics in regard to standing committees'. The Victorian executive was not prepared to compromise and finally recommended that council accept the resignation 'with very much regret'.[13]

In the latter part of 1915, NCWV went still further, adopting what came very close to a party political position, and one that interfered with the autonomy of member organisations. In August, the council refused to admit outspoken pacifist Adela Pankhurst as the Women's Political Association (WPA) delegate because she 'had taken a prominent part in much peace propaganda' and 'had expressed sentiments with which the majority of the Council felt that they could not in any way agree'. One prominent member even asserted that 'working for peace at the present time was little short of treasonable'. A special by-law was passed making all delegates subject to council's approval. It was challenged by Vida Goldstein and some others at subsequent meetings, and police were finally called to evict Pankhurst from the October council assembly.[14]

---

13 NCWV Council Minutes, 11 and 27 May 1915, 8 and 24 June 1915, 13 July 1915, 26 August 1915, NCWV Papers, SLV (classification pending); NCWV, *Report for 1915*, p. 6; *Weekly Times*, 3 July 1915, p. 10; *Argus*, 27 August 1915, p. 9. For more detailed discussion about internal conflicts, see Kate Gray, 'The Acceptable Face of Feminism: The National Council of Women of Victoria, 1902–18', MA thesis, University of Melbourne, 1988, pp. 109–10, and Judith Smart, 'Women Waging War: The National Council of Women of Victoria 1914–1920', *Victorian Historical Journal*, 85 (1), June 2015, pp. 61–82. SIP was to become the first branch of the Women's International League for Peace and Freedom (WILPF) in Australia.

14 NCWV Council Minutes, 23 September 1915, NCWV Papers, SLV (classification pending); *Argus*, 24 September 1915, p. 6, and 29 October 1915, p. 6; NCWV, *Report for 1915*, p. 5. See also Gray, 'Acceptable Face', pp. 111–16.

Rejection of the women's section of the Socialist Party as 'unsuitable' for affiliation, resolutions against all things German including the German NCW, and outright support for conscription in the referendum campaigns of 1916 and 1917 were even clearer indications that the NCWV had forsaken internationalist principles for militarist and patriotic ones.[15]

Neither the New South Wales nor the Western Australian councils took such a strong position against peace work, instead setting up study circles on international relations and arbitration, as Lady Aberdeen suggested, while also giving staunch support to the war effort. Nevertheless in Western Australia there was considerable conflict and division during 1915 and 1916, in part over war-driven state legislation for compulsory notification of venereal disease and mandatory treatment, and in part over questions of autonomy and presidential authority. The three largest affiliates—the Women's Service Guild led by Bessie Rischbieth, the Woman's Christian Temperance Union, and the Women's Labour Social Club—eventually withdrew from the council in 1916, depriving it of its leading voices of moderation. NCWWA now also gave unalloyed support to the campaigns for conscription.[16] In NSW, too, there was conflict over compulsory military service with Rose Scott leading the opponents, but a majority of delegates voted for council to affiliate with the pro-conscription Universal Service League.[17] Queensland's council was also hostile to peace activism and in April/May 1916 refused to grant affiliation to the local branch of the Women's Peace Army led by Margaret Thorp, drawing attention to the fact that NCWQ's own peace and arbitration committee was

---

15 Gray, 'Acceptable Face', pp. 116, 120–1; Smart, 'Women Waging War', pp. 70–4.
16 Noreen Sher, *The Spirit Lives On: A History of the National Council of Women of Western Australia 1911–1999*, Perth, NCWWA, 1999, chap. II.
17 NCWNSW Executive Minutes, 26 August 1915, 1 and 20 September 1915, and NCWNSW Council Minutes, 5 and 12 August 1915, Box MLK03009, MS3739, NCWNSW Papers, SLNSW.

'in abeyance'.[18] In Hobart, the 1916 annual meeting of the Tasmanian council focused much of its attention on women's duty in war time, applauding a suggestion that they should 'instil into the minds of all … the righteousness of the cause in overcoming the German dragon of destruction'.[19] By 1917, then, all of the Australian NCWs seem to have become mouthpieces for pro-war political conservatism and patriotism, though not without varying degrees of dissent from within.

Nationality of Married Women

Some international contacts and matters of concern apart from the war did persist during these years of conflict. Domicile was a matter of international as well as national concern because, in most countries, a married woman was required to take on her husband's nationality. At the very least, marriage to a foreigner or alien meant loss of citizenship in her own country, and, in some circumstances, she could also be rendered stateless and without recourse to any law. Within the British Empire, the 1914 British Nationality and Status of Aliens Act provided the model adopted by all the dominions, and it was deeply gendered. In establishing that all individuals born or naturalised within 'His Majesty's dominions and allegiance' acquired British nationality, it also stipulated that a married woman had no such entitlement. With some specified exceptions, a British woman who married an alien became an alien herself, losing the rights, privileges and welfare benefits to which British nationals were entitled.[20]

In Australia, the NSW council took note of the problem almost straight away when it became clear that the British act would override

---

18   NCWQ Executive Minutes, 17 May 1916, and NCWQ Council Minutes, 12 May 1916, Box 16045, 7266 NCWQ Minute Books, NCWQ Papers, State Library of Queensland (SLQ).

19   *Mercury*, 3 March 1916, p. 7.

20   M. Page Baldwin, 'Subject to Empire: Married Women and the British Nationality and Status of Aliens Act', *Journal of British Studies*, 40 (4), October 2001, pp. 522–56.

existing Australian law. Its leaders were somewhat comforted by new prime minister Andrew Fisher's inclusion of 'this question of the naturalisation of Australian women in his programme for the session' for 1914, believing that 'Australian women, like Australian men [should] not lose their rights as citizens because they happen to marry foreigners'.[21] War stymied the government's pursuit of the issue and the state councils next took it up in 1916, not specifically in relation to Australian women's situation but this time in response to a letter from the Netherlands council.[22] In reply to a request for information by NCWNSW laws convenor Rose Scott, the minister for defence, Senator Pearce, now expressed the view that Australian women ought to lose their nationality in such circumstances, a position contrary to that his government had taken when first elected.[23] The Victorian council sought legal advice from women lawyers and was addressed by Anna Brennan, who confirmed the disabilities suffered by women married to aliens.[24] The following year, the Australian councils were asked by their British counterpart to urge the Australian government to pass independent legislation enabling married women to retain their nationality, and to raise the issue at the next Imperial conference. NCWNSW made the approach without hesitation but the request was rejected by Prime Minister Hughes.[25] The Queensland council sent a memorial directly to the Imperial conference in London in 1918, arguing in support of uniformity in the Empire but

---

21 NCWNSW, *Biennial Reports for 1913–1914*, p. 7.
22 See NCWV Executive Minutes, 6 August 1916, NCWV Papers, SLV (classification pending); NCWNSW Council Minutes, 3 August 1916, Box MLK03009, MS3739, NCWNSW Papers, SLNSW.
23 NCWNSW Council Minutes, 24 and 31 August 1916, Box MLK03009, MS3739, NCWNSW Papers, SLNSW.
24 NCWV Executive Minutes, 6 August 1916, and NCWV Council Minutes, 31 August 1916, NCWV Papers, SLV (classification pending); Ada Norris, *Champions of the Impossible: A History of the National Council of Women of Victoria, 1902–1977*, Melbourne, Hawthorn Press, 1978, p. 175.
25 NCWNSW Minutes, 1 and 29 November 1917, 4 July 1918, Box MLK03009, MS3739, NCWNSW Papers, SLNSW.

asking that 'women married to non Britishers be not forced against their will to take husband's nationality'.[26] The request was ignored.

In 1920, rather than trying to redress the problem as had been intended in 1914, the Australian government introduced legislation modelled on the British Act of 1914. The NSW council sent a resolution on the issue to ICW for discussion at the first post-war conference.[27] ICW for its part resolved that councils should promote legislation in their own countries but agreed to 'draw up proposals for international agreement regarding the nationality of women married to aliens, for presentation to the Governments and to the League of Nations'.[28] The Australian NCWs meanwhile continued their agitation at home. On NCWNSW's initiative, the councils sent a resolution to the federal government in connection with the new nationality bill, asking that 'women be given the same right to retain their own nationality … as men'.[29]

The conservative Nationalist Party government was more interested in preserving uniformity within the Empire and unity within families than giving women equal nationality rights, and, though Labor Party representatives protested against the injustice meted out to married women, government MPs were generally unconcerned. The most trenchant critic was Labor's Frank Brennan, who commented that the designation of the 'an Australian girl' who married a foreigner as 'a citizen of a foreign country' was 'an utterly unjust one' and gave notice of an amendment 'that no woman born in Australia shall become an alien or forfeit her nationality by reason of her marriage'. The government declined to accept Brennan's amendment, the minister for home and territories commenting that it was 'no hardship to say that [a woman]

---

26   NCWQ Minutes, 27 April, 19 and 27 May 1918, Box 16045, 7266 NCWQ Minute Books, NCWQ Papers, SLQ.

27   NCWNSW Council Minutes, 1 July 1920, Box MLK03009, MS3739, NCWNSW Papers, SLNSW.

28   Kristiania 1920, 'ICW Resolutions', http://www.ncwcanada.com/ncwc2/wp-content/uploads/2014/02/ICW-CIF_Resolutions1.pdf, p. 115.

29   NCWV Council Minutes, 30 September 1920, NCWV Papers, SLV (classification pending).

shall take on the nationality of her husband', and that to accept the amendment would render the bill 'null and void' because it would 'destroy the uniformity of our law with that of the Empire'.[30]

With the formation of the Federal Council of the National Councils of Women of Australia (FCNCWA) in 1925, councils were able to discuss international issues in concert, though there was wariness on some matters, given that standing committee activities as well as direct contact with ICW remained under the aegis of the state councils. But there was little difference of opinion within Australian council circles on the question of the independent nationality of married women,[31] and resolutions demanding equal nationality rights were passed regularly by the federal council from 1925 and then by the National Council of Women of Australia (NCWA) from 1932.

The approach to the nationality question, as in Britain, was necessarily three-pronged.[32] The councils, together with other women's groups, urged the federal government to take a lead in legislating for the rights of Australian married women, but also urged government representatives at Imperial conferences to take up the cudgels for all British women. At the broader international level, Australian NCWs followed ICW in trying to influence the League of Nations Conference on the Codification of International Laws held in The Hague in 1930, and thereafter, when the resulting convention failed to include nationality

---

30   *Commonweatlh Parliamentary Debates* (*CPD*), House of Representatives, 28 October 1920, pp. 6063, 6100, 6140. Labor members also rejected as undemocratic the requirement that they conform to legislation just because it was part of an Imperial plan (p. 6140).

31   The only quibble we have discovered came from Queensland's conservative president of the late 1920s and early 1930s, Zina Cumbrae-Stewart, whose background was the Mothers' Union. She persisted in arguing that different nationalities 'might mean dissension in the home', long after even the most conservative politicians had given up on this argument. See NCWA Conference Minutes, November 1932, Box 12, MS7583, NCWA Papers, NLA.

32   Page Baldwin, 'Subject to Empire', pp. 522*ff*.

rights for married women,[33] focused on working with ICW and the league-created Women's Consultative Committee on Nationality. The first NCWA conference in 1932 resolved:

> That the National Council of Women of Australia support the international organisations in their proposed plan of action so outlined in the I.C.W. Bulletin, in order to further the claims for equality of women under the Nationality Laws in all countries of the world.[34]

The Australian councils had some limited success at the national and Imperial levels. In 1925, the British House of Commons unanimously agreed that British women should not lose their nationality by the act of marriage to an alien. As a result of approaches by the Australian NCWs, together with other nationally organised women's groups, the same resolution was moved in federal parliament in February 1926. It was passed on the voices, Prime Minister Bruce agreeing that Australia's representative at the next Imperial conference would 'certainly be prepared to move in the matter, in the hope that all the parts of the British Empire may agree to an alteration of the law in the direction suggested'.[35] However, he made a proviso parallel to that of the British government, that:

> The Government regards ... uniformity as essential, and if this motion be agreed to, will not be prepared to bring down a bill for the amendment of the Nationalization Act until the change is approved by other portions of the Empire, so that uniformity may continue.[36]

---

33 Except where they had been rendered stateless.
34 See resolution at NCWA Conference Minutes, November 1932, Box 12, MS7583, NCWA Papers, NLA. NCWQ, however, abstained.
35 *CPD*, House of Representatives, 2 February 1926, pp. 677–85; 25 February 1926, pp. 1140–1.
36 *CPD*, House of Representatives, 25 February 1926, p. 1139.

Though Britain, Australia and New Zealand were all prepared to move on this issue, successive Imperial conferences were unable to agree and, given the fragility of consensus on shared British nationality, with the Irish Free State, Canada and South Africa threatening to break away, Britain's political leaders opted for the status quo.[37] The nationality question thus remained unresolved at all levels when the NCWA came into being in 1931.

The League of Nations and the Politics of Peace

Interest in international arbitration as a means of preserving peace gradually revived in Australian council circles after the war, most slowly in Victoria. Lady Aberdeen's active and successful representations on behalf of women at the Versailles Peace Conference in 1919,[38] her subsequent enthusiastic support for the League of Nations, and her work in urging ICW affiliates to lobby for women delegates to represent their nations were all instrumental in overcoming persistent anti-German feeling among councils in the former allied nations, including Australia.[39] Aberdeen kept the councils informed about this work[40] and encouraged representatives to come to London to meet with her

---

37 Page Baldwin, 'Subject to Empire', pp. 522*ff*.
38 Aberdeen and the representatives of IWSA with whom she worked were rewarded by the provision in Article 7 of the Covenant of the League that 'All positions under or in connection with the League, including the Secretariat, shall be open equally to men and women'. Leila Rupp, *Worlds of Women: The Making of an International Women's Movement*, Princeton, Princeton University Press, 1997, pp. 211–12.
39 As late as March 1920, as preparations were underway for the first post-war ICW congress, the Victorian council told Emily Dobson that they would only support representation by allied and neutral nations. NCWV Council Minutes, 26 March 1920, NCWV Papers, SLV (classification pending).
40 In describing the achievements, she also commented that 'it was the first deputation of women ever received by any peace conference'. NCWV Council Minutes, 24 June 1919, NCWV Papers, SLV (classification pending). See also reports in NCWNSW Executive Minutes, 3 July 1919, Box MLK03009, MS3739, NCWNSW Papers, SLNSW; and NCWQ Minutes, 28 July 1919, Box 16045, 7266 NCWQ Minute Books, NCWQ Papers, SLQ.

in June 1919,[41] where, according to Victorian delegate Alice Michaelis, they made an 'exhaustive study of the Peace Conference' and began to plan for the ICW congress the following year. It was at this point that NCWV decided to revive its standing committees, including peace and arbitration.[42] And, after the Kristiania conference resolution that 'all States Members of the League ... send forward a woman as one of the three delegates to the First Assembly of the League in November 1920',[43] all the Australian councils began to lobby for a woman representative on the Australian delegation.

A further stimulus to council interest came from the League of Nations Unions (LNU), formed between 1920 and 1922 in all the Australian states. Significantly, both ICW and NCW peace and arbitration standing committees were now rebadged to include League of Nations in their titles.[44] The Australian LNUs, in recognition of the NCWs' wide reach among women, invited council presidents (or their nominees) to join, usually as vice-presidents. Rose Scott, though elderly and frail, was made a vice-president of the NSW LNU formed in Sydney in 1920, and NCWV president Jessie Henderson was appointed vice-president in Victoria in 1921.[45] Given the domination of LNU branches by conservative and previously pro-war politicians, leading clergymen and even military commanders, the NCWs were reassured as to their patriotic credentials, quite different from the grassroots anti-

---

41 NCWV Council Minutes, 22 May 1919, NCWV Papers, SLV (classification pending).

42 NCWV Council Minutes, 24 June 1919, NCWV Papers, SLV (classification pending). Other representatives at the London meeting included Mary Bage from Victoria and Mrs Vickery from NSW. Australia's ICW delegation president, Emily Dobson from Tasmania, may have been there too.

43 Kristiania 1920, 'ICW Resolutions', http://www.ncwcanada.com/ncwc2/wp-content/uploads/2014/02/ICW-CIF_Resolutions1.pdf, p. 87.

44 Noted in NCWV Council Minutes, 20 July 1920, NCWV Papers, SLV (classification pending), as an agenda item for the ICW quinquennial conference. See also Norris, *Champions*, p. 45.

45 League of Nations Union (Victoria) Minutes, 23 March and 12 April 1921, MS2198, League of Nations Union (Victoria) Papers, NLA.

war and peace groups of the war years.⁴⁶ Though key women peace activists in Melbourne remained alienated from NCWV, which they saw as harbouring a 'hard, vengeful, narrow spirit', they welcomed this change of sentiment: 'If the National Council joins in this work, so much the better for the cause'.⁴⁷ Suspicion was also evident in Western Australia where Bessie Rischbieth worked for the LNU but also formed her Australian Federation of Women's Societies (AFWS) to promote women's international awareness and peace activism more actively than the Australian national councils.

Queensland seems to have been the first council to take up the issue of a woman representative on the Australian delegation to the League of Nations, writing to the prime minister in March 1921.⁴⁸ A Council for the Representation of Women in the League of Nations emerged some months later, probably on the suggestion of Rischbieth and the newly formed AFWS.⁴⁹ The Australian NCWs were approached to affiliate and their response was discussed at the Hobart interstate conference in January 1922.⁵⁰ They agreed that each would prepare nominations for the prime minister to consider. Given that there was as yet no nation-wide organisation to co-ordinate council responses, they all lobbied the government individually, though each made efforts to garner support from the others for particular candidates.⁵¹ No woman was appointed

---

46 Hilary Summy, 'From Hope … To Hope: Story of the Australian League of Nations Union, Featuring the Victorian Branch, 1921–1945', PhD thesis, University of Queensland, 2007.
47 *Commonweal*, October 1919, p. 11.
48 NCWQ Council Minutes, 1 March 1921, Box 16045, 7266 NCWQ Minute Books, NCWQ Papers, SLQ.
49 NCWT Executive Minutes, 19 September 1921, NS325, NCWT Papers, Tasmanian Archive and Heritage Office (TAHO), LINC Tasmania; NCWNSW Executive Minutes, 1 September 1921, Box MLK03009, MS3739, NCWNSW Papers, SLNSW.
50 NCWNSW Executive Minutes, 20 October 1921, Box MLK03009, MS3739, NCWNSW Papers, SLNSW; NCWT Executive Minutes, 24 October 1921, NS325, NCWT Papers, TAHO, LINC Tasmania.
51 For example, Tasmania nominated Emily Dobson, who was supported by South Australia too. Victoria nominated Lady Novar (the retiring governor general's wife),

a full delegate, though the government did agree to a female alternate/substitute delegate. But the disunity among the councils meant that none of their nominees was chosen; that honour went to Marguerite Dale, the candidate of the AFWS.[52] Dale was quite acceptable to the NCWs since she was actually a prominent member of the NSW council and at various times chaired two of its standing committees. But she had not been nominated by them and this was taken as a rebuff to their assumed right to speak for Australian women internationally as well as nationally.

Despite the growing interest in international matters and the League of Nations in particular, the National Councils of Women were preoccupied with domestic concerns in these years, and this to some extent accounts for the failure to co-ordinate their efforts in the matter of international representation. Paradoxically, it was their very success in drawing in new member organisations and fostering the growth of others that caused them at first to disregard the manoeuvrings of Bessie Rischbieth's much smaller federation for recognition in the international arena.

In 1923, a group of twelve Australian women led by Mrs Rischbieth set sail for Europe to attend the International Woman Suffrage Alliance (IWSA) conference in May in Rome. Shortly thereafter, the national councils in Australia received a letter from Lady Aberdeen intimating that she would be attending the IWSA conference to propose that the two transnational organisations amalgamate.[53] This had been foreshadowed at the 1922 Hague ICW executive meeting[54] but seems not to have penetrated council awareness in Australia. In this light,

---

and NSW nominated educationist Louisa Macdonald, who had returned to Britain in 1919.

52 Lake, *Getting Equal*, p. 159.
53 NCWV Council Minutes, 26 April 1923, NCWV Papers, SLV (classification pending); NCWQ Executive Minutes, 30 April 1923, Box 16045, 7266 NCWQ Minute Books, NCWQ Papers, SLQ.
54 Hague 1922, 'ICW Resolutions', http://www.ncwcanada.com/ncwc2/wp-content/uploads/2014/02/ICW-CIF_Resolutions1.pdf, p. 5.

the claim, reported in the press, that Rischbieth's delegation would represent the women of Australia at the Rome conference, now assumed a more sinister character. As they feared, Rischbieth and her delegation 'strongly oppose[d] the federation' between ICW and IWSA; she was reported to have told the congress that 'the National Councils in Australia were old-fashioned and mainly interested in questions of philanthropy, health and education, and therefore not prepared to press for legislative reforms, and to claim equal rights for women in all relations of life'.[55]

Rischbieth's extremist statements brought the councils together. They now co-ordinated their lobbying for the substitute League of Nations delegate to succeed Dale, each council voting on the various nominees before they all agreed to put up Victoria's Jessie Webb. Webb won government appointment for 1923, indicating to Rischbieth that AFWS did not have a monopoly on political strategy and influence. The subsequent formation of the federal council, and later NCWA, helped strengthen the chance that the alternate delegate to the League Assembly would come from one of the councils, rather than from the more radical AFWS or WILPF. It also increased the likelihood that the chosen representative would report her experiences in all states on her return to Australia.[56]

In 1924, the councils began to show interest in a wider peace activism, largely in response to Lady Aberdeen's call for them to hold a Prevention of Causes of War conference at the same time as the gathering she was convening in Wembley, England, from 5 to 8 May. In Sydney, the churches were asked to declare Sunday 4 May Peace Sunday to precede a two-day conference on 5 and 6 May, and the papers

---

55 'Statement by the Executive of the W.A. National Council of Women', NCWWA Council Minutes, 26 November 1923, Vols 1–7, MS1389A, NCWWA Papers, State Library of Western Australia (SLWA).
56 For example, see resolution at 1929 FCNNCW conference, which also requested that the federal government fund her travel expenses in Australia. FCNCWA Conference Minutes, September 1929, Box 12, MS7583, NCWA Papers, NLA.

from the conference were printed in the NCWNSW's biennial report.⁵⁷ South Australia simply made it the discussion subject of its meeting on 8 May and passed two resolutions about the necessity for schools to place 'more stress on the triumphs of peace and less on glorification of war', as well as emphasising the work of the League of Nations.⁵⁸ In Victoria, Lady Forster emphasised the importance of councils taking simultaneous and parallel action,⁵⁹ and NCWV arranged a conference for 8 May at which well-known speakers addressed the large audience on the subjects set down for Wembley. These included: democratic control of foreign affairs; the interests and duties of motherhood in all countries in regard to the prevention of war; the rights of women to full citizenship; women's support for an all-inclusive League of Nations; universal reduction of armaments and ultimate disarmament; and the reference of all disputes to arbitration.⁶⁰

The broad-ranging peace issues discussed in the parallel 'prevention of war' conferences in 1924 came to occupy a larger part of discussion over time, initiated by the NSW peace convenor, Madeline Wood, wife of historian Professor G.A. Wood. In 1926, she was responsible for the federal council resolving to urge the inclusion of teaching about the League of Nations in all schools, to find new text books to replace 'old-style history', and to co-operate with the various branches of the LNU to publicise the work and objects of the league throughout Australia.⁶¹ The 1927 meeting also discussed at length the proposal of the NSW council for all Australian schools to adopt a textbook on the League of Nations and to add to their libraries 'any new publications about the League

---

57   NSWNCW Council Minutes, 3 April 1924, MLK03009, MS3739, NCWNSW Papers, SLNSW; NCWNSW *Biennial Reports for 1923–1924*, pp. 26–37.
58   NCWSA Council Minutes, 8 May 1924, Box 3, SRG297, NCWSA Papers, State Library of South Australia (SLSA).
59   *Argus*, 1 April 1924.
60   NCWV Council Minutes, 8 May 1924, NCWV Papers, SLV (classification pending).
61   FCNCWA Conference Minutes, July 1926, Box 12, MS7583, NCWA Papers, NLA.

... and other books of international interest'. The teaching of history and civics must be brought up to date rather than stopping in 1914, for 'no child should leave school without a knowledge of the League'. Wood went further. Young people needed '*peace* marches', she claimed; 'We must fight the idea of the inevitableness of war'. Representatives from all states except Queensland were keen to report they had already made considerable progress with local education departments, and the resolution was carried unanimously.[62]

Activities outside the councils continued to turn their attention to broader matters of peace. In Melbourne in February 1928, '[a] gathering of the friends and members of the League of Nations took place ... to inaugurate monthly meetings to further the interests of the League'. May Moss, 1927 alternate delegate to the League of Nations and soon to become NCWV president, was elected vice-president of the Victorian LNU soon after. In July 1928, another meeting was organised by the Society of Friends to 'arrange public demonstrations ... in favour of permanent peace and world disarmament on the tenth anniversary of Armistice Day, November 11, 1928'.[63] NCWV appointed a representative to participate in the peace demonstration and also a delegate to the World Disarmament Movement.[64] The NSW council was following a similar track, resolving in favour of the World Disarmament Conference and expressing appreciation of the Commonwealth government's readiness to accede to the Kellogg Renunciation of War Pact, while South Australia's peace committee had made the Kellogg Pact a special object of study.[65]

At the 1929 meeting of FCNCWA, May Moss proposed:

---

62 FCNCWA Conference Minutes, September 1927, Box 12, MS7583, NCWA Papers, NLA. Emphasis in the original.
63 *White Ribbon Signal*, 8 October 1928, p. 150.
64 NCWV, *Report for 1928*, p. 8.
65 NCWNSW, *Biennial Reports for 1926–1928*, p. 13; NCWSA, *Report for 1928*, p. 16.

May Moss
NCWA President 1931–1936

May Moss was the first president of the National Council of Women of Australia, elected in 1931. Coming from a privileged background Moss was nevertheless a strong campaigner for the rights of all women. Born in 1869 in Victoria, she was educated at the Presbyterian Ladies' College in Melbourne and the Sorbonne in Paris.

In 1906 Moss campaigned for female suffrage in Victoria, despite being vice-president of the conservative and anti-suffrage Australian Women's National League. Other issues she took up were technical education for girls, equal pay for female teachers, opportunities for girls to work in public transport, the problem of white slave trafficking.

During the Great War in 1914 she became the only female member of the Victorian recruiting committee for the armed services.

In 1927, the Australian government appointed Moss as the alternate delegate to the Assembly of the League of Nations in Geneva. She was the first female member of the League's finance committee. Her fluency in French and German rapidly led to other appointments within the League, as well as participation in the International Council of Women. She was elected a vice-president of ICW in 1928.

When the National Council of Women of Australia was formed in 1931, Moss was an ideal candidate as inaugural president. NCWA had been envisaged as an umbrella organisation, to speak to government with one voice on federal issues on behalf of all the women of Australia. Its structure of state councils and broad affiliate organisations gave women a path of action to advocate issues such as a uniform federal marriage law, full nationality rights for married women and the right of married women to work. Its link with the ICW gave it global influence.

In 1934 Moss was appointed to the Victorian Centenary Celebrations executive as its only female member, and promptly called together the presidents of all women's organisations in the state. After broad consultation, they decided to mark the state's centenary by holding an international conference of women and establishing the Pioneer Women's Memorial Garden in Melbourne's Domain gardens. A moving ceremony is held in this garden every year by way of tribute to these women. The Women's Centenary Council also produced a *Book of Remembrance* and a *Centenary Gift Book* featuring the part played by women in public life.

In 1934 Moss was appointed CBE and was awarded the NCWV gold badge (still worn by presidents today) for distinguished service. She died in 1948.

Explore further resources about May Moss in the Australian Women's Register.

> That disarmament is an ideal to be worked for, realising that armaments tend not to make for security and peace, but rather become a stimulus for war, and that with this end in view steps be taken to co-operate with any approved campaign with the object of achieving disarmament and world-wide peace.

Moss sketched for delegates the post-war history of strategies to reduce armaments through the League of Nations. 'The whole Assembly of 1927', she said, 'ricochetted [sic] towards the great goal—the Outlawry of War. In 1928, the Kellogg Pact was signed by 15 Powers', and now, 'In 1929, the greatest move since the War ended will be made' with the proposed conference on naval disarmament: 'If Naval disarmament takes place there, then [there] is land and air disarmament to be discussed. Women must do all they can to promote international peace'. ICW, after all, as Mildred Muscio noted in her federal council presidential address that year, had been called the 'Mother of the League of Nations'.[66] The ensuing discussion of Moss's motion nevertheless indicated some reservations among delegates. From NSW, Labor Party member May Matthews was firmly in support of the motion, but Mrs Bailey from the Queensland council was opposed to anything more radical than a 'publicity campaign'. The final resolution was eventually watered down by the addition after 'achieving disarmament' of the words 'to a point consistent with national safety'. But they did all agree on the necessity for a full-time minister for external affairs.[67]

Australian YWCA president Georgina Sweet's attendance at the final conference of the federal council early in 1931, and her eloquent plea for involvement in the Pan-Pacific women's conference movement (of which she was president), did much to keep questions of peace and internationalism before members and delegates. So too did federal and

---

66   FCNCWA Conference Minutes, September 1929, Box 12, MS7583, NCWA Papers, NLA. The appellation came from Austen Chamberlain.
67   The amendment was the work of Victoria's Lillias Skene and South Australia's Lottie Leal, with WA's Edith Cowan speaking in support. FCNCWA Conference Minutes, September 1929, Box 12, MS7583, NCWA Papers, NLA.

DEVELOPING INTERNATIONAL IDENTITY

NSW president Mildred Muscio's report of proceedings at the ICW conference she had attended in Vienna the previous year.[68] In response, the federal council resolved on 'a National Peace Day' to be observed in conjunction with an annual 'League of Nations Day'. Once again the emphasis was on 'more systematic instruction in the schools regarding international relations and the League', one delegate even arguing that 'Peace teaching should begin with the kindergarten'. Australian Federation of University Women delegate, Gladys Marks, noted an alarming 'spirit among youth ... which regarded war as romance'. 'The horrors of war should be stressed; peace must be organised for. It was no use stopping at pious resolutions, especially in this distant and insular country.' Interestingly, Victoria's Jessie Henderson stressed that peace teaching 'must be apart from Empire Day', an unusual departure from the general council presumption about the leading role of the British Empire in matters of international order.[69]

With the creation of the National Council of Women of Australia in 1931, direct international communication with ICW and responsibility for international policy was taken out of the hands of the state councils and concentrated in the new national body. But for nearly three decades, the local councils had been directly responsible for peace work, war-time mobilisation, and post-war engagement with issues such as international arbitration and disarmament, as well as those specific to women such as the nationality question. This experience had provided council leaders and many members with the knowledge and interest to make for a degree of sophistication in the discussion among national delegates.

---

68   FCNCWA Conference Minutes, January 1931, Box 12, NCWA Papers, MS7583, NLA.
69   FCNCWA Conference Minutes, January 1931, Box 12, NCWA Papers, MS7583, NLA.

Though some of the state councils thereafter lamented their loss of direct connection to ICW, they persisted with discussing international matters, as well as formulating resolutions on a range of broad social, economic and political issues for their national delegates to take to international conferences. Many in the councils had thus formed an awareness of the transnational character of the interests and experiences of women and children that could be employed to bring about change at local, national and international level. This was evident in the nature and topics of many debates and the direction much NCWA work took in the two decades considered in the next section of this history.

PART TWO
NCWA TAKES SHAPE

Consolidation and the Challenge of Depression and War
1931–1950

After the first national conference of the NCWA was held in Melbourne in November 1932, the *Argus* published a reflective piece by its women's affairs columnist, 'Vesta'. 'Vesta', or Stella Allan, was well equipped to comment, having been an early member of NCWV and the government-appointed alternate delegate to the fifth assembly of the League of Nations in 1924.[1]

The conference, she wrote, 'mark[ed] the beginning of a new era' and was 'a great stride in the right direction' for women's organisation in this country. Previously Australian women travelling abroad and meeting leaders of women's movements in other countries had 'felt themselves at a loss when invited to discuss women's work in the Commonwealth'. They had quickly realised that 'their outlook [was] limited by the conditions in their own States, and that very few of our women were competent to represent Australian women generally, or even to speak with authority about the work done or opinions held in all of the States'.

While there were some exceptions—notably Emily Dobson and Bessie Rischbieth—the observation was a just one. 'Vesta' acknowledged that the national councils had been making 'very strong efforts' 'to break down the walls' over the past six to eight years, and that considerable progress had been made, but there was much more to be done 'before the women of this country can hope to exercise their influence in national or

---

1   Patricia Keep, 'Allan, Stella May (1871–1962)', *Australian Dictionary of Biography*, http://adb.anu.edu.au/biography/allan-stella-may-4998/text8307.

international affairs at full strength'. The potential was enormous, she believed, because of the 'great body of women ... associated with the council[s]' for whom the new body might claim to act and speak. But any such claim, she warned, rested on an obligation for the leaders to be certain that they understood the attitudes and knew the opinions of their members. She doubted that that was the case on many issues. If the NCWA and the constituent councils were to become 'actual leaders of opinion', they must be able to stimulate 'enthusiasm for study' and 'really close co-operation and intimate discussion' among delegates and within affiliated organisations. Only then could they be sure that broad-based and well-informed opinion underpinned their representations.[2]

The two challenges 'Vesta' identified—overcoming a focus on state or region, and ensuring effective communication with and participation of the grassroots membership—were recognised and broached early by NCWA leaders. But these twin problems continued to test and temper the representative claims of the council movement throughout the twentieth century and beyond.

The formation of NCWA was a major achievement but the timing of its birth was hardly auspicious: in the depths of the Great Depression, a period of major political crisis and national division. It is testimony to the determination of its leaders that the new organisation survived and gradually grew in strength, as the upheavals of the depression were succeeded by the challenges and frustrations arising from Australia's involvement in the Second World War. The growth was uneven among NCWA constituent councils; both Tasmania and Western Australia struggled with financial and leadership difficulties and divisions. Communication between the states was problematic during the war, and much of the energy within the state councils was diverted to war-related work. Nevertheless, with its national imperative reinvigorated

---

2   'Vesta', 'Australian National Council: A New Era', in 'Women to Women', *Argus*, 30 November 1932, pp. 13–14.

in the post-war years, NCWA stood on the threshold of an era of unprecedented growth and influence at the end of the 1940s.

This section examines that historical trajectory in three chapters. The first will trace the organisational development of the new national body in terms of its evolving methods of governance and its claims to be the leading voice of Australia's organised women. The second will examine how far the national body was able to co-ordinate and express the constituent councils' views on what had always been regarded as the association's core concern—home and family. The third will focus on NCWA's commitment to the mainstream feminist equality agenda, and its achievements and limitations in the challenging national and international contexts in which it represented Australian women during the 1930s and 40s. It will also consider the overwhelming issues of peace and war that dominated this period, and examine NCWA's engagement in national debates and causes relating to Australian women's part in international relations.

Chapter 5

ORGANISATIONAL CHALLENGES AND ACHIEVEMENTS

The first officers of the National Council of Women of Australia were elected in October 1931. This occurred in Melbourne when ICW president Lady Aberdeen's acknowledgement of the new constitution was received; the constitution was then formally adopted, and Victoria's May Moss was elected president.[1] A member of the Victorian council since 1904 and its president from 1928 to 1938, Moss was also active in the conservative Australian Women's National League, but she was more dedicated to women's rights and equality than most of the league's leaders. Unusually for an Australian woman in this period, she was fluent in French and German. Moss represented the Australian government as alternate delegate to the League of Nations in 1927 and as the councils' representative at the ICW executive meeting in Geneva in the same year.[2] She was thus well equipped to take on the presidency of the new national body.

---

1   NCWA, *First Annual Report*, November 1932. NCWA formally came into being in July 1931 after ratification of the constitution by all states except WA. Muriel Muscio, last president of FCNCWA, acted as president of the new body until the election of the first board.
2   'May Moss', *Stirrers with Style! Presidents of the National Council of Women of Australia and Its Predecessors*, http://www.womenaustralia.info/exhib/ncwa/presidents-20.html.

ORGANISATIONAL CHALLENGES AND ACHIEVEMENTS

Bringing in the West

The formation of NCWA was not the celebratory occasion the founders might have hoped. The dampening effects of the Great Depression were compounded by persisting organisational problems. The main topic of discussion at the early executive meetings was a strategy to deal with Western Australia's decision not to join the national body.[3] Over the ensuing months, the WA council made unsuccessful overtures to NCWA to change its constitution to allow more state autonomy, and approached ICW requesting separate affiliation. The issue of affiliation had coincided and became entangled with the Western Australian secessionist movement and the 'present financial crisis', which was the pretext NCWWA used throughout 1931 for postponing further consideration to 'more normal times'.

In addition, there was grave internal dissent within the Western Australian council and executive over the powers of former president, now honorary vice-president, Edith Cowan. In March 1932 Cowan's refusal to relinquish her authority triggered the resignation of ten out of fourteen members of the council's governing body. Cowan had opposed affiliation to NCWA and angered the majority of the executive by sending an unauthorised letter to Lady Aberdeen asserting parallels between national unification and 'sovietism'. Among the ten who resigned was president Roberta Jull, as well as former presidents Gwenyfred James and Phoebe Holmes. Jull had represented Australia as alternate delegate to the League of Nations in 1929, and, with this experience at national and international levels, she was supportive of NCWA affiliation. Of all the office bearers only the home secretary, Ruby Pratt, a firm supporter of Cowan, did not resign. Council felt it had no choice but to accept the ten resignations 'with very great regret'. Cowan was elected president but was by then too ill to officiate and was succeeded by Pratt herself in April. Cowan died in early June 1932 but

---

3   NCWA Board Minutes, Melbourne, 13–14 October 1931, NCWA Papers, Box 12, MS7583, National Library of Australia (NLA).

the divisions were by now too deep to mend. Jull continued as a council member but did not thereafter hold office, except briefly as the convenor of the national health standing committee.[4]

Ironically, the WA council did reluctantly surrender its autonomy later that month, when, at the Australian council's urging, Lady Aberdeen finally decreed that the international council's acceptance of the new national body automatically cancelled individual state council membership of ICW, along with rights of direct communication. Left with no viable alternative, WA resolved in favour of affiliating with NCWA on 27 June, albeit by a very narrow margin, and a telegram to that effect was sent to the national board.[5] The decision did not, however, prevent WA continuing to propose constitutional changes directed towards greater autonomy.[6] The long-drawn-out negotiations with NCWWA meant that the inaugural NCWA conference did not take place until fifteen months after the national body was formed, but, when it did so in Melbourne in November 1932, it had a full complement of state delegates (though WA appointed a proxy). Moss could thus say with some conviction that 'they came together with optimism in their hearts'.[7]

---

4   NCWWA Council Minutes, 28, 29 May, 29 June, 27 July, 31 August, 28 September, 26 October and 30 November 1931; 19 February and 21 March 1932; MS1389A, NCWWA Papers, State Library of Western Australia (SLWA). Cowan died on 9 June 1932. Noreen Sher, *The Spirit Lives On: A History of the National Council of Women of Western Australia 1911–1999*, Perth, NCWWA, 1999, pp. 41–4.

5   The vote was 22 in favour and 19 against. NCWWA Council Minutes, 27 June 1932, MS1389A, NCWWA Papers, SLWA; NCWA Board Minutes, 19 July 1932, Box 12, MS7583 NCWA Papers, NLA.

6   NCWA Conference Minutes, 22–25 November 1932, Box 11, MS7583, NCWA Papers, NLA; NCWA Board Minutes, 12 June 1933, Box 12, MS7583, NCWA Papers, NLA.

7   NCWA Conference Minutes, Melbourne, 22–25 November 1932, Box 11, MS7583, NCWA Papers, NLA.

ORGANISATIONAL CHALLENGES AND ACHIEVEMENTS

The Tyranny of Distance

Three years later, at the end of her tenure, Moss affirmed the value of the new organisation as the means of ensuring regular contact between the nation's organised women: 'Contact is one of the most valuable contributions we can make to life'. But although 'connecting the long distances of the various states' in a national organisation was a major achievement and successive presidents worked hard at improving communications, active participation in NCWA by all the councils was difficult to sustain during this period. While Moss believed that the Australian council was now on a 'very sure foundation',[8] the constituent councils' influence and strength varied from state to state. Some residual resentment remained concerning their diminished autonomy and all states needed to be reminded that they must now channel communications with ICW through NCWA standing committees.[9] The effects of the depression were felt in all councils and travel funds were hard to come by. Financial deprivation was felt most keenly in the weakened Western Australian council, which lost a number of affiliations and was close to collapse in 1934–35 and again in 1937.[10] Tasmania also struggled; the death in 1934 of the Australian council movement's early leader, Emily Dobson, deprived the local branch of its principal guarantee against funding shortfalls.[11] South Australia also

---

8 May Moss, Presidential Address, NCWA Conference Minutes, August 1935, Box 11, MS7583, NCWA Papers, NLA.

9 For example, NCWA Board Minutes, 18 January 1934, Box 12, MS7583, NCWA Papers, NLA; NCWA Conference Minutes, 21 November 1934, Box 11, MS7583, NCWA Papers, NLA; NCWA Conference Minutes, August 1935, Box 11, MS7583, NCWA Papers, NLA; *Report of Biennial Conference Held in Melbourne, Victoria, October 15–18th, 1946*, p. 33, Box 31, MSAcc07/96, NCWA Papers, NLA.

10 Sher, *The Spirit Lives On*, p. 45; Letter read to NCWA conference delegates, NCWA Conference Minutes, 21 November 1934, Box 11, MS7583, NCWA Papers, NLA. Fees were remitted for one year as noted in the minutes of the 1935 conference. NCWA Conference Minutes, 27 August 1935, Box 11, MS7583, NCWA Papers, NLA. See also NCWA Board Minutes, 5 February 1937, Box 12, MS7583, NCWA Papers, NLA.

11 Comment from Tasmanian delegate that because of their size they felt the affiliation fee was too high: Mrs Dobson 'was very generous' but they did not now have her

felt the pinch though it maintained its membership.[12] The Victorian council was the largest, the wealthiest and perhaps the most innovative. By 1935, it had 108 affiliated societies, which had grown to 113 by 1944 but dropped back to 108 in 1949;[13] the next largest council, NSW, had 71 in 1934 and 73 in 1940.[14] South Australia had 53 in 1936, seems to have lost members during the war years, then experienced a resurgence to 82 in 1949.[15] The Queensland Council recorded 62 affiliates in 1932 but no figures are available for the later years in this period.[16] Tasmania continued to languish, with only 14 affiliates in 1943.[17]

NCWV had established a travel fund in the 1920s (as had NSW's council) and this underwrote large enough delegations to supply proxies for the poorer states at national conferences, notably at the Brisbane conference in 1935 when both the South Australia and Western Australian councils, citing the handicap of distance, were represented by Victorians.[18] NCWV also hosted three of the five national conferences during the 1930s (1932, 1934, 1938), as well as the reduced wartime conference in early 1941, when Victorians acted as proxies for Queensland, Tasmania and Western Australia. Melbourne was the venue too for an extended board meeting (including representatives or proxies for all

---

support to fall back on. NCWA Conference Minutes, 23 November 1934, Box 11, MS7583, NCWA Papers, NLA.

12 Barbara J. Pitt, 'The History of the National Council of Women in South Australia 1902–1980', typescript, Adelaide, NCWSA, 1986, p. 45.
13 NCWV, *Report for 1935*, p. 7; NCWV, *Summary of the Activities of the National Council of Women of Victoria during the years 1940, 1941, 1942, 1943, 1944, In lieu of the Annual Reports*, p. 14; NCWV, *Annual Report 1949*, p. 7.
14 NCWNSW, *Biennial Reports for 1933–1934*, pp. 47–8; *Biennial Reports for 1938–1940*, pp. 16–17. There are no NSW reports available for 1941–66.
15 Pitt, 'The History of the National Council of Women in South Australia 1902–1980', pp. 50, 59. Pitt asserts 62 affiliates in 1936, but the annual report lists only 53 for the period covered by the annual report of 1936–37. Pitt does not provide a source but it is possible that numbers fell off after the centenary celebrations of 1936. NCWSA, *Report for 1936–37*, pp. 5–7; *Report for 1948–49*, pp. 4–7.
16 NCWQ, *Report August, 1931–1932*, p. 15.
17 NCWA Board Minutes, 1 July 1943, Box 12, MS7583, NCWA Papers, NLA.
18 NCWA Conference Minutes, 27 August 1935, Box 11, MS7583, NCWA Papers, NLA.

councils) that saw the reins transferred from South Australia to the NSW Council in November 1942. Though the next full conference was held in Sydney in October 1944 after travel restrictions were eased, the first post-war conference in 1946 was again in Melbourne. NCWV provided proxies for Western Australia at most of these conferences as well as at the Brisbane one in 1948.

The growth of NCWV can partly be explained by its location. Although Melbourne was no longer the national capital of Australia after 1927, federal government departments and the head offices of many organisations and businesses continued to be located there until well into the 1960s. In addition, it was the hub of a network of large towns spread throughout the state of Victoria but within easy reach by train. As well as being central for lobbying purposes, Melbourne was geographically the most convenient national meeting spot in terms of the distance interstate delegates needed to travel.

NCWV was also strong because of the initiative of its leaders, who pioneered regional councils in the major country towns, The first was in Ballarat in June 1927, the next in Geelong was formed during the war in April 1944, and the third, in Bendigo, was established in July 1948. It was also the Victorian council that took the leading role in founding an Australian Capital Territory council in 1939, with new state president Ivy Brookes and vice president May Couchman providing advice and expertise.[19] Victoria-based presidents bookend this first period of NCWA's history—May Moss (1931–1936) and Ivy Brookes (1948–1952)—though the council was concerned to spread the leadership to all the states as far as possible, Adelaide Miethke representing South Australia (1936–1942), Ruby Board New South Wales (1942–1944), and Elsie Byth Queensland (1945–1948). The only Tasmanian president in NCWA's history was not elected till the 1960s (and then from

---

19 *From Vision to Reality: Histories of the Affiliates of the National Council of Women of Victoria*, Melbourne, NCWV, 1987, G1–3, 6, 15; Freda Stephenson, *Capital Women: A History of the Work of the National Council of Women (ACT) in Canberra 1939–1979*, Canberra, Highland Press for NCWACT, 1992, p. 5.

Adelaide Miethke
NCWA President 1936–1942

Elected the second president of the National Council of Women of Australia in 1936, Miethke was born in 1881 to a large family in Manoora SA. She was educated in country schools and the University Training College, gaining a BA in 1924. Unlike her predecessors in NCWA Miethke followed a full-time career as a teacher and later inspector in the state Department of Education. She was active in union affairs, working to improve conditions for women teachers and to open wider educational opportunities for girls.

In 1915, she was founding president of the Women Teachers' Progressive League and it was as their delegate that, in 1920, she came to the NCWSA. She also served as commissioner of the Girl Guides Association from 1925 to 1939. As president of the NCWSA (1934–1940) she was appointed president of the Women's Centenary Council of SA, raising in that role £5000 to finance the Alice Springs base of the Royal Flying Doctor Service. As president of the Flying Doctor Service Miethke inaugurated the world's first school of the air, linking distant stations by pedal-radio.

As national president of NCWA Miethke worked to overcome the 'tyranny of distance' between state councils. She established the 'Quarterly Bulletin', and tried to fund the travel of delegates from the far distant states. But the intervention of the second world war made national action almost impossible. Delegates managed to meet for a scheduled national conference in January 1941 and Miethke was elected for another term of office in the interests of stability. A planned conference in 1942 had to be abandoned and it was not until November 1942 that the management of the council could be handed over to a Sydney-based board. In all the councils the pre-war concerns of members were deferred as they turned their attention to local war work and issues related to the war effort.

In 1941, Miethke retired from her position as South Australian Inspector of Schools. She established the Adelaide Miethke House, a city hostel for country students, and edited both *Country Hour* and *Air Doctor* to be distributed to remote children. In 1942, as president of the Woodville District Child Welfare Association, she established four pre-schools, and the Adelaide Miethke Kindergarten still flourishes. She once admitted 'I fear work has become a disease with me!' She was appointed an Officer of the Order of the British Empire in 1937 and died at her home in 1962.

Explore further resources about Adelaide Miethke in the Australian Women's Register.

ORGANISATIONAL CHALLENGES AND ACHIEVEMENTS

Launceston), and distance remained a major obstacle to a Western Australian presidency until teleconferencing in the 1990s.

Adelaide Miethke, the first national president outside the two dominant states, took the problems of distance, communication and travel seriously. Elected in 1936, she held office until 1942. Miethke was the first, and one of the few, among NCWA presidents to also hold down a full-time paid job (as the first woman inspector in the South Australian education department). Problems of distance prompted her early interest in the Royal Flying Doctor Service and remained one of her principal concerns in her retirement, when she established the School of the Air for outback children.[20] On becoming NCWA president in 1936, she made improved communications between the state councils a priority. Initiatives included a fund to allow the president to visit each state once every six years and to assist delegates from the distant ones to attend national conferences: 'If we are to reflect an AUSTRALIAN opinion, then it must be possible for all States to be represented by attendance'.[21] The board suggested a contribution of £2 per annum from each state towards the president's travel and the gradual build-up of a delegates' fund, each state contributing according to its ability. A more permanent communication strategy put into effect under Miethke in 1937, and continued up to the present, was a quarterly newsletter distributed to all state councils by the NCWA board. Its object was to report on council activities at state, national and international levels. All states expressed satisfaction with this attempt to extend their work beyond 'watertight compartments'.[22]

Reaching beyond print, Miethke's board, urged by ICW, also discussed the value of radio as a national 'boundary-breaking medium'

---

20 'Adelaide Miethke', *Stirrers with Style! Presidents of the National Council of Women of Australia and Its Predecessors*, http://www.womenaustralia.info/exhib/ncwa/presidents-18.html.
21 *ANCW Bulletin*, no. 1, 4 March 1937, p. 2. Emphasis in original.
22 NCWA Board Minutes, 5 February 1937, Box 12, MS7583, NCWA Papers, NLA; *ANCW Bulletin*, no. 2, 1937, p. 8.

and the possibility of regular broadcasts by the president. The board reported a positive response from the ABC to a Western Australian proposal that the national president broadcast a speech to their annual meeting in Perth. As it turned out, notice was too short for the ABC on that occasion but General Manager Charles Moses told Miethke that, with two months notice, it could be arranged for future meetings. The Queensland council was already broadcasting weekly, while NCWNSW had experimented with radio from 1928 and was running a weekly session through 2GB from mid-1933, but all councils except WA expressed doubts about the practicality of nation-wide broadcasts, and it is unclear if national programs eventuated at this time. Certainly the councils involved in ABC state women's sessions expressed disappointment at their replacement by a new daily national women's program in 1946.[23] Their lobbying, along with that of country women, saw the concession of an extra ten minutes of local news on Fridays.[24] Radio aside, Miethke's broad communication initiatives during 1937–38 seem to have paid off for, at the 1938 NCWA conference in Melbourne, she could report with some satisfaction that delegates from both Western Australia and Tasmania were present—the first time all states were directly represented.[25]

The 1938 conference saw Miethke and the Adelaide-based board elected for another term. Delegates must have sensed the shrinking of international distance as well as that between the states when it was suggested in the same year that the next ICW triennial conference be held in Australia in 1942. Part of Miethke's brief was to begin the

---

23 On discussion of communication strategies, see *ANCW Bulletin*, no. 1, 4 March 1937, p. 3; no. 2, 1937, pp. 2–3, 5, 8; NCWA Board Minutes, 10 May 1937, 24 May 1937, 11 August 1937, Box 12, MS7583, NCWA Papers, NLA. Also: NCWNSW, *Biennial Reports for 1926–1928*, p. 8, and *Biennial Reports for 1933–1934*, pp. 5, 18; *NCWA Report of Biennial Conference Held in Melbourne, October 15th–18th, 1946*, pp. 13–14, Box 31, NCWA Papers, MSAcc07/96, NLA.

24 Minutes of Biennial Conference of the National Council of Women of Australia, Held in Brisbane September 1st–3rd 1948, typescript, NCWV Papers, SLV (classification pending).

25 *ANCW Bulletin*, no. 5, 1938, p. 3; *Argus*, 15 September 1938.

process of organising for this major international event, which was planned to be one of several international gatherings that included the Country Women's Associations of the World, the International Federation of Women Graduates and the International Federation of Nurses.[26] But anticipation of war was already evident at the 1938 ANCW conference; delegates considered plans for the voluntary enrolment of girls and women for national service in the case of emergency.[27] Within a year, all thought of international gatherings of women in Australia had been abandoned with the disintegration of ICW organisation and the dispersal of its leaders in occupied Europe.

The Disruptions of War

Within Australia, the lines of contact May Moss had envisioned and Miethke had worked to strengthen began to unravel. With interstate civilian travel subject to restrictions owing to the priority accorded to the armed forces, politicians and public service personnel, the executive meeting scheduled for September 1939 in Adelaide and the conference planned for Sydney in September 1940 had to be abandoned.[28] A meeting consisting of the board and just two delegates from each state was held in Melbourne in January 1941. In reality, only NSW, Victoria and South Australia were directly represented, the other three states having proxies appointed from Victoria. Discussion revealed that council activity in all states showed a 'marked falling-off' as both leaders and affiliates focused on locally based war service; standing committees had effectively gone into abeyance in the absence of calls for replies to ICW questionnaires. All councils reported on their war work, typically focused on the Red Cross, the Australian Comforts Fund, the Women's National Voluntary Register (which the NCWs initiated) and family welfare for soldiers'

---

26   *Argus*, 15 September 1938.
27   *Argus*, 15 September 1938.
28   See NCWNSW, *Biennial Reports for 1938–1940*, p. 12.

dependants.[29] The decline in record-keeping and reporting in all states in the war years indicates the extent to which council activities were redirected. The January 1941 meeting re-elected Miethke and her board in the interests of wartime stability and continuity but, by July, the difficulties of travel to and from Adelaide had frustrated their efforts to hold even an executive meeting and induced the South Australians to suggest transferring control to a Sydney-based board.[30]

It was another sixteen months before this occurred, despite Miethke's urging.[31] A conference planned for Easter 1942 in Sydney had to be abandoned in the wake of the onset of war with Japan and the arrival of large numbers of American troops. The new board, headed by Ruby Board, was not elected until an executive meeting could be held in November—once again in Melbourne—to hand over the reins.[32] Ruby Board, a long-term office bearer in NSW's council and state president from 1938 to 1948, seems to have delayed taking on the national presidency because of her workload co-ordinating NSW women's organisations for the war effort. But she recognised that the councils could find national purpose and common direction in considering the long-term goals of their work. At the 1941 Melbourne conference, she introduced and chaired a session, 'Planning for Post-war Reconstruction', at which it was agreed that the national councils would 'pursue a plan of study and discussion during the next year or two', conceived of at least in part as a means of providing a broad unifying focus on 'what we consider the fundamental needs of our social life after the war'.[33]

---

29 *Report of Biennial Conference Held in Melbourne, Victoria, January 21st to 23rd, 1941*, pp. 9, 14–16.
30 NCWA Board Minutes, 3 July 1941, Box 12, MS7583, NCWA Papers, NLA.
31 NCWA Board Minutes, 27 February, 6 and 13 March, 10 April 1942, Box 12, MS7583, NCWA Papers, NLA.
32 NCWA Board Minutes, 23 October 1941, Box 12, MS7583, NCWA Papers, NLA; *Sydney Morning Herald*, 12 November 1942, p. 3.
33 *Report of Biennial Conference Held in Melbourne, Victoria, January 21st to 23rd, 1941*, pp. 17–18.

Ruby Board
NCWA President 1942–1944

Ruby Board was the third president of National Council of Women of Australia, assuming office in the depths of World War II. She provided steady leadership on issues relating to the treatment and pay of women in the services, post-war reconstruction (especially housing) and the perennial matters of uniform marriage and divorce laws.

Born in 1880, Ruby Board was educated in Sydney, Berlin and Paris. She was an only child, born in Gunning NSW, and her social conscience was moulded in her small and closely linked family. Her father was the NSW director of education and her maternal grandmother was Euphemia Bowes, a founder and early president of the Woman's Christian Temperance Union and a perfect role model for community commitment.

Ruby Board was a member of the National Council of Women of NSW for 50 years, serving as general secretary, interstate secretary, president from 1938 to 1948, and state delegate to national conferences in 1946 and 1948. She led the Australian delegation to the sixth quinquennial convention of the International Council of Women in Washington in 1925. In 1931, she was interim treasurer of NCWA, becoming its president from 1942 to 1944 and then the national convenor for home economics from 1944 to 1952.

With no need to work for a living, Board devoted her life to social welfare and achieving justice for women. In addition to carrying out her NCW work, she played a leading war-time role in NSW as president of the Women's Voluntary National Register, as an executive of the Australian Comforts Fund, as defence director of the Women's Auxiliary National Service and as president of the Housekeepers' Emergency Service. She was a leader of the Country Women's Association in the 1930s and on the board of the Rachel Forster Hospital. She was a founding president of the Diabetic Association of Australia and chaired its first conference in Sydney. A diabetic herself from the 1930s, she demonstrated how little this condition need interfere with a busy and productive life.

Selfless and generous with boundless energy, she inspired those around her to similar enthusiasm for social welfare for women. She died in 1963 and her obituarist judged her 'balanced, judicious, tolerant and serene'. Her work for diabetics was honoured by the naming of the diabetic wing of the Rachel Forster Hospital after her.

Explore further resources about Ruby Board in the Australian Women's Register.

The importance of this work was reinforced in July 1941 by a letter from the Department of Labour and National Service requesting that the councils consider questions of post-war reconstruction. State councils were thus urged to hold special meetings.[34] It had been hoped this would be the central theme of the 1942 conference, at which Ruby Board was to become president, but the abandonment of the conference and the delay in transferring NCWA's administration to NSW slowed progress. On becoming president at the end of 1942, Board took up reconstruction again as a unifying strategy, urging all councils to hold their own conferences on aspects of the question with a view to formulating a co-ordinated approach at the next national conference—yet to be arranged. In the event, NCWA leadership on this issue was pre-empted by Jessie Street's National Women's Conference for Victory in War and Peace, held in Board's home town of Sydney in November 1943 and representing approximately ninety women's organisations, many of them NCW affiliates and in at least one case a state council. This highly publicised event produced a 'Charter' of principles for post-war reconstruction, including rights for women, which was circulated to all state and federal politicians and local governments. It was followed up over the ensuing months by state conferences in Perth, Melbourne and Adelaide.[35]

Though apprised of Street's plans by Victorian president Ivy Brookes in September 1943—two months before the Charter conference—Ruby Board procrastinated. Her belated approach to the prime minister in January 1944 for his co-operation in holding a conference organised by NCWA to consider the issues in the Charter was coldly received, and no help was offered.[36] Telegrams to the prime minister from NCWA and the constituent councils in March protesting that the Charter had not been considered or approved by the national councils and did not

---

34 NCWA Board Minutes, 3 July 1941, Box 12, MS7583, NCWA Papers, NLA.
35 Marilyn Lake, *Getting Equal: The History of Australian Feminism*, Sydney, Allen & Unwin, 1999, p. 190.
36 NCWA Board Minutes, 16 September 1943, 20 January 1944, Box 12, MS7583, NCWA Papers, NLA.

represent the views of the majority of women's organisations sounded like sour grapes.[37] Nevertheless, Board, believing the issues were unifying and potentially empowering, urged all the councils to hold their own conferences in May and planned a national conference for October 'to clarify and develop our combined aims for the post-war period'.[38] Although the resulting discussions and resolutions were wide-ranging and future oriented, they did not attract the publicity gained by the Charter movement. It was left to a new national president and board to find other ways of fostering unity and national communication among the councils, and to re-establish NCWA's representative claims.

Post-war Organisation

Elsie Byth, elected national president at the October 1944 conference, was the first Queenslander to take on the role and, like Miethke, she was concerned to overcome barriers of distance between the state councils. One of the first actions of her board was to institute the use of telephone communication with interstate presidents and other members of the NCWA executive, and to mandate the use of airmail letters, especially to Western Australia. Byth's board also requested ICW officers to use airmail in their communications with Australia, pointing out that surface mail could take up to three months to arrive.[39] As president of NCWQ from 1940 to 1945, Byth like Miethke and Board was prominent in the state war effort, playing leading roles in organisations like the Women's Voluntary National Register and the Australian Comforts Fund. As national president, she was concerned to re-establish council activities on a more normal footing after the

---

37 NCWA Board Minutes, 2 and 16 March 1944, Box 12, MS7583, NCWA Papers, NLA.
38 NCWA Board Minutes, 16 March and 7 July 1944, Box 12, MS7583, NCWA Papers, NLA.
39 NCWA Board Minutes, 2 December 1943, 7 February 1945, Box 12, MS7583, NCWA Papers, NLA; International Secretary's report, Minutes of Biennial Conference of the National Council of Women of Australia Held in Brisbane September 1st – 3rd 1948, typescript, NCWV Papers, SLV (classification pending).

Elsie Byth
NCWA President 1944–1948

Elsie Byth was the first Queenslander to hold the position of national president, and saw NCWA through the final stages of the Second World War. She was responsible for the re-establishment of international links with the International Council of Women and the Pan Pacific Women's Association. She maintained her commitment to international co-operation for the remainder of her life.

Born in 1988, Byth was educated at Brisbane Girls' Grammar School and Sydney University and married George L. Byth in 1917; they had three sons and one daughter. She was president of NCW Queensland twice, from 1940 to 1945 and later from 1948 to 1952, being national president in the years between. As part of her global focus, Byth was a member of the United Nations Association of Australia for 30 years, serving as president of the Queensland division from 1945 to 1959. In 1949, the Australian government chose her as its representative to attend the third session of the Status of Women Commission (CSW) in Lebanon. When voting took place on equal pay, she was placed in a difficult position between the official government line and her own and the NCWA's views. Following government instructions, she abstained from the vote. This government attitude to the question of equal pay continued to be a problem faced by Australian women delegates to CSW during the 50s and 60s. Within Australia, however, Byth and her successors continued to agitate for remuneration without discrimination based on sex.

Byth also became involved in many other community groups. For example, she was a member of UNICEF, the Brisbane Women's Club (as president from 1933 to 1936), vice-president of the Queensland division of the Australian Comforts Fund from 1940 to 1945, vice-president of the war-time state Women's Voluntary Register, the Management Committee of the Queensland Patriotic Club and the War Savings Committee. She also held a number of government appointments; these included membership of the federal committee on Imports Licensing Control, the Commonwealth Council of Medical Benefits Fund and the ABC.

She was appointed an Officer of the Order of the British Empire in 1953 and died in Brisbane in 1988.

Explore more resources about Elsie Byth in the Australia Women's Register.

ORGANISATIONAL CHALLENGES AND ACHIEVEMENTS

war and to revive the national organisation's influence, particularly by revitalising the work of standing committees. She urged members to pay heed to traditional as well as new areas of concern in such matters as health, housing, education, family welfare, immigration, equal pay, and uniform marriage and divorce laws. Byth stressed the need to 'teach women generally the difference between politics and party issues' so they understood that 'Politics, the body politic, provides the whole framework of our living; scarcely anything we do is divorced from politics'. They must be able to work with different governments in 'dealing with public matters of all kinds … No one can help being "mixed up in politics"'.[40]

In addition to working to strengthen interstate contact and national focus, Byth sought to cement national identity and unity among the constituent councils by elevating NCWA's international credentials and hence its claim to recognition as the majority voice of Australian women. As will be seen in a later chapter, it was Byth's board that cabled the United Nations conference at San Francisco to adopt the principle of equal status and opportunity for women, restored ICW contacts, revived the Australian Liaison Committee, took an initially hostile NCWA into the newly established Australian National Council for the United Nations (ANCUN), and, finally, in September 1948, organised a 'Pacific Assembly'—the NCWA's first serious engagement with the Asia-Pacific region.[41] Byth continued her international engagement after the end of her presidency, serving as the second Australian delegate to the UN Status of Women Commission in 1949, and participating in the new Pan Pacific and Southeast Asia Women's Association during the 1950s and 60s.

40　Presidential address, Minutes of Biennial Conference of the National Council of Women of Australia Held in Brisbane September 1st – 3rd 1948.

41　NCWA Board Minutes, February1945 – December 1948, Box 13, NCWA Papers, MS7583, NLA; 'Elsie Byth', *Stirrers with Style! Presidents of the National Council of Women of Australia and Its Predecessors*, http://www.womenaustralia.info/exhib/ncwa/presidents-06.html.

Ironically, it was Byth's presidency that also saw the beginnings of perhaps the most divisive issue in NCWA's history—what became known as 'the Tasmanian problem'. In a formal sense this stemmed from an innovation at the conference held in Melbourne in January 1941, when the term 'regional' was substituted for 'state' in describing the constituent councils in the NCWA constitution. This derived from ICW concern about the confusion the use of the term 'state' caused in correspondence with other national councils, and it also served to resolve the anomalous status of the new ACT council, which was not state based. However, the term 'regional' opened up the possibility that new councils formed within the various states could contest the representative status of the existing constituent councils. This amendment laid the foundation for problems that followed the re-emergence of a Launceston-based council in Tasmania. Reincarnated in 1942 from the ashes of an earlier northern branch, it expanded steadily and by late 1944 was requesting local autonomy from the existing constituent council based in Hobart.[42]

Hostility between Hobart and Launceston was evident in the earliest available minutes for NCWT. Council discussions in 1905 were preoccupied with squabbles about notice and location of meetings, accuracy of minutes, missing correspondence, the right of Launceston to conduct correspondence without NCWT approval, composition of delegations to mainland conferences, and the good faith of particular individuals, including the founder and president, Emily Dobson. Dobson's executive investigated whether any other national council was 'carried on in two divisions' but found that 'No record of such procedure appears in the literature of any of the National Councils in the Bureau though such literature has been carefully searched'.[43] Nearly all the

---

42 For example, *Mercury*, 22 September 1944, p. 7, and letters, 30 September 1944, p 3. See also letter from Launceston president Margaret McIntyre, *Mercury*, 2 October 1944, p. 13.
43 Special meeting of Council, 26 September 1905, NCWT Minute Book 1905–1910, NS325/1/8, NS325 Correspondence, Minutes and Associated Papers of the National Council of Women of Tasmania, Tasmanian Archive and Heritage Office, LINC Tasmania.

ORGANISATIONAL CHALLENGES AND ACHIEVEMENTS

themes of subsequent conflicts were rehearsed here, including attempts to find a constitutional solution consistent with ICW procedures. Conflict seems to have broken out periodically in the ensuing two decades but Launceston then went into recess and finally disbanded during the 1930s. Its re-emergence during the war years when councils were described as regional rather than state thus presaged a new period of conflict.

The issue of the Launceston council and its status was broached at national level at the first post-war NCWA conference held in Melbourne in October 1946, under Elsie Byth's presidency. Margaret McIntyre, president of Launceston, proposed:

> That when twelve or more organisations of women are affiliated to the National Council of Women as a branch, that that branch be permitted to form an independent and autonomous council of the National Council of Women irrespective of the State in which it is functioning.

In support of her proposal, McIntyre argued 'such an arrangement would give more independence and responsibility, and as well create more interest and keenness'. Delegates responded warily, and it was agreed that 'details of the proposed status should be formulated and circulated to the States for any further discussion and agreement'. Speakers stressed the need for collaboration where intra-state divisions existed and proposed various ways of achieving this. Byth herself suggested 'independence in their own matters' with a joint state council for 'co-operation in State affairs' but when a 'rotation of control' was proposed she retreated to a more conventional hierarchical model, arguing that a 'vigorous branch' applying to NCWA for autonomy 'should still work with the parent branch as head branch in the State'.[44] In clarifying the situation later, the NCWA secretary decreed that the concession

---

44 *NCWA Report of Biennial Conference Held in Melbourne, October 15th – 18th, 1946*, p. 22, Box 31, MSAcc07/96, NCWA Papers, NLA.

to Launceston council of semi-autonomous status was limited by the obligation to 'send to the parent body copies of all such letters sent to the Australian Board' and that it 'must co-operate with the parent Branch on all matters of State policy'.[45] It was the beginning of, rather than the solution to, a problem that persisted into the 1990s and arguably has still not been satisfactorily resolved.

---

45   Hilda Brotherton, Hon. Australian Secretary, to Mrs Vimpany, President, NCWT, 14 December 1946. Photocopy held in Mollie Campbell-Smith Papers (private collection).

Chapter 6

HOME AND SOCIETY

Depression, War and Post-War Reconstruction

President May Moss instructed delegates to the 1935 conference of the National Council of Women of Australia (NCWA) that they should 'not [be] deterred by depression'; rather, they were 'here to discuss problems relating particularly to women and children' and to do so with 'the best of motives—Social Service for others'. She also noted that: 'Some of our subjects are very wide and very embracing and some are decidedly controversial'.[1] The major issues occupying the council's attention during the 1930s and 40s were: unemployment and national insurance; child welfare; domicile and maintenance; population issues; post-war reconstruction as it affected families; and, in addition to the ongoing health and morality issues relating to alcohol consumption and venereal disease, an increasing concern with the cultural and moral impact of mass entertainment represented by the moving picture industry. All this was framed by the continuing belief that the welfare of home and family was the basis of the nation's strength.

Unemployment and National Insurance

The Australian economy was in decline from the mid-1920s, with unemployment rising consistently in the two years before the Wall

---

1   'Presidential Address', NCWA Conference Minutes, August 1935, Box 11, MS7583, NCWA Papers, National Library of Australia (NLA).

Street collapse in October 1929. The depression in Australia reached its nadir between 1931 and 1933, and it was not until 1938 that the nation significantly increased its productivity. At its highest point in 1931–32, unemployment was probably between 30 and 35 per cent, though it varied widely according to state, city, industry, class, occupation, region, age, skill, sex and religion. According to historian Geoffrey Spenceley, the worst affected states were the urban–industrial ones of New South Wales, South Australia and Victoria, and worklessness was twice as high in the city as in the country. Preference was given to married men so that the unemployment levels were higher among the young and the old, and it was the older workers who were most heavily represented among the long-term unemployed. Though men were probably more affected than women because of the industries in which they worked, preference to married men saw women lose jobs in many less gender-specific areas of employment. Unskilled workers were more likely to lose jobs than skilled, as is evident in the suburban distribution of unemployment. In Melbourne, the 1933 census showed an unemployment rate of over 32 per cent in suburbs like Fitzroy and Port Melbourne, compared with less than 20 per cent in suburbs like Hawthorn and Kew. In the Sydney suburb of Balmain, the male unemployed figure was 38 per cent compared with Woollarah at 18 per cent. Overall, as Spenceley writes, 'Australia was one of the countries most severely affected by the depression. Indeed, in terms of unemployment, only Germany appears to have fared worse'.[2]

Although the leaders of the National Councils of Women were probably not personally affected by unemployment, the effects of the slump were too serious and extensive for them to ignore or attribute to unwillingness to work and thriftlessness. At the last meeting of the Federal Council of the National Councils of Women of Australia

---

2 G.F.R. Spenceley, *A Bad Smash: Australia in the Depression of the 1930s*, Melbourne, McPhee Gribble, 1990, pp. 41–2; see also John Murphy, *A Decent Provision: Australian Welfare Policy, 1870–1949*, Farnham, Ashgate, 2011, pp. 158–61.

(FCNCWA) in January 1931, the president, Mildred Muscio, devoted her address to the 'disastrous change [that] has come over the economic life of our country'. She observed that the attitude of councils and their affiliated organisations 'will reflect the attitude of the individuals who are members of them, of ourselves as citizens of the State'. They should refrain from attributing blame to any party or group or other scapegoat, for the depression was world wide and, although some problems might have been 'accentuated by certain policies, the total situation is one beyond our control'. But they should at least try to understand the economic underpinnings, for 'Knowledge is the beginning of concerted action' and, in the case of the NCWs, their main purpose depended on it: 'Legislation for child welfare and public health and education costs money, and those who desire these things must understand why there is not an adequate national income'. Muscio acknowledged the call for 'immediate practical action', the 'direct call to help', while warning that what was needed was 'not the mere charity of those who have more', but 'the solidarity of sympathy and a common life which makes us a civilised and progressive unit of humanity'. She cited the example of her own council in NSW where members had instituted 'schemes for securing employment and relief' that had 'benefited thousands of women'. In eschewing the paternalism of traditional charity activities, she called on councils to work to ensure that 'national suffering does not fall only on the weak, that loss of income and resources is not borne by those who have least … but that all share in bad as well as in good times'. This might involve sacrifices and, since women were 'the practical economists of the nation' and were accustomed to 'making the money go round', their expertise should be exploited in public policy: 'Our national housekeeping has to be adjusted to meet the times and we ought to have more women in Parliaments to give their voice in these affairs'.[3]

---

3   'President's Address', FCNCWA Conference Minutes, January 1931, Box 12, MS7583, NCWA Papers, NLA.

The councils, with their strong philanthropic roots, struggled to find ways to deal with the suffering outside the framework of charity. At the first conference of NCWA at the end of 1932, unemployment was still a major preoccupation. Prime minister's wife Enid Lyons, in opening the conference, was comfortingly reassuring to the traditionalists. They were not a group of 'stern faced feminists gathered together' to assert their 'rights'; rather they were 'banded together with … a sense of our privileges and our duties'. Dealing with the depression was not 'just a matter of economic theories and monetary policies; it is also a matter of spirit', the spirit and philosophy of Christian love, of 'helping those who cannot help themselves'.[4]

All state councils reported on their activities to assist the unemployed, particularly young women and girls. In Queensland and most other states the emphasis was on relief, but in Victoria and NSW council members also canvassed work for sewing depots. NCWNSW helped run short training schemes in co-operation with the NSW Education Department, the aim being to provide girls with certificates of competence to fill jobs in domestic service. And South Australia's council reported that a 'home school' established in Adelaide by Dr Ethel Hillier, and funded by a patron scheme, was training unemployed girls. The council itself was conducting classes for girls on how to cook their rations, and NCWV, too, was helping teach hundreds of girls how to cook at cooking centres run by its affiliate, the Victorian Ladies Benevolent Society.[5] But this type of work and training was modelled on what middle-class women benefactors believed unemployed girls and women should be doing, rather than providing them with opportunities.

This point was made to the 1932 conference by Rowena Chisholm, the principal of Melbourne's Emily McPherson College of Domestic Economy, who reported that the girls occupying free places at her

---

4   *Argus*, 23 November 1932, p. 14.
5   FCNCWA Conference Minutes, January 1931, Box 12, MS7583, NCWA Papers, NLA; NCWA Conference Minutes, November 1932, Box 11, MS7583, NCWA Papers, NLA.

college were not choosing household courses. Chisholm, like Muscio the year before, argued against focusing on relief and stressed the need to look more deeply at causes of unemployment, including the extent to which they should tolerate 'the present social order'. Delegates agreed to include such a discussion in the program of the next conference. Further, on the urging of NSW's May Matthews, the first NCWA conference also passed a resolution in support of 'a contributory system of national insurance to cover health and unemployment administered under and subsidised by the Federal Government'.[6]

Matthews was unusual among Labor Party women in joining the NCW. She convened the NCWNSW trades and professions standing committee for many years, and served on the executive of the NSW Progressive Housewives Association in the 1930s. Though staunchly opposed to conscription during the Great War and a supporter of the railways strikers in 1917, she was not afraid to criticise unions for their ambivalence towards schemes such as national insurance, which she saw as a rational and scientific instrument for replacing demeaning relief and charity with entitlement:[7]

> It was high time that people generally recognised that unemployment under present conditions was inevitable. Continued and improved use of machines, overproduction and under-consumption, tariffs, changes of currency, changes of fashion, all contributed their quota to unemployment. It was something that could not be solved. It could be only dealt with in a proper scientific way, as a phenomenon of modern industrial conditions.[8]

---

6   NCWA Conference Minutes, November 1932, Box 11, MS7583, NCWA Papers, NLA.
7   Lyn Brignell and Heather Radi, 'Matthews, Susan May (1877–1935)', *Australian Dictionary of Biography (ADB)*, http://adb.anu.edu.au/biography/matthews-susan-may-7525/text13127; NCWA Conference Minutes, November 1932, Box 11, MS7583, NCWA Papers, NLA; *Argus*, 24 November 1932, p. 3.
8   *Argus*, 24 November 1932, p. 3.

As historian John Murphy writes, conservative federal governments in the interwar years made two attempts, in 1928–29 and 1938–39, 'to shift the funding of welfare onto a contributory insurance model in which workers, employers and the state compulsorily saved for future needs'. The 1928 legislation would have created a scheme of sickness, invalidity, widows' and orphans' pensions, and old-age payments, but not unemployment benefits, even though there was a degree of cross-party consensus on this. A working model—albeit a limited one—had existed in Queensland from 1919, and the Victorian Labor government had tried and failed three times to introduce a similar scheme between 1927 and 1930.[9] The 1928 federal NCW conference supported the insurance principle but resolved unanimously to 'stress the necessity to the Federal Government of making provision in the proposed National Insurance Scheme for unemployment—also to provide that pensions be paid to necessitous widows with dependent children'.[10]

In the event, the bill was postponed in late August 1929 in the face of the shrinking economy and concerted opposition from employer organisations and friendly societies.[11] Nevertheless, as Matthews' resolution demonstrates, NCWA support for contributory national insurance—including for unemployment—remained constant. Given the largely middle-class composition of the national councils' leadership and the increasing influence in council circles of modern, rational, progressivist thinking, the contributory model's emphasis on self-help and self-respect, rather than dependence on the state alone or charity, was ideologically attractive. As Murphy astutely comments, national insurance married progressive policy with the moral virtue of thrift.[12] It would have taken social welfare provision on a different path from that already established in Australia by 'a tradition of state intervention

---

9   Murphy, *A Decent Provision*, pp. 129–30, 135–6, 151.
10 FCNCW Conference Minutes, July 1928, Box 12, MS7583, NCWA Papers, NLA.
11 Murphy, *A Decent Provision*, p. 154.
12 Murphy, *A Decent Provision*, pp. 130–1.

in the economy … particularly as a consequence of a legal system for setting the basic wage through arbitration'.[13]

When the government considered contributory insurance again in 1937, NCWA reiterated its support for the proposal while protesting to the treasurer 'against any sex differentiation in payment of pensions for men and women', arguing that this would be a retrograde step given that 'no Australian pension scheme had introduced such a principle'.[14] In 1938, when legislation was being debated in federal parliament, the Australian councils meeting in Melbourne urged that the bill's coverage be extended beyond health to include unemployment. Mildred Muscio, in moving 'That the Commonwealth Government be asked to introduce as soon as practicable a comprehensive unemployment insurance scheme for Australia', acknowledged that this was the government's long-term intention after health insurance was on a secure basis. But, confident of NCWA's representative status, she argued that a resolution from the national conference would demonstrate support from most women's organisations and thus strengthen the government's hand.[15] Miethke reported that her board had been successful in its approach to the treasurer to allow women to contribute on an equal basis with men so that they might draw a pension of £1 rather than 15s.[16] However, the councils remained concerned that there was no provision in the bill for wives and mothers of families unless they were on the payroll of an independent employer.

The United Australia Party government, facing the resistance of the medical profession as well as internal division and opposition from the Country Party, watered down the scheme's scope in March 1939 but remained split over its cost and implementation. Labor now opposed

---

13 Murphy, *A Decent Provision*, p. 3.
14 NCWA Board Minutes, 17 November 1937, Box 12, MS7583, NCWA Papers, NLA; *NCWA Bulletin*, no. 4, 1937, p. 1.
15 *Argus*, 16 September 1938, p. 4.
16 NCWA Board Minutes, 17 May and 28 June 1938, Box 12, MS7583, NCWA Papers, NLA; *Argus*, 15 September 1938, p. 7.

any scheme involving employee contributions because its new leader, John Curtin, was committed to a tax-based welfare model. Robert Menzies, who became prime minister after Joseph Lyons' death in April 1939, had resigned from cabinet when the contributory scheme was emasculated but he now postponed implementation indefinitely on the pretext that defence expenditure must take priority. Although cabinet agreed to the health minister devising a new and more comprehensive health plan that would include women and children, the proposal was overtaken by the demands of war and did not see the light of day. The NSW council was especially irate when postponement was mooted but the NCWA board decided at this point not to intervene, significantly noting 'the controversial views held by NCW members themselves'.[17]

From 1941, the new federal Labor government, with Ben Chifley as treasurer and minister for postwar reconstruction, began to devise a welfare state premised on Keynesian economic principles, and a conviction that it was a primary responsibility of the state to provide for its less fortunate citizens as their right. This would be funded by progressive taxation rather than by what John Curtin saw as a regressive contributory insurance system. Interestingly, the expanded tax system introduced from 1941 included working-class taxpayers, and was justified as a social service contribution giving entitlement to means-tested benefits, including unemployment relief.[18] NCWA seems to have made no objection to this approach, although in June 1950 the Brookes board proposed to write to the new Liberal minister for social services to express council's opinion that 'instead of a means test, a contributory scheme should be established with regard to all pensions'.[19]

In the meantime, NCWA and its constituent councils continued to discuss the depression's impact on unemployment, focusing principally on young people and on married women workers unfairly dismissed

---

17 NCWA Board Minutes, 3 March 1939, Box 12, MS7583, NCWA Papers, NLA.
18 Murphy, *A Decent Provision*, pp. 5, 203, and chap. 9.
19 NCWA Board Minutes, 26 June 1950, Box 13, MS7583, NCWA Papers, NLA.

to give preference to unemployed male breadwinners. Partly they were influenced by ICW resolutions on these subjects and partly by domestic concerns. The injustice experienced by married women in the workforce was incorporated into the councils' equality agenda during the 1930s despite an ongoing ambivalence, evident in May Moss's 1935 presidential address, about the desirability of encouraging mothers with dependent children to work outside the home.[20] The councils' concern for unemployed young people was particularly focused on girls. In 1935, the Victorian council urged the state government to extend its assistance programs for unemployed boys to include girls, arguing that helping them to find work was 'equally important'.[21] A Victorian motion at the 1935 NCWA conference to persuade all governments to place youth unemployment at the 'forefront' of their legislative agendas was described by the president as the 'most important resolution on our agenda'. Victorian Lillias Skene argued that the situation for girls was especially concerning given that the government had put very little money into assisting them. The point of the motion was to 'enable us to go to the Government on behalf of the girls'.[22] Two years later, in 1937, the Western Australians requested that the federal body send a protest to the government about the omission of girls from its youth unemployment scheme.[23]

As economic conditions improved and the outbreak of war created unprecedented demand for women workers, the problem of unemployment receded without the discriminatory treatment of girls during the depression years being tackled. National council concerns about young women of working age during the war and post-war years were

---

20   NCWA Conference Minutes, August 1935, Box 11, MS7583. NCWA Papers, NLA.
21   Helen Gillan, *A Brief History of the National Council of Women of Victoria 1902–1945*, Melbourne, Spectator Publishing, 1945, p. 46.
22   NCWA Conference Minutes, August 1935, Box 11, MS7583, NCWA Papers, NLA.
23   NCWA Board Minutes,11 August 1937, Box 12, MS7583, NCWA Papers, NLA.

directed more to pay and conditions, and to questions of sexuality and public morality.

Child Welfare

The Great Depression magnified the inadequacies of the child welfare and maternal support system, with the growing gap between cost-of-living increases and boarding-out allowances making it unattractive for families to take in a child and difficult for widowed and deserted women to retain care of their own children. From 1928 boarding out began to decline and more children were taken into institutional care.[24] This was a matter for the individual state councils rather than NCWA, but it was closely related to the issues of the 'baby bonus', child endowment, and maintenance for widows and deserted wives with children, all of which continued to be debated at national level. Despite financial stringencies, a major interest in the health and education of pre-school children also emerged in the depression period and was extended into the post-war years to include disabled children, then commonly referred to as 'handicapped'.

The 'baby bonus', the one-off payment received by a woman on the birth of a child, was strongly supported by women's organisations across the spectrum, as was evident in the 1923 national conference organised by NCW Victoria, which rejected the views of medical women that it should be replaced by funding ante- and post-natal services. While such services were desirable, they should be funded in addition to, not instead of, the baby bonus. When the baby bonus was reduced by the federal government from £5 to £4 and subjected to means testing as a cost-cutting measure, the NCWA conference of 1934 readily co-operated with Labor women and the Australian Federation of Women Voters in lobbying the government to have its value restored. The conference also proposed that the federal government should 'subsidise all State

---

24 Nell Musgrove, *The Scars Remain: A Long History of Forgotten Australians and Children's Institutions*, Melbourne, Australian Scholarly Publishing, 2013, chap. 2.

Governments in order that ... the States which have been unable to establish Departments of Maternal Hygiene may be enabled to do so'.[25] A further case was made in 1935 for restoration of the bonus to £5, with delegates who worked for women's hospitals making a special appeal. Ivy Brookes, for example, was president of the Women's Hospital in Melbourne, and argued that the women there 'do have a difficult struggle, and after all maternity is such a big factor in the progress of our nation'. Mrs Fossett of the Queen Victoria Hospital, also in Melbourne, pointed out that the nursing, medical attention, food and clothing the women received took £3 out of their bonus. The resolution passed in 1935 affirmed the council's support for restoration of the full amount and abolition of 'the present income limit'.[26] This did not occur until 1943. The bonus was finally abolished in 1978, superseded as Treasurer John Howard argued, 'by health care and family allowances'. Important though it was in the interwar and war years for enabling women to afford medical assistance during and immediately after childbirth, the baby bonus never provided the ongoing support for the welfare of children that child endowment promised.

In 1928, as we have seen, the majority report of the royal commission set up to consider a national scheme of child endowment or family allowances recommended against any separate ongoing state payment to mothers, whether in recognition of their contribution to the state as maternal citizens, as many women argued, or simply as child support.[27] In the context of depression and government retrenchment, including cuts to existing allowances, endowment was not vigorously pursued by NCWA in the first half of the 1930s. With signs of economic recovery finally occurring, Adelaide Miethke resumed lobbying on the

---

25   NCWA Board Minutes, 20 March 1934, Box 12, MS 7583, NCWA Papers, NLA; NCWA Conference Minutes, November 1934, Box 11, MS7583, NCWA Papers, NLA; *Australian Women's Weekly*, 17 August 1935, p. 2.

26   NCWA Conference Minutes, August 1935, Box 11, MS7583, NCWA Papers, NLA.

27   Marilyn Lake, *Getting Equal: The History of Australian Feminism*, Sydney, Allen & Unwin, 1999, pp. 103–109.

issue, though noticeably not in terms of women's unique citizenship. Rather, she devoted most of her 1938 presidential address to 'endowed families', arguing that larger families could be made more attractive by 'a flat basic wage, plus endowment in an increasing scale for each successive child'. A basic wage grounded in an assumption of a 'four-family unit' only encouraged a man 'to feel that he is better off single', she suggested, whereas 'a child endowment system ... would relieve the family of financial troubles when a child was born' and assist much-needed population growth.[28] It was not a position Labor Party women could endorse, as we have seen, but financing provision for children by readjustment of the family wage had considerable support in the mainstream and more radical feminist movements, even if it was not explicitly couched in terms of economic independence for wives.

The impasse about funding, as John Murphy notes, was finally broken when the first Menzies government introduced a government-funded universal system of child endowment in January 1941. It was apparently done on the suggestion of one of the wartime economic advisors, D.G. Copland, who represented it as a counter-inflation measure that could be used to dissuade the arbitration court from awarding wage increases in the context of the war-time shortage of labour.[29] Murphy's comment is apt: 'There is some irony that child endowment, so long stalled because of its relationship to the wage-fixing system, had now been introduced as a solution to wage pressures'.[30] NCWA made a point of expressing its approval that the allowance was being paid to women and resolved to write to the prime minister endorsing the proposed scheme.[31]

Only when sources of family support were further expanded with the war and post-war introduction of Commonwealth widows' pensions,

---

28 *Argus*, 16 September 1938.
29 Rob Watts, *The Foundations of the National Welfare State*, Sydney, Allen & Unwin, 1987, p. 54; Murphy, *A Decent Provision*, pp. 203–04.
30 Murphy, *A Decent Provision*, p. 204.
31 *Age*, 23 January 1942; NCWA Board Minutes, 28 March 1941, Box 12, MS 7583, NCWA Papers, NLA.

and sickness and unemployment benefits did poverty cease to be the major real cause of children being taken into 'care', whatever other reasons might have been given by traditional child rescuers and the new profession of social workers. During most of this period, values about parenting and appropriate care and carers continued to be underpinned by codes of morality that had changed but little since the nineteenth century, though the language was modernised as the profession of social work and the discourse of psychology became more influential.[32] The NCWs attitudes and responses during this period reflected both traditional moral values and the growing impact of professional and scientific expertise, as well as a woman-centred approach to public policy in a period of economic stress that triggered concern about the wellbeing of the nation's children. This can be seen in a new focus on pre-school children's health and education, as well as on 'mental deficiency' and the education of 'handicapped' children.

At the first NCWA conference in 1932, the NSW delegation moved 'That Baby Health Centres in all States should expand their work to include supervision of the child of pre-school age'. The detailed discussion that followed demonstrated the value of a national organisation and national exchange of views. It revealed the different directions taken by the various states, as well as the common objectives emerging in the mainstream women's movement with regard to policy and practice, including both a self-consciously modern stress on physical surveillance and a broader concern with educational development. It also revealed the problems of achieving uniformity. The NSW representatives reported a gap in state 'supervision' of the physical health, psychological development and 'moral and emotional values' of the child between the ages of two and seven. Although some machinery existed within day nursery schools, free kindergartens and through training provided by the social studies board the NCW itself had helped establish, it was not systematic or available to all. The Victorians and South Australians

---

32   Musgrove, *The Scars Remain*, chap. 2.

reported a complex mix of clinics, day nurseries and kindergartens, some state administered and others voluntary, as well as variability in the specific training of nurses and carers, with the infant welfare field catered for best. Both the Victorians and the South Australians were at pains to stress the educational as well as physical needs of the pre-school child to avoid the danger of 'bringing up a race of animals ... without there being anything beyond [their] physical welfare'. The result was a less prescriptive, more inclusive but also non-specific resolution: 'That steps be taken by the National Council of Women in each State to secure arrangements for the supervision of the health, and also for the education of the pre-school child'.[33]

An underlying purpose not explicitly discussed was the opening up or extension of fields of professional opportunity for women. For example, while kindergarten training colleges already existed in all states by the 1920s, lobbying at a national level saw the federal government fund a new national organisation for pre-school children and their education in 1938 that continues today as Early Childhood Australia. This new body fostered the establishment of Lady Gowrie Child Centres in all states from 1939, the only childhood centres to receive federal funding for decades, and recognised from the beginning as 'a benchmark for the best standards of childcare and pre-school education' and training.[34]

While supporting the agitation for government-funded war-time crèche, childcare and children's services to assist married women now entering the labour market in much greater numbers, the national councils were anxious to keep the necessity for this to a minimum, arguing that women with children under sixteen should be protected against pressures to take paid work in the auxiliary services or industry.[35]

---

33 NCWA Conference Minutes, November 1932, Box 11, MS7583, NCWA Papers, NLA.
34 Deborah Townsend, 'Kindergarten Teaching and Pre-school Education', in Judith Smart and Shurlee Swain (eds), *The Encyclopedia of Women and Leadership in Twentieth-century Australia*, http://www.womenaustralia.info/leaders/biogs/WLE0335b.htm. The centres were named for the wife of the governor general.
35 *Age*, 17 November 1942.

Although the government conceded the request that such women be exempt from manpower regulations, married women with pre-school and school-age children were still encouraged to take work where possible. And, indeed, many were obliged to do so when their husbands enlisted, since the military allotment they received was below the basic wage.[36] NCWA was thus anxious to participate in the investigation into child welfare conducted by Constance Duncan for the National Health and Medical Research Council during 1942 and 1943, providing content for her 1944 report recommending a national program of maternal and child welfare, more support services for mothers, better pay for domestic workers, crèches and subsidised kindergarten training colleges, as well as uniform divorce laws to enable maintenance orders to be enforced.[37] While it would be too harsh to say the report fell on deaf ears, government support remained grossly inadequate; it was mostly directed to extending the operations of existing voluntary services and did not lead to any marked increase in public childcare facilities.[38]

With the end of the war, the revival of ICW and the reestablishment of state and national standing committees, NCWA, in preparing a response to an international council questionnaire, devoted a session at the 1946 conference to child welfare. The Australian convenor, Queensland's Edna Hill,[39] deplored the way 'the children dragged up in 1939–1946 have suffered'. She argued the need 'not only to work for additional [government-funded] facilities, but also to publicise, co-ordinate and extend the work of all existing voluntary organisations', which served to 'act as a spur to Government departments' and were, she argued, more

---

36 Kate Darian-Smith, *On the Home Front: Melbourne in Wartime 1939–1945*, Melbourne, Oxford University Press, 1990, pp. 122–3.
37 NCWA Board Minutes, 6 August 1942, Box 12, MS7583, NCWA Papers, NLA; Diane Langmore, 'Duncan, Ada Constance (1896–1970)', *ADB*, http://adb.anu.edu.au/biography/duncan-ada-constance-10061/text17747.
38 Darian-Smith, *On the Home Front*, pp. 125–9.
39 Hill was a kindergarten teacher and life-long advocate for early childhood education. She was involved with the Crèche and Kindergarten Association of Queensland and the Queensland Spastic Children's Welfare League.

humane in their operation than 'officialdom'. Reiterating the mantra that 'the welfare of society is dependent on its attitude towards, and treatment of, its children', she emphasised the need to fight malnutrition and disease and was also adamant about the importance of education and play: 'To-day society is reaching the logical conclusion that the kindergarten and nursery school, with trained supervisors, are neither a charity organisation nor a rich man's privilege, but the foundation stone of community life'. Provision for such services should be a 'first charge' on post-war reconstruction.

Hill was supported by leading Victorian pre-school educationist and founder of the Australian Association for Pre-school Child Development (1936) Ada à Beckett, who seconded the resolutions passed urging the Commonwealth government to formulate a national program for the welfare of children, to establish a council to implement it, and, along with state and municipal governments, to

> give special consideration to the increase of pre-school child care facilities throughout Australia as part of a considered policy to conserve and increase the physical, mental and moral wellbeing of children and to disseminate sound principles of child management, happy parenthood and congenial home life.[40]

The 1948 conference, in discussing the matter once again, stressed the lack of sufficient trained personnel to keep up with the expanded enrolments in pre-school education, a concern that persisted into Ivy Brookes's presidency when her board recommended that each state council take separate action with its Department of Education.[41]

---

40 NCWA, *Report of Biennial Conference Held in Melbourne, Victoria, October 15th–18th, 1946*, pp. 27–8; Julie Marginson, 'à Beckett, Ada Mary (1872–1948)', *ADB*, http://adb.anu.edu.au/biography/a-beckett-ada-mary-4963/text8235.

41 NCWA, Minutes of Biennial Conference of the National Council of Women of Australia, Held in Brisbane September 1st–3rd 1948, typescript, NCWV Papers, SLV (pending classification); NCWA Board Minutes, 10 July 1950, Box 13, MS7583, NCWA Papers, NLA.

A concern with science, expertise and national efficiency was also evident in an emerging discussion about the care and education of 'handicapped' or 'defective' children. In Victoria, such education is dated from 1918 when Methodist missionary and NCWV delegate Sister Faith founded 'Yooralla', a free kindergarten in inner Melbourne for children with a disability. The depression awakened more widespread concern and saw the foundation between 1929 and 1939 of societies for 'crippled children' in all states—NSW (1929), Queensland (1932), Tasmania (1935), Victoria (1935), Western Australia (1938) and South Australia (1939). The first honorary secretary of the Victorian Society for Crippled Children, Ada Norris (NCWA president 1967–70), was also appointed the organisation's delegate to the National Council of Women of Victoria in 1935 and remained engaged with disability services throughout her long public life.[42]

Although physical, psychological and social categories of disability were not specifically included in the eugenics discussions about mental deficiency in the 1930s, some of the language and concepts subsequently used to talk about 'handicapped' children were similar, with a greater emphasis on environmental factors becoming evident over time. ICW resolutions reported to the 1936 NCWA conference in Adelaide urged 'education and training' for 'crippled children',[43] issues already being broached by the new state societies dedicated to their welfare. But these were not discussed in detail by NCWA until after World War II. While the 'handicapped' might be 'incapable of achieving normality', convenor Edna Hill told the 1946 NCWA conference, such men and women had been 'useful in war', and it was 'inconceivable' that they could not be 'retained in peace-time industry'. Thus, by implication, future generations of disabled children should be educated to take their place. Conceding that some efforts were already being made, she pointed to

---

42 'Ada Norris', *Stirrers with Style! Presidents of the National Council of Women of Australia and Its Predecessors*, http://www.womenaustralia.info/exhib/ncwa/presidents-22.html.
43 *Advertiser*, 17 September 1936.

Ada Norris
NCWA President 1967–1970

Ada Norris was national president of the National Council of Women from 1967 to 1970, but, for decades before and after that, she was a force for change in the national councils and the wider Australian community.

Born in 1901 in Western Australia, she was educated at Melbourne High School and Melbourne University. She taught until 1929 when she married John Norris, later a judge of the Supreme Court in Victoria.

Concerned for children in need, she joined the Children's Hospital Auxiliary, then became secretary to the newly established Victorian Society for Crippled Children, and was appointed the VSCC's delegate to the National Council of Women of Victoria. In 1944, she became both vice-president of NCWV and foundation secretary of the Advisory Council for the Physically Handicapped.

From the 1950s, Norris developed expertise and leadership in three key policy areas: ageing, immigration, and status of women issues. As NCWV president (1951–54), she initiated the Victorian Council for the Ageing, working to provide government-funded home help, hot meals and recreation centres. Positions as convenor of migration for NCW Victoria and then for NCWA led to her appointment in 1966 as convener of migration with the International Council of Women. She was a leading member of the Good Neighbour Council of Victoria, and of the Commonwealth Immigration Advisory Council, serving on this for more than twenty years. She wrote histories of both the VSCC and the NCWV.

Within the National Council of Women she took a leading role in national campaigns to advance the status of women, in particular equal pay and equality within marriage. This led to her appointment as Australia's official delegate to the United Nations Status of Women Commission over an unprecedented three sessions, from 1961 to 1963. She was president of the United Nations Association of Australia's Victorian division from 1961–1971, and chaired the UNAA National Committee for International Women's Year, and the Committee for the Decade of Women.

Norris was appointed OBE in 1954 and Dame Commander of the British Empire in 1976. In 1969, she became the first Australian woman to be appointed a Companion of the Order of St Michael and St George, for services to the community. She was also awarded the UN Peace Medal in 1975, and in 1980 Melbourne University honoured her with a Doctorate of Laws.

Explore further resources about Ada Norris in the Australian Women's Register.

their failure to 'cover all children handicapped'. Under existing state provisions, she said, 'only seriously defective children can be dealt with' and then only in terms of detention 'if they have broken the law'—they were never dealt with from 'the educational or social betterment angle'. Moreover, 'the socially handicapped child', she added, referring to adopted and fostered children, 'demands attention'. Thus conference passed a resolution in which 'handicap' was defined very broadly: 'That increased attention be given to the care of the handicapped child, and further facilities be provided for the physically, the psychologically, the legally and socially handicapped child throughout Australia'.[44]

The 1948 conference also paid attention to disability. Delegates agreed on the importance of child guidance clinics to identify and deal with environmental and family factors in treating the 'neurotic child', and commended the increased endeavours for the 'blind, deaf and dumb' resulting from the visit by famed American activist Helen Keller. But they feared a focus on these activities would be at the expense of 'facilities for other types [of disability]—mental defectives, delinquents, retarded and orphaned children', which were 'totally inadequate'. Edna Hill emphasised the importance, too, of a 'scientific' approach, starting with the need to press for governments to spend more on research and preventive measures 'rather than solely on care', and extending to 'widespread education of the public ... regarding the cause and prevention of these abnormal conditions'.[45]

Domicile and Maintenance

Although maintenance for widows and deserted wives with children was intimately connected with issues of child welfare, as we have seen, it is a matter that deserves separate discussion here because of its wider

---

44 NCWA, *Report of Biennial Conference Held in Melbourne, Victoria, October 15th–18th, 1946*, pp. 27–8.
45 NCWA, Minutes of Biennial Conference of the National Council of Women of Australia, Held in Brisbane September 1st–3rd 1948, typescript, NCWV Papers, SLV (classification pending).

links to marriage law and the problem of domicile pursued by NCWA in this period. In the latter half of the pre-war depression decade, the board again took up the issue of economic independence with respect to deserted wives and mothers, specifically the seemingly intractable problem of enforcing maintenance orders rather than the more idealistic recasting of marriage itself as an equal economic partnership that they had been considering in 1928 and 1929. They continued then to lobby for a uniform national marriage law, referring to specific problems arising from anomalies between the state marriage laws as well the widespread difficulties arising from the lack of a national domicile. The corresponding problem of enforcing court orders was 'prejudicially affecting women's rights'.[46] Attorney General John Latham was apparently 'sympathetic' to the idea of instituting an Australian domicile when approached in 1934 but he left politics for the High Court soon after.[47] Thus, when Maurice Blackburn offered to introduce a private members' bill to establish an Australia-wide matrimonial domicile, the 1935 NCWA conference took up his offer, reaffirming earlier resolutions on the subject and recommending that delegates 'urge Federal Members to support it'.[48] Though the resolution Blackburn proposed was supported by the House of Representatives in March 1936, it was not taken up by the government in its legislative program.[49]

At the 1938 national conference, maintenance—together with the difficulty of enforcing orders with or without a national domicile—was again a major discussion point, Victoria's Lillias Skene commenting

---

46 *Age*, 24 November 1932. For the ongoing concern, see NCWA Conference Minutes, November 1932, Box 11, MS7583, NCWA Papers, NLA; NCWA Board Minutes, 13 November 1933, 10 December 1940, 28 February 1941, 16 December 1943, 3 February 1944, Box 12, MS7583, NCWA Papers, NLA.

47 NCWA Board Minutes, 9 April 1934, Box 12, MS7583, NCWA Papers, NLA.

48 NCWA Conference Minutes, August 1935, Box 11, MS7583, NCWA Papers, NLA.

49 Henry Finlay, *To Have but not to Hold: A History of Attitudes to Marriage and Divorce in Australia 1858–1975*, Sydney, Federation Press, 2005, p. 319; see also *Commonwealth Parliamentary Debates* (*CPD*), House of Representatives, 26 March 1936, pp. 592–9.

that defaulting men were rarely committed to prison because they were then unable to earn but noting that some men actually 'preferred to go to prison to evade their responsibilities'. President Adelaide Miethke suggested all councils should send a report on family maintenance in their respective states to be published in the *Quarterly Bulletin* as a basis for working out a solution. A resolution was passed to that effect, together with a request for information about widows' pensions that might assist those states without them.[50]

The problem of maintenance continued unresolved both nationally and internationally, ICW reiterating the need for an international convention, and the NCWA board in 1939 again rather helplessly asking the laws committee to investigate and make suggestions to the executive about how, in the absence of an Australian domicile, the position of deserted wives could be improved.[51] At the 1941 conference, a comparison was presented of the reports from all states on maintenance legislation; it 'showed that no State could find any solution to cope with the problem of a husband who deserted his wife and against whom orders had been served, if the man had moved to another State'. Once again, NCWA resolved to 'recommend to the Prime Minister that legislation be introduced for all-Australian domicile'.[52]

The problem of support for children of deserted wives was somewhat alleviated by the introduction of child endowment. Widows were assisted in 1942 when the Curtin government introduced means-tested pensions. The definition of a widow was broad, including those who had been separated or divorced at the time of the husband's death, as well as those who had been in de facto relationships, and those with a husband in a hospital for the insane. All were required to be of 'good character', and specified categories of Aboriginal women—those judged

---

50 *Argus*, 16 September 1938.
51 NCWA Board Minutes, 3 July 1939, Box 12, MS7583, NCWA Papers, NLA; Geneva 1927, Vienna 1930, 'ICW Resolutions', http://www.ncwcanada.com/ncwc2/wp-content/uploads/2014/02/ICW-CIF_Resolutions1.pdf, pp. 116–17.
52 *Argus*, 22 January 1941.

to be 'assimilated'—were included, as was also now the case for child endowment, maternity allowances and the aged and invalid pensions. Women deemed eligible for the benefit who had a child or children under sixteen were entitled to the same rate as the aged pension, while the others received less and, for those under fifty and without children, the period was limited to six months after the husband's death.[53] The NCWA board's response was consistent with its conservative stance on protecting the institution of marriage. It vehemently opposed the inclusion of de facto wives and resolved to write to the prime minister 'expressing appreciation of the assistance to necessitous widows, but deploring the inclusion of the "de facto" widow, since such provision undermines the sanctity & stability of marriage upon which rests the foundation of our national life'.[54]

The widows pension did not, however, apply to the deserted or divorced wife and mother whose husband was still alive but refusing to pay maintenance. Though she now had access to the limited amount provided by government endowment for her children, she often had insufficient income for her own support and her family's housing and other expenses. Thus the NCWA board continued regularly to lobby the federal government on the broader question of a uniform marriage and divorce law, emphasising its urgency to resolve domicile and maintenance issues. Though equality still informed the arguments of laws convenors in the councils, a stress on maintenance, following ICW policy, served to reassure those for whom concern about 'easy divorce' remained strong.[55] This coupling of divorce reform with the domicile and maintenance issues continued to mark the point on which radicals and conservatives could agree: the need to relieve the problems, particularly

---

53 Murphy, *A Decent Provision*, pp. 208, 212–13.
54 NCWA Board Minutes, 6 August 1942, Box 12, MS7583, NCWA Papers, NLA.
55 Rome 1914, Copenhagen 1924, Geneva 1927, Vienna 1930, 'ICW Resolutions', http://www.ncwcanada.com/ncwc2/wp-content/uploads/2014/02/ICW-CIF_Resolutions1.pdf, pp. 114–17.

the economic problems, of women whose marriages had irretrievably broken down.

The board's actions in approaching the government in 1943–44 were stimulated by a motion put to federal parliament by the first woman elected to the Senate, Labor's Dorothy Tangney. Tangney was primarily concerned with the plight of Australian wives deserted by their US servicemen husbands and was advised by long-term legal associate of the Victorian NCW, Anna Brennan. Tangney recalled later that she raised 'the subject of uniform divorce laws' because 'I experienced the greatest difficulty in trying to get justice for the deserted wives due to variations between the different State laws concerning matrimonial causes'. Although NCWA leaders supported this position, Tangney remembered that many others did not:

> I was very broadly criticised throughout Australia by many people who thought my main objective was to make divorce easier. I had to issue a public statement to show that that was not my intention, and that I did not think that if there were divorce laws in Australia any woman should be penalised merely because of geographical situation.[56]

In 1944, the Labor government's attorney-general told the NCWA board that consideration would be given to their views concerning uniformity of divorce laws and Australian domicile,[57] but, although another long battle for equal nationality rights for married women was won in Australia in 1946,[58] there were no corresponding moves towards uniform federal laws on marriage and divorce as such. When in May 1950 the NCWA secretary wrote to the new Liberal government's attorney-general requesting 'That the Commonwealth Government

---

56   *CPD*, Senate, 25 November 1959, p. 1834.
57   NCWA Board Minutes, 16 December 1943, 20 January 1944, 2 February 1944, NLA Box 12, MS7583, NCWA Papers, NLA.
58   M. Page Baldwin, 'Subject to Empire: Married Women and the British Nationality and Status of Aliens Act', *Journal of British Studies*, 40 (4), 2001, pp. 522–56. See also below chapter 7 for an account of some continuing limitations in the law.

will bring down legislation granting Australia a common domicile and a uniform marriage and divorce law', she noted dryly that, 'From the time of the formation of the ANCW, in 1924, we have sent this resolution to the Government in office'[59]—without effect.

Population and Race

As with their concerns about handicapped children, the national councils' emphasis on adequate support for mothers and children can in part be understood as a concern to counter the declining birth rate and the associated evils of abortion and contraception. This in turn was symptomatic of a broader anxiety about population quality as well as quantity. All were intimately connected with the widespread preoccupation with the health and survival of the race, understood as white and overwhelmingly British in origin.

Once again, debates about population in NCW circles were couched in contemporary progressivist terms that emphasised science and efficiency. The widespread discourses of eugenics were especially influential in the pre-war decade, though older moral values still had considerable purchase in relation to abortion and contraception. The main interwar focus of eugenic reformers was 'mental deficiency'. In Victoria, the national council was involved in discussion of this topic from the time the first mental deficiency bill was introduced into state parliament in 1926. Although many in the science and medical communities favoured sterilisation of those deemed mentally deficient (especially children), politicians were wary of the public reaction and preferred to confine legislative measures to segregation in secure institutions in order to prevent procreation.[60]

---

59 Attorney-General to Sec. NCWA, 20 May 1950, Correspondence 1936–1971, Folder 1, MS5193, NCWA Papers, NLA. On nationality, see chapter 7 below.
60 Ross L. Jones, 'The Master Potter and the Rejected Pots: Eugenic Legislation in Victoria, 1918–1939', *Australian Historical Studies*, 30 (113), 1999, pp. 324–30.

This ambivalence was reflected in NCW discussions, which saw the federal council urge unified Commonwealth and state action in 1926.[61] Queensland delegates raised the issue again at the 1929 Perth conference of the federated council,[62] then pushed for a full discussion at the first NCWA conference in Melbourne in 1932, explicitly requesting consideration of 'mental deficiency with regard to segregation and sterilisation' and recommending 'that a resolution be introduced dealing with the problem in accordance with the most recent finding of experts'. Subsequent discussion elicited views opposed to sterilisation from NSW's Lillie Goodisson, founder of the Racial Hygiene Association of NSW, and resulted in agreement on a resolution to ICW seeking 'reliable information' from other countries' councils about its efficacy.[63]

The decision of the ICW Agenda Committee to delete reference to sterilisation from the resolution put to the Paris conference in 1934 aroused the ire of delegates to the NCWA conference in Melbourne later that year. They were not seeking 'an opinion as to whether it was the right thing to do but information as to whether it was successful in those countries where it was practised', commented one delegate, and it would have been preferable to delete the whole resolution rather than censoring mention of sterilisation. Victoria's May Couchman, who had headed the Australian delegation to Paris, explained that the decision not to discuss sterilisation 'in any shape or form' was taken because the 'Latin countries would have simply walked out' and it was judged that it was not worth insisting on the issue if it would disrupt the whole congress. Thus discussion was confined to segregation. For NCWA, however, it was a matter of principle and conference resolved: 'That

---

61 NCWV, *Report for 1926*, p. 19.
62 FCNCWA Conference Minutes, September 1929, Box 12, MS7583, NCWA Papers, NLA.
63 NCWA Conference Minutes, November 1932, Box 11, MS7583, NCWA Papers, NLA.

when a resolution is sent from a country, that resolution should either be submitted in its entirety or disallowed'.⁶⁴

Refusing to be put off by the international council's decision not to discuss sterilisation, the NCWA board devised another resolution, approved at the 1935 national conference, requesting ICW's health committee to circularise all affiliated councils 'for information on the subject of sterilisation of mentally deficient where this treatment has been tested'. And an 'emergency resolution', passed unanimously, urged all ICW affiliates 'to make enquiries into the incidence of mental deficiency and the methods used to lessen it in their respective countries'. Queensland president Zina Cumbrae Stewart was not alone in arguing the necessity for prevention in preference to continually 'having to build more institutions to hold them'. Dr Ellice Dart, however, was more positive about treatments, especially since some of the causes (like parental alcohol consumption and venereal disease) were already known and were not appropriately treated by sterilisation; she suggested the NCWs collect statistical data for other nations to use, as well as lobbying for mental defectives legislation in all states. She pointed out that compulsory detention and training were having positive outcomes in institutions where occupational therapy was employed to 'astounding' effect.⁶⁵ At the ensuing conference in Adelaide in 1936, a resolution of support for segregation was passed. There is no indication that ICW discussed the matter of sterilisation again, and, although it continued to be a matter of concern among the state NCWs in the late 1930s,⁶⁶ the outbreak of war and the legacy of Nazi eugenic experiments saw subsequent discussion confined to segregation, with an increase in

---

64 NCWA Conference Minutes, November 1934, Box 11, MS7583, NCWA Papers, NLA; Paris 1934, 'ICW Resolutions', http://www.ncwcanada.com/ncwc2/wp-content/uploads/2014/02/ICW-CIF_Resolutions1.pdf, p. 71.
65 NCWA Conference Minutes, August 1935, Box 11, MS7583, NCWA Papers, NLA.
66 NCWNSW, *Biennial Reports for 1937–1938*, p. 13. Evidence of continuing discussion comes from Victorian convenor of laws, M.A. Williamson, who told the *Argus* that it was 'a live issue' among NCWV affiliates. See *Argus*, 22 November 1939, cited in Jones, 'The Master Potter', p. 340.

moves towards palliative treatment and education analogous to the general approach to disability evident at the 1948 NCWA conference.

Also intricately bound up with eugenic understandings of population questions in the 1930s were national council attitudes to the place and treatment of Australian Aboriginal people in contemporary society and the nation's future. Gendered humanitarian considerations were mingled with racial assumptions. The mix of attitudes came to the surface in the Australian council at the 1934 Melbourne conference, in discussion of a proposal to bring 'Octoroon' girls from the Northern Territory to Victoria for adoption by organisations or individuals with a view to their being absorbed into the population and, ultimately, marrying white men.[67] While Victoria's May Couchman was concerned that these girls would be exploited as cheap labour and be subject to sexual abuse, the chair, citing 'Mendelian law', believed it would give them a 'chance' since 'the Australian aborigine does not show traces of any black blood at the octoroon degree'—'These girls are as fair as any of us … and who is to know of the stigma of their birth?' Of greater concern would be transmission of 'the traits of the fathers', presumably white, who were 'the scum of the Northern Territory'. This produced a response from another Victorian delegate that importing the girls would be 'most dangerous' and 'It would be much better to sterilize them'.

A crude and distasteful exchange about 'throwbacks' and the accuracy of Mendelian theory as applied to Aboriginal peoples ensued. Only the South Australian delegates, reflecting the more humanitarian approach of women's organisations in that state, argued that 'They are splendid girls … and would not contaminate us'; after all, 'We do not know what our ancestors were three or four generations ago', so 'why should we be scared of a little bit of black blood. We have many nationalities in our race. Our aborigines are fine people really'. Couchman had the last word,

---

67 NCWA Board Minutes, 20 August 1934, Box 12, and NCWA Conference Minutes, November 1934, Box 11, MS7583, NCWA Papers, NLA.

saying that there was 'a great difference between mixed nationalities and mixed races' and the girls should not 'be brought among the white people in the south'; however, 'they are our fellow-women and it is our duty to help them'.[68] Fear of miscegenation and a maternalist sense of duty were also behind another major concern for NCWA in the 1930s: ensuring measures were taken to keep Aboriginal women away from railway workers' camps during the construction of the north–south rail line. There was no questioning here of the need for Aboriginal women and children to be 'protected' and controlled. At best NCWA conference delegates recommended that the white male protectors of Aborigines should be married and living with their wives and that white women should also be appointed as official protectors.[69]

National discussion in NCWA, as in other national women's organisations like the Australian Federation of Women Voters and the Woman's Christian Temperance Union, saw gathering support for uniform national policy on Aboriginal affairs. But doing away with state authority altogether was still a step too far for the councils before the war. At the 1938 Melbourne conference, a number of states submitted resolutions on the subject and the one finally agreed on urged 'both Federal and State governmental action to better conditions of life for aborigines' with regard to health, education and opportunities. It further recommended the co-operation of all the states in carrying into effect 'a broad Australian policy', though this was qualified by the addition of the words 'in a manner suited to the special conditions in each State'.[70] It was 1950 before the NCWA board came out in favour of Commonwealth control; the Victorian Council requested the matter be considered by the premiers' conference, though the Queensland and

---

68 NCWA Conference Minutes, November 1934, Box 11, MS7583, NCWA Papers, NLA.
69 NCWA Conference, November 1932, Box 11, MS7583, NCWA Papers, NLA; *Argus*, 17 September 1938; NCWA, *Report of Biennial Conference Held in Melbourne, Victoria, January 21st to 23rd 1941*, p. 12, and inside back cover.
70 *Argus*, 17 September 1938.

Western Australian councils, in the states with the largest Indigenous populations, seem to have remained unenthusiastic.[71]

Alongside eugenic concerns about the quality of children being born and the composition of the race was an ongoing preoccupation with quantity, manifested in council discussions during the 1930s about abortion and widespread use of contraceptive devices. By this time, infanticide and 'baby-farming' had declined dramatically but so too had the birth rate. The available evidence suggests a steep increase in abortions, and the sale of contraceptives to those who could afford them also increased, despite the prohibition on their importation. The onset of depression from the late 1920s saw a further downturn in births, the rate of decline in fertility more than doubling between 1929 and 1934. Women of all classes were apparently resisting pronatalist pressures to have more children. The limited evidence we have from NSW and Victoria suggests that the woman most commonly seeking abortion was not the stereotypical young single girl; rather, she was married and over thirty with three or more children.[72] The Melbourne District Nursing Service acknowledged this in establishing 'Mothers' Welfare Clinics' in 1934 to supply contraceptives to its married women patients, a service pioneered in New South Wales by the explicitly named 'Birth Control Clinics' operated by the Racial Hygiene Association.[73]

---

71 NCWA Board Minutes, 14 June 1950, 24 July 1950, 11 September 1950, Box 13, MS7583, NCWA Papers, NLA.

72 Robyn V. Gregory, 'Corrupt Cops. Crooked Docs. Prevaricating Pollies and "Mad Radicals": A History of Abortion Law Reform in Victoria, 1959–1974', PhD, RMIT University, 2004, chap. 2; Shurlee Swain with Renate Howe, *Single Mothers and their Children: Disposal, Punishment and Survival in Australia*, Melbourne, Cambridge University Press, 1995; Judith Allen, *Sex and Secrets: Crimes Involving Australian Women since 1880*, Melbourne, Oxford University Press, 1990; R.G.S. Worcester, 'The Problem of Abortion', Appendix II, *Report of the National Health and Medical Research Council*, 3rd session, November 1937, Canberra, Commonwealth Government Printer.

73 Jessie Henderson,NCWA Conference Minutes, August 1935, Box 11, MS7583, NCWA Papers, NLA; Lillie E. Goodisson, 'Racial Hygiene Association of NSW', in NCWNSW, *Biennial Reports for 1937–1938*, p. 43.

The 1935 NCWA conference saw a lengthy discussion on abortion and contraception; it was, according to the president, May Moss, 'almost the most interesting debate we have yet had'. Victoria had submitted resolutions seeking the prevention of abortion and a ban on the advertisement of contraceptives[74] and Queensland introduced an 'emergency resolution' asking the councils to gather information about law and practice in the various states with a view to deciding the best means to check it. Delegates agreed that abortion was an 'evil' that should be prevented, but disagreed about how best to do this—and especially about the place of contraception in this process. The Queensland resolution originated with Irene Longman, former Queensland president and the state's first woman MP. Longman was moved by the plight of women seeking abortion: 'not wicked women, or irresponsible women, but almost always women who had had several children, and they were driven by economic stress to get whatever help they could'.

Delegates sympathetic to these women's needs suggested measures like child endowment to make childbearing more affordable, and also the provision of 'scientific information … about the spacing of families'. Lillie Goodisson of the NSW Racial Hygiene Association also supported birth control measures to minimise abortions, but Queensland's Dr Ellice Dart arguing against this, claimed that the demand for abortion was 'more prevalent' among single women 'and more unforgiveable'. She proposed the teaching of sex hygiene in schools by 'proper people', including mothercraft experts and religious professionals. Instruction in birth control should come from the family doctor, and the poor who had no doctor could get sympathetic advice at public hospitals. Dart believed that the stricter enforcement of laws against advertisement and sale of contraceptives would be the best

---

74 NCWV, *Report for 1935*, pp. 9–10.

remedy against abortion.[75] Other delegates thought that some part of the blame lay with the medical profession itself. Lillias Skene, who was on the Women's Hospital Committee's Board of Management in Melbourne, was confident of women doctors' 'very high standard' of professionalism, but believed that the 'wholesale practice' of abortion by certain male doctors was making abortion safer and therefore compromising the effectiveness of education in persuading 'the boys and girls that they are wrong in what they are doing'.[76]

The general tone of the discussion was not sympathetic to family limitation. Queensland's Zina Cumbrae Stewart and Victoria's Cecilia Downing, both dedicated Christians and moral conservatives, emphasised the inculcation of the 'Christian ideal' of 'self-control right from the early years' and the importance of education 'to counteract the low moral tone which was bringing about such a terrible state of affairs'. In addition to opposing abortion, 'As Christian women we should set our faces against birth control. The happiest families are the biggest families', asserted Downing. 'It was agreed that all State Councils undertake to endeavour to get legislation enacted which will make the distribution of advertising matter for contraceptives etc. a punishable offence.' At the ensuing conference in Adelaide in 1936, the delegates went further, recommending 'that each State council urge its government to press for legislation concerning the sale, advertisement, exhibition and distribution of contraceptives similar to the Victorian Act of 1935'.[77] This was not, however, the same as advocating a ban on contraceptives or birth control advice as such, both of which were tolerated so long as information and access remained under strict medical control.

---

75 NCWA Conference Minutes, August 1935, Box 11, MS7583, NCWA Papers, NLA.
76 NCWA Conference Minutes, August 1935, Box 11, MS7583, NCWA Papers, NLA.
77 *Advertiser*, 19 September 1936.

There was little further direct discussion of these matters in the NCWA before the war but the related concern about the decline in the birth rate persisted. The 1938 conference in Melbourne identified the causes of 'the population problem' as the continuing excess of unmarried men over 30, the housing shortage as a factor discouraging young couples from having children, the still too-readily available information about contraception for engaged couples, the dangers of childbirth, and the lack of child endowment to ease financial concerns. May Moss, the only women representative on the National Health and Medical Research Council (NHMRC), also reported to the conference that the research council had commenced an inquiry into the root causes of the problem.[78]

Abortion continued to be an issue during the war years, perhaps aggravated by the prohibition of contraceptive sales through the post under the National Security Regulations in 1942. The introduction of child endowment in 1942 and a rapid decline in maternal mortality figures following the introduction of antibiotics in the early 1940s saw a slight rise in the birth rate but that was from a very low base in the 1930s. As a result, a more broad-based discussion of 'the population problem' gathered momentum in the councils as well as in government circles.[79] The major object was to ensure that a return to normality after the war would see women resuming domestic roles and especially child bearing.

This was the purpose of the report compiled in 1944 by Dame Enid Lyons, MHR, and Dr Phyllis Cilento for the NHMRC's inquiry into reasons for the declining birth rate. Causes the report identified included the changing attitudes among young women towards motherhood and family—changes derived from images of Hollywood glamour, fears of being locked into domestic drudgery like their mothers, and a desire for

---

78 *Argus*, 16 September 1938.
79 See Darian-Smith, *On the Home Front*, pp. 193–202; Gregory, 'Abortion Law Reform in Victoria', chap. 2.

material comfort.[80] Lyons and Cilento might well have added a wish for sexual fulfilment. This came to be recognised in the 1950s and has been analysed by later feminist historians as one of the outcomes of the greater independence experienced by young women during the war years.[81]

Lyons and Cilento's report was considered by J.H. Cumpston, director general of health, in preparing the NHMRC's recommendations to the minister. Lyons and Cilento favoured compulsory education for all girls in mothercraft and home management, a professional domestic training scheme (in effect recruitment of a new generation of domestic servants), establishment of 'fertility clinics', a propaganda campaign in favour of 'the development of a vigorous family life', and a guaranteed secure family income via non-means-tested unemployment, sickness and superannuation benefits and extended child endowment. The NHMRC report accepted most of these proposals, but added to them access to secure home ownership and improvement of hospital, medical and nursing maternity services. It was wary of any 'simple solution', and rejected a propaganda campaign in favour of 'mitigating the economic and social disadvantages experienced by both the children and parents of larger families' and transferring costs to 'the community as a whole'. The report acknowledged the possibility that none of these strategies might be successful since a further major reason for the widespread practice of birth control, including abortion, was the 'decreasing dependence of women'.[82] And to that there was no easy solution.

Between June and November 1945, the NCWA board received a number of letters from Tasmanian vice-president and president of the Tasmanian Council for Mother and Child, Edith Waterworth. Waterworth urged support for a deputation to the prime minister in the wake of the alleged failure of the government to act on the NHMRC's

---

80 *Advertiser*, 28 November 1944, p. 5.
81 See especially Marilyn Lake, 'Female Desires: The Meaning of World War II', *Australian Historical Studies*, 24 (95), October 1990, pp. 267–84.
82 Darian-Smith, *On the Home* Front, pp. 193–201; *Advertiser*, 25 November 1944, p. 7.

recommendation for an immediate investigation in every state. Her object was a national body to deal with the population question as it related to maternal and child welfare, and to ensure mothers were represented on it. Her underlying concern was that the 'white races' were being outbred by 'coloured peoples', and that Australia was particularly vulnerable. In commending the objects of the campaign, NCWA secretary Hilda Brotherton suggested to all state councils that they communicate with Waterworth directly and nominate a delegate to join a deputation to the prime minister. She also wrote to the prime minister formally stating the support of the NCWA for the objects of the deputation. Prime Minister Chifley refused to meet a deputation, arguing that the NHMRC specialist committee had included mothers and that 'everything possible will be done to safeguard the interests of both mothers & their children'. Waterworth's subsequent threat to hold public protest meetings raised alarm signals among NCWA board members and they acted quickly to distance themselves from her actions. It was council policy to work in co-operation with governments, Brotherton explained to her, and state investigations into the decline in the birth rate detailed by the NHMRC were in fact underway.[83]

Although some state councils seem to have continued their support for Waterworth, the issue was not discussed at the 1946 NCWA conference. Council interest in birth-rate and population issues thereafter focused on ways of providing home help for mothers, on extending and professionalising child welfare facilities, on improving and increasing the stock of housing and, increasingly, on migration policy. The most challenging and eventually the most transformative of these approaches to population expansion was migration.

NCWA migration convenor, South Australia's Mrs Brimblecombe, told the 1946 conference that the birth rate was not going to 'solve the

---

83   Correspondence between Edith Waterworth and Hilda Brotherton, 1945–46, Correspondence Files, Miscellaneous NCWQ Papers, in possession of the authors; NCWA Board Minutes, 6 June 1945, Box 13, MS7583, NCWA Papers, NLA.

population problem', and 'Australia stood in vital need of migrants of the right type'.[84] From 1944, the federal government and other public bodies had been acknowledging the need for a large migrant intake as part of post-war reconstruction. In its submission to the NHMRC inquiry into the declining birth rate, the Commonwealth Bureau of Census and Statistics acknowledged that any government attempts to restrict access to contraception would be not only ineffective but constitute 'a serious intrusion on the freedom of individuals in their most private affairs'. The only viable solution was a program of immigration. Like the committee established by Information Minister Arthur Calwell, the submission's authors, Roland Wilson and 'Nugget' Coombs, foresaw that a large migrant intake would of necessity extend beyond Britain and into Europe. As with attempts to improve the local birth rate, the nation's ability to draw the 'right type', preferably British, would, however, depend on making conditions of living and working attractive.[85]

At the 1946 NCWA conference, Mrs Brimblecombe acknowledged the need to provide conditions and services that would entice the most desirable migrants, urging delegates to vote for the establishment of state bodies to take responsibility for immigrants, especially women and children.[86] At the 1948 conference, Elsie Byth, in her presidential address, emphasised council's keen interest 'in the numbers and in the various types of migrants and in their absorption into the community'. The focus clearly was on British migrants. NCWA had some success in its request for two women to be appointed to Australia House in London as 'selection officers' 'to assist intending migrants', the first appointment being NSW council's nominee, Miss Swinney.[87] Calwell also formed

---

84   NCWA, *Report of Biennial Conference Held in Melbourne, October 15th–18th, 1946*, pp. 16–17.
85   *Advertiser*, 22 November 1944, p. 5; 28 November 1944, p. 5.
86   NCWA, *Report of Biennial Conference Held in Melbourne, October 15th–18th, 1946*, pp. 16–17.
87   NCWA, Minutes of Biennial Conference of the National Council of Women of Australia, Held in Brisbane September 1st–3rd 1948, typescript, NCWV Papers, SLV (classification pending).

the Commonwealth Immigration Advisory Council (CIAC) in 1947 'in order to have a channel through which the opinions of different important sections of the community could be expressed'. NCWA immediately requested the inclusion of at least one woman. Calwell's initial appointment, Jessie Street, resigned soon after to become Australia's first delegate to the UN Status of Women Commission and was replaced in 1950 by the national council's nominee, Ada Norris. The CIAC was responsible, among many other things, for organising the annual government-sponsored citizenship conventions held between 1950 and 1968, essentially assimilationist occasions that Norris attended as a delegate from both NCWA and the advisory council, usually along with the NCWA president.[88]

Public Health and Morals

During the 1930s and 40s, the main health matters discussed by the national councils at federal level were maternal and child welfare and population quality, matters already dealt with here. Another concern was physical fitness, the NSW and Victorian councils taking a particular interest in school programs and university courses for training physical education teachers but this was not an issue that was much canvassed at the national level. Concerns about alcohol consumption still persisted and were most evident in the war years when the issues of 'shouting' and 'dry' or 'wet' canteens were discussed nationally,[89] and state councils lobbied and petitioned their governments for a variety of local controls over access to alcohol. NCWA was wary of engaging in the debates. In 1940, the board first declined to comment on supply of alcohol to

---

88   'The Commonwealth Immigration Advisory Council', August 1965, Box 4, MS90/190, Papers of Mrs J.G. Norris (Norris Papers), University of Melbourne Archives (UMA). This document includes terms of reference, a brief history, functions and a list of the 28 members. See also NCWA, Minutes of Biennial Conference of the National Council of Women of Australia, Held in Brisbane September 1st–3rd 1948, typescript, NCWV Papers, SLV (classification pending).

89   NCWA Board Minutes, 23 April 1940, 24 September 1940, 24 October 1940, 11 November 1940, 19 August 1941, Box 12, MS7583, NCWA Papers, NLA.

the 'fighting forces', then acknowledged that the introduction of wet canteens rendered agitation about shouting redundant;[90] and the 1941 national conference maintained that individual state laws were outside NCWA's gamut. Conference could only consider the general question and provide 'a lead'. It resolved on investigation into 'the general charge of excessive increase in drunkenness, and the reasons for such increase', and on following up the overall 'problem of liquor reform' when they next met, but, as in the first war, alcohol restrictions on the home front remained largely the province of the states.[91]

More evident at national level was anxiety about sexual morality and the effects of the greater sexual freedoms that accompanied war at home and overseas. This was expressed in council opposition to the eligibility of de facto wives and widows for Commonwealth benefits ('a reward for immorality'), in questions about the treatment of pregnant women in the auxiliary services, and in concern about the prevalence of venereal diseases.[92] Although home-front historians have identified the same gendered pattern of discrimination as occurred in the Great War discussion and treatment of VD, NCWA records show little direct council involvement in the debates during the second war. National Security (Venereal Diseases and Contraception) Regulations passed in 1942 enabled civil health authorities to detain and examine persons—invariably they were young women—suspected of carrying VD.[93] There is no evidence that the federal body opposed these additional powers and, given its previous stance on the issue, it almost certainly supported them. The Victorian council had joined a deputation in 1940 requesting

---

90 NCWA Board Minutes, 24 September 1940, 11 November 1940, Box 12, MS7583, NCWA Papers, NLA.
91 NCWA, *Report of Biennial Conference Held in Melbourne, Victoria, January 21st to 23rd, 1941*, p. 19.
92 NCWA Board Minutes, 23 April 1940, 19 August 1941, 6 August 1942, 3 June 1943, Box 12, MS7583, NCWA Papers, NLA.
93 See Darian-Smith, *On the Home Front*, pp. 186–93 for further detail.

amendment to the state venereal diseases act to increase its powers.[94] Only on the matter of broadcasting information did NCWA express a general opinion, one that confirmed its long-held commitment to the view that such information must be sourced and prepared by medically qualified men and women. In any case, the availability of penicillin for civilians in the last two years of the war meant that VD was no longer categorised as a major health issue.[95] It was rarely discussed in the post-war period.

The issue of greatest moral concern among NCWA conference delegates throughout the 1930s and 40s was the ongoing challenge of cinema. According to Michael McKernan, in one twelve-month period in the 1930s, admissions to cinemas in Australia totalled 68 million, while, in comparison, combined racing and theatre attendances amounted to slightly fewer than 16 million.[96] Although cinema was increasingly discussed by the national councils and the Good Film Society in terms of desirable directions for Australian culture, effective censorship remained the driving imperative in view of the huge appeal of film and 'the effects ... upon the minds of the young'.[97] This was one of the first issues to receive the attention of the new NCWA interim board in July 1932, which called on the federal government to appoint a board similar to the Australian Broadcasting Commission for the purpose of censoring and controlling production, introduction and exhibition of all films and posters, and acting as an appeal board. The minister was sympathetic and, seeing the council as a potential ally for achieving national control, advised the board to frame a conference resolution that included strategies for dealing with the states' resistance to a consequent

---

94 NCWV, *Summary of the Activities of the National Council of Women of Victoria during the Years 1940, 1941, 1942, 1943, 1944*, p. 4.
95 NCWA Board Minutes, 7 July 1944, Box 12, MS7583, NCWA Papers, NLA; Darian-Smith, *On the Home Front*, p. 93.
96 Michael McKernan, *All In! Australia during the Second World War*, Melbourne, Nelson, 1983.
97 NCWA Conference Minutes, November 1932, Box 11, MS7583, NCWA Papers, NLA.

loss of powers.[98] The first NCWA conference in 1932, on the initiative of the NSW and Victorian councils, devoted a full session to the proposal for uniformity in censorship, citing the recommendations of the 1927/28 royal commission on the moving picture industry. This would, in the view of most speakers, be best achieved by assignment of all censorship powers to a reconstituted Commonwealth board. The conference finally agreed to a resolution recommending national uniformity, supervision over advertising in connection with films, the inclusion of at least one woman of the board, the addition of a separate appeals board, and selection criteria based on qualifications for the job; also that 'an Enabling Act be passed in each State to transfer to the Commonwealth the powers of regulation'.[99]

They did not achieve this goal for some years. NCWNSW's May Matthews was right in expressing scepticism during the debates about the willingness of the states to surrender their powers.[100] State censorship continued to operate alongside the Commonwealth board throughout the 1930s and the war years except in Victoria, which had handed responsibility to the Commonwealth in 1927. NCWA turned its attention during this time to supporting efforts to improve the quality of films produced and imported and to fix quotas for, or otherwise reduce the dominance of, Hollywood. At the 1935 conference in Brisbane, a Tasmanian motion for 'a concerted move' on the part of NCWA 'to secure better films … which would uplift by beauty and goodness rather than degrade by ugliness and sin' was carried unanimously, Lillie Goodisson, a founder of the Good Film League in NSW, urging the formation of similar bodies in all the states.[101] It was a resolution that

---

98 NCWA Board Minutes, 18 July 1932, 24 October 1932, Box 11, MS7583, NCWA Papers, NLA.
99 NCWA Conference Minutes, November 1932, Box 11, MS7583, NCWA Papers, NLA; NCWNSW, *Biennial Reports for 1933–1934*, p. 10.
100 NCWA Conference Minutes, November 1932, Box 11, MS7583, NCWA Papers, NLA.
101 NCWA Conference Minutes, August 1935, Box 11, MS7583, NCWA Papers, NLA.

allowed delegates whose concerns about 'Hollywood vulgarisation' were primarily aesthetic to co-operate with those, like Queensland's Zina Cumbrae Stewart and Victoria's Cecilia Downing, whose fears of the popular appeal of film were rooted in conservative Christian moral values.

There was similar support at the 1938 conference for measures to ensure greater diversity of films available to Australian audiences, after a public meeting in association with the conference heard evidence from New South Wales' Evelyn Tildesley that 90 per cent of the films seen were produced in Hollywood. 'English films were gradually being squeezed out', she claimed, and children's understanding of important matters such as 'the administration of justice and the rule of law were being formed by films that attached non-British meanings' to them. Quota legislation in NSW had been ignored, she continued, and pressure was now being mounted for a tax on American films to assist Australian producers.[102] NCWA also agreed on a resolution to ICW 'that good films should be available from all countries'. It was not among those passed at Edinburgh in 1938, though it was consistent with the emphasis there on 'the education of public taste' and encouragement of 'films of high moral and artistic value'.[103] As war increased nationalist feeling, NCWA again argued variously for Commonwealth investigation of the film industry and for legislation or other action to safeguard British and Australian film interests against 'the uninterrupted flood' of Hollywood films during and after the war—by quota if necessary. It was still a matter of concern in the post-war years but, by 1948, film convenor Evelyn Tildesley was taking heart from the appearance of more British films on Australian screens; the next step, she believed, was for state cinema

---

102 *Argus*, 16 September 1946.
103 *NCWA Bulletin*, No. 5, 1938, p. 1; Edinburgh, 'ICW Resolutions', http://www.ncwcanada.com/ncwc2/wp-content/uploads/2014/02/ICW-CIF_Resolutions1.pdf, p. 141.

committees to encourage the showing of European and independent films.[104]

With the heightened anxieties about a loosening of morals in the war years, NCWA also revived agitation about the relationship between film and the corruption of children, the 'alarming wave of sex offences' being attributed to dark theatres and 'the influence of American films on adolescents'.[105] Thus the councils turned their attention once more to censorship and the necessity for national uniformity to make it effective. With the end of war, and in the context of the expansion of Commonwealth powers it had brought about, the prospect of the states surrendering film classification and censorship to the national body seemed more promising.[106] In August 1946, at the state premiers conference, all states except South Australia agreed to enact uniform film censorship legislation on the Victorian model, whereby the Commonwealth film censorship authority would act on behalf of the states. This was to come into force in 1949.[107] NCWA president Elsie Byth and film convenor Evelyn Tildseley met with the chief censor in October 1947 and reported agreement that censorship policy should follow accepted social attitudes rather than try to mould public opinion, that classification (A for adult and G for general exhibition) should be given more publicity, and that the best way of dealing with the problem of children seeing suitable films was to educate the parents. The secretary reported to the 1948 conference that the council's recommendations

---

104 NCWA Board Minutes, 13 June 1940, 15 July 1943; 7 July 1944, Box 12, MS7583, NCWA papers, NLA; *Argus*, 23 January 1941; NCWA, *Report of Biennial Conference Held in Melbourne, Victoria, January 21st to 23rd 1941*, pp. 16–17; NCWA, Minutes of Biennial Conference of the National Council of Women of Australia, Held in Brisbane September 1st–3rd 1948, typescript, NCWV Papers, SLV (classification pending), p. 21.

105 *Sydney Morning Herald*, 28 October 1944.

106 NCWA, *Report of Biennial Conference Held in Melbourne, Victoria, October 15th–18th, 1946*, pp. 10, 13; NCWA Board Minutes, 3 December 1946, Box 13, MS7583, NCWA Papers, NLA; NCWA, Minutes of Biennial Conference of the National Council of Women of Australia, Held in Brisbane September 1st–3rd 1948, typescript, NCWV Papers, SLV (classification pending), p. 13.

107 *Canberra Times*, 22 August 1946, p. 4.

had been adopted by the chief censor and 'would be put into effect when agreement is reached between States and necessary laws passed'.[108] In the event, the legislation commenced operation in 1949 without South Australia and New South Wales, which do not seem to have authorised the Commonwealth censors to act on their behalf until 1972.[109] Although the commencement of uniform national censorship was not perfect, it did, as Tildesley told the 1948 conference, 'close a chapter on N.C.W. agitation' in Australia.

A remarkably wide range of issues relating to the welfare of home and family occupied the attention of the state and national councils in this period of economic and political crisis and post-war reconstruction. Approaches to these issues drew on a self-consciously modern and scientific discourse of reform led by an expanding body of professionally qualified women in the councils, while still having recourse to the traditional Christian moral values espoused by many ordinary delegates and their affiliated organisations. While the latter tended to restrain the impact of the former, it is surprising to see how often the councils were able to reach a consensus on appropriate policy and action. This pattern continued into the 1950s and 60s before showing major signs of fracture in the 1970s and 80s. The other important feature of NCWA discussions about home and welfare in this period was the growing emphasis on national uniformity. While a commitment to states rights was still evident, the sense of national interest had a much firmer foundation in 1950 than when NCWA was established two decades earlier.

---

108 NCWA, Minutes of Biennial Conference of the National Council of Women of Australia, Held in Brisbane September 1st–3rd 1948, typescript, NCWV Papers, SLV (classification pending), pp. 10, 21.

109 See also Ina Bertrand, *Film Censorship in Australia*, Brisbane, University of Queensland Press, 1978.

Chapter 7

RIGHTS, EQUALITY AND INTERNATIONAL AFFAIRS

In developing a national focus on domestic issues during the first decades of its existence, the National Council of Women of Australia (NCWA) came also to identify many of its concerns as shared with women of other nations, and to see the value of working internationally. This process was perhaps most pertinent to issues of legal and economic discrimination and inequity, and to threats to international order. During the depression, war and post-war years from 1931 to 1950, the main equality and rights issues that occupied the attention of NCWA were entangled to varying degrees with the ongoing international crises, and the post-war attempt to create a new world order through the United Nations. This chapter first considers the two major equal rights issues of the period—nationality of married women, and equal pay and employment opportunities—and relates them to ICW policy, Imperial relations and post-war United Nations principles, as well as to the domestic context. It then examines NCWA efforts in the 1930s to maintain peace through support for disarmament and the League of Nations, the response of council to the outbreak of war and loss of international links, post-war revival of its international engagement through ICW and the United Nations Commission on the Status of Women (CSW), and, towards the end of the period, early steps taken by its leaders to pave the way for a regional role and identity.

Equal Nationality Rights

During the 1930s, Australian national councils persisted with the three-pronged approach to fighting for married women to have the same entitlement to choice of nationality as men. In addition to continuing their pressure on the Australian government, then on the British and the other dominions through the Imperial conferences, they worked in accord with ICW and with the League of Nations Women's Consultative Committee on Nationality. This committee, though a useful forum for discussion, had no power and was offered as a sop to the international women's movement after the Conference on the Codification of International Laws held in the Hague in 1930 failed to take the issue beyond the problem of statelessness. The Australian council was also represented on a federal government war-time inquiry into the nationality problem, and pursued it further in the 1940s and 50s through the United Nations Commission on the Status of Women.

As we have seen, Britain, Australia and New Zealand were, by the late 1920s, all willing to legislate for married women to have the same choice of nationality rights and place of residence as men—at least within the jurisdictions of the British Empire. The House of Commons passed a resolution of in-principle support in 1926, but the government declined to go further when several dominions refused support, giving higher priority to preserving common British subject status across the Empire.[1] When the decisions of the Hague Codification of Laws conference in 1930 required further legislation, the government proposed a change to the law that would prevent a British woman who married an alien from becoming stateless if she did not automatically acquire his nationality on marriage. Australia's major women's organisations, including NCWA, mobilised behind the British women's campaign for a much more inclusive non-discriminatory nationality law but, in 1934,

---

1   M. Page Baldwin, 'Subject to Empire: Married Women and the British Nationality and Status of Aliens Act', *Journal of British Studies*, 40 (4), 2001, pp. 522–56. They were the Irish Free State, Canada and South Africa.

RIGHTS, EQUALITY AND INTERNATIONAL AFFAIRS

Australia's prime minister, Joseph Lyons, told NCWA president May Moss in a private interview that he viewed

> the whole question with grave concern. He did not give much hope. This was just between himself and me. It is a sort of see-saw between the Dominions and the British Empire. South Africa and Canada are standing aloof on the religious side of the question, and we say we will fall behind it if Great Britain does.[2]

Britain did not fall behind it. To the fury of the women's organisations in the United Kingdom, the parliament had, in 1933, passed an amendment to the Nationality Act dealing only with the problem of statelessness and ignoring the rights of married women. This enabled the British government then to ratify the Hague Convention and it refused to take the matter further at this stage. New Zealand and Australia followed suit in 1935 and 1936 respectively but with a significant modification in their legislation.[3] That Australian women lobbyists had some effect on this is indicated by the shift in the government's position since deputy prime minister Earl Page had written to them in August 1935, stating that he 'would not be prepared to do anything further than that no woman shall be "stateless"'.[4] The modification now conceded by the government provided that a woman who became an alien by marriage could retain the rights and obligations of a British subject while resident in Australia if she so requested.[5] Senator George Pearce, who had carriage of the bill in the Senate, rather patronisingly claimed that it went 'a long way towards meeting … the wishes of those women's organizations in regard to the national status of married women', but, as he also made very clear, 'Strictly speaking, she would still be regarded

---

2   NCWA Conference Minutes, November 1934, Box 11, MS7583, NCWA Papers, NLA.
3   Page Baldwin, 'Subject to Empire', pp. 522–56.
4   NCWA Conference Minutes, August 1935, Box 11, MS7583, NCWA Papers, NLA.
5   *Commonwealth Parliamentary Debates* (*CPD*), House of Representatives, 13 November 1936, p. 1865.

in the eye of the law as an alien outside Australia'.[6] Tasmania's Senator Herbert Payne more accurately observed of the reaction of the lobbyists:

> I know that these organizations have been working very hard, and ... I feel sure that they will not be content until they get all that they require ... There does not appear to be any good reason why women should not have the same rights as men.[7]

On the international stage, ICW continued to push to amend or eliminate those articles in the Hague convention that discriminated against women.[8] This had to be achieved before the convention was ratified by sufficient nations to enter into force. ICW's instrument was the Women's Consultative Committee on Nationality on which it was represented alongside the other major international women's organisations. NCWA's first national conference in 1932 resolved:

> That the National Council of Women of Australia support the international organisations in their proposed plan of action so outlined in the I.C.W. Bulletin, in order to further the claims for equality of women under the Nationality Laws in all countries of the world.[9]

It was ICW's pressure and the commitment to the international movement among NCWA's leaders that kept this fundamental equality issue alive in Australia. Councils loyally passed resolutions of support but it is doubtful that most members had more than a passing understanding of or interest in the issue. It is revealing that the board minutes for September 1933 note that at an 'afternoon party' at which many delegates and members were present, 'when Mrs Moss spoke of work which NCWs had put in to the question of nationality ... it

---

6 *CPD*, Senate, 25 November 1936, p. 2072.
7 *CPD*, Senate, 25 November 1936, p. 2250.
8 NCWA Conference Minutes, November 1932, and November 1934, Box 11, MS7583, NCWA Papers, NLA; NCWA Executive Minutes, 18 January 1934, Box 11, MS7583, NCWA Papers, NLA.
9 NCWA Conference Minutes, November 1932, Box 11, MS7583, NCWA Papers, NLA. NCWQ delegates abstained.

seemed to be of no further interest'.[10] Moss and her board nevertheless persisted. In November 1934 she told conference that although the leader of Australia's delegation to the League of Nations, John Latham, had agreed to bring the question forward at the next league assembly, he was leaving parliament and would be unable to do fulfil his promise. Moss went on to say they must persevere:

> 1936 will see this brought before the League of Nations for further consideration. The women throughout the world must see that something definite is done between now and then, and not leave it to the American women who stormed the League in 1931–32 determined that this question which so affects them should be brought before the Assembly.[11]

The women's consultative committee's reports and recommendations on equal nationality rights were repeatedly rejected by the League of Nations Assembly, and the unamended Hague convention was finally ratified in 1937. Though women's international pressure tactics were unsuccessful, they had some long-term consequences. A committee of experts set up by the League in 1937 to inquire into the status of women paved the way for the formation of the United Nations Commission on the Status of Women after the Second World War.[12]

Nothing further was achieved in Australia either, until the marriage of Australian women to American servicemen during World War II made reconsideration of the issue a matter of some urgency, since under American law they did not automatically acquire American nationality.

---

10   NCWA Board Minutes, 13 September 1933, Box 12, MS7583, NCWA Papers, NLA.
11   NCWA Conference Minutes, November 1934, Box 11, MS7583, NCWA Papers, NLA.
12   Katarina Leppännen, 'The Conflicting Interest of Women's Organizations and the League of Nations on the Question of Married Women's Nationality in the 1930s', *Nora: Nordic Journal of Feminist and Gender Research*, 17 (4), 2009, pp. 240–55; Candice Lewis Bredbenner, *A Nationality of Her Own: Women, Marriage and the Law of Citizenship*, Berkeley and Los Angeles, University of California Press, 1998, chap. 6 and epilogue.

NCWA noted with approval newly elected Senator Dorothy Tangney's success in persuading the government to attend to this matter.[13] A very brief act that became law in April 1946 amended the 1936 legislation to provide for automatic and retrospective retention of British nationality by Australian women married to aliens; in other words they now had to opt out rather than in.[14] But, as NCWA's president noted, it still applied 'only while the wife is resident in Australia and would not be recognized as valid in many countries outside Australia'. To deal with this problem, among others, Tangney was appointed by the minister for immigration to head a committee 'to consider the practical and legal difficulties involved in the possession, by husband and wife, of different nationalities'. It was a mark of NCWA's influence that it was specifically represented on the committee—by Melbourne lawyer and NCWV associate Anna Brennan. The full report was published in the minutes of the 1946 NCWA conference.[15] The Tangney committee detailed the problems, congratulated the minister on the recent legislation, noted specifically that the position could only be 'wholly overcome by all [Nation] States adopting uniform procedure', and recommended that

> the Australian delegation to the forthcoming dominion conference in London of nationality experts of British countries be instructed to move that a united approach be made by the British Commonwealth in the United Nations Organisation with a view to universal adoption of the principle that a woman shall be free to determine her own nationality irrespective of that of her husband.[16]

---

13 NCWA Board Minutes, 16 December 1943, Box 12, MS7583, NCWA Papers, NLA.
14 An Act to Provide for the Retention or Acquisition of British Nationality by Women Married to Aliens, No. 9, 1946.
15 NCWA, *Report of Biennial Conference Held in Melbourne, October 15th–18th, 1946*, pp. 2–7.
16 NCWA, *Report of Biennial Conference Held in Melbourne, October 15th–18th, 1946*, pp. 4–7.

RIGHTS, EQUALITY AND INTERNATIONAL AFFAIRS

When the dominion leaders met in London to reconsider the question in 1946, Canada and South Africa had already gone their own way with national citizenship legislation. The war had thus sounded the death knell of uniform British nationality and the illusion that it would continue to take precedence over dominion nationalism. Nevertheless, the conference agreed in principle to retain a common national status throughout the Commonwealth while simultaneously condoning independent nationality laws.[17] From there, it was a short road to separate citizenship legislation in Australia, which in 1948 incorporated equal nationality rights for all those defined as citizens.[18] The laws standing committee convenor, in reporting on this to NCWA's 1948 conference, noted that the councils had been working on the issue for thirty years.[19] But the legislation finally enacted, as with American nationality law, specifically excluded alien women married to Australians from the automatic entitlement to citizenship (or British subject status) they had previously possessed. And it did little to resolve the contradictory situations in which married women found themselves in other parts of the world.

At the international level, the newly created Commission for the Status of Women pushed for an equal nationality convention under article 15 of the Universal Declaration of Human Rights, which stipulated equal rights for women. ICW rejoiced in 1951 'to see that the International Law Commission of the UN has agreed to draft a convention on the nationality of married women at the request of the Economic and Social Council of the UN'. Thereafter its work in this area was dedicated to securing support for the passage and ratification

---

17 Page Baldwin, 'Subject to Empire', pp. 522–56. British subject status was abolished for Australian citizens in 1984.
18 Nationality and Citizenship Act 1948 (in 1973 renamed Australian Citizenship Act 1948).
19 Minutes of Biennial Conference of the National Council of Women of Australia, Held in Brisbane September 1st–3rd 1948, typescript, NCWV Papers, SLV (classification pending).

of the Convention by member nations.[20] It was a step too far for the Australian government, however. Though it had granted these rights to its own female citizens, it opposed signing up for an international obligation to recognise them for immigrant wives on the delicately racist grounds that 'to allow unrestricted entry in all such cases would seriously weaken the universally recognised right of each country to determine the composition of its own population'.[21] The UN Convention on the subject was finally passed in 1957 and entered into force in 1958, but was only ratified in Australia in March 1961, as the White Australia policy was entering its death throes. The final recognition of the universality of this right by her own country was a matter for rejoicing by NCW stalwart and Australian delegate to CSW, Ada Norris.[22]

Equal Pay and Employment Opportunities

Australia's minimum wage fixing machinery had made the Australian system a model for reformers in other countries in the early decades of the century. The process by which the industrial court arbitrated the competing claims of employers and unionists was universally admired. But, as we have seen, the adversarial system locked out women workers, and the gendering of the minimum wage kept the basic women's wage at 54 per cent of the male rate, with the differential understood as constituting the 'family wage' part of male remuneration. The court's awards set in concrete a heavily gendered workplace in which men and

---

20 Athens 1951, Helsinki 1954, 'ICW Resolutions', http://www.ncwcanada.com/ncwc2/wp-content/uploads/2014/02/ICW-CIF_Resolutions1.pdf, pp. 119–20, 122.
21 Secretary Immigration Department to Secretary External Affairs, 15 March 1949, Folder 'Preparation for Delegation to Lebanon, Feb.–March 1949', Status of Women Commission, Department of External Affairs, A1838/1 856/15/5/4, National Archives of Australia (NAA).
22 'Report of the Australian Representative Mrs J.G. Norris to the Fifteenth Session of the Commission on the Status of Women Held at the European Office of the United Nations, Geneva, 13th–30th March 1961', Canberra, Department of External Affairs, 1961, p. 20; Gwenda Tavan, *The Long, Slow Death of White Australia*, Melbourne, Scribe, 2005.

women rarely did the same work, and women's skills were consistently undervalued.[23]

From just before World War I, Australia's national councils took up the cause of equal pay, though mainly in the interests of teachers and other professionals. Only after the war did ICW start to agitate on the issue, working with the International Labour Organization to devise a clear position. And, by 1930, ICW was recommending that all National Councils of Women should push for 'minimum wage fixing machinery' to raise the standards of living of the poor, 'always having regard to the principle accepted in Article 427 of the Treaty of Versailles "that men and women should receive equal remuneration for work of equal value"'.[24] During the 1930s and 40s, NCWA—held steadfast in part by ICW policy—maintained its support for equal pay and an individual rather than a family basis for wage fixation. Councils did not campaign actively on this in the depression years, when many affiliates and members had reservations about agitating for equal pay in the context of widespread unemployment of male breadwinners. Nevertheless, resolutions of support for salary equality as well as equal employment and promotion opportunities for women in the federal public service were passed at the federal council meetings in 1928 and 1929, when the economic downturn in Australia was well underway.[25] And the councils extended their concern to the employment rights of married women during the 1930s.

As in other parts of the world in the decade of the Great Depression, Australian employers, including governments, discriminated against all women workers, but especially married ones. Committed to the primary

---

23   Edna Ryan and Anne Conlon, *Gentle Invaders: Australian Women at Work*, Melbourne, Penguin, 1989, chapter 4.

24   Vienna 1930, 'ICW Resolutions', www.ncwcanada.com/ncwc2/wp-content/uploads/2014/02/ICW-CIF_Resolutions1.pdf, p. 177.

25   Ada Norris, *Champions of the Impossible: A History of the National Council of Women of Victoria 1902–1977*, Melbourne, Hawthorn Press, 1978, p. 64; FCNCWA Conference Minutes, July 1928, and September 1929, Box 12, MS7583, NCWA Papers, NLA. The marriage bar was not lifted until 1966.

responsibility of women to home and family, the Australian national councils had studiously avoided considering the right of married women to work, even though ICW resolutions of support dated from 1925.[26] But, in view of the overt discrimination now being practised and the hardship it was causing, delegates to the nation-wide conference in Brisbane in 1935 affirmed the ICW position that any woman, 'married or unmarried', should 'have the same right as a man to keep or obtain paid work', as well as resolving 'to promote equal conditions of work between men and women'. The conference further added that it 'look[ed] upon this matter as one of extreme importance in view of the conditions in Australia at present'. Delegates then unanimously condemned the dismissal of married women teachers by act of parliament in New South Wales and restrictions imposed on married women teachers in several other states, as well as a proposal from the Shop Assistants Union in Queensland that married women be debarred from industrial work.[27]

Muriel Heagney's detailed indictment of the targeting of women workers, *Are Women Taking Men's Jobs?*, published in the same year, was widely read and recommended to members by a number of affiliated women's organisations, including the Housewives' Associations and the Woman's Christian Temperance Union.[28] Its effect was evident at the 1936 NCWA conference in Adelaide, which, following Heagney's argument as well as an ICW resolution, declared its opposition to 'any restrictions on the women's right to work', believing 'that the hope that

---

26   See May Moss's presidential address at the 1935 NCWA conference, and ICW resolutions affirmed at the conference, 29 August 1935, Box 11, MS7583, NLA. For ICW resolutions, see http://www.ncwcanada.com/ncwc2/wp-content/uploads/2014/02/ICW-CIF_Resolutions1.pdf, pp. 176–80. The only evidence we have found of previous discussion of the issue is in the NCWV syllabus for 1915, when 'That women on marriage shall not have to give up their position in the Public Service' was listed for debate. NCWV Executive Minutes, 18 February 1915, NCWV Papers, SLV (classification pending).
27   NCWA Conference Minutes, August 1935, Box 11, MS7583, NCWA Papers, NLA.
28   See, for example, *White Ribbon Signal*, 1 April 1936, p. 62, and *Housewife* (Victoria), 5 (7), June 1937, p. 33.

unemployed men will be absorbed into the vacated positions is illusory, and restriction of women only shifts the problem of unemployment without solving it'.[29] However, there is no evidence of NCWA co-operation with Heagney's Council of Action for Equal Pay, formed in 1937, despite the council's ongoing commitment to the principle.

Before the outbreak of war, and in the face of an initially discouraging response from the federal government, state councils, urged by NCWA, established and ran voluntary registers of women available for emergency services. After the government was persuaded of their value, the registers—still run by the national councils—worked first under the Defence Department and then under Manpower. In Victoria, the registration office remained open until November 1944, during which time over 30,000 women and girls enrolled, trained and carried out canteen work, maintained and drove vehicles, and did evening clerical and typing work for service and production departments. The voluntary service continued even though many of the women were eventually absorbed into paid work; some, however, continued to volunteer in their spare time.[30]

As the demand for women's paid employment expanded, the climate for arguing the case for gender equity in pay and opportunities would seem to have improved. A resolution from NCWNSW to the NCWA board in December 1940 recommended an expression of support for equal pay to the basic wage commission hearing about to open in Melbourne. After consulting the other councils, NCWA sent a telegram to the arbitration court 'announcing the unanimous approval of New South Wales, Victoria, Queensland, Tasmania and West Australia for equal pay'.[31] But equal pay was not supported by all the councils, South

---

29   *Advertiser*, 17 September 1936.
30   Norris, *Champions*, pp. 86–7.
31   NCWA Board Minutes, 10 December 1940, Box 12, MS7583, NCWA Papers, NLA; NCWA, *Report of Biennial Conference Held in Melbourne, Victoria, January 21st to 23rd, 1941*, p. 12.

Australia refusing its consent. NCWSA requested consideration of the issue at the January 1941 national conference.

It is significant that NCWA's international secretary took the lead in arguing the case during what was described as a 'vigorous discussion'. The South Australians were informed in no uncertain terms of their obligation to support ICW policy. Not only had equal pay 'long been affirmed by the Australian Council', it was also a 'a strong plank in the platform of the International Council, was considered a matter of vital reform in Britain, and was strongly held in all but the backward countries'. South Australia was also informed that two-thirds of the councils constituted a majority for adoption of NCWA policy and that all councils were thereby committed to its support. Conference then affirmed equal pay but did so in terms of 'the principle of "the rate for the job"', a formulation adopted from the British national council that did not commit them to the family basis of male basic wage fixation about which they had long held doubts.[32] But it was to no avail in any case. Neither the court nor the government was convinced. The Menzies government regarded the new child endowment allowance as not only an argument against any increase by the court in the basic wage, as we have seen, but also as a reason for failing to ask the court to consider equal pay.

The NCWA board, together with other women's groups, continued its agitation.[33] But all of them were stymied by the decision of the new Labor government to sidestep the arbitration court and avoid challenges to the existing rationale and structure of wage fixing by establishing the Women's Employment Board (WEB) in May 1942. WEB's authority was limited. Its decisions were confined to the period of the war and were not applicable to traditional pre-war women's work; moreover, employers sought and found ways of avoiding compliance with its determinations.

---

32   NCWA, *Report of Biennial Conference Held in Melbourne, Victoria, January 21st to 23rd, 1941*, pp. 14–15.
33   NCWA Board Minutes, 27 February, 6 and 13 March 1942, Box 12, MS7583, NCWA Papers, NLA.

Awards made by WEB to the comparatively small proportion of women taking over men's jobs—just 9 per cent of the female workforce—were between 60 and 90 per cent of the male rate. It only rarely awarded equal pay.[34] Those in jobs traditionally done by women still mostly got the 54 per cent awarded by Justice Higgins in 1912, though war-time loadings and overtime saw higher wages for many, especially in textiles and clothing.[35]

NCWA's view was that all women war workers and especially those in the fighting services should be awarded equal pay and the board referred the question to all state councils to elicit their support.[36] Though the Labor Party had paid lip service to equal pay while in opposition, Curtin's government was not going to sacrifice the huge savings it made from paying most women in the military only 56 per cent of the male rate, even where the same tasks were performed. An appeal to patriotism and the provision of uniforms would, they believed, attract enough women to the auxiliary and other services without offering equal pay.[37] NCWA took up some small cases of wage injustice and loss of status incurred by professional women transferred from one part of the armed services to another—from the medical corps to the women's medical corps for example—but had little impact.[38]

Although some sections of the union movement supported equal pay during the war years, others did not, and the Australian Council of Trade Unions took the middle course of accepting WEB determinations while supporting equal pay in principle. When WEB was disbanded

---

34 Kate Darian-Smith, *On the Home Front: Melbourne in Wartime 1939–1945*, Melbourne, Oxford University Press, 1990, pp. 62–4.
35 Marian Aveling [Quartly] and Joy Damousi (eds), *Stepping out of History: Documents of Women at Work in Australia*, Sydney, Allen & Unwin, 1991, p. 136; Darian-Smith, *On the Home Front*, p. 65.
36 NCWA Board Minutes, 29 June 1942, Box 12, MS7583, NCWA Papers, NLA; Norris, *Champions*, p. 85.
37 Darian-Smith, *On the Home Front*, pp. 61–2.
38 NCWA Board Minutes, 5 and 19 August 1943, 16 March 1944, Box 12, MS7583, NCWA Papers, NLA.

and responsibility for all women's wages was shifted back to the arbitration court in 1944, WEB processes continued to be followed and the case for equal pay was arguably thereby impeded.[39] Towards the end of the war, there was general support on the NCWA board for the Queensland council's request that the federal government be asked to legislate a minimum female wage rate of 75 per cent of the male standard but with the proviso that it be seen as a step towards equal pay for the sexes.[40] This was discussed at the 1946 conference, where the rate for the job with allowances for dependants was proposed again as an alternative to equal pay based on the existing family wage system, but conference decided not to press that particular issue. Instead, delegates agreed on a letter to the prime minister congratulating him on his stated intention of advancing the female rate of pay to 75 per cent of the male rate, but only 'as a step towards the aims of the A.N.C.W. ... equal pay for similar work'.[41] The convenor for trades and professions meanwhile noted that much of the war-time work for women in the trades no longer existed and, although women in the professions were 'in a slightly better position' with respect to continued availability of work, in 'very few cases are the salaries offered to women equal to those of men'.[42] As historian Kate Darian-Smith has concluded, women were not 'abruptly ejected' from the workforce so much as consigned to the traditional pre-war female occupations where the fight for equal pay had not progressed during the war years.[43]

Little change occurred in the immediate post-war years. As NCWA secretary Hilda Brotherton observed at the 1948 conference in Brisbane, 'So far equality of pay in industry and in the Public Services (together

---

39   Darian-Smith, *On the Home Front*, pp. 64–5.
40   NCWA Board Minutes, 1 August 1945, Box 13, MS7583, NCWA Papers, NLA.
41   NCWA, *Report of Biennial Conference Held in Melbourne, October 15th–18th, 1946*, p. 26.
42   NCWA, *Report of Biennial Conference Held in Melbourne, October 15th–18th, 1946*, p. 13.
43   Darian-Smith, *On the Home Front*, p. 67.

RIGHTS, EQUALITY AND INTERNATIONAL AFFAIRS

with equal opportunity for advancement) has not yet been achieved'.[44] There was, however, a gradual acceptance by the Arbitration Court of the 75 per cent standard for women's wage determinations, and, at the 1949–50 basic wage enquiry, women's base rate was formally set at 75 per cent of a man's. NCWA joined many women's organisations in intervening—though in rather tokenistic terms—it being agreed that international secretary Marie Breen should write to the court requesting intervention to make a statement that equal pay had long been on the platform of the Australian councils and ICW.[45]

The council's next intervention, to protect the 75 per cent determination from a concerted assault by employers at the 1952/53 hearing, was a much more serious and detailed one conducted in concert with the Australian Federation of Business and Professional Women.[46] Throughout NCWA's fight for equal pay during this period, advocates always used their obligation to ICW policy to bolster their argument. So it was particularly galling for the 1948 conference to hear that Australia had voted against equal pay in the forums of the United Nations, despite being signatories to the UN Charter.[47] It was even more so for Elsie Byth, as delegate to the Commission for the Status of Women in 1949; not only was she forced to abstain, she also had to argue a case she did not believe in conformity with Australian government policy.

Peace, Disarmament and International Co-operation

The creation of NCWA in 1931 saw the national body assume primary responsibility for co-ordinating international policy. The board of

---

44 NCWA, Minutes of Biennial Conference of the National Council of Women of Australia, Held in Brisbane September 1st–3rd 1948, typescript, NCWV Papers, SLV (classification pending).
45 NCWA Board Minutes, 28 November 1949, Box 12, MS7583, NCWA Papers, NLA.
46 Norris, *Champions*, pp. 104–05.
47 Presidential Address, NCWA, Minutes of Biennial Conference of the National Council of Women of Australia, Held in Brisbane September 1st–3rd 1948, typescript, NCWV Papers, SLV (classification pending).

officers took its new role seriously. At its third meeting in December, it decided to forward a resolution to the prime minister expressing the view that it was 'of vital importance that an Australian-born woman be appointed to the Disarmament Conference, and one who is qualified by her association with women's work to represent the feelings and ideals of the women of Australia'. NCWA had taken up peace activism in the late 1920s, as we have seen, and had supported the world-wide petition for disarmament organised by the Women's International League for Peace and Freedom. When the request for a woman delegate to the Geneva conference was refused 'due to the financial stringency', the board despatched a letter to the conference with the minister for external affairs and head of Australia's delegation to the league, John Latham. On the suggestion of Lady Aberdeen, a cable was also sent to the conference, due to begin at Geneva in February 1932.[48]

The first NCWA conference in November 1932 also took up international questions with some enthusiasm. Delegates demanded that the Australian government include 'women on all delegations to the League of Nations Assembly or I.L.O. [International Labour Organization] meetings or to other international conferences, and to appoint a woman as full delegate to the Assembly meetings'. In order to assist their work, they voted to request copies of the business papers of the League of Nations assemblies from the government. In addition conference resolved to write both to the secretary general of the league and to the ILO requesting the appointment of more women. A major concern, according to the chair, was the 'gradual attempt to supersede women in all departments of the League'. 'This Australian conference' was thus determined to 'strengthen the hands of the I.C.W. and all women's international organisations overseas by pressing for the carrying out not only in spirit but in action of Article 7' of the League of Nations Covenant, known as the 'women's charter'. With Secretary General Sir

---

48 NCWA Board Minutes, 21 December 1931 and 23 February 1932, Box 12, MS7583, NCWA Papers, NLA.

RIGHTS, EQUALITY AND INTERNATIONAL AFFAIRS

Eric Drummond's term of office coming to an end, concern mounted that the league's previous sympathy with women's organisations and claims for equality would weaken in the transition from a British secretary general to a French one.[49]

Despite this rush of enthusiasm, NCWA's international work was constrained by continuing hostility to Bessie Rischbieth and the Australian Women's Co-operating Committee (AWCC) she had initiated. Refusal to join restricted NCWA's ability to take advantage of the 1931 League of Nations resolution to co-operate with women's organisations, and also limited its capacity to influence the choice of Australia's alternate delegate to league assemblies. Pressure came in the form of a letter from ICW president Lady Aberdeen in July 1932. In it she urged NCWA to confer with the Co-operating Committee, and the NSW council also counselled working together. Since ICW's chosen agents of co-operation for lobbying the League of Nations were the Joint Standing Committee of Women's International Organisations, formed in 1925, and, from 1931, the Liaison Committee of Women's International Organisations, Aberdeen saw no advantage in double-handling by keeping open separate channels with all the constituent national councils on these matters. Given that AWCC was modelled on the Joint Standing Committee, it made sense for it to be the sole channel for League of Nations and Joint Standing Committee communication with Australian women.[50] Only after NCWA finally swallowed its pride and agreed to become a full member of AWCC in January 1934 was a national council nominee, May Couchman, once again appointed

---

49 NCWA Conference Minutes, November 1932, Box 11, MS7583, NCWA Papers, NLA.
50 NCWA Board Minutes, 13 July 1932, 15 August 1932, Box 12, MS7583, NCWA Papers, NLA. The Joint Standing Committee of Women's International Organisations dealt specifically with appointments of women to League of Nations bodies, while the Liaison Committee had a much broader brief. Originally a subcommittee of the Liaison Committee, the Disarmament (later Peace and Disarmament) Committee, formed to agitate at the League of Nations Disarmament Conference in 1933, took on a life of its own under the leadership of Mary Dingman.

to Australia's League of Nations delegation.[51] NCWA's May Moss accepted the presidency of the Co-operating Committee soon after—an appropriate recognition, the councils believed, of their representative status.[52]

Hopes for disarmament faded with Germany's withdrawal from the Geneva conference and the League of Nations in October 1933, leaving more limited arbitration work and the idea of 'collective security' as the only realistic options for maintaining peace between nations. Doubts about the league's continuing efficacy were evident in NCWA president May Moss's address to conference delegates in 1935. Referring to Italian actions in Abyssinia, she noted that 'before we have really settled to what peace is like … we are on the brink of something which may darken our spiritual and mental horizon perhaps for a long time to come'. The only gleam of hope', she concluded,

> is the fact that our Empire, and the heart of the Empire in Great Britain, is going to stand firm to … Article 16 of the League of Nations … Great Britain could be trusted, and it made one proud to think they belonged, as a unit, to such a nation.[53]

The conference then agreed, on the motion of Mildred Muscio, to a resolution that the Australian government should follow 'the precedent set by the British Government' and 'immediately appoint a Minister without Portfolio for the League of Nations affairs', a suggestion Muscio argued was 'more practical' than a ministry for peace: 'There was nothing like strengthening the one instrument they had in the world for collective security'. They also agreed to endorse a similar resolution from

---

51 NCWA Board Minutes, 18 January 1934, and 21 May 1934, Box 12, MS7583, NCWA Papers, NLA.
52 NCWA Conference Melbourne November 1934, Box 11, MS7583, NCWA Papers, NLA.
53 Presidential Address, NCWA Conference Minutes, August 1935, Box 11, MS7583, NCWA Papers, NLA. Article 16 refers to sanctions and collective contribution to armed forces to protect the Covenants of the League should any member of the League resort to war in disregard of articles 12, 13 and 15 stipulating measures for resolution of disputes.

the Australian League of Nations Union, which further 'urge[d] the Commonwealth Government to instruct the Australian representative to stand solidly behind the representative of the British Government'.[54] Significantly, Muscio was appointed Australia's alternate delegate to the league in 1937.

In the final years before the outbreak of the second world war, NCWA continued to give its support to ICW resolutions about peace and the need to support the League of Nations. At the 1936 Adelaide conference, it endorsed the international council's 'deep disappointment' with the failure of statesmen to 'maintain the main object of the League—the preservation of peace', but also supported its appeal to members for their 'unflinching allegiance to the principles of the League' by bringing 'their influence to bear on Governments'. It gave its backing too to ICW's call for a new peace settlement and a reinvigorated league, affirming 'wholehearted opposition to war, and its faith in international collaboration for promotion of peace and the common welfare'.[55] As late as 1938, Mildred Muscio, now returned from her time in Geneva, reiterated that 'the necessity for standing by the League was greater than ever', since 'it offered the only expression of the great ideal of working together for the benefit of all'.[56] Conference that year again reaffirmed 'its adherence to the principles of international co-operation and arbitration in the cause of peace', and appealed to women 'not to lose their vision or courage, but to exert their collective influence on behalf of justice, peace and harmony among the nations of the world'.[57] But by this time NCWA seems mostly to have retreated from involvement in the broader peace movement at home, and its leaders increasingly advocated taking closer shelter under the umbrella of Britain both within the league and outside. When war finally broke out in September, council's resolution

---

54   NCWA Conference Minutes, August 1935, Box 11, MS7583, NCWA Papers, NLA.
55   *Advertiser*, 17 September 1936.
56   *Argus*, 15 September 1938.
57   *Argus*, 17 September 1938.

of loyalty was sent to 'His Majesty and His Majesty's Government ... in support of the stand taken by Great Britain'.[58] A lone dissentient was the convenor of the NSW council's Peace and Arbitration Committee, Madeline Wood, who, unable to reconcile support for war with her position, tendered her resignation as an acknowledgement of failure.[59]

War and the Fragmentation of International Links

World War II fragmented the international women's movement, including the international council, even more seriously than did the Great War. In Europe, ICW fell victim to the rapid spread of German occupation forces from 1939, many of its leaders fleeing, joining resistance movements or disappearing, while national councils on the continent mostly collapsed. The president, Baroness Marthe Boël of Belgium, transferred the presidency to Switzerland's Renée Girod in April 1940 in the wake of German invasion and occupation of her homeland. Temporary headquarters were set up in Geneva, and London also took on a leadership role, as did the United States. Relations between London and Geneva were not always harmonious but contacts were maintained with and between councils in unoccupied countries and outside Europe.[60] In May 1940, NCWA sent messages to all the European councils except Germany and Italy and, after many months, received replies from Dr Girod, Countess Apponyi in Hungary, and Lady Nunburnholme in Britain. The councils everywhere else 'were stricken into silence' and ICW communications were limited to a 'valiant little news-sheet' from London and 'a brave but attenuated form of the International Bulletin' from Geneva. NCWA nevertheless decided that

---

58   NCWA Board Minutes, 7 September 1939, Box 12, MS7583, NCWA Papers, NLA.
59   NCWA Board Minutes, 26 October and 5 December 1939, Box 12, MS7583, NCWA Papers, NLA.
60   Catherine Jacques and Sylvie Lefebvre, 'The Working Methods of the ICW from its Creation to the Second World War', in Eliane Gubin and Leen Van Molle (eds), *Women Changing the World: A History of the International Council of Women*, Brussels, Éditions Racine, 2005, pp. 113–20.

the Australian national councils 'should continue to pay their fees into an accumulating fund which would be a great help to the I.C.W., when the war was over'.[61]

While acknowledging that 'the need is greater than ever for international co-operation', NCWA leaders' Anglo-Australian loyalism remained uppermost in their hearts and minds during the war years. Messages were sent to the King and Queen and the British government conveying their loyalty and 'the sympathy and prayers of the women of Australia'. Their 'first and foremost effort', said president Adelaide Miethke, must be to 'add to the national effort of Australia' and to 'fight the good fight—for democracy'. The councils of Europe would be rescued and 'would rise again when Britain and her kinsmen have dealt with the aggressor'. NCWA was regretful that the ICW conference planned for Australia in 1942 would not now go ahead and hoped that it was 'only postponed, not cancelled'. Miethke nevertheless saw opportunities in the demise of the European councils for the international council movement to be 'rebuilt, in a newer design, maybe—more modern in its ideas, more vigorous'. And Australia could play a key part in that process. Miethke envisioned a new role for NCWA and its constituents as regional leaders and agents for change, perhaps even for re-centring the international council.[62] But, in the immediate context of war, the resolution passed on the subject by the conference in Melbourne in January 1941 can also be interpreted as offering NCWA's networks for propagandising the allied and national cause. It was, they agreed,

> desirable that the A.N.C. should awaken to the responsibility of its geographical position as a regional centre, and take steps to contact the Councils of South Africa, Rhodesia, Egypt, New Zealand, Burma, India, Netherlands East Indies, Chile, Argentina, Peru, Brazil and any other councils established in

---

61 NCWA, *Report of Biennial Conference Held in Melbourne, Victoria, January 21st to 23rd, 1941*, pp. 2–3, 14.
62 NCWA, *Report of Biennial Conference Held in Melbourne, Victoria, January 21st to 23rd, 1941*, pp. 3, 7.

the region with the idea of presenting to them the Australian point of view on current affairs and promoting closer friendship and understanding with the idea of ultimate co-operation.⁶³

Each of the state councils was then assigned a contact with one or more of these countries' councils and asked to prepare and send a newsletter as the first step to more extended and detailed communication of 'what we are doing, and why we are doing it'.⁶⁴ However, much of Southeast Asia and the nearest Pacific countries were overrun by the Japanese from the end of 1941 and the Pan Pacific conference movement collapsed, so realisation of these ambitions was constrained. Although NCWA interest in the Pacific region resurfaced in the years after the war, as we shall see, concrete moves to become the regional centre for a cluster of national councils only began to take form in the 1960s and 70s.

The other major pre-war focus for council's internationalist activism, the League of Nations, lost its purpose when the war started in earnest in 1939, though it continued reduced operations through the secretary general. While some associated bodies such as the International Labour Organization continued to function, NCWA made no effort to work through them in the absence of ICW and the Liaison Committee of Women's International Organisations as mediators. The league assembly did not meet again until April 1946 when it dissolved itself and handed over its assets to the new United Nations. NCWA had expressed its 'satisfaction' that the Australian substitute delegate to the League of Nations for 1940 was 'once again a member of the National Council'. But Mrs Paul McGuire, assistant secretary to the board, was, of course, now unable to take up the position. NCWA conferences kept alive the principles of the league on peace negotiations, and those of ICW on gender equality,

---

63   *Argus*, 24 January 1941; NCWA, *Report of Biennial Conference Held in Melbourne, Victoria, January 21st to 23rd 1941*, p. 19.
64   NCWA, *Report of Biennial Conference Held in Melbourne, Victoria, January 21st to 23rd 1941*, pp. 20–21.

resolving in 1941 'That when the time arises for a Peace Conference, women be represented thereon and given full voting rights'. Further clauses instructed the board to convey the resolution to the federal government, ICW and all other councils 'inviting co-operation at the right time'. In discussing post-war reconstruction, conference delegates also recommended League of Nations research reports in order to establish 'basic principles' for a program of action.[65] But, given the comparative isolation from traditional international sources of influence and the threat posed by war in the Pacific, NCWA and the constituent national councils turned their focus inwards for the remainder of the war and devoted most of their energies to supporting the national war effort.

Post-war International Revival

Elsie Byth's board cabled the United Nations conference at San Francisco in 1945 to adopt the principle of equal status and opportunity for women,[66] restored ICW contacts, revived the Australian Liaison Committee (formerly AWCC), and took an initially hostile NCWA into the newly established Australian National Council for the United Nations (ANCUN). The Australian council soon became the dominant women's voice in ANCUN, effectively sidelining Jessie Street and, in the process, tagging her as a communist sympathiser. Finally, in September 1948, Byth organised a 'Pacific Assembly'—the NCWA's first serious engagement with the Asia-Pacific region.[67] Byth

---

65 NCWA, *Report of Biennial Conference Held in Melbourne, Victoria, January 21st to 23rd 1941*, pp. 3, 13–14, 18, 20–21; NCWA Board Minutes, 12 February 1941, Box 12, MS7583, NCWA Papers, NLA.

66 AFWV and other Australian women's organisations associated with the Women's Charter movement did so too. Marilyn Lake, *Getting Equal: The History of Australian Feminism*, Sydney, Allen & Unwin, 1999, p. 191.

67 NCWA Board Minutes, February1945 – December 1948, Box 13, MS7583, NCWA Papers, NLA; 'Elsie Byth', *Stirrers with Style! Presidents of the National Council of Women of Australia and Its Predecessors*, http://www.womenaustralia.info/exhib/ncwa/presidents-06.html.

herself, in the wake of her NCWA presidency, became the second Australian delegate to the UN Commission for the Status of Women (CSW) in 1949, thus beginning a pattern of NCW dominance of this role.

ICW Reconnection

By early 1946, the International Council of Women was re-emerging, though not without conflict and difficulties. These related to the wartime friction between the London and Geneva centres, to the delicate problem of the reaffiliation of councils in former Nazi and Fascist countries, and to the problem of councils in Eastern Bloc countries being taken over by the new Women's International Democratic Federation (WIDF), which ICW increasingly saw as a threat to its international influence. Given WIDF's claim to represent 80 million women, this threat was not without substance. In May, the councils of Canada and the United States of America organised a conference in New York on the future of ICW and the international solidarity of women generally, and a reduced executive met in Brussels in June. Contacts were made with representatives of the United Nations Organisation and its specialised agencies, and, in March 1947, ICW was accorded consultative status B with the UN Economic and Social Council (ECOSOC) (elevated to A in 1968). Soon the constituent councils were asked to consider how best to implement a resolution from a meeting of non-government organisations with consultative status that national governments should consult affiliates to such NGOs in their own countries.[68] This was to remain a problem for NCWA, which constantly demanded information and reports from the Australian government, as well as

---

68 Catherine Jacques and Sylvie Lefebvre, 'In the Wake of the United Nations Organisation: The Reconstruction and New Working Methods from the Second World War up to the Present', in Gubin and Van Molle (eds), *Women Changing the World*, pp. 121–32; NCWA, Minutes of Biennial Conference of the National Council of Women of Australia, Held in Brisbane September 1st–3rd 1948, typescript, NCWV Papers, SLV (classification pending).

consultation rather than instruction about the positions to be adopted at UN forums such as CSW and ILO.

The initial post-war meetings of ICW revived and reorganised its standing committees, requesting national councils to reply to questionnaires from the end of 1945. NCWA responded quickly to these requests, instructing all states to revive their committees or set up new ones, and sending collated reports on child care, suffrage, peace and arbitration, domestic economy, migration and cinema to ICW convenors before the end of 1946. And, although the council could not afford to send a delegation to the first post-war conference in Philadelphia in 1947, it was represented by NCWNSW's Joyce Cocks, who was visiting America at the time. Titles of standing committees were subsequently changed to accord with the new nomenclature adopted in Philadelphia and names of all the convenors collated for ease of communication. ICW, now centred in Zürich under the presidency of Jeanne Eder, published its first postwar *Bulletin* in May 1948, partly to counter the threat of WIDF among its constituents. NCWA board urged all the state councils to increase the circulation of the *Bulletin* among their members since, apart from standing committee activity and correspondence, 'it was the chief means of making the I.C.W. real to us here in Australia where we are largely deprived of personal contacts so invaluable in international work'.[69]

The Liaison Committee, ANCUN and the UN Status of Women Commission

In the years after the Second World War, NCWA and ICW both found themselves challenged from the left wing of the women's movement, and both responded by setting up avenues for co-operation with more centrally placed organisations. At the international level, ICW was now

---

69   Jacques and Lefebvre, 'In the Wake of the United Nations Organisation', pp. 121–32; NCWA Board Minutes, 6 February 1946, Box 13, MS7583, NCWA Papers, NLA; NCWA, *Report of Biennial Conference Held in Melbourne, October 15th–18th, 1946*, pp. 8–10; NCWA, Minutes of Biennial Conference of the National Council of Women of Australia, Held in Brisbane September 1st–3rd 1948, typescript, NCWV Papers, SLV (classification pending).

competing with dozens of internationally based women's organisations to claim consultative status with the United Nations.

The international council responded by reviving the London-based Liaison Committee of Women's International Organisations (ILC), originally established to bring women's affairs before the League of Nations, and now intended to handle relations with the UN.[70] NCWA followed this lead and revived the Australian Committee of the Liaison Committee of Women's International Organisations (ALC). Invitations were accepted by the national presidents of all the Australian women's organisations with international representation: the Australian Federation of University Women, the Young Women's Christian Association, the Girl Guides, the Woman's Christian Temperance Union, the Australian Federation of Women Voters (AFWV), the Australian Nursing Federation and the Country Women's Association. Others such as the St Joan's International Alliance and the Business and Professional Women's Club joined a little later. The first meeting, chaired by Elsie Byth, took place in Sydney in April 1947 and a delegate from ILC, Australia-based Betty Archdale, was also present to explain 'the need for increased watchfulness in the present U.N. set-up' and the greater effectiveness of approaches made by an international body with consultative status than by national bodies acting alone.[71]

ALC, like AWCC before it, was intended to function as the channel through which women's organisations could co-operate to advise the federal and state governments on the appointment of women to state, regional, national and international committees, as well as representing women's views on questions of international importance. Of particular import was the appointment of Australian representatives to United

---

70 President's Address, NCWA, Minutes of Biennial Conference of the National Council of Women of Australia, Held in Brisbane September 1st–3rd 1948, typescript, NCWV Papers, SLV (classification pending).

71 NCWA Board Minutes, 20 November 1946, Box 12, MS7583, NCWA Papers, NLA; ALC Minutes, 11 April, 27 June, and 22 July 1947, Box 1, MS1082, Liaison Committee of Women's International Organisations, Australian Group, 1947–1963 (ALC) Records, NLA.

RIGHTS, EQUALITY AND INTERNATIONAL AFFAIRS

Nations committees and commissions. Nevertheless, when AFWV delegate Ruby Rich asked if Jessie Street's proposal for another organisation to arrange representation on the UN Commission on the Status of Women (CSW) would duplicate ALC work, she was told that the liaison committee's work was broader and co-operation with Street would be unproblematic.[72] This was not to be the case.

Jessie Street, long-term president of Sydney's United Associations of Women, had organised the Women's Charter Conference on post-war reconstruction in 1943 and upstaged NCWA in doing so. She had also been selected against NCWA nominations as Australia's only woman delegate to the first UN gathering in San Francisco in 1945, where she was instrumental, with others, in having gender equality written into the UN Charter and laying the foundation for CSW. Street organised a further large Australian Women's Charter Conference in Sydney in 1946. Having attracted a wide array of national representatives as well as a substantial international contingent, she again succeeded in putting NCWA's claims to represent Australian women into the shade. The Australian council stood aloof. Street was subsequently appointed Australia's first representative to CSW, which met initially at Lake Success, New York, in February 1947.

Street played a significant role in the work of CSW, especially in the redrafting of the Universal Declaration of Human Rights in new inclusive language.[73] But she also attended the founding congress of WIDF in Paris in 1945 and remained involved even as suspicions deepened during the Cold War that it was a tool of the Soviet Union, and she took on the presidency of the Australian Russian Society in 1946. For these reasons, she was seen by significant sections of the Australian women's

---

72 ALC Minutes, 11 April 1947, Box 1, MS1082, ALC Records, NLA.
73 Heather Radi, 'Street, Jessie Mary (1889–1970)', *Australian Dictionary of Biography* (*ADB*), http://adb.anu.edu.au/biography/street-jessie-mary-11789/text21089; Lake, *Getting Equal*, pp. 191–8; NCWA Board Minutes, 19 June 1946, Box 13, MS7583, NCWA Papers, NLA; *Short History of the Commission on the Status of Women*, http://www.un.org/womenwatch/daw/CSW60YRS/index.htm.

movement as having moved too far to the left on the political spectrum; she had, moreover, alienated former allies in the Australian Federation of Women Voters, including Bessie Rischbieth, and the AFWV now found itself in much greater sympathy with NCWA than had been the case since its foundation over two decades earlier.[74]

These dissensions were aggravated by Street's apparent determination in mid-1947 to push forward with her own reporting organisation for UN and CSW matters, to be drawn from Women's Charter movement participants, and to ignore the existence of ALC as an appropriate co-ordinating body. Press reports and ALC minutes allude to deliberate attempts to exclude Liaison Committee representatives from meetings she called to set up the alternative body.[75] ALC letters to the minister for external affairs and the prime minister claimed a right to recognition as the appropriate organisation for CSW matters. Meanwhile, Labor Senator Dorothy Tangney had also protested to Mr Chifley about Street's re-appointment to CSW and introduced a deputation of representative women, including NCWWA's Mrs Pratt and AFWV's Bessie Rischbieth as well as trade unionists, to contest the appropriateness of the choice as well as the exclusion of ALC from consultations. Elsie Byth followed this up with a letter to the prime minister laying out NCWA's position, and the board engaged in further correspondence with Tangney as well as new Liberal Senator Annabelle Rankin. For all Street's achievements at the UN, the government could not ignore the opposition from a wide range of organisations in the women's movement to Street's continuing role. It was decided not to renew her appointment to the second session of CSW, and instead to call for nominations from the broad spectrum of women's associations.[76]

---

74 Radi, 'Street'; Lenore Coltheart, 'Citizens of the World: Jessie Street and International Feminism', *Hecate*, 31, 2005, pp. 182–94; NCWA Board Minutes, 19 June 1946, Box 13, MS7583, NCWA Papers, NLA.
75 ALC Minutes, 13, 24 and 27 June, 10, 15, 22 and 25 July 1947, Box 1, MS1082, ALC Records, NLA.
76 ALC Minutes, 15 and 25 July, 1 August, 9 September, 17 October 1947, Box 1, MS1082, ALC Records, NLA; NCWA Board Minutes, 2 and 19 July, 6 and 20

RIGHTS, EQUALITY AND INTERNATIONAL AFFAIRS

The national councils initially forwarded their nominations through the Australian Liaison Committee, but were promptly informed that the federal government wished to receive them through a co-ordinating committee set up by the government itself, the Australian National Council of the United Nations (ANCUN). The government established and funded this new peak body to give reliable and non-controversial advice on matters relating to the United Nations, and, in November 1947, invited eleven non-government organisations, including NCWA, to participate. Embracing this new opportunity, Elsie Byth took a position on the executive committee.[77] When the Australian Liaison Committee protested the loss of its function to ANCUN, the NCWA board suggested that ALC should 'go into recess during the active functioning of ANCUN, as we hear the position causes the Government great confusion': 'ANCUN should be given a chance to prove itself, and in the meantime the ALC should not attempt to dictate to Canberra'. After all, there was considerable duplication of personnel.[78]

This advice was perhaps somewhat disingenuous. The board had already submitted its nominations through ANCUN, and may well have been confident of success. Isabel McCorkindale, the national president of the Woman's Christian Temperance Union, wrote to the Department of External Affairs in December 1948 complaining that NCWA was exercising undue influence within ANCUN.

> I understand that at the meeting of the Federal Committee of ANCUN, held last week in Melbourne, a small committee was appointed to screen names sent forward to the Department of External Affairs, of women considered suitable for appointment as delegates to meetings of UNO.

August 1947, Box 13, MS7583, NCWA Papers, NLA.

77   NCWA Board Minutes, 5 November 1947, 16 December 1948, Box 13, MS7583, NCWA Papers, NLA.
78   NCWA Board Minutes, 10 February 1949, Box 13, MS7583, NCWA Papers, NLA.

It would seem that with one exception all are officers of the
National Council of Women.[79]

McCorkindale's ire arose from the fact that she was a contender for the
CSW position, with strong support amongst Women's Charter organisations, especially in Victoria and Western Australia. In the event, the
government decided to appoint Elsie Byth, recently retired as NCWA
president. But McCorkindale's complaint won her the consolation
prize. When the prime minister announced Byth's appointment to the
Third Session of the Status of Women Commission, he simultaneously
announced McCorkindale's appointment as delegate to the Fourth
Session in 1950.[80]

Byth's instructions made it clear that as an Australian representative
she would have to 'acquaint herself thoroughly with the matters to be
discussed at the sessions and the Government's views thereon ... [and
would] not commit the Australian government on any specific issue
unless authorised to do so'.[81] In several matters, the government's views
did not coincide with those of the national councils, and Byth, like her
predecessors at the League of Nations and her successors to CSW, had to
argue cases that the association did not support. One such case was the
proposed Convention on the nationality of married women, a right that
the Australian government now applied to its own citizens, as we have
seen, but opposed as a universal obligation on the grounds that it might
interfere with the operation of its racially selective immigration policy.[82]
The issue of equal pay was just as difficult. Byth found herself attempting
to divert Russian criticism of the entrenched differences in male and female

---

79 Isabel McCorkindale to Dr Burton, 4 December 1948, Folder 'UN—Status of Women Commission—4th Session', A1838 (A1838/283), National Archives of Australia (NAA).
80 Memo for Minister of External Affairs, 27 February 1950, Folder 'UN—Status of Women Commission—4th Session', A1838 (A1838/283), NAA.
81 John Dedman (for the PM) to Mrs I. Brookes, President NCWA, 13 January 1949, Folder 1: 1949–52, Correspondence 1936–71, MS5193, NCWA Papers, NLA.
82 Secretary Immigration Department to Secretary External Affairs, 15 March 1949, Folder 'Preparation for Delegation to Lebanon, Feb. – March 1949', Status of Women Commission, Department of External Affairs, A1838/1, 856/15/5/4, NAA.

wages in Australia by arguing that an appropriately assessed 'family wage' would remove the need for married women to work in order to 'supplement the family income'. It was not a position she believed, but, as instructed, she abstained from voting on the resolution supporting equal pay.[83] These issues continued to vex the women delegates appointed to the commission in this period—McCorkindale in 1950, and Jean Daly from the Catholic St Joan's Alliance in 1951.

The deepening Cold War exacerbated the problems of international engagement. NCWA became involved in the political controversy that erupted over the abduction of some 28,000 Greek children by communist-affiliated guerrilla troops in 1947–48 during the Greek Civil War. The National Council of Women of Greece wrote to NCWA early in 1948 asking for help to recover children 'who had already been forcibly removed to communist controlled countries'.[84] NCWA immediately took up the cause, forwarding the letters to the ICW president and UN secretary general, as well as to the minister for external affairs, H.V. Evatt, with a request for investigation by the UN Commission for Human Rights.[85] In his reply, Evatt assured the councils that the UN special committee for the Balkans had investigated the matter and the states concerned had been instructed to return the children to their homes.[86] Evatt was central in pushing several resolutions on this issue through the UN in his capacity as president of the UN General Assembly 1948–49. But, as the problem dragged on into 1950–51, the councils began to have doubts about pursuing it. In the context of attempts by the new Menzies Liberal government to ban the Communist Party in Australia, Cold

---

83 'Elsie Byth', *Stirrers with Style!*
84 NCWA, Minutes of Biennial Conference of the National Council of Women of Australia, Held in Brisbane September 1st–3rd 1948, typescript, NCWV Papers, SLV (classification pending).
85 NCWA Board Minutes, 10 March 1948, Box 13, MS5783, NCWA Papers, NLA; NCWA, Minutes of Biennial Conference of the National Council of Women of Australia, Held in Brisbane September 1st–3rd 1948, typescript, NCWV Papers, SLV (classification pending).
86 NCWQ Executive Minutes, 19 July 1948, Box 16045, 7266 NCWQ Minute Books, NCWQ Papers, State Library of Queensland (SLQ).

War polarities became more extreme. Newspapers reporting reunions of some of the children with parents who had since migrated to Australia emphasised their exposure to communist brainwashing; in November 1951, NCWA board member Ada Norris, who was on the government's Immigration Advisory Committee, warned of the 'need for utmost caution' in any move to aid abducted Greek children, 'especially where these children had possibly been Communist indoctrinated'.[87]

Steps towards Regional Identity

Although Elsie Byth can be credited with NCWA's first serious engagement with the Asia-Pacific region in 1948, some earlier groundwork had been carried out through the Pan Pacific Women's Conference movement. Australia's Georgina Sweet was the first president of the Pan Pacific Women's Association formed in 1930, and she represented YWCA at the final conference of the Federated Council of the National Councils of Women of Australia (FCNCWA) in 1931. At her urging, the federal council agreed to maintain its observer status with the local Pan Pacific committee while state councils were asked to consider the desirability of full membership. Victoria's council assumed responsibility for representing the federal body at the Melbourne-based committee meetings and all councils were kept informed about events and topics of discussion.[88] With the formation of NCWA and its assumption of responsibility for international matters, the executive agreed to become a full member of the Pan Pacific Women's Committee in January 1934. And, when NCWA president May Moss became chair of the Australian Women's Co-operating Committee, which oversaw appointment of Australian delegations to Pan Pacific conferences and other international gatherings, Sweet expressed her 'very great joy'

---

87 Joy Damousi, 'Aileen Fitzpatrick, UN, International Refugees', paper presented at Women and Leadership Conference, 2 December 2011, Museum of Australian Democracy, Canberra; NCWA Board Minutes, 9 November 1951, Box 13, MS7583, NCWA Papers, NLA.

88 FCNCWA Conference Minutes, January 1931, Box 12, MS7583, NCWA Papers, NLA; NCWA Conference Minutes, November 1932, Box 11, MS7583, NCWA Papers, NLA.

at the appointment.[89] The council's leaders were therefore conversant during the 1930s with subjects planned and discussed by the Pan Pacific women's movement both in Australia and at the pre-war conferences. But they did not support holding the conference in Australia when it was suggested,[90] and there is little evidence that they engaged seriously with regional women's interests before the war, May Couchman noting ruefully in 1936 that 'with our minds set on Europe … we forget that we live in the Pacific zone'.[91] Historian Fiona Paisley observes that although Western participants in Pan Pacific meetings commonly used the language of 'inter-cultural exchange' and co-operation, most assumed a Eurocentric guiding role for western women in this relationship.[92] NCWA representatives are unlikely to have questioned this.

Although NCWA voted to continue affiliation with the Pan Pacific Women's Association at the council's January 1941 conference, war in the Pacific caused the abandonment of Pan Pacific conferences and the suspension of the Pan Pacific committee,[93] but it also quickened council's concern to have some influence in the region. With most of Western Europe occupied, NCWA, as we have noted, talked about taking on greater regional responsibility, even before the Japanese attack on Pearl Harbour. The region President Adelaide Miethke had in mind extended, as we have seen, to the Americas, southern Africa, India,

---

89   NCWA Executive Minutes, 18 January 1934, Box 11, MS7583, NCWA Papers, NLA; Pan Pacific Women's Committee Minutes, MS4973, Pan Pacific and Southeast Asia Women's Association of Australia Papers, NLA; NCWA Conference Minutes, November 1934, Box 11, MS7583, NCWA Papers, NLA.

90   NCWA Conference Minutes, November 1934, Box 11, MS7583, NCWA Papers, NLA.

91   NCWA Conference Minutes, September 1936, Box 11, MS7583, NCWA Papers, NLA.

92   Fiona Paisley, 'A Geneva in the Pacific: Reflecting on the First Three Decades of the Pan Pacific and Southeast Asia Women's Association (PPSEAWA)', in Kathryn Kish Sklar and Thomas Dublin (eds), *Women and Social Movements International, 1840 to Present*, http://wasi.alexanderstreet.com/help/view/a_geneva_in_the_pacific_reflecting_on_the_first_three_decades_of_the_panpacific_and_south_east_asia_womens_association_ppseawa.

93   NCWA Board Minutes, 28 June 1940, Box 12, MS7583, NCWA Papers, NLA.

China and Japan, and the Netherlands Indies. However, in the wake of Japan's occupation of much of China and Southeast Asia, council by 1943 was making overtures to just a few Pacific nations for 'a regular interchange of ideas'.[94] Interest quickly revived with the end of the war and the first post-war NCWA conference in October 1946 resolved to consider 'the possibility of establishing a Pan Pacific Committee to bring into closer touch the interests of those countries that border the Pacific'. Minnie Williamson of Victoria suggested it might take the form of a 'Regional Liaison Committee of women's international organisations round the Pacific'.[95]

In order to kick-start Australian claims to leadership in regional engagement, NCWA president Elsie Byth undertook the organisation of a three-day 'Pacific Assembly', held in Brisbane in September 1948. Speakers included the high commissioners of New Zealand, Canada, the Netherlands, Pakistan and Hong Kong and women with experience in Malaya, Indonesia, Siam and Fiji.[96] The assembly brought together politicians, academics, and bureaucrats to speak on topics ranging from democratising Japan to the status of women in the Pacific.[97] Speakers set out the aims of the assembly as 'increasing knowledge, enhancing understanding, promoting an awareness of the dependence upon each other of the Pacific peoples, and arousing a sense of personal interest, greater tolerance, and desire to be "a good neighbour"'. Resolutions were passed suggesting 'the teaching of International affairs in schools and universities, the interchange of students with Pacific countries', and 'that the Governments and peoples of the Commonwealth take a greater interest in Pacific affairs and problems'. Representatives

---

94 NCWA Board Minutes, 16 September 1943, Box 12, MS7583, NCWA Papers, NLA.
95 NCWA, *Report of Biennial Conference Held in Melbourne, October 15th–18th, 1946*, p. 18.
96 NCWQ Council Minutes, 28 July 1948, Box 16045, 7266 NCWQ Minute Books, NCWQ Papers, SLQ.
97 Program, *Pacific Assembly, September 6th, 7th and 8th*, Brisbane Telegraph Typ. Item in A9108, ROLL 10/18, NAA.

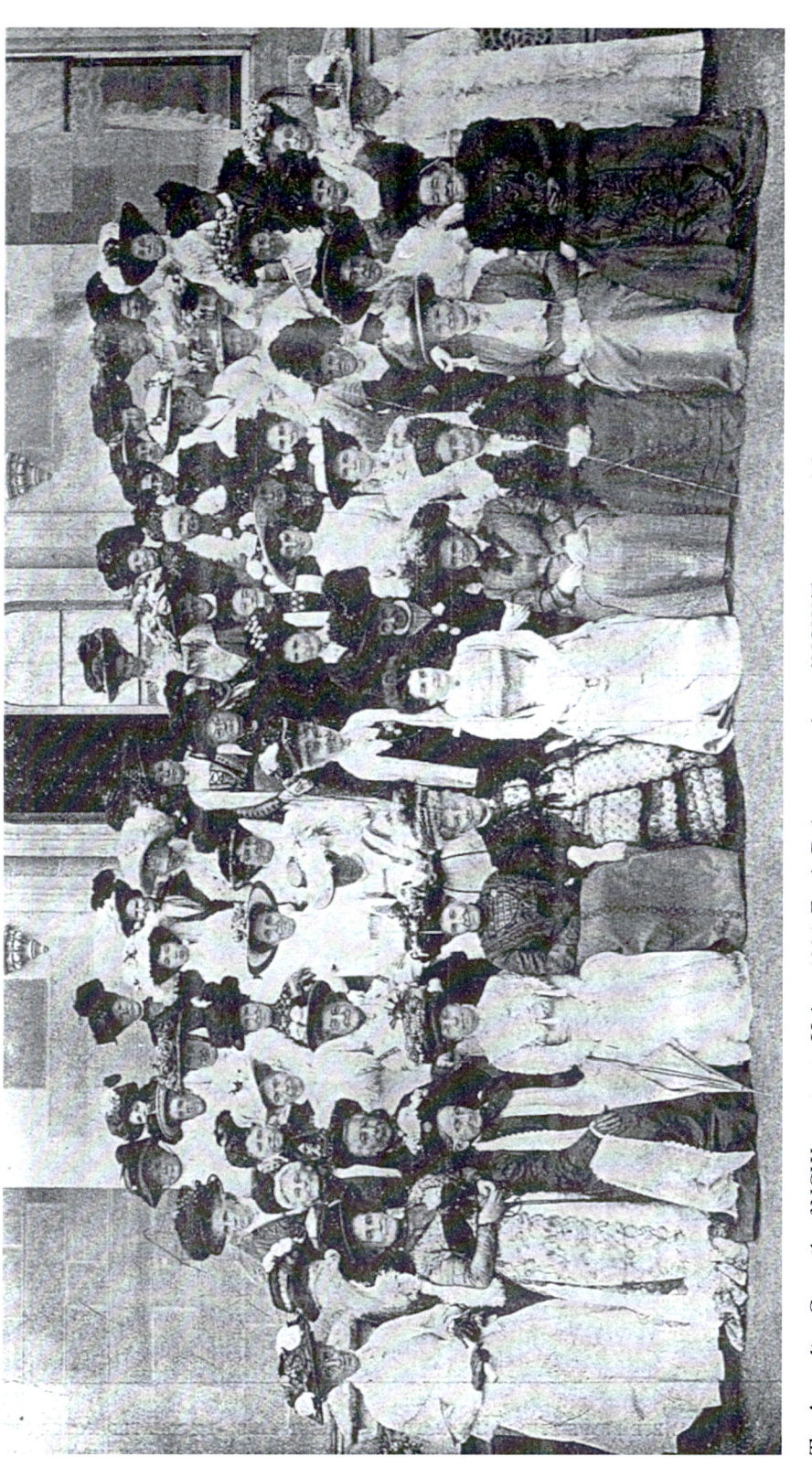

The Australian Councils of NCW meeting in Hobart 1906. Emily Dobson, president of NCW Tasmania and for many years president of Australia's delegation to ICW, is seated 4th from the left in the front row. Courtesy of Naomi Wilson, from the Dobson family collection.

The International Council of Women meeting at the Hague in 1922. Emily Dobson is seated at the table on the far right. Courtesy of Naomi Wilson, from the Dobson family collection

Delegates to the 1928 Annual Meeting of the FCNCWA at a party given by Lady MacCallum at the University of Sydney. Front row (from left to right): Miss E. Tildesley, (Federal Hon. Secretary), Mrs Glencross (Vic.), Mrs Christophers (SA), Mrs Mond (Tas.), Mrs Skene (Vic.), Mrs Muscio (Federal President), Lady MacCallum, Mrs Cumbrae Setwart (Q.), Miss Holmes (WA.), Mrs I.H. Moss (Vic)., Miss Ruby Board (Federal Hon. Treasurer). Miss Poole (SA) is on the extreme right. From the collections of the National Library of Australia.

Members of the NCWA with Dame Maria Ogilvie Gordon in Melbourne in January 1938. Front row (from left to right): Mrs Robertson (Q.), Mrs Muscio (NSW), Mrs Moss (Vic.), Dame Maria Ogilvie Gordon (England), Miss Miethke (SA), Miss Tildesley (NSW) Back row (from left to right): Lady Yseult Bailey, Miss Williamson, Mrs Brookes (Vic.). Second to back row on the left Mrs Couchman (Vic.) and Miss Watson (SA); others unknown. Dame Maria Ogilvie Gordon was a Vice-President of the International Council of Women, and an official guest at the Australian Sesqicentennial Celebrations of 1938. From the Brookes collection, National Library of Australia.

Mrs Tilley from the National Council of Women of Victoria presenting a mobile unit to the Australian Comforts Fund. Mrs Herbert Brookes accepts the unit on behalf of the Australian Comforts Fund. Melbourne, Victoria, 3 November 1943. From the collection of the Australian War Memorial.

Mrs Brookes and her board at the 1952 Conference of the Australian National Council of Women. NCWA Board members present, from the left: Miss M.A. Williamson (Life Vice-President); Mrs R.T. Breen (Hon. International Secretary), Mrs F.G. Kumm (Deputy President), Mrs Herbert Brookes (President), Mrs C.H. Hall (Hon. Secretary), Mrs J.G. Norris (Hon. Treasurer), and Mrs A.E. Hall (Assistant Hon. Secretary). From the collection of the National Council of Women of Australia.

Mrs Dorothy Edwards with her NCWA Board members, 1964. From left to right: Mrs E.S. Padman, Mrs W.E. Northey, Mrs J.M. Parker, Alderman D. Edwards President, Mrs L.B. Hooper, Mrs P.M. Hart. From the collection of the National Council of Women of Australia.

NCW ACT reception for government visitor from East Pakistan 1963. Begum Salima Ahmed from East Pakistan (second left) was met in Canberra by NCWACT committee members (from left) Mrs J. Smart, Secretary; Mrs H.G. McConnell, President; and Mrs J. Bourke, Treasurer. From the collection of the National Archives of Australia.

ICW Regional Conference, Brisbane 1964—delegates outside Town Hall. President Dorothy Edwards with delegates to the 1964 International Council of Women Regional Conference in Brisbane. From the collection of the National Archives of Australia.

ICW Regional Conference, Brisbane 1964—delegates with hats. Ruth Gibson (on the left) with two fellow delegates. From the collection of the National Archives of Australia.

NCWA President Necia Moccatta with conference delegates 1988. NCWA members have tentatively identified amongst these delegates Mary Whitehead; Myra Knight; Yvonne Bain; Joyce Murray; Necia Mocatta (centre front); Maureen Giddings; Margaret Davey; Heidi Taylor; Betty Davy; Barbara Grealy; Daryl Feather; Sylvia Gelman; Shirley Hartley; Lois Brock; Phyllis Wilson. From the NCWA collection.

Delegates at Triennial NCWA Conference Melbourne 2000. From the left: Sylvia Gelman NCWV, Gracia Baylor NCWA President. From the NCWA collection.

Delegates at ICW Asian Regional Conference Auckland 2004. From the left: NCWA Past President Judith Parker, NCWA President Leonie Christopherson with Olivia Bunari from NCW Papua New Guinea. From the NCWA collection.

Presidential handover, 8 October 2006, Melbourne. Incoming NCW President Hean Bee Wee, outgoing President Leonie Christopherson. From the NCWA collection.

A selection of NCWA publications and leaflets.

NATIONAL COUNCIL OF WOMEN OF AUSTRALIA INC LTD

THREE MILLION WOMEN THROUGHOUT AUSTRALIA BELONG TO ORGANISATIONS ASSOCIATED WITH THE NATIONAL COUNCIL OF WOMEN OF AUSTRALIA

ACN 061 777 937
AFFILIATED WITH
THE INTERNATIONAL
COUNCIL OF WOMEN

PRESIDENT MRS GRACIA BAYLOR

PATRON (AUSTRALIA)
HER EXCELLENCY LADY DEANE

NATIONAL COUNCIL OF WOMEN OF AUSTRALIA INC LIMITED
ACN 061 777 937

SUITE 1.06
QUEEN VICTORIA
WOMEN'S CENTRE
210 LONSDALE STREET
MELBOURNE
VICTORIA 3000

TELEPHONE
61 3 9662 9177

FACSIMILE
61 3 96629477

EMAIL NCWA@bigpond.com.au

DONNE MOZZAFIATO

SENSIBILIZZAZIONE ALL'ASMA

Il presente opuscolo è stato messo a punto specificamente per le donne di 50 anni e più.

This information is provided with the assistance of the National Council of Women of Australia Inc Ltd

eating disorders

WHAT'S THE STORY?

This brochure includes the true story of one girl's struggle with Bulimia. It might help you to understand why eating disorders affect many young women. Anorexia usually starts when a person is in their early teens but Bulimia is more common among the 17-25 years group.

Eating Disorders Foundation of Victoria (Inc)
1513 High Street, Glen Iris, 3146
Phone: (03) 9885 0318 or toll free
for non-metro callers 1300 550 236
www.eatingdisorders.org.au
edfv@eatingdisorders.org.au

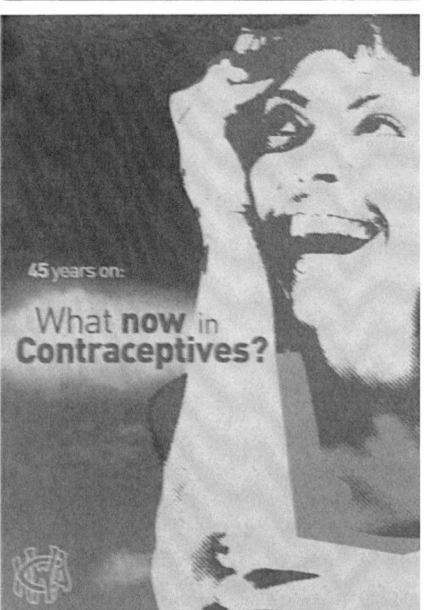

45 years on:

What **now** in **Contraceptives?**

RIGHTS, EQUALITY AND INTERNATIONAL AFFAIRS

of the Commonwealth Investigation Service, ASIO's predecessor, were interested to attend and report the event, it being assumed that engagement with the Asia–Pacific region was potentially subversive.[98]

Although it was sixteen years before another such gathering was organised in Australia, the 1950s saw a rising interest in a regional role for Australia among national council leaders. In April 1950, for example, Minnie Williamson, now a member of Ivy Brookes's board, suggested pursuing the idea of a National Council of Women of the Pacific.[99] A number of council leaders also became involved in reconstituting what became the Pan Pacific and Southeast Asia Women's Association in Australia, and NCWA was keen to send a representative to the first post-war Pan Pacific Women's Conference in New Zealand in 1952. Their choice, appropriately, was Elsie Byth.[100]

The first two decades of NCWA's existence saw an impressive expansion of engagement in international issues ranging from transnational organisational co-operation in strategies for peace and arbitration to exploring possibilities for a closer regional identity. In the process there was a gradual weakening of ties with Britain, a corresponding strengthening of national awareness and common interest among the states, and a tentative reaching out to Pacific and Southeast Asian women. In the post-war years, however, these trends were coloured by the divisions of the Cold War and fears of communism both at home and internationally.

---

98 R.F.B. Wake, Deputy Director, to Director, Commonwealth Investigation Service, Canberra, 16 September 1948, A9108, ROLL 10/18, NAA; 'Elsie Byth', *Stirrers with Style!*
99 NCWA Board Minutes, 28 April 1950, Box 13, MS7583, NCWA Papers, NLA.
100 'Elsie Byth', *Stirrers with Style!*

By 1950, NCWA and its constituent councils had weathered the Great Depression and the challenges of World War II, and, despite major challenges from rival women's coalitions, they were still recognised by government as a force to be respected and consulted. In the period of what has been seen as NCWA's golden age during the 1950s and 60s, council leaders continued to explore strategies, including their international commitment to ICW and UN policies, for redressing inequality and improving social and family welfare in the gradualist manner judged necessary to bring affiliated organisations along with them.

PART THREE
THE GOLDEN YEARS
1950–1970

The 1952 biennial conference of the National Council of Women of Australia opened with a special prayer.

> Oh God, Father of all men, we thank Thee for the International Council of Women, for the vision and wisdom of those who founded and maintained it, and for Thy continued blessing on it throughout its history. We thank Thee for what the International Council of Women has achieved, and for the hopes and possibilities of the future. Grant us here assembled faith and wisdom to do our share of the task in this our land ...
>
> In fellowship with our sisters in the National Councils of Women of many generations and in many countries let us say together the Lord's Prayer.[1]

A reader in the twenty-first century may question the ready assumption here that all the women of the world would want 'fellowship' offered in these terms, would find Christianity relevant to their concerns and needs. But in the middle decades of the twentieth century, the benign maternalism of white Christian women towards their coloured and often heathen 'sisters' was unchallenged and unquestioned. And the internationalism that flowed from this Christian commitment was a positive force in that time and place. The ideal of universal equality captured in the United Nations Declaration of Human Rights was based for many of these Australian women on the equality of all people before the Christian God.

---

1   *NCWA Report 1949–1952*, Melbourne, 1952, p. 1.

The prayer was followed by a reading of the 'Loyal Resolution', which affirmed the NCWA's 'sincere loyalty' to Queen Elizabeth, 'Supreme Liege Lady in and over the Commonwealth of Australia', and assured her 'that a warm welcome awaits her when she visits Australia'.

Ivy Brookes continued the themes of equality, loyalty and morality in her presidential address.[2] Her first concern was the status of women. Her approach was straightforwardly feminist; the problem was the male monopoly on rights and power, perpetuated by male selfishness and ignorance.

> All those who have worked for women's emancipation know that this battle has to be won by women themselves ... it has been rare for rights to be conceded voluntarily by those who monopolise them. Chivalry has never excluded women from the operation of this harsh historical law ... women have had to battle for their political, legal and social rights and they are still battling, as much as a result of ignorance as selfishness.

'Selfishness' is a key term here. Historians have noted a tension in the language of the day between 'selfishness' and 'citizenship', between 'the pursuit of happiness and social demands';[3] Brookes is typical of maternal feminists in gendering the dichotomy male and female.

Brookes went on to celebrate the achievement of formal equality in the charter of the United Nations; 'for the first time in history', a declaration that 'the pursuit of fundamental freedoms for all without distinction as to race, sex, language or religion, is part of international morality'. But she noted that this was 'only on paper as yet', recognised 'by lip-service only'. And, in Australia, women 'must continue to press for equal opportunity being allowed to women in all fields'. Brookes described the role of NCWA in tackling 'injustices and problems

---

2   *NCWA Report 1949–1952*, Melbourne, 1952, pp. 5-8.
3   John Murphy, *Imagining the Fifties: Private Sentiment and Political Culture in Menzies' Australia*, Sydney, UNSW Press, 2000, p. 23; Nicholas Brown, *Governing Prosperity: Social Change and Social Analysis in Australia in the 1950s*, Melbourne, Cambridge University Press, 1995, chapter 1.

Ivy Brookes
NCWA President 1948–1952

Ivy Brookes was born in 1883 in Melbourne, the eldest daughter of Alfred Deakin, Australia's second prime minister, and his wife Pattie. Her family's political connections gave her a commitment to a life of public service, and a good measure of political influence. Her husband Herbert was a powerful figure in conservative politics for many years. Ivy Brookes was active as a leader of the Women's Section of the Commonwealth Liberal Party from its foundation in 1909, and in the 1940s she worked with Robert Menzies to form the Liberal Party of Australia, establishing a powerful base for women within the party structures.

Brookes was elected to the executive of the National Council of Women of Victoria in 1912, and remained involved in council affairs for the rest of her life. A major interest was the pursuit of women's rights, and during her national presidency from 1948 to 1952 she led the association's campaigns for equality in marriage and equal pay, and formally changed its title to the Australian National Council of Women (it reverted to NCWA in 1970).

Brookes was the founding president (1915) and later patron of the Housewives' Cooperative Society, the first consumer watch body in Australia and the largest women's organisation in the country by the 1960s. She was also the founding president of the International Club of Victoria, president of the Women's Hospital Board for many years, president of the Playgrounds & Recreation Association of Victoria and vice-president of the United Nations Association of Victoria from 1945 to 1963. Brookes represented Australia at the ICW's 50th Anniversary Conference in Edinburgh in 1938. Appointed to the early Canberra Citizenship Conventions from 1950, she was also a member of the national Women's Committee for the Jubilee Celebrations.

A talented musician, Brookes won the Ormond Scholarship for singing in 1904 and for some years played first violin in the orchestra of the Melbourne Conservatorium of Music. From 1906 Brookes and her husband were deeply involved in founding and supporting the Melbourne Symphony Orchestra.

Ivy Brookes died in 1970, aged 87. In her time she gave strength, intellectual stimulus and cultural inspiration to those around her, and used her political influence to advance the interests of the mainstream women's movement. She was one of the first women included on the Victorian Honour Roll of Women when it began in 2001.

Explore further resources about Ivy Brookes in the Australian Women's Register.

affecting the lives and welfare of our citizens' as one of duty, 'a watchful stewardship'. The model to be emulated here was the British Crown:

> Our young Queen is fully conscious of her stewardship, like her late father, King George VI, who was so faithful to his high calling. She will lead us, and we, I hope and believe, will follow her and support her in her fine ideals.

The 'principal work' of Brookes' stewardship—in addition to 'our efforts to improve the status of women'—had been 'for the aged and for the amelioration of the lot of the young mother and housewife', and here, she said, more work needed to be done.

In concluding her address, Brookes called her audience's attention to a larger challenge: the 'desperate uneasiness and confusion' apparent across the globe. She quoted a document put out by a group that included the leaders of the major Christian denominations in Australia, and most of the leading judges: 'A Call to the People of Australia'. The Call was for a renewal of 'moral strength and moral unity' in Australia, 'a restoration of the moral order from which alone true social order can derive'. This was comfortable, familiar language to the members of the Australian councils. Dangers 'at home and abroad' required this renewal: 'evil designs and aggressions', 'evil dissensions'. The solutions proposed were equally imprecise: 'a new effort to advance moral standards', 'a duty of honest work', 'an adequate understanding of the nature of law and of its necessity as the principle of order in a free society'.[4]

> We call on our people to remember those whose labours opened this land to the use of mankind: those who bore and reared the children of a new nation; those who died in battle for us, bringing splendour to Australian arms; those who worked with mind and muscle for the heritage which we, please God, shall hold and enlarge for our children and their children.

---

4   'The Call' was printed in various forms in 1951 and 1952; these quotes are taken from the version printed in the *Longreach Leader*, 16 November 1951, p. 1.

And that this may be so, we ask that each shall renew in himself the full meanings of the call which has inspired our people in their highest tasks and in their days of danger:

FEAR GOD, HONOUR THE KING.

The Call campaign was in fact a product of the Cold War, the work of ultra-conservative men with connections to the clandestine paramilitary groups of the 1930s, and the aims of the campaign were deeply political.[5] The women in Brookes' audience probably did not share the extreme anti-communism that fuelled the Call, but all would have affirmed its sonorous conclusion. For these women, communism was the enemy of God and King both. They would have been appalled to know that their council meetings were of interest to the Commonwealth Investigation Service (CIS), the forerunner of ASIO, the Australian Security Intelligence Organisation. As we have seen, the main account we have of Elsie Byth's 'Pacific Assembly' in 1948 comes from the records of the CIS.[6] Security agents regularly attended meetings organised by the national councils. In 1950, two female operatives attended a women's rally organised by NCW Queensland to protest against rising prices; they noted approvingly that an attempt by a representative from the Trades Hall to raise the issue of peace had been met with cries of 'Communist Propaganda'.[7]

---

5   Andrew Moore, 'Doyle, Alec Broughton (1888–1984)', *Australian Dictionary of Biography* (*ADB*), http://adb.anu.edu.au/biography/doyle-alec-broughton-12436; Geoff Browne, 'Herring, Sir Edmund Francis (Ned) (1892–1982)', *ADB*, http://adb.anu.edu.au/biography/herring-sir-edmund-francis-ned-12626. Moore describes the campaign as 'A Cold War project'.

6   Program, *Pacific Assembly, September 6th, 7th and 8th*, Brisbane, Brisbane Telegraph Typ., 1948; R.F.B. Wake, Deputy Director, to Director, Commonwealth Investigation Service, Canberra, 10 September 1948, A9108, ROLL 10/18, NAA.

7   NCWQ Special Executive Minutes, 12 September 1950, Box 16045, 7266 NCWQ Minute Books, NCWQ Papers, State Library of Queensland (SLQ); Report to the Officer in Charge, "D" Branch, Queensland, 25th September 1950, A9108, ROLL 10/18, NAA.

The next two decades were to be the golden years of the Australian National Council of Women. Membership, affiliated organisations, and branches grew to an extent not exceeded in later years. Under a Liberal government, the council's claims to represent Australian women took on new force, though this was always under challenge and often ineffective. The beliefs and attitudes displayed at the 1952 conference continued to move the members of the Australian councils across these decades. International fellowship, gender equality and moral reform were as important to NCWA in 1970 as they were in 1950. But the content and direction of these imperatives expanded and shifted across the period, reflecting major changes in Australia's society, culture and place in the world.

This section will chart these changes across four major areas of association activity. Chapter 8 looks at the changing shape and structure of NCWA, at the way it was shaped by and adjusted to its relationship to government and to other women's organisations. Chapter 9 follows the making of policy and practice with regard to women, home and family: a field of action in which the association simultaneously refused and embraced change. The councils' commitment to the traditional family as the central element of society never wavered, but they continued to be strong advocates for divorce reform—in the interests both of gender equality and the strengthening of the family. Chapter 10 looks at a parallel set of equally vexed issues: policies that concerned women at work outside the home. Commitment to equal pay for equal work had long been on the councils' agenda, along with support in principle for married women's right to work, but alongside both ran a suspicion that working mothers caused delinquency and worse. Chapter 11 maps NCWA's changing understanding of the ways that organisation and nation should relate to the world beyond Australia: a growing focus on action within the region—Asia and the Pacific. This shift involved a movement away from the ready assumption of white racial superiority made by the women of 1952, as the councils came to countenance an Australian population with a small admixture of people who were not white.

Chapter 8

ORGANISATIONAL DEVELOPMENTS

The Presidents

In her history of the National Council of Women of Victoria, Ada Norris characterised the leadership of the Australian councils in the early 1950s as on the cusp of change. The older generation were 'leisured' women representing 'a way of life that was not to return'. The entry of young women into the professions and the disappearance of the domestic servant meant that 'the woman who could give practically her whole time to voluntary work was becoming rare'. Norris wrote with feeling of her own generation that: 'The next series of presidents would not have complete home help or their own private secretaries. They would be younger women, with home duties of their own, children still at school, and busy husbands'.[1]

In the official photo of the NCWA board presiding over the 1952 conference, Ivy Brookes, standing, and deputy president Gertrude Kumm, at Brookes's right hand, personify Norris's older generation.[2] Both were born in the 1880s to well-to-do families active in Melbourne's cultural and political life, both devoted most of their lives to philanthropic work and, in Brookes's case, to political activity. Ada

---

1   Ada Norris, *Champions of the Impossible: A History of the National Council of Women of Victoria*, Melbourne, Hawthorn Press, 1978, p. 93.
2   Photo of the Board of Officers, Australian National Council of Women, *NCWA Report, 1949–1952*, p. 2. See p. 232 above.

Norris herself, at this point treasurer of NCWA, is seated second on Brookes's left, and Marie Breen, the international secretary, is second on her right. These women were both born in the first years of the twentieth century, married ambitious husbands in the late 1920s, and had children still at school when they became active in the national councils. Live-in servants and governesses were almost unknown after the Second World War, and these younger women certainly had a more difficult task in juggling home duties and voluntary work. But it is a measure of the greater opportunities available to women in public life after the war that both Breen and Norris would go on to more powerful positions—in at least a formal sense—than anything achieved by their elders: Breen to the Australian Senate, and Norris to the Immigration Advisory Committee and the United Nations Commission for the Status of Women (CSW).

The personal lives of the five national presidents who succeeded Brookes mostly followed the pattern that Norris suggests, balancing voluntary work against home duties. They also shared a common thread that Norris does not mention; unlike the 'leisured ladies' of earlier decades, these women worked outside the home before they married. Unremarkably, four out of five worked as teachers, almost the only profession open to middle-class women. Norris herself taught in Victorian high schools for several years before resigning to marry a talented lawyer who was to become a judge of the Supreme Court of Victoria. She took up voluntary work while her children were still in primary school—an unusual step for women of her class and generation. In his eulogy on her death, her son-in-law noted that 'a trained and restless mind, and a degree of ambition, was not to be satisfied by the cares of managing a house, children and a husband … she wanted to play a part in the wider community also'.[3]

---

3   'Ada Norris', *Stirrers with Style! Presidents of the National Council of Women of Australia and Its Predecessors*, http://www.womenaustralia.info/exhib/NCWA/presidents-22.html .

ORGANISATIONAL DEVELOPMENTS

Ruth Gibson, the South Australian who succeeded Brookes in 1952, was unusual in choosing career rather than marriage; like her mentor and predecessor, Adelaide Miethke, she trained as a teacher and was working as a school inspector during her presidential term. No president after her took on this double burden until Laurel Macintosh, in the 1980s. Gibson was the eldest of four children and took over the care of the family when her mother died young; her biographer notes that she 'became a source of strength in a close-knit family for the rest of her life'.[4] Gibson's successor, Thelma Metcalfe, also trained and worked as a secondary teacher of languages, but gave up her career when she married an ambitious husband who was to become New South Wales state librarian. There were no children to the marriage. Metcalfe shared her husband's enthusiasms, working with him in the movement for free public libraries; she also initiated a wide range of voluntary activities directed to the support of the family, from Meals on Wheels to the Children's Film Council.[5] Dorothy Edwards, who followed Metcalfe, was yet another teacher; she taught Latin and Literature at Launceston High School but was forced to resign from the Education Department when she married. Once her sons were in school, she took up an active public life that included a career in local government and a spell as one of the first female city mayors in Australia.[6] Her successor, Anne Hamilton, was exceptional in not being a teacher; she took a business course and worked as a secretary and briefly as a dressmaker. She too married an ambitious husband who became the Brisbane city architect, and she too 'found the domestic routine unstimulating', moving into

---

4   'Ruth Gibson', *Stirrers with Style! Presidents of the National Council of Women of Australia and Its Predecessors*, http://www.womenaustralia.info/exhib/NCWA/presidents-11.html.
5   'Thelma Metcalfe', *Stirrers with Style! Presidents of the National Council of Women of Australia and Its Predecessors*, http://www.womenaustralia.info/exhib/NCWA/presidents-17.html.
6   'Dorothy Edwards', *Stirrers with Style! Presidents of the National Council of Women of Australia and Its Predecessors*, http://www.womenaustralia.info/exhib/NCWA/presidents-10.html.

public life when her two children reached school age.[7] Hamilton is remembered by Laurel Macintosh, a member of her board, as a 'feisty lady'[8]—a description that fits all of these remarkable women.

Hamilton was followed by Ada Norris herself. NCW Victoria's turn to claim the national presidency did not come until 1967, by which time Norris—the obvious candidate—was already of an older generation than the presidents before and after her: ten years older than Hamilton and nearly twenty years older than her successor, Jessie Scotford. Scotford's presidency was to see change in Australian society and politics more rapid and more dramatic than anything during the 1960s, but that is the subject of the next section of the book.

Organisational Growth

In 1952 Ada Norris told the federal arbitration court that NCWA represented some 500,000 Australian women. In 1969 she claimed 'three-quarters of a million'.[9] Such a claim was always somewhat rhetorical, based as it was on the collective membership of the women's organisations that affiliated with the state councils. The number of organisations affiliated across this period increased from some 490 in the early fifties to more than 600 in the early seventies. The state councils grew at different rates; South Australia, Victoria and Queensland all began the decade with about 100 affiliates, trailed by New South Wales with 80, Launceston 45, Hobart 26, Western Australia only 16 and the recently founded ACT council 30.[10] By the late 1960s Victoria was

---

7 'Anne Hamilton', *Stirrers with Style! Presidents of the National Council of Women of Australia and Its Predecessors*, http://www.womenaustralia.info/exhib/NCWA/presidents-13.html.
8 Interview with Laurel Macintosh, 26 June 2009, Brisbane, NCWA History Project.
9 'Basic Wage Case—1952–53' and 'Equal Pay for Equal Work' [1969], typescripts, Box 33, MS90/190, Papers of Mrs J.G. Norris (Norris Papers), University of Melbourne Archives (UMA).
10 NCWA Executive Minutes, 9 October 1954, Box 13, MS7583, NCWA Papers, National Library of Australia (NLA); Finance Report, *NCWA Biennial Conference, 1954*, Adelaide.

the largest state council, with some 140 affiliates; New South Wales, South Australia and Queensland all had about 90; Launceston had 60, Tasmania and Western Australia both about 30,[11] and the recently founded Northern Territory council 15 affiliates.[12]

The period was also marked by a large increase in the numbers of associate members: women who joined the councils not as representatives of affiliated organisations but in their own right. This kind of membership had been introduced as a way of allowing women whose affiliate membership had lapsed to continue their NCW activities. Associate members soon outnumbered affiliates; in 1966, Queensland was typical of the state councils with 81 affiliated organisations and 182 associate members.[13] Constitutionally, associates had limited voting rights during this period, but the experience of these women within the councils gave weight to their voices.

Growth also came through the founding of new branches in country areas—though long-term success came mostly in Victoria. This was due to the comparatively high density of population across that state, and the size and location of country towns serving that population—far enough from Melbourne to grow local pride, but not too far for regular contact between the state council and branch executives. The Geelong, Ballarat and Bendigo councils were well established by 1950, and by 1965 branches covered most of the state, from Sunraysia and the Murray Valley in the north, to Corangamite and the Wimmera in the west, and the South Gippsland and Central Gippsland branches to the east. All had their local affiliates and associate members, and branches like Ballarat attracted larger attendances to their monthly council meetings than struggling state councils like Western Australian and Tasmania.

---

11   Financial Report, *NCWA Triennial Conference*, Melbourne, 12–19 August 1970; Secretary's Report, *NCWNSW Biennial Report, 1968–70*, p. 5.

12   *NCWNT Annual Reports*, 1967–70, Box 2, NTRS836P1, NCWNT Papers, Northern Territory Archives Service (NTAS).

13   *61st Annual State Report of the National Council of Women of Queensland*, 23 November 1966 p. 3.

Other state councils tried to follow Victoria's example: NCWNSW launched a South Coast and Tableland Branch in 1967 but it did not survive the year. Queensland formed its Townsville Regional Branch in 1963, and, though 'beset with problems', its members were considering the formation of a Cairns Branch in 1966.[14] Townsville did not prosper in the 1970s, and the NCWA board failed to revive it in 1979.[15]

The sixties saw affiliated national councils operating in every state and territory of Australia—and, as we have seen, two in Tasmania. A council was established in Darwin in 1964, with the active assistance of members of the National Council of Women of the Australian Capital Territory. The steering committee drafting the constitution for the new council wrote to the board in some confusion. The ACT constitution, which they were using as a guide, referred to the region covered by the council as a 'State'—but neither the Australian Capital Territory nor the Northern Territory were in fact 'states'. Furthermore, the committee was reluctant to take on the name 'Northern Territory'. Given 'the immense distance, 1000 miles between the two main Centres of the Northern Territory viz. Darwin and Alice Springs', they preferred to call themselves 'National Council of the Women of Darwin'.[16] In the event, the NCWA board required the use of 'Northern Territory'.

It was perhaps ironic that the board that dealt with the Northern Territory's request was located in Launceston. We have seen how the rapid expansion of the Launceston branch in the 1940s—mirroring the growth of the city and its ambition to displace the official capital at Hobart—led NCWA to allow NCWL a semi-autonomous position in relation to its parent council, the NCW of Tasmania. However, the Launceston council was not satisfied with a situation in which it was

---

14 NCWQ Executive Minutes, 5 December 1966, Box 16045, 7266 NCWQ Minute Books, NCWQ Papers, State Library of Queensland (SLQ).
15 NCWQ Council Minutes, 28 July 1979, Box 16045, 7266 NCWQ Minute Books, NCWQ Papers, SLQ.
16 Lyn Berlowitz, letter to President Dorothy Edwards, 29 December 1964, Folder 5, MS5193, NCWA Papers, NLA.

still obliged to 'send to the parent body copies of all such letters sent to the Australian Board and must co-operate with the parent Branch on all matters of State policy'.[17] In 1952, Ivy Brookes, as NCWA president, oversaw an agreement between 'N.C.W. of Tasmania, State Council, and Launceston Council' stipulating that 'the Launceston Council has autonomy', but insisting in somewhat contradictory terms that 'the State Council retain its "status quo"' and its right to control the forwarding of submissions and resolutions from Tasmania.[18] Dorothy Edwards short-circuited this arrangement by winning the national board and the national presidency for Launceston in 1960—an outcome that might have been thought to strain the constitutional framework of both NCW Tasmania and NCWA. But goodwill and the comparative strength of the Launceston council papered over the cracks, and the contradictions remained to trouble the association from the 1970s into the 1990s and beyond.

Representing Women

In July 1950, the board of the Australian National Council of Women made an unusually detailed minute concerning their intention to contact the prime minister, Robert Menzies. The issue was the council's representation on the committees established to plan activities marking the jubilee of Australian federation in 1951. President Ivy Brookes had attended the first planning meeting on the personal invitation of the prime minister, only to be excluded from its executive committee. When the board wrote to the secretary of the Prime Minister's Department

---

17   Hilda Brotherton, Hon. Australian Secretary, to Mrs Vimpany, President, NCWT, 14 December 1946. Photocopy held in Mollie Campbell-Smith Papers (private collection).

18   Agreement between N.C.W. of Tasmania, State Council, and Launceston Council at Hobart on Friday 23 February 1952 under the Chairmanship of Mrs Herbert Brookes J.P., President A.N.C.W. Photocopy held in Mollie Campbell-Smith Papers (private collection). A minor amendment was made in Hobart in June 1959 regarding Launceston's right to seek information from the state government without first going through NCWT.

querying this omission,[19] they were told that they should 'recognise the impracticality of including representatives of all organisations on the Executive Committee'.[20]

The board's minute captures Mrs Brookes's annoyance at this double slight, to her personal status and to the standing of the NCWA.

> NCWA to write again, addressing letter to the Prime Minister's Lodge, by hand, in a plain envelope, to R.G. Menzies, Esq. Subject: that we had written to his Department, and had received letter, copy enclosed of both ... We should like to know ... what reason we can give to our various affiliated societies as to why the NCWA has not been included when individual societies have. The Celebrations are Commonwealth wide, and amongst our affiliated societies are many also Commonwealth wide, with very large memberships, e.g. Housewives Association, Young Women's Christian Association, Girl Guides Association, etc. ... Above letter to be posted to reach the Prime Minister when he returns from England, but not to be posted beforehand to be diverted to Departmental channels.[21]

Ivy Brookes, daughter of second Australian prime minister Alfred Deakin and wife of Herbert Brookes, had worked for more than thirty years in various organisations supporting the non-Labor side of politics, and she had been instrumental in the founding of Menzies' new Liberal Party in 1944.[22] The new prime minister and his wife were personal friends of long-standing. While relations with the previous Labor government had been reasonably cordial, Brookes clearly expected more of the new prime minister. She was annoyed by the intervention of a

---

19   NCWA Hon. Sec. to Sec. Prime Minister's Department, 6 June 1950, Folder 1, MS5193, NCWA Papers, NLA.

20   Sec. Prime Minister's Department to NCWA Hon. Sec., 14 June 1950, Folder 1, MS5193, NCWA Papers, NLA.

21   NCWA Board Minutes, 10 July 1950, Box 13, MS7583, NCWA Papers, NLA. The letter drafted here was sent on 23 August 1950; see R.G. Menzies to Mrs. F. Howard, Folder 1, MS5193, NCWA Papers, NLA.

22   Alison Patrick, 'Brookes, Ivy (1883–1970)', *ADB*, http://adb.anu.edu.au/biography/brookes-ivy-5640.

departmental secretary, and infuriated by this minion's lack of respect for NCWA. To reduce its status to that of an ordinary organisation was to ignore its national standing and the hundreds of women's organisations that it represented.

Menzies' response was cordial. He wrote asking NCWA to 'nominate a representative to act on the Jubilee Executive Committee'.[23]

> I am, of course, aware of the representative nature of the National Council of Women and feel that as your Organisation is desirous of having a delegate to undertake this appointment in addition to that of membership of the Jubilee Council it would be in the best interests of the Celebrations that this should be done.

This incident is instructive about the political style of NCWA as this had developed in the first half of the century, and as it would continue in the third quarter of the century. One can read on both sides of the exchange a ready acceptance of the authority of the National Council of Women of Australia to speak to government and to speak for Australian women. This authority was confirmed by a close relationship with the Australian Liberal Party, especially in Victoria. Members of the Victorian board had been active alongside Ivy Brookes in the foundation of Menzies' new Liberal Party in 1944. Marie Breen would go on to be chairman of the Women's Section of the Liberal Party, state vice president, and a Liberal member of the Commonwealth Senate in the 1960s.[24] Breen's career was typical of women elected to state and federal parliament before the 1970s. In the absence of Labor women (usually blocked by their party from affiliation), women from political parties opposed to Labor were often the most active office bearers in the national councils. And, while the councils never directly supported political

---

23 R.G. Menzies to Gen. Sec. NCWA, 10 October 1950, Folder 1, MS5193, NCWA Papers, NLA.

24 Anne Heywood, 'Breen, Marie Freda', *Australian Women's Register*, National Foundation for Australian Women, http://www.womenaustralia.info/biogs/IMP0013b.htm.

candidates, the non-Labor women first elected to state parliaments were nearly all publicly associated with the national councils.[25] After World War II, the story was repeated at the federal level; the only woman elected to the House of Representatives before 1967 (Dame Enid Lyons) and five out of six of the first women Senators were non-Labor women with NCWA connections.[26] The NCWA board was always ready to use those connections in lobbying the government. Victorian Senator Ivy Wedgwood was particularly helpful, regularly forwarding requests and leading deputations to ministers, and the correspondence files of NCWA in the National Archives make it clear that the senatorial intervention guaranteed a bureaucratic response—though, as we shall see later, the response was by no means always favourable.

The claim of NCWA to represent Australian women internationally was equally as important to its leaders as their assertion of national representivity. We have seen in the previous section how this claim came to be focused in the late 1940s on the government's appointment of an Australian woman delegate to the UN Commission on the Status of Women, and how the association worked with and around other women's organisations to secure the appointment for an NCWA representative—with varying degrees of success.

This pattern continued in the 1950s, in a political climate more favourable to NCWA. The rivalry between the Australian Liaison Committee (ALC) and the Australian National Committee of the United Nations (ANCUN) that marked the last years of the 1940s effectively ended in late 1950 when ANCUN's Commonwealth funding was much reduced, and it was reconstituted as the Australian

---

25   Edith Cowan in Western Australia; Millicent Preston-Stanley in New South Wales; Irene Longman in Queensland; Ivy Weber in Victoria; Margaret McIntyre in Tasmania.

26   Annabelle Rankin (1947), Agnes Robertson (1949), Ivy Wedgwood (1950), Nancy Buttfield (1955), and Marie Breen (1962), were all non-Labor women; Robertson, Wedgwood and Breen had close NCWA connections. Dorothy Tangney (1943) was a Labor senator. See *ADB* and Parliament of Australia, The Senate, Senate Brief no. 3, *Women in Parliament*, July 2008.

ORGANISATIONAL DEVELOPMENTS

Association for the UN.[27] NCWA influence was strong within ALC. In Sydney the committee met in the comfortable rooms of the New South Wales National Council of Women in Phillip Street, and meetings were generally chaired by Thelma Metcalfe of NCWNSW. In 1952, Ruth Gibson, on taking over the presidency of NCWA, suggested the relocation of ALC to her home city of Adelaide, an offer gratefully accepted.[28] Gibson generally chaired the Adelaide meetings, but tactfully located them in the rooms of the South Australian branch of the Australian Federation of Women Voters (AFWV). AFWV locally and the International Alliance of Women internationally remained the only organisations rivalling the International and National Councils of Women's claims to representivity, but co-operation was more common than conflict after 1950, when AFWV and NCWA both opposed Jessie Street's radicalism and the new Soviet-aligned Women's International Democratic Federation.

NCWA often pursued its international aims through the Australian Liaison Committee, and just as often took independent action. When Australia's term on CSW came to an end in 1951, NCWA wrote to remind the Department of External Affairs of the importance of maintaining Australian representation. The department secretary's response was cordial and expansive, explaining in some detail why 'the Australian Government did not feel it could ask for re-election just now', and assuring the board that 'The Australian Government greatly

---

27 See correspondence between Isabel McCorkindale and the Federal Secretariat of AAUN, November/December 1950, Folder 'UN Status of Women Commission, 4th Session', A1838 (A1838/283), National Archives of Australia (NAA). The Australian Liaison Committee was in its turn reconstituted in 1954 as the Liaison Committee of Women's International Organisations (Australia Group) (ALC) with a membership restricted to organisations that were affiliates of international organisations represented on the London-based ILC. See Ruth Gibson to A.H. Loomes, Department of External Affairs, 24 August 1955, Folder 'Status of Women Commission 9th Session', A1838 (A1838/1), NAA.

28 Australian Liaison Committee of Women's International Organisations (ALC) Minutes, 7 July 1952, Box 1, MS1082, ALC Papers, NLA.

Ruth Gibson
NCWA President 1952–1956

Ruth Gibson served as national president of the Australian National Council of Women from 1953 to 1956, the second South Australian to do so. She was born in Goodwood Park in 1901 and educated at the Teachers' Training College and Adelaide University.

Gibson's main area of interest and expertise was education. Trained as a teacher, she was mentored by and succeeded Adelaide Miethke as the SA Inspector of Schools (girls' departments) in 1941, eventually becoming Inspector of Secondary Schools in 1953. She continued working fulltime in this role while leading the ANCW at state, federal and international levels. She was appointed a Fellow of Australian College of Education in 1963 and with her energy, dedication and commitment was able to improve the conditions and status of women teachers. Her encouragement promoted the careers of many promising young female teachers in the Education Department.

As national president, she united the state councils in a campaign for federal legislation to bring about equal pay and equal marriage and divorce laws. During her period in office she was honoured to represent Australian women at the coronation of Queen Elizabeth II in 1953 and played a leading role in welcoming the Queen to Australia during the royal tour of 1954.

Gibson played a key role in the decision to purchase NCW House ('a home of our own') in Adelaide in 1957, where the Council continues to meet to this day. She also played an active role in a large number of other groups such as the United Nations Association, the Royal Flying Doctor Service, the ABC, the Junior Red Cross and served on the state council of the Girls Guides Association for many years.

Gibson's work with ICW began in 1938 as one of ten Australian delegates to their Jubilee Conference in Edinburgh, and her activism culminated in her election as vice-president from 1953 to 1956 and her elevation to the Council's Committee of Honour. Her international expertise was also recognised in her appointment as Australia's delegate to the UN Status of Women Commission (CSW) in Geneva (1956) and New York (1957).

Gibson was awarded the OBE in the coronation honours list of 1953 and the CBE in 1970. She died in 1972 and women of South Australia erected a sundial in her memory at the Adelaide Festival Centre in 1973. A Ruth Gibson Memorial Fund continues to provide assistance for projects of benefit to the women of South Australia.

Explore further resources about Ruth Gibson in the Australian Women's Register.

appreciates the contribution by the women's organisations of Australia to the work of the United Nations'.[29]

The following year, Brookes was at her most charming in a letter to the minister for external affairs, R.G. Casey, inviting him to address the association's biennial conference—'We would much prefer to have you to anyone else'—and complaining gently about his department's decision not to send a non-government woman delegate to the United Nations Assembly; a handwritten postscript observed, 'I trust the policy for Paris will not always be the procedure'.[30] In this case, Brookes demonstrated her ease of access to the Liberal government by bypassing ALC and going directly to Casey seeking funding to send one delegate—Elsie Byth—to a meeting of the Pan Pacific Women's Conference in New Zealand.[31] On the success of this application, ALC wrote to the board suggesting that the money should be shared between all the Australian delegates; the board politely declined.[32]

Casey moved to revive Australian representation on CSW in 1953 and achieved this the following year. Rather than go through a process of consultation, the department chose to send the previous delegate, Jean Daly, to the 9th session in 1955. Daly's performance was conscientious and obedient, and officials in the department recommended that she should serve a third term in 1956; they noted that some women's organisations had previously complained about not being consulted, but that others including the National Council of Women of Australia had welcomed Daly's second appointment.[33] Casey gave Daly to understand

---

29 Secretary Department of External Affairs to Secretary NCWA, 14 November 1951, Folder 1, MS5193, NCWA Papers, NLA.
30 Ivy Brookes to R.G. Casey, 15 May 1951, Folder 1, MS5193, NCWA Papers, NLA.
31 NCWA Board Minutes, 11 September 1951, Box 13, MS7583, NCWA Papers, NLA.
32 NCWA Board Minutes, 18 December 1951, Box 13, MS7583, NCWA Papers, NLA.
33 Memo to Minister from Patrick Shaw, Acting Secretary of the Department of External Affairs, 20 July 1955, Folder 'Status of Women Commission 9th Session', A1838 (A1838/1), NAA.

that she would serve a third term, then in July 1955 suddenly changed his mind upon receiving a confidential letter from the Federal Secretariat of the Liberal Party of Australia. Eileen Furley, chairman of the Federal Women's Committee, wrote strongly recommending 'further consideration' of the Daly appointment, and noting that 'The greatest importance should be attached to the opinion of my Committee, the members of which individually are representative of the major women's organisations in Australia'.[34]

Furley's intervention was most likely politically based. Daly's home organisation, the St Joan's Alliance, represented the radical wing of Catholic women. Furley's 'major women's organisations' certainly included NCWA, but the council does not seem to have initiated the move against Daly. When consulted in May 1955, Elsie Byth went out of her way to stress that the NCWA biennial conference had 'unanimously approved' of Daly's reappointment.[35] The prime mover in this case was probably the Australian Women's Movement Against Socialisation, a Liberal Party affiliate whose politics were of the extreme right.[36]

NCWA played a somewhat magisterial role in the negotiations that followed. Shaw flew to Melbourne to seek the advice of Ivy Brookes on how to proceed with the appointment. She suggested that the department should 'seek recommendations from the principal women's bodies with associations in the international field'.[37] Shaw contacted the Australian Liaison Committee, the body that had originally recommended Daly's

---

34 Eileen Furley to R.G. Casey, 7 July 1955, Folder 'Status of Women Commission 9th Session', A1838 (A1838/1), NAA.

35 Elsie Byth to Patrick Shaw, 11 May 1955, Folder 'Status of Women Commission 9th Session', A1838 (A1838/1), NAA.

36 Inward printergram, Patrick Shaw to the Minister, 9 August 55, Folder 'Status of Women Commission 9th Session', A1838 (A1838/1), NAA. See also Warwick Eather, 'The Liberal Party of Australia and the Australian Women's Movement Against Socialisation 1947–54', *Australian Journal of Politics and History*, 44 (2), 1998, pp. 191–207.

37 Inward printergram. Patrick Shaw to the Minister, 5 August 1955, Folder 'Status of Women Commission 9th Session', A1838 (A1838/1), NAA. Shaw also consulted Frances Pennington of the Australian Federation of University Women.

appointment in 1950.³⁸ The discussion at that committee, chaired by Ruth Gibson, debated the virtues of continuity of representation against the need for change; in the end they put forward the names of Ruth Gibson and two others. Gibson's appointment to the 10th session of the UN Commission for the Status of Women was announced in February 1956.³⁹

Ruth Gibson held the position until 1957, when Australia's three-year term on CSW again expired. When Australia was next represented, in 1961, NCWA's nomination was again successful. Ada Norris's appointment was as much in recognition of her own status as it was a feather in the cap of Australian council. Norris was not president of the council at this point; she was convenor and deputy convenor respectively of the NCWA and the ICW committees on migration, and represented NCWA on the Commonwealth Immigration Advisory Committee, where she was vice-chairman.⁴⁰ She held her position on CSW for an unprecedented three terms, from 1961 to 1963. The UN Section of the External Affairs Department came to rely on Norris for information and advice about women's affairs both international and national, and she acted as a channel so that, in her words:

> The NCW of Victoria and Australia, and other organisations also, had readily available up-to-date international information on various subjects such as equal pay and discrimination on the grounds of marital status at a time when the drive for reform in these areas were [sic] gaining great impetus.⁴¹

---

38   ALC Minutes, 1 August 1955, Box 1, MS1082, ALC Papers, NLA.
39   NCWA Board Minutes, 22 October 1955, 28 November 1955, and newscuttings inserted into minutes 11–14 February 1956, Box 13, MS7583, NCWA Papers, NLA.
40   Judith Smart, 'Ada Norris (1901–1989): Champion of the Impossible', in Fiona Davis, Nell Musgrove and Judith Smart (eds), *Founders, Firsts and Feminists: Women Leaders in Twentieth-century Australia*, Australian Women's Archives Project, 2011, http://www.womenaustralia.info/leaders/fff.
41   Norris, *Champions*, p. 126.

When Norris took on the NCWA presidency in 1967, she and the council enjoyed an access to government as direct and as cordial as Brookes had given them in 1950—though it is a reflection of the changing nature of politics and administration across this period that, where Brookes worked to avoid dealing with bureaucrats, her protégée Norris developed those relationships to a fine art. But access to powerful men did not guarantee success. When the government next appointed an Australian woman representative to the UN Commission for the Status of Women, in 1967, women's organisations were not consulted, and when in 1969 Norris wrote as NCWA president to the relevant minister hoping 'that a return to the former practice of consultation would be contemplated', it was without effect.[42]

---

42 Memo to T. Shand, E.A., 22 October 1968, and Norris to Gordon Freeth, 22 February 1969, Folder 'Status of Women Commission—Nomination of Australian Representatives', 931/3/1 Part 1A, A1838 (A1838/1), NAA.

Chapter 9

WOMEN, HOME AND FAMILY

From the inception of ICW and the Australian councils, members understood woman's relationship to home and family as the secure centre of the moral universe, the well-spring of moral action. By the 1950s, the stability of the family was seen to be under threat, in Australia and the western world. In 1954, Pope Pius XII told Catholics that 'if the world is to survive this present crisis satisfactorily and not labour in vain once more it must begin by rebuilding families'.[1] In the same year, the International Council of Women, meeting in Helsinki, adopted a resolution on 'Mental Hygiene' that focused on the same problem.

> The ICW, considering the knowledge recently acquired in the domain of mental hygiene, requests the National Councils to watch over the diffusion and application of all that pertains to mental hygiene: … by encouraging the further education of parents, teachers and social workers, insisting particularly on the influence of the mother on the mental and emotional development of young children from their earliest years …[2]

Knowledges old and new constructed the family as damaged, in need of the expert assistance that only their practitioners could give. Religion might be thought to typify 'old knowledge', and certainly the expertise of popes and archbishops generally promoted past traditions and practices. But progressive Protestant clergymen allied themselves

---

1 'Rebuild Family if World Is to Survive Crisis', *Catholic Weekly*, 7 October 1954, p. 3.
2 Helsinki 1954, 'ICW Resolutions', www.ncwcanada.com/ncwc2/wp-content/uploads/2014/02/ICW-CIF_Resolutions1.pdf, p. 28.

with the new knowledges of psychology and sociology, presenting what historian John Murphy has called 'secular expertise, based especially in psychology, but framed within religious values'.[3] In Australia, Allan Walker, Methodist minister and marriage guidance counsellor, told audiences across the country that: 'The religion of Jesus Christ was necessary to their needs today because of what could be done on the level of the family. Stability of the family in the end affected the stability of governments and the people'.[4]

The signs of family instability were considered to be the same across the western world: declining moral values, divorce, materialism, increasing rates of illegitimacy, single parenthood, desertion, and especially juvenile delinquency.[5] And mothers were most commonly blamed for family instability and moral decay—especially mothers who worked. The Melbourne *Argus* ran a centre spread in July 1956 under the oversized headline—'DON'T BLAME THE WORKING MOTHERS'—and then proceeded to do exactly that:

> One of the problems of our time is the steady increase in women employed in breadwinning jobs and the wave of juvenile delinquency which sweeps the country. It is obvious that one should link these two phenomena. Many people call the working mother, straightout, a homebreaker.[6]

In the same year *Woman's Day* asked for readers' opinions on married women working, and found them six to one against.[7]

This section looks at the national councils' attempts across the 1950s and 1960s to redress problems understood as relating to morality and

---

3   John Murphy, *Imagining the Fifties: Private Sentiment and Political Culture in Menzies' Australia*, Sydney, UNSW Press, 2000, p. 37.
4   'Turn to God: Mission to Nation Appeal', *Central Queensland Herald*, 6 August 1953, p. 9.
5   David Hilliard, 'God in the Suburbs: The Religious Culture of Australian Cities in the 1950s', *Australian Historical Studies*, 24 (97) 1991, pp. 399–419.
6   Dr Irma Schnierer, child psychologist, 'Don't Blame the Working Mothers', *Argus*, 20 July 1956, p. 4.
7   Murphy, *Imagining the Fifties*, p. 48.

family life. It first considers a range of moral concerns that troubled the councils: old problems like alcohol and prostitution; new problems like working mothers and delinquency. The councils could find no obvious solutions to these problems; rather they struggled with a tangle of languages to define them: languages of morality, of law and criminology, of psychology and sociology. Only one family-related problem presented itself with its solution in place: the matter of legal inequalities within marriage and divorce law. Unlike suggested cures for delinquency, uniform and equal divorce law was an achievable end—though its achievement was long in coming.

Fighting Moral Decay

The defence of moral standards within the national councils was traditionally done by the Moral Welfare Standing Committees. The local nature of most this work—delegations to cinemas to protest against sexually explicit posters, complaints to wine saloons about children on their premises—should not blind us to its international frame within the councils. Like all council standing committees, moral welfare committees operated at all three levels of the association, and much of the business of the local committees was determined by decisions in Geneva. Historians Catherine Jacques and Sylvie Lefebvre make it clear that moral issues were always high on the agenda of the International Council of Women; during the 1950s, these included prostitution, women in prison, the provision of female police, pornography, and juvenile delinquency.[8] Fact-seeking questionnaires from the ICW Moral Welfare Standing Committee directed the attention of the Australian committees to problem areas and gave them new language to identify the problems. Thus, in 1957, Phyllis Frost reported as the convenor of the national Moral Welfare Standing Committee that her committee

---

8   Catherine Jacques and Sylvie Lefebvre, 'From Philanthropy to Social Commitment', in Eliane Gubin and Leen Van Molle (eds), *Women Changing the World: A History of the International Council of Women*, Brussels, Éditions Racine, 2005, pp. 166–7.

had produced one report for ICW on the need for sex education and premarital instruction, another on adult probation and the parole system, and a third on 'The Sex Offender'.[9] A few years before, the issues referred to here would have been described as teenage immorality, recidivism and male depravity.

The division of powers between state and federal governments in Australia gave the conduct of moral and welfare issues to the state governments, and kept most NCW activity in this area to the level of the state councils. The pattern was the same across the states; moral issues were redefined as matters requiring legislation and government action. Thus, in 1955, the Victorian state government set up a Child Advisory Committee to supervise the implementation of its new Child Welfare Act—a comprehensive measure consolidating and reforming legislation concerning Victorian children under the care of the state. NCW Victoria had been involved in the drafting of the act and was asked to nominate a representative to the advisory committee. That representative, laws convenor and lawyer Ethleen King, regularly reported back to the Victorian council, and members found themselves discussing topics like fostering, adoption and institutional reform in this new context.[10]

Old-style moral indignation did not disappear from the councils. President Marie Breen was enthusiastically applauded when she told the annual general meeting of the Victorian council in 1956 that moral problems were still rife in the state:

> Young children are frequently locked in cars at night as well as day while parents are in hotels. During intervals at theatres there is a rush to the nearest hotel by many patrons. Numbers of cars on the roads have trebled at night and night accidents have increased, many due to the effects of liquor. Employment of

---

9 *NCWA Biennial Conference*, January 1957.
10 Mrs R.T. Breen, 'Victorian Report', *NCWA Biennial Conference*, January 1957.

mothers is causing concern and juvenile delinquency. Emotional security is required more and more for children.[11]

But conference also heard an address from an academic social worker on 'Family Instability and Social Welfare', which spoke the language of 'psychosocial disturbance', 'pyschological maladjustment', and their remedy, 'positive mental health' for the whole community. The focus of action remained 'the family', the 'basic unit of our society'. But all families were not equal; some were identified as 'problem families', a 'hard core' that 'demand most of health and social welfare services and provide an undue proportion of ... cases of delinquency, psychological maladjustment ... etc.'.[12] At the 1958 annual general meeting, Phyllis Frost made a similar point in similar language; she 'stressed again the need for strengthening the family unit to combat anti-social elements in the community'.[13]

Interest in the issue of family instability was so high that the Victorian council took up a suggestion from ICW to establish an additional standing committee, on family welfare. The retiring president, Marie Breen, took on the convenorship, and 22 affiliated organisations 'agreed unanimously that action should be taken' and joined the new committee. Its first resolution, forwarded to the national board in May 1958, was stronger on good intentions than explicit policy objectives.

> In order to help preserve and strengthen family life it is resolved that all National Councils of Women impress on their Governments and on the community the need to ascertain what factors tend to cause the breakdown of the family and when this

---

11 NCWV Annual General Meeting, 15 March 1956, in NCWV Council Minutes, NCWV Papers, State Library of Victoria (SLV) (accession pending).

12 'Family Stability and Social Welfare', roneoed paper inserted in Annual General Meeting, 15 March 1956, NCWV Council Minutes, NCWV Papers, SLV (accession pending).

13 NCWV Council Minutes, 26 April 1958, NCWV Minutes, NCWV Papers, SLV (accession pending).

knowledge is available that active steps be taken to combat these factors.[14]

But Breen had a more concrete outcome in mind. In September she convened a public meeting 'to consider the problems of breakdown in family life'. The result was the formation of the Victorian Family Council, bringing together representatives from community organisations, welfare groups, government agencies and the churches, together with concerned health professionals and academics. Its objects were:

> To help safeguard and strengthen family life; to study those factors which promote sound family life and those which tend to cause its breakdown; to take any appropriate action to promote family welfare, and; to cooperate with and assist the work of statutory, governmental, municipal and other bodies, voluntary organisations and interested persons who are concerned with family welfare.[15]

With Breen as president, it quickly became the preferred channel of communication with government for those in the child and family welfare field. In May 1959 Breen took a delegation from the Family Council to the chief secretary, Arthur Rylah, on behalf of the Child Advisory Committee complaining about lack of consultation; in April 1960, she intervened in the administration of the Department of Health with a plea that, in the interests of 'family life' and 'good motherhood',

> the Maternal and Infant Welfare and Pre-school Division [should] remain a separate Division of the Department of Health, and continue as at present under the direction of a Woman Medical Director experienced in this field, whose status shall not be diminished.[16]

---

14 NCWV Annual General Meeting, 15 March 1956, NCWV Council Minutes, NCWV Papers, SLV (accession pending).

15 Cate O'Neill, 'Victorian Family Council (1958–)', *Find and Connect*, http://www.findandconnect.gov.au/ref/vic/biogs/E000630b.htm.

16 NCWV Council Minutes, 14 May 1959, 14 April 1960, NCWV Papers, SLV (accession pending).

Thus the concerns of NCWV for the wellbeing of families and of women within families became subsumed in the interests of welfare professionals in shaping policy and defending their professional status.

Federal action on moral welfare issues was constitutionally limited. The major Commonwealth power of relevance to the defence of moral standards was the power to control and prohibit imports, as we have seen with respect to contraceptives and films. NCWA regularly lobbied the minister for customs asking for further action in this area; in 1963 the board wrote supporting the prohibition of 'gambling toys' and 'pornographic literature' such as *Playboy*, and the introduction of uniform censorship of both film and print.[17] Broader policy formation proved difficult at the federal level. The national Standing Committee on Child and the Family heeded the ICW call to strengthen family as a means of preventing delinquency, and took up 'Family Stability in a Decade of Development' as the theme for the national program of work for the 1963–66 triennium.[18] But three years later at the 1967 triennial conference, the convenor for child and the family found it hard to point to specific areas of improvement. She reported that, while the work of the committee was 'motivated by a deep desire to attain and maintain "Family Stability"', the theme had 'proved much too wide for one triennium and has been continued in the 1966–69 plan of work under the title "Progress towards Family Stability"'.[19]

Phyllis Frost, speaking at the same conference as the national convenor for social and moral welfare, looked as always for practical policy outcomes. She argued that the problem of

> increased violence, particularly amongst young people … increased illegitimate births, sexual promiscuity and rise in venereal disease makes it imperative that constructive and firm educational and practical action must be taken to counteract the

---

17   *NCWA Report 1963–64*, Launceston.
18   *NCWA Report 1963–64*, Launceston.
19   *NCWA Conference 1967*, Brisbane.

adverse influences which we believe are being exerted on the community, particularly on youth today.

But, in the end, Frost put her faith less in social action than in the work of individual women in the home:

> Increasing pressures are being exerted on us all, but particularly on young people, and we must reiterate that it is the first responsibility of women to preserve high moral standards and to pass them on to future generations through the family unit.[20]

The 1967 triennial conference was particularly coloured by fear of social disintegration. Anne Hamilton's presidential address took up the essentially optimistic theme proposed by ICW, 'The Significance of Communication in Development', and her presentation looked to a better future for women in developing countries. But her view of her own affluent society was bleak: 'There is a sickness in our society'. Road accidents were caused by 'immature, selfish egoism, a callous disregard for human life, and for the rights of others'. 'Brutal attacks on women in their own homes' were also a kind of sickness. 'Destructive, twisted egoism' had its beginning in a loveless infancy.[21] The conference concluded with a half-day seminar on 'Ethical Standards for Modern Living'. Pioneering psychiatrist Alan Stoller opened the proceedings with a view of 'Society and Moral Values' almost as bleak as Hamilton's. He predicted the decline of the monogamous family, the policing of populations by psychological profiling, a huge growth in urbanisation and a concomitant growth of 'a conforming society of individuals, less involved with children and families, more selfishly isolated', and moved by mass media to 'selfish emotion'.[22]

The discussion that followed involved all the seminar participants. Given the aim 'to define morals from the point of view of NCW

---

20 *NCWA Conference 1967*, Brisbane.
21 Anne Hamilton, 'President's Address', *NCWA Conference 1967*, Brisbane, p. 3.
22 Alan Stoller, 'Society and Moral Values', *NCWA Conference 1967*, Brisbane. pp. 29–34.

members', the participants chose to deal with Stoller's dire predictions by voting to reassert the values of their class and culture, with a nod towards difference in the conclusion.

> There was general agreement on the desirability of honesty, integrity, truthfulness, chastity, faithfulness in marriage; a consideration for the rights of others and a respect for the right of each person to develop according to the individual potential within the discipline of community welfare; a recognition of the obligation to contribute towards community welfare and promote loyal, reasoned behaviour in both personal relations and community attitudes. Courage to hold to and practise beliefs of right and wrong was essential. It was also a responsibility of each person to take opportunities available to acquire knowledge and understanding of society here and abroad as it is, because it was recognised that what is right in one place and time is not necessarily so for ever and everywhere.[23]

Marriage and Divorce

The story of NCWA's campaign for equal and uniform divorce legislation is by contrast one of concrete achievement—but in this case the goal was clearly defined and achievable. The councils' understandings were shaped by the equal rights language that came down to them from ICW, and by the legal rights language framed for them by the women lawyers who sat on their laws standing committees. The tensions aroused by women's changing relationship to home and family had no purchase within this legal language. But, for all that, fear of family instability also plays its part in this story.

We have already seen how intractable problems with prosecuting divorce and obtaining maintenance across state borders, together with the impossibility of amending state legislation, moved the Federal

---

23 'Study Report: Ethical Standards for Modern Living', *NCWA Conference 1967*, Brisbane. pp. 35–8.

Council of the National Councils of Women of Australia to seek a federal marriage and divorce law from as early as 1925.[24] The problem of domicile was of particular concern—that provision by which:

> If a husband deserts a wife, to live in another State, she must live in that State to divorce him. But if he lives in Timbuctoo, he can divorce a wife in Australia, though she is not in Timbuctoo to defend herself.[25]

Reformers also targeted specific cases of discrimination in state legislation. The Victorian law was particularly objectionable, preserving as it did the old inequitable provision that allowed a husband to divorce a wife for a single act of adultery, while a wife had to prove 'aggravated adultery' on the husband's part. There was sharp debate about which state provisions should be included in any uniform federal law.[26] The most contentious was the Western Australian provision allowing as a ground for divorce five years of separation with no reasonable likelihood of reconciliation: a step towards 'no-fault' divorce'.[27]

In 1951, the International Council of Women welcomed the enunciation of the principle of equality in marriage in the United Nations Declaration of Human Rights, and looked forward to a Convention supporting equality between spouses. In Australia, this strengthened the voices of NCWA leaders concerned primarily with women's rights in marriage. Brookes's board moved to initiate federal legislation, asking all states to comment on what grounds for divorce should be included.[28] At the same time they sought advice on drafting a suitable bill from

---

24 Ada Norris, *Champions of the Impossible: A History of the National Council of Women of Victoria*, Melbourne, Hawthorn Press, 1978, p. 57.
25 Lawyer Joan Rosanove in an address to NCWV in 1933, cited in Norris, *Champions*, p. 77.
26 Norris, *Champions*, p. 63.
27 James Walter, 'Designing Families and Solid Citizens: The Dialectic of Modernity and the Matrimonial Causes Bill of 1959', *Australian Historical Studies*, 32 (116), April 2001, p. 48.
28 NCWA Board Minutes, 28 August 1951, Box 13, MS7583, NCWA Papers, National Library of Australia (NLA).

a Victorian federal member of parliament, Percy Joske, who had been working for years for uniform federal legislation.[29] In the next months, the board decided to give general support to a bill that Joske was drafting, and Marie Breen, the NCWA international secretary, joined Joske in radio broadcasts promoting reform.[30] In September 1952, the board was told that Joske was almost ready to put the bill before parliament and that the NCWA Laws Standing Committee was providing him with further information.[31]

In the state councils, commitment to reform was much more hesitant. The affiliates whose delegates made up these councils included many organisations representing or based on religious denominations, like the Catholic St Joan's Social and Political Alliance and the Anglican Mothers' Union, together with generically Christian groups like the Woman's Christian Temperance Union and the Young Women's Christian Association. Some of these groups were totally opposed to any federal divorce legislation. The St Joan's Alliance feared that federal action would 'suggest to the people of Australia that there is no body of public opinion in Australia sufficiently strong to preserve the binding power of marriage'; more specifically they believed that: 'Such legislation must inevitably widen the scope of divorce because all the grounds of divorce in all the States would be made grounds of divorce under Commonwealth Law'.[32]

A special meeting of the Queensland council called to discuss Joske's draft bill heard this same argument, that 'the allowable grounds for divorce in the various states totalled 23, but that Queensland had only 7 grounds' and that 'to achieve uniformity Queensland might have

---

29 NCWA Board Minutes, 11 September 1951, Box 13, MS7583, NCWA Papers, NLA.
30 NCWA Board Minutes, 11 March and 13 May 1952, Box 13, MS7583, NCWA Papers, NLA.
31 NCWA Board Minutes, 23 September 1952, Box 13, MS7583, NCWA Papers, NLA.
32 Statement by St Joan's Alliance, Marriage and Divorce Bill 1947, A432 1956/2207, National Archives of Australia (NAA).

to accept additional grounds which might make divorce easier'. One response was 'that, as Queensland has fewer grounds than any other State it would be better to keep our present status and let the women of other States fight their own battles'. But others argued for federal legislation because 'grounds should be uniform for men and women' and across the states. The note taker even-handedly summed up the feeling of the meeting: 'Most members were in favour of the principle of uniformity, no one wanted divorce in general made easier, everyone agreed that the first care should be to the happiness of home and family'.[33]

Leaders at a national level paid due respect to this unstable mix of opinion. In her president's report to the 1954 conference, Ruth Gibson celebrated the fact that 'in the matter of divorce laws ... the NCWA has long since taken the lead in urging reforms', then promptly qualified this with a defence of home and family:

> Lest there should be the slightest misapprehension as to the stand taken by the NCWA as regards the home and family, let me here reiterate our belief that the home is the very foundation stone of national life, and we at all times give our support to anything that will foster and strengthen happy home life.

At the same time, she stood by the equality model: 'Whatever our views on divorce, the fact remains that marked inequalities exist in law as between men and women and as between States, and it seems only fair and just that these should be removed'. And, in concluding, she paid specific attention to the issue of 'easier divorce': 'It does not automatically follow that with uniformity will come easier divorce, as some people fear, but the solution may probably lie in a suitable compromise between the existing State laws'.[34]

This careful defence of uniformity and equity proved effective; the conference minutes record that, yet again: 'NCWA reaffirmed its belief

---

33   NCWQ Council Minutes of Special Meeting, 4 November 1953, Box 16045, 7266 NCWQ Minute Books, NCWQ Papers, State Library of Queensland (SLQ).
34   *NCWA Biennial Conference, 1954*, Adelaide, p. 2.

in the desirability of the establishment of Australian domicile and of uniform divorce laws for Australia. The Board was asked to advise Federal Government accordingly, asking them to take early action'.[35]

Yet again, the federal government took no immediate action. In 1955, Percy Joske pushed through a limited marriage act that achieved a national domicile for women. It was not until 1957 that his more wide-ranging bill seeking to establish uniform national marriage and divorce legislation was finally introduced to parliament.[36] Again the commitment of NCWA was tested by principled opposition within its own ranks. The South Australian council, previously strongly in support of national legislation,[37] was advised by its own legal subcommittee to reject the Joske bill. The issue was not grounds for divorce, but the absence from the bill of provision for judicial separation. Lawyer Roma Mitchell, the state convenor on legal matters, was both a champion of equal rights and a practising Catholic. She argued in a private memorandum to the executive that judicial separation on the South Australian model provided a dignified alternative to deserted and abused wives who did not wish for moral or religious reasons to seek divorce; this provision would disappear with the passage of the Joske bill. The executive gave a vote of thanks to Miss Mitchell, but minuted that 'General feeling that opposition to the Bill of Mr Joske should not be stirred up, as it is most desirable there should be an Australian Act on Matrimonial Causes'.[38]

In the event, Joske's bill stalled in the House of Representatives, and he withdrew it when Prime Minister Robert Menzies promised that the attorney-general, Garfield Barwick, would bring in a 'commensurate'

---

35 *NCWA Biennial Conference, 1954*, Adelaide, p. 31.
36 The origins of the Joske bill go back to 1947 when Evatt appointed Joske and two other lawyers to draft a uniform federal marriage and divorce law. See the file Marriage and Divorce Bill 1947, A432 1956/2207, NAA; also Henry Finlay, *To Have But Not To Hold: A History of Attitudes to Marriage and Divorce in Australia 1858–1975*, Sydney, Federation Press, 2005, pp. 304–7.
37 See, for example, NCWSA Executive Minutes, 4 November 1952, SRG297, NCWSA Papers, State Library of South Australia (SLSA).
38 NCWSA Executive Minutes, 30 July 1957, 12 September 1957 (insert), Series 1, SRG297, NCWSA Papers, SLSA.

government measure.³⁹ Barwick's Matrimonial Causes Bill was in fact much more radical than Joske's. Where Joske repeated state provisions assuming men to be the 'natural' breadwinners,⁴⁰ Barwick's grounds for divorce were scrupulously non-discriminatory in gender terms, to the extent of expecting a guilty wife to pay children's maintenance.

Barwick also included the Western Australian provision for divorce after five years separation. The clause had been controversial when it was introduced in Western Australia, and church groups loudly condemned its presence in the federal legislation. Members of parliament from both sides of the house criticised it during the debates on the bill. Many women wanted legal responsibility firmly sheeted home to the guilty (male) party, in the hope that public shaming might promote reform and save the marriage, or at least inspire a healthy maintenance award from the court. Senator Dorothy Tangney, who otherwise supported marriage and divorce law equality, fiercely opposed the no-fault clause on the grounds that 'in nine cases out of ten, in Western Australia, it is the women who suffer under this provision'.

> I could give you example after example ... of women who have borne children, who have helped their husbands in their businesses or other enterprises and who have grown old in the doing of it and who have found, when success has been attained, that they have been dumped for some bright young thing.⁴¹

One might expect to find this kind of opposition in the national councils, and the no-fault clause certainly caused some disquiet. In South Australia conservatives expressed concern that a guilty person could seek divorce after five years, and the president commented that this could prove to be 'a stumbling block to the new Bill'.⁴²

---

39   Margaret Fitzherbert, *So Many Firsts: Liberal Women from Enid Lyons to the Turnball Era*, Sydney, Federation Press, 2009, p. 56.
40   Marriage and Divorce Bill 1947, A432 1956/2207, NAA.
41   *Commonwealth Parliamentary Debates* (*CPD*), Senate, 25 November 1959, p. 1835.
42   NCWSA Council Minutes, 1 September 1959, September 1957 – September 1963, SRG297, NCWSA Papers, SLSA.

The board seems to have asked the convenor of the national Laws Standing Committee for advice on the impact of the no-fault clause on innocent parties to the divorce. Sesca Zelling advised the board that the only provision under which an application for divorce by separation might be refused was one in which 'the particular circumstances of the case [would] be harsh and oppressive to the respondent or contrary to the public interest', specifically in the case of adultery 'not condoned by the respondent'. It was Zelling's opinion that while the clause:

> certainly imports a new concept into the law relating to matrimonial causes ... some members of the National Council of Women may feel nevertheless (as the draftsman of the bill undoubtedly must feel) that it is better in such a case as that postulated to permit the [guilty] husband to remarry because it is unlikely that the husband and wife will resume cohabitation in the future. [43]

The board reluctantly accepted the logic of this advice. They sent on Zelling's report to Barwick, with a cover note affirming the need for 'uniformity in the Divorce Laws', recognising 'the efforts which have been made to protect the welfare of children', and noting that 'The provision of adequate safeguards in connection with [the no-fault clause] is essential for the protection of innocent parties in such cases'.[44] Barwick's non-committal response to the board's letter was summarised without comment in the December 1959 issue of the *NCWA Newsletter*.

By 1960, the convenorship of the national Laws and Suffrage Standing Committee had passed from Sesca Zelling to Roma Mitchell. Mitchell had criticised Joske's bill for not including a provision for judicial separation, something also lacking in Barwick's Matrimonial

---

43 'Re Matrimonial Causes Bill 1959', report of Convenor of Laws to NCWA Board, NCWA Correspondence, Folder 'Attorney General and Human Rights Commission', Box 4, MS7583, NCWA Papers, NLA.

44 President of NCWA to Barwick, 22 November 1959, cover letter to report of Convenor of Laws to NCWA Board, NCWA Correspondence, Folder 'Attorney General and Human Rights Commission', Box 4, MS7583, NCWA Papers, NLA.

Causes Act. But the summary of the act that Mitchell presented to the 1960 biennial conference was largely positive. After noting that 'there are some provisions which may appear to render divorce easier to attain and to lead to an easier breakup of marriage', Mitchell detailed some of the 'many provisions in the Act which must be a benefit to the family as a unit, and which are in accord with the recommendations which have been made by the NCWA', including: 'the attachment of wages to enforce maintenance', 'the settlement of the property including the matrimonial home', 'conciliation whenever it appears at all likely that the marriage may be saved', and the refusal of a divorce until 'proper provisions have been made for the children'.[45] There was much there to satisfy the Australian councils.

The creation of uniform and equal divorce legislation was necessarily the work of lawyers. Beyond providing a platform and support for feminist women lawyers, the national councils had little impact on the detailed content of the act. But their consistent public advocacy over more than three decades, together with their identification of the particular problems faced by women, helped keep the issue politically alive in Canberra. In the wider community, the most significant result of the long years of debates within the councils may have been the tacit agreement that ending unhappy marriages could strengthen happy ones.

---

45   Roma Mitchell, Report of the Convenor Laws and Suffrage Standing Committee, *NCWA Biennial Conference, Adelaide, 29 October – 4 November, 1960*, p. 64.

Chapter 10

WOMEN IN THE WORKFORCE

The story of how NCWA helped win equal pay for Australian women is still celebrated within the association as a tale of obstacles overcome and principles vindicated. Less remembered is the fact that obstacles existed within the councils as well as without. Women representing affiliates with a religious base tended to see the presence of women in the workforce, especially married women, as a threat to family life. Even among women who supported equal pay, there was, as we have seen, no necessary agreement on the form that it should take. Social liberals argued from an egalitarian position that looked to remove all barriers to working women's equality with working men. More conservative women might support the principle only in so far as it related to the wages of professional women, or implied a lowering of men's wages by abandoning the family basis of wage fixation to accommodate better pay for women. The chapter tells how the leaders of the association negotiated the thorny moral and emotional issues raised by working women, and brought the councils to a full endorsement of gender equality in the workplace—a principle involving the removal of barriers to the employment of married women as well as the achievement of equal pay. The story also tells how an organisation largely representing middle-class women broadened its understanding of equity to embrace all women who worked.

The International Council of Women's long and close association with the International Labour Organization since the early 1920s brought an early recognition that the liberal proposition of 'equal pay' had to be elaborated into a concept with some traction in courts and tribunals—'equal pay for work of equal value'—and this was reflected in resolutions such as that passed in Vienna in 1930, as we have seen. At the first conference after World War II in 1947, a new resolution proposed: 'That irrespective of sex, equal pay for equal work and equal opportunities for promotion should become a reality in all gainful employment', and further: 'That neither marriage nor child-bearing should debar women from having full opportunities in trades and professions, including the Civil Services, and that all existing barriers should be abolished'.[1]

During the Second World War, the creation of the Australian Women's Employment Board to deal with the wages of women replacing men as well as those going into new war industries allowed a small minority of women to achieve 90 per cent of the male rate, as we have seen. And, in the post-war years, the Arbitration Court commonly awarded women 75 per cent in cases that came before it.[2] Alarmed by this trend, in 1949, employers argued at the Arbitration Court's inquiry into the basic wage that women's wages should return to pre-war levels. The Australian Council of Trade Unions claimed equal pay for women, but the logic of their position was somewhat undermined by a parallel demand for a male basic wage sufficient to support a family of five. Professional women's associations sought leave to intervene in defence of women's wages, and NCWA followed suit—though only in terms of a simple statement that 'equal pay had been a plank of the platform of the National Councils for many years'.[3] The court ruled that, given

---

1   Philadelphia 1947, 'ICW Resolutions', www.ncwcanada.com/ncwc2/wp-content/uploads/2014/02/ICW-CIF_Resolutions1.pdf, p. 180.
2   Edna Ryan and Anne Conlon, *Gentle Invaders: Australian Women at Work*, Melbourne, Penguin, 1989, chapter 5.
3   NCWA Board Minutes, 28 November 1949, Box 13, MS7583, NCWA Papers, National Library of Australia (NLA).

that the male was 'normally' the breadwinner of an Australian family, 'the question of relative efficiency or productivity between males and females was not relevant', but it did not agree to a return to pre-war levels, setting the female basic wage at 75 per cent of the male wage.[4]

The first years of the fifties saw important gains for women workers at the international level, and Australian feminists were keen to promote these back home. Australian delegate Isabel McCorkindale returned from the 4th session of the Commission on the Status of Women (CSW) to tell the *Argus* in September 1950 that the 'Biggest thrill for me was being present … when 117 delegates accepted the report for equal remuneration for work of equal value'.[5] The following year her successor, Jean Daly, just back from the 5th session of CSW, reported to the *Sydney Morning Herald* that a high point of her trip had been the recommendation by the International Labour Organization of a Convention guaranteeing 'equal remuneration of men and women doing work of equal value';[6] she did not mention that the forty members of the ILO conference who abstained from the vote approving the equal pay Convention included Australia and most of the British Commonwealth.[7] Mary Tenison Woods, the Australian-born bureaucrat in charge of CSW, back in Sydney for a holiday, told the *Sydney Morning Herald* in September 1951 that the 5th session of the commission had passed a resolution 'deprecating the fact that Australia was one of the few nations where women public servants were paid lower wages than men' and, further, that the Commonwealth government would shortly receive notice about this from the United Nations.[8]

---

4   Ryan and Conlon, *Gentle Invaders*, p. 141.
5   'World Conference on Equality: "a momentous year for women"', *Argus*, 20 September 1950, p. 9.
6   'Delegate to UN on Status of Women: Mrs Harry Daly back from 5th Session of Status of Women Commission', *Sydney Morning Herald*, 9 August 1951, p. 3.
7   'Convention on Equal Pay', *Sydney Morning Herald*, 30 June 1951 p. 3.
8   'Women Public Servants Entitled to Equal Pay', *Sydney Morning Herald*, 20 September 1951, p. 14.

Given the international gains, Australian women's organisations were indignant when in July 1952 a group of employers' organisations brought a case before the Commonwealth Arbitration Court seeking a reduction in the basic wage and, with that, a reduction of women's wages from 75 to 60 per cent of the male rate. It was, as Jean Daly said in a letter to the *Sydney Morning Herald*, 'strange that at this time, when an upward trend is taking place, a retrograde step of a further reduction in the rate should even be considered'.[9] In Victoria, the Women Graduates Association raised the matter at a meeting of Victoria's National Council of Women. Frances Pennington from the VWGA 'pointed out that it was only simple justice that was sought in asking for equal pay for equal work instead of the proposed cut in women's wages'. She asked the council to support a protest against the Victorian Chamber of Manufactures, one of the groups involved in in the court case. When the meeting enthusiastically agreed, lawyer Molly Kingston suggested a further move, 'that steps be taken to intervene at the Arbitration Court', and again 'all agreed'.[10]

From asserting 'simple justice' to mounting an intervention before the Arbitration Court was not a simple matter. To be effective, an intervention needed to be made on the opening day of the case, in this instance Tuesday 5 August. Victorian president Ada Norris and convenor of laws Ethleen King investigated the circumstances of the case and the legal procedures involved, and decided that action was possible and useful. On their recommendation, the Victorian executive asked the Australian National Council of Women to make a formal intervention in the case. The national board met on Monday 4 August and decided that action should be taken 'as a natural corollary of the Councils' policy, viz "Equal Pay for Equal Work"'. Time was too short to contact all the state councils, but the August *NCWA News Sheet* reported that

---

9   Mrs Jean Daly, 'Wage for Women', *Sydney Morning Herald*, 22 September 1952, p. 2.
10 NCWV Council Minutes, 10 July 1952, NCWV Papers, State Library of Victoria (SLV) (accession pending).

'telegrams to State Councils brought unanimous confirmation of the board's action'.[11] The news sheet informed members, with quiet pride, that 'Miss M. Kingston, Solicitor, and member of NCW was authorised by NCWA to act on our behalf, and at the opening session of the case on Tuesday 5th August, she successfully applied for "leave to intervene"'.

The board was careful to make it clear, at this point and later, that the intervention was purely directed towards the issue of women's inequality.

> We wish to stress that the Council is not opposing the other matters being considered at the same time, nor is it protesting against the general wage reduction. The point on which we have lodged the protest is the unfair discrimination against women in the application for a further reduction from 75% of the male basic wage to 60%.[12]

There would be a continuing need to reassure the membership of councils and affiliated organisations that working for equal pay did not mean an alliance with the trade union movement, commonly seen by Liberal voters as run by communists.

Much work remained to be done. Kingston based her case on equity and disadvantage. She asked the councils for help in finding suitable witnesses to take the stand: women who were 21 years old or more and earning the basic wage; middle-aged women; and elderly women. In each case they should be able to give evidence of hardship.[13] The Legal Women's Association and Molly Kingston volunteered their services, but Ruth Gibson, soon to take over the national presidency from Ivy Brookes, believed that 'at least an honorarium should be paid'. She distributed a notice to delegates to the South Australian council, pointing out that the intervention was 'a vast undertaking, requiring

---

11 'NCWA Intervention in Arbitration Court', *NCWA News Sheet*, August 1952.
12 'NCWA Intervention in Arbitration Court', *NCWA News Sheet*, August 1952 (emphasis in the original).
13 *NCWSA* Executive Minutes, 2 September 1952, Box 4, SRG297, NCWSA Papers, State Library of South Australia (SLSA).

expert evidence on economic factors, as well as legal procedures', and estimating costs at £250—£50 per council. 'The appeal is therefore to every woman to do what she can, to give what she can, and for every women's organisation to give every possible support to this appeal.'[14] The appeal was answered, in South Australia and the other states.

In NSW, Joyce Cocks, convenor of the laws committee, donated 2 guineas to the cause, on the understanding that 'NCW supports the principle of the rate for the job for single men and women—this would bring the wages of men down to the wages of women'.[15] Cocks's reading of the effects of equal pay serves as a reminder that conservative women could support women's equality in the workplace without any expectation of economic levelling. Liberal feminists wrote equal opportunity into the policy platform of the Liberal Party in 1948, but economic equality was hedged with qualifications. The party committed itself only to: 'The elimination of anomalies in employment opportunities for women, and the institution of further enquiries into the principles of assessing women's wage rates, with a view to the correction of existing injustices'.[16] The term used by Miss Cocks—'the rate for the job'—was the same used in Senate debates in 1958, by Liberal Senator Agnes Robertson to distinguish her claim from that of Labor members who were calling for 'equal pay for the sexes'. Robertson declared that 'The demand by women's organisations is for equal pay for equal work or the rate for the job'.[17] The leaders of NCWA never publicly supported a reading of equal pay that would bring down men's wages, but some councils were more enthusiastic than others for 'equal pay for the sexes' without these constraints. But others—in particular NCWNSW

---

14 Single loose sheet inserted in NCWSA Executive Minutes, 4 November 1952, Box 4, SRG297, NCWSA Papers, SLSA.
15 NCWNSW Executive Minutes, 30 October 1952, 24 September 1954, Box MLK03009, MS3739, NCWNSW Papers, State Library of New South Wales (SLNSW).
16 Fitzherbert, *So Many Firsts*, p. 28.
17 *CPD*, Senate, Senator Agnes Robertson, 18 September 1958, p. 1.

during the 1950s—seem to have been more interested in wage equity for professional women than equality across the board.

Some indication of the extent of women's organisations ready to support the case for equal pay can be seen in the minutes of the Australian Liaison Committee. This peak body met in Sydney until mid-1952, at which point it was reconstituted in Adelaide with Ruth Gibson in the chair. At its first Adelaide meeting, the committee considered a letter from Jean Daly, suggesting that the time was ripe to press the federal government to ratify the ILO Convention on equal remuneration for work of equal value. A motion to this effect was supported by members representing the Australian Federation of Women Voters, the National Council of Women of Australia, the Australian Federation of Business and Professional Women's Clubs, and the Australian Federation of University Women. Of these, the Business and Professional Women and the University Women represented professional women. Daly also recommended support for NCWA in their Arbitration Court intervention; in this case: 'It was resolved unanimously that the members of the Committee support member bodies who are intervening in the proceedings before the Federal Arbitration Court ... but the Committee is not in a position at present itself to intervene'.[18]

In the event, Molly Kingston presented a submission to the Arbitration Court on behalf of two organisations: the National Council of Women of Australia and the Australian Federation of Business and Professional Women's Clubs. The submission was made 'in regard to so much of the employers' case as relates to the application to reduce the female basic wage from 75% to 60% of the male basic wage'.[19] The case submitted was shaped as a response to the employers' case, and so had little to do with 'simple justice'. Rather, Kingston argued that no evidence had been introduced to support a reduction in wages beyond

---

18   ALC Minutes, 25 August 1952, MS1082, ALC Papers, NLA.
19   'Basic Wage Case—1952–53', typescript, Box 33, MS90/190, Papers of Mrs J.G. Norris (Norris Papers), University of Melbourne Archives (UMA).

a vague gesturing towards needs; that 'the relative needs of the female as opposed to the male have risen', rather than declined; and that to fix female wages 'as a proportion of the male wage assessed on the needs of a single female' is 'neither "just" nor "reasonable" to the individual female worker or to the community'. She defended the decision in 1950 to raise the female rate to 75 per cent as 'a recognition by the Court (albeit rather tardily) of the fact that the average female employee was a very different person from the itinerant fruit picker or seamstress considered by Mr Justice Higgins'. The stenographers and teachers and nurses in the workforce *deserved* more pay.

> The female worker of this country has by her efforts decreased largely the former responsibility of males for dependants, partly by removing herself from the dependent class and partly by undertaking what was previously solely male responsibility, namely the provision of support for dependants.

When, after much delay, Justice Foster handed down the Arbitration Court's decision on the case, women workers were pleased to find that the court declined to lower the ratio of female to male wages below 75 per cent. Kingston would have been less pleased with the court's reasoning; the judgement was based entirely on industry's capacity to pay. The *Sydney Morning Herald* reported that: 'No question of adjudging what should be the relationship to the male basic-wage was involved in the decision, although Foster J. did expressly reject the claim for "complete equality immediately" as being in the circumstances "socially undesirable"'.[20]

The federal government agreed. The brief provided to Jean Daly as the Australian representative to the ninth session of the UN Status of Women Commission included a detailed explanation of Australia's inability to ratify the ILO Convention concerning Equal Remuneration; the matter properly belonged to the courts, and 'At present a large

---

20 'Basic Hours and Wages Judgment', *Sydney Morning Herald*, 28 October 1953, p. 8.

section of the Australian public remains unconvinced that women should be granted equal rights with men in the matter of remuneration'.[21]

Despite the commitment of the leadership of NCWA to equality in the workplace, many within the councils were concerned about the 'socially undesirable effects' of working mothers, especially the mothers of small children. Ruth Gibson told the 1954 biennial conference of NCWA that 'there was no doubt that ... as far as humanly possible, [mothers] should be in the home with their children'.[22] Other moral concerns could also cloud the issue. In 1955, a meeting of the National Council of Women of South Australia discussed a proposal 'that the NCW should protest against the re-introduction of the employment of women as barmaids'. When this was reported to the Australian Liaison Committee its members were appalled: 'Such an attitude is contrary to the principles of equal opportunity and there should be no discrimination against women'. Recognising that this view was not widely shared across the women's movement, the committee put it on record that they considered it 'desirable that women's organisations in South Australia should be made aware of the principles of equal opportunity and equal pay', and prepared a brochure to this effect.[23]

Ruth Gibson also took the issue to the NCW state councils, writing as national president to ask 'What is each state doing to bring about Equal Pay for Equal Work? Are we being sufficiently vocal and active?'[24] State councils responded with varying degrees of knowledge and interest. In Queensland, executive members were already working with an Equal Pay Committee organised by the Brisbane Trades and Labour Council, and undertook with them a publicity campaign with radio talks, public

---

21 SWC9/Item 6—Equal Pay for Equal Work, Background notes for the Australian representative Mrs Jean Daly, United Nations Commission of the Status of Women New York Ninth Session—14th March – 1st April, 1955, 856/15/10/2 Annex, External Affairs, A1838/1, National Archives of Australia (NAA).
22 *NCWA Biennial Conference*, Adelaide, 1954, p. 15.
23 ALC Minutes, 18 April 1955, Box 1, MS1082, ALC Papers, NLA.
24 NCWNSW Executive Minutes, 25 August 1955, Box MLK03009, MS3739, NCWNSW Papers, SLNSW.

meetings and a petition to the state premier.[25] The Victorians were more gradualist in their approach. They began with their own affiliates, holding a special council meeting to 'inform members of the principle of Equal Pay for Work of Equal Value', and offering the services of board members to any organisation wanting a speaker on this issue. They progressed to co-operating with an Equal Pay Committee formed by the Victorian Teachers' Union, then formed their own committee, chaired by Ada Norris, to 'inform and develop public opinion on the question of equal pay for equal work'.[26] Members of the NCWSA executive were understandably well informed, with Gibson in their midst. Their minutes record a discussion about the issue raised by Joyce Cocks in NSW: that the removal of the family wage differential from the male wage would bring down men's wages to the level of women's. Unlike Miss Cocks, they feared this outcome and canvassed various ways of avoiding it: 'a family endowment, or pay on the basis of two people, with family endowment'; 'child endowment ... Maternity Allowance'.[27] In the end, they referred the issue to the NCWA conference in Tasmania in January 1957.

The conference devoted a whole session to the issue of workplace equality. A motion from Victoria picked up on a resolution listed for discussion at the 1957 ICW conference in Montreal: 'The ICW upholds the principle that a woman, whether married or single, has the right to take up paid employment'.[28] The Victorian resolution required the state and federal governments to amend their public service regulations so that 'marriage of itself shall be no bar to access to, or retention in, and promotion in employment of women'.[29] The motion was not carried

---

25 NCWQ Executive Minutes 5 April 1956, 21 May 1956, 2 July 1956, 16 July 1956, Box 16045, 7266 NCWQ Minute Books, NCWQ Papers, SLQ.
26 NCWV Council Minutes, 9 September 1957, 8 August 1957, 10 October 1957, NCWV Papers, SLV (accession pending).
27 NCWSA Council Minutes, 3 July 1956, Box 4, SRG297, NCWSA Papers, SLSA.
28 Montreal 1957, 'ICW Resolutions', www.ncwcanada.com/ncwc2/wp-content/uploads/2014/02/ICW-CIF_Resolutions1.pdf, p. 182.
29 *NCWA Biennial Conference*, Hobart and Launceston, 12–19 January 1957.

without debate. When, prior to the conference, this motion had been circulated to the state councils for discussion, country delegates told the South Australian council that married women did not always accept the full responsibilities of employment; 'single women are more likely to be sent to the country, as married women insist on staying near their home'. The delegate from Women Graduates suggested an amendment: that 'marriage shall be no bar to promotion "provided [married women] are employed under the same conditions as single women"'.[30] At the NCWA conference, South Australia moved this amendment and the motion was carried as amended.

Its passage was immediately followed by the discussion of the topic that had long vexed NCWSA:

> That NCWA discuss and endeavour to reconcile two Council policies which at present seem to conflict: 1. That men and women should receive equal pay for equal work. 2. That a satisfactory home life be maintained as being the basis of good community and home life.

The introductory statement set out the issues as the South Australians understood them.

> If the basis of pay is equal for men and women [and men are not paid a family wage], it means that in many cases a man, wife, and several children would have to live on the same income as a single man or woman. The consequence is bound to be that more married women would feel impelled to enter into money earning jobs outside the homes so that their standard of living could be maintained. This would mean increased lack of security for children without real family life. What is the solution? Do married women work because of the economic position, or because they prefer the outside job to home life? What can ensure security of home life for children?

---

30   NCWSA Council Minutes, 8 October 1956, Box 4, SRG297, NCWSA Papers, SLSA.

Unfortunately there is no record of the conference discussion. We only know that the president Ruth Gibson intervened, suggesting that the subject 'required a good deal of research', and referred it back to the individual councils for further consideration.[31]

By 1958, the issue of equal pay and equal opportunity seemed less and less a matter of 'simple justice', and more a moral conundrum. NCWA's position was further complicated by political and industrial moves to claim the issue for the Australian Labor Party and the union movement. In March, the Australian Council of Trade Unions endorsed equal pay for work of equal value, and in the same month the Labor government in New South Wales announced that it would legislate for equal pay for all men and women working under state awards. At federal level the minister for labour, Harold Holt, responded that the government 'did not oppose the principle of equal pay', but believed that the matter should be decided by the appropriate tribunals.[32] Threats of strikes and demonstrations kept the issue prominently in the news. Within the national councils, co-operation with unionists came under challenge. In Brisbane, a member of the executive complained about the conduct of the Equal Pay Committee:

> She went as an observer to the last meeting of this Committee, and she considered that a number of the speeches made were simply rabble-rousers. The subject was treated from a militant Trades Union angle, with talk of Australia-wide strikes, etc. She felt it was not the sort of thing the NCW wanted.[33]

In Melbourne, Ada Norris spoke on behalf of NCW Victoria at an equal pay rally organised by the Trades Hall, then came under criticism from within the new NCWA board—now based in New South Wales—for

---

31 *NCWA Biennial Conference*, Hobart and Launceston, 12–19 January 1957.
32 'Tribunals Place for Equal Pay Issue, Says Holt', *Canberra Times*, 16 June 1958, p. 3.
33 NCWQ Executive Minutes, 2 September 1957, Box 16045, 7266 NCWQ Minute Books, NCWQ Papers, SLQ.

associating NCW publicly with the union movement.[34] In Perth, Leila Roberts, representing the WA Equal Pay Conference, was generally well received at a NCWWA meeting, but one listener complained that 'Unions were ruling the world and charitable organisations worked for nothing'.[35]

None of these interventions derailed the NCWA campaign for equal pay. Protests were met politely then set aside. Ada Norris recommended to the national board, now led by Thelma Metcalfe, that the best way to implement conference's recommendation was to undertake a national campaign for equal pay that included 'the fact that the NCW was a supporter of equal pay long before it was the policy of the Trade Union Movement or of any political party'.[36] Given the location of the Arbitration Court in Melbourne, Metcalfe tended to depute equal pay matters to Norris, who pursued them vigorously within trade union circles and beyond. In May 1960, she reported to the board that she had attended the annual ACTU conference to discuss equal pay and other issues relating to women in paid employment. The greatest difficulty hampering the campaign was, she said, the lack of reliable data on which to build one's case.[37]

Opening the NCWA biennial conference in October 1960, Thelma Metcalfe was optimistic about the equal pay campaign: 'After many years Equal Pay is on the way and the 1958 N.S.Wales Act points the way'.[38] Metcalfe's comment suggests that the first concern of the New South Wales Council was the pay rates of professional women. In effect, the 1959 Industrial Arbitration (Female Rates) Amendment Act gave

---

34 NCWV Council Minutes, 13 February 1958, and Executive Minutes, 26 April 1958, NCWV Papers, SLV (accession pending).
35 NCWWA Council Minutes, 25 August 1958, ACC7678A/17, NCWWA Papers, State Library of Western Australia (SLWA).
36 'A.N.C.W. Conference: September, 1958', single sheet, inserted in NCWA Board Minutes, Box 13, MS7583, NCWA Papers, NLA.
37 NCWA Board Minutes, 9 May 1960, Box 13, MS7583, NCWA Papers, NLA.
38 'Presidential Address', *NCWA Biennial Conference*, Canberra, 29 October – 4 November 1960, p. 15.

Thelma Metcalfe
NCWA President 1957–1960

Thelma Metcalfe was born in Melbourne in 1898 and educated at Albury District School and the University of Melbourne. After her marriage in 1934 to the deputy principal librarian of NSW, John Metcalfe, they worked together in the Free Library Movement to lobby for a system of public libraries nationwide. Her teaching experience, interest in languages and libraries and overseas travel gave her an international awareness that she brought to her leadership role in the National Council of Women.

Metcalfe was an office bearer in the NSW and national councils for over 40 years, serving as national president from 1957 to 1960. During the war years her work with NCWNSW led to the founding of the Nutritional Advisory Council. She and Ruby Board started the Housekeepers' Emergency Service and later Meals on Wheels. As national president she stressed the importance of regional activism and work towards improving social and economic conditions, particularly for women in the Asia-Pacific area. She also worked to redress inequality issues in Australia such as discrimination against married women in the work force, varying education standards, the declining value of child endowment, and the financial hardships of deserted wives.

Metcalfe also held office in a great many other organisations, remaining active in most until her last illness. She was a long-term member and president of the Lyceum Club, a founding member and later president of the Good Neighbour Council of NSW, an early member of the NSW Pan-Pacific and South East Asia Women's Association from its re-establishment in 1954, and its president from 1963 until 1968. She was NCW delegate to the NSW branch of the UN Association of Australia becoming its vice-president, as well as belonging to the British Drama League, the NSW committee for International Children's Book Week and the Arts Council of Australia, NSW. She once said that she was the 'best annual meeting attender in Australia'.

Metcalfe's wide range of work was acknowledged by an MBE in 1956 and NCWNSW marked her 30 years of service to the organisation with an honorary life-presidency. She died in 1984. Her NCW obituarist, Jean Arnot, wrote that Thelma Metcalfe would be remembered for her 'significant work in the cause of human welfare, for her perseverance, for her tolerance, for her good humour and for her great capacity for objectivity.'

Explore further resources about Thelma Metcalfe in the Australian Women's Register.

equal pay to only a tiny proportion of women working in New South Wales. Women seeking equal pay had to relate their wage value to that of men working in the same occupation.[39] A clause in the amending bill made it specific that

> This section shall not apply to and in respect of those provisions of any award and industrial agreements which are applicable to persons engaged in work essentially or usually performed by females but upon which male employees may also be employed.[40]

The gender divisions in the workforce meant that almost the only women who benefited were the secondary school teachers, who had been pushing vigorously for equal pay within the trade union movement. The historians of women's battle for workplace equality note that 'The equal pay campaign in New South Wales received no further encouragement from the official trade union movement after this'.[41] There is equally no evidence of local action on the issue from NCWNSW.

Delegates at the 1960 NCWA conference showed no antipathy towards unions. A motion from Queensland called on state councils to press trade unions to take up the ILO call within local arbitration courts.[42] Nobody spoke against union involvement, and delegates from Tasmania, ACT and South Australia supported the idea—'to have the industrial unions helping ... would get it much quicker'. Queenslanders suggested that state councils should themselves intervene in arbitration cases, and were supported by New South Wales. Ada Norris cited NCWA's 1952 intervention to argue against this idea; 'I would not recommend any National Council of Women to take on such an experience unless it had adequate free legal aid, as Mrs King and I

---

39   Ryan and Conlon, *Gentle Invaders*, p. 147.
40   Clause 9(b), Section 88D, New South Wales Industrial Arbitration (Female Rates) Amendment Act, cited in Ryan and Conlon, *Gentle Invaders*, p. 147.
41   Ryan and Conlon, *Gentle Invaders*, p. 148.
42   *NCWA Biennial Conference*, Canberra, 29 October – 4 November 1960, p. 41.

had'. In the end, an amended motion authorised state councils to take whatever actions they thought fit 'in support of this principle'.

Motions were also passed calling on the Commonwealth government to ratify the ILO Convention on equality in the workplace, and to remove the marriage bar in the Commonwealth public service. NCWs in South Australia and Victoria had already taken up this issue with their state governments,[43] and at the national level Metcalfe had written to the Prime Minister's Department on the issue.[44] Conference speakers in favour of the motion pointed to the fact that the Boyer report into promotion in the Commonwealth public service (CPS) had recommended in February 1959 that all the disabilities suffered by married women in the CPS—loss of permanency, promotion and superannuation—should be removed.[45]

The Menzies government promised to consider the views of women's organisations when they came to respond to the Boyer report.[46] But the Public Service Bill that came before the federal parliament late in 1960 proposed no change to the status of married women. Help came unasked from the Labor opposition. On 8 December, Senator Don Willesee moved:

> That the bill be recommitted for the purpose of establishing in the bill the principle that the rates, or scales of rates, of salary payable to female officers shall not be less than the rates, or scales of rates, of salary payable to male officers performing equivalent duties.[47]

Willesee's motion would have been carried in the Senate if the four women senators representing non-Labor parties had chosen to vote

---

43   NCWSA Council Minutes, 10 July 1958, Box 4, SRG297, NCWSA Papers, SLSA; NCWV Executive Minutes, 26 April 1958, NCWV Papers, SLV (accession pending).
44   *NCWA News*, February 1959, p. 2.
45   *NCWA Biennial Conference*, Canberra, 29 October – 4 November 1960, pp. 22–3.
46   *NCWA News*, February 1959, p. 2.
47   *CPD*, Senate, Senator Don Willesee, 8 December 1960, p. 1.

against the government. The national councils were appalled at this lost opportunity. The ACT council wrote asking the new Launceston-based NCWA board to protest. The board, now led by the strong-minded Dorothy Edwards, wrote a sharp letter of rebuke to the four senators: Nancy Buttfield, Agnes Robertson, Ivy Wedgwood and Annabelle Rankin. The letter concluded: 'This protest is in conformity with NCWA's policy on equal pay for women'.[48]

A reply came from Agnes Robertson, senator from Western Australia.[49] She made some effort to defend the political appropriateness of the women's vote—the amendment was a Labor Party 'red herring' to delay the passage of the bill—but the crucial point was that Menzies himself had declared that the government would not accept the amendment: 'So you can see that we had no option but to uphold the Government's decision at this particular time'. Robertson made it clear that this was not a decision she approved of—'I would remind you that I have worked all my life for equal pay for equal work'. She had written to the government leader in the Senate 'asking for information'; she quoted in full his infuriatingly contradictory reply:

> As you know, the official platform of the Liberal Party of Australia includes "acceptance of the principle of equal remuneration for men and women for work of equal value". The Government's attitude to this question has been stated on many occasions and was put quite clearly during the recent debates in Parliament on the Public Service Bill. That view is that it is for the Commonwealth Conciliation and Arbitration Commission

---

48 NCWA Board Minutes, 27 February 1961, Box 13, MS7583, NCWA Papers, NLA.

49 Robertson was perhaps the senator most immediately associated with NCWA at this point, her daughter, Jess, having recently held the position of state president of the NCWWA and currently being international president (1961–64) of the NCWA-backed Pan-Pacific and Southeast Asia Women's Association. For their biographies, see Wendy Birman, 'Robertson, Agnes Robertson (1882–1968)', *Australian Dictionary of Biography* (*ADB*), http://adb.anu.edu.au/biography/robertson-agnes-robertson-11540; and Michael Sturma, 'Robertson, Jessie Marian (1909–1976)', *ADB*, http://adb.anu.edu.au/biography/robertson-jessie-marian-11543.

Dorothy Edwards
NCWA President 1960–1964

Dorothy Edwards broke new ground for women and was an outstanding ambassador for the council movement worldwide. Born in Deloraine, Tasmania, in 1907, she was educated at Launceston High School, the University of Tasmania and the London School of Economics. A gifted teacher, she married in 1933 and, because of the regulations of the time, was forced to resign from the Education Department. Once her sons were in school, she found other outlets for her talents and leadership qualities.

Edwards had a long-standing interest in local government, and, on joining the NCW of Launceston as secretary from 1947 to 1956, she actively campaigned to allow women to stand as aldermen. In 1945, the Corporations Act was amended and, in 1949, she became not only the first woman to stand but also the first to be elected. She was an alderman for fifteen years and one of the first female mayors in Australia. She was the first Tasmanian woman to be elected president of the Australian National Council of Women, in 1960. Because Edwards' base was in the autonomous Launceston council, her election had implications for the status of the constituent state council of Tasmania based in Hobart. This aggravated tension over the constitutional position of the two Tasmanian councils.

Edwards' period in office was impressive at local, national and international levels. She enthusiastically promoted close relations between Australia and the national councils of Thailand, Fiji and Papua New Guinea. With regard to Australian issues, Edwards pulled no punches, fighting for equal pay and the removal of the marriage bar to the employment of women. After relinquishing the Australian presidency, she concentrated on ICW activity. At the 1963 ICW Washington conference, she was elected vice-treasurer, serving in that position from 1963 to 1970 and as vice-president from 1963 to 1979, as well as convenor of the finance committee.

Edwards was a member of many other organisations. In addition to being president of the Launceston branch of the United Nations Association of Australia, she served on the ABC Board, the State Library Board, Decimal Currency Committee, Queen Victoria Hospital Board and the Tasmanian Orchestra Advisory Committee.

Edwards was awarded an OBE in 1958 and a CBE in 1979. She was appointed a life vice-president of NCWA in 1973, admitted as an honorary freeman of the City of Launceston in 1984 and named on the Tasmanian Honour Roll of Women in 2005. She died in 2006.

Explore further resources about Dorothy Edwards in the Australian Women's Register.

and its associated tribunals in particular fields to determine the rates of remuneration for both men and women.[50]

Over the next few years, the Menzies government gave this same response to every call for it to act on the issue of equal pay and the related question of ratifying ILO Convention no. 100. There was perhaps some logic to this position in the latter case; the power to bring Australia in line with the requirements of the Convention lay mainly with the courts and the state governments. But the federal government did have the power to determine the remuneration and conditions of its own public servants, and to support a case for equal pay before the Arbitration Court.[51] NCWA and other women's organisations repeatedly pressed the federal government to remove the disabilities suffered by married women in the Commonwealth public service, and each time they were refused.[52] Margaret Fitzherbert, historian of women within the Liberal Party, places the blame for this squarely with Robert Menzies. She tells how the Liberal and Country Party women senators met with the prime minister in 1959 and again in 1962 to press for 'the end of the marriage bar, equal pay for equal work and equal opportunity for women', to no avail. 'Menzies held out against eliminating the marriage bar until only a few months before he stepped down as Prime Minister', in February 1966. The new leader Harold Holt legislated in October of the same year to give married women full access to all employment benefits in the Commonwealth public service—though not yet to equal pay.[53]

The government's insistence that equal pay had to be sought through the arbitration system pushed the National Councils of Women further

---

50   Agnes Robertson to NCWA, 10 March 1961, NCWA Correspondence, Box 7, MS5193, NCWA Papers, NLA.
51   Tom Sheridan and Pat Stretton, 'Pragmatic Procrastination: Governments, Unions and Equal Pay', *Labour History*, 94, May 2008, pp. 133–56.
52   See, for example, Secretary of the Prime Minister's Department to Secretary of NCWA, 5 May 1964, Folder 3: 1957–1967 'Correspondence with Government Departments', NCWA Correspondence 1936–1971, MS5193, NCWA Papers, NLA.
53   Fitzherbert, *So Many Firsts*, pp. 58–9.

towards co-operation with the trade union movement and intervention in the courts. In the early years of the 1960s, all the councils except New South Wales and Western Australia worked actively with the ACTU-based Equal Pay Committees in their states. Reading the minutes of the South Australian council, one can see that the executive moved cautiously, at first sending only observers to the meetings of the Equal Pay Committee, then establishing a small subcommittee of council to vet the committee's program.[54] A circular was distributed to all affiliated organisations, followed by a special council meeting that voted to support the principles of equal pay and 'any State action for their implementation'.[55] In April 1962, the council and its affiliates announced their support for the Equal Pay Week project organised across the nation by the ACTU and a new player in the game, the Australian Council of Salaried and Professional Associations.[56] NCWSA remained cautious about public association with the union movement. In March 1963, the executive held a special meeting to discuss 'whether the invitation to join a deputation being led by the ACTU ... can be accepted'. The executive decided that 'as long as the deputation is not dominated by the ACTU we would be in favour', and left it to Ruth Gibson to decide. The April meeting of council was happy to learn that the deputation to Sir Thomas Playford was 'well received'.[57] By such careful strategies, the fears of conservative women's organisations were soothed, and middle-class suspicion of equal pay and equal opportunity gradually defused.

The first half of the 1960s also saw changing attitudes within the councils and their affiliates to the issue of working mothers. The

---

54 NCWSA Executive Minutes, 26 May 1961; Council Minutes, 8 June 1961; Special Executive Minutes, 15 June 1961; Council Minutes, 4 July 1961; Box 1, SRG297, NCWSA Papers, SLSA.
55 NCWSA Council Minutes 10 August 1961, 09 November 1961, Box 1, SRG297, NCWSA Papers, SLSA.
56 NCWSA Council Minutes 12 April 1962, Box 1, SRG297, NCWSA Papers, SLSA.
57 NCWSA Executive Minutes 3 March 1963; Council Minutes 9 April 1963, Box 1, SRG297, NCWSA Papers, SLSA.

International Council of Women helped focus this shift by circulating a questionnaire to all councils on working women with family responsibilities. In Victoria, the convenor of the Trades and Professions Standing Committee, Shirley Horne, told a council meeting that this required a decision 'whether we think women should have the right to choose whether they stay in the home or have a career as well as the home'.[58] Horne, a full time academic, had no doubts about the answer. In New South Wales the questionnaire helped generate a lengthy report to the NCWA biennial conference, held in Brisbane in September 1964. Under the title 'The Responsibilities of a Woman to Her Community', the paper moved from the old equity arguments to the new science of management:

> Woman's right to work should be guaranteed and made effective. No woman should be forced by economic circumstances to work outside her home, but she should be free and enabled to do so if she chooses …
>
> If we are not to waste the services of trained women, there must be development of child care facilities, better housing and more labour-saving devices'.[59]

Similar themes were pursued in 1966 by a national conference held in Melbourne on 'The Status of Women in Employment', which aimed to educate employers and the general public about 'the role women can play in the development of Australia'.[60] The Victorian Employers' Federation was the major sponsor of the conference, and NCW Victoria was represented on the planning committee. In a report on the conference in *NCWA News*, the vice-chairman of the NCWA board, Helen Keays, wrote:

---

58   NCWV Council Minutes, 9 July 1964, NCWV Papers, SLV (classification pending).
59   *NCWA Biennial Conference*, Brisbane, September 1964, section 3, p. 8.
60   'Women at Work', *NCWA News*, April 1966.

> In brief, the economic health of Australia depends on the best use of its manpower. Employers at long last recognise that they must try to overcome their prejudice against the employment of women, and in particular, encourage and prepare older, married women to resume work outside the home.

Keays called for 'equal pay, removal of the marriage bar in the public service, flexible hours, adequate retraining ... but on the other hand women must belong to unions and actively participate in their own advancement'.[61] Here was a new interpretation of the theme of the responsible woman worker, looking back to NCWA's first full intervention in 1952, and forward to their next entry into the Arbitration Court in 1969.

In 1967 the NCWA board moved to Melbourne, with Ada Norris as president. Norris's participation in the equal pay campaigns had raised her profile in the trade union movement, and late in 1967 she was asked by the Fuel and Fodder Workers' Union to give evidence as an NCWA representative in support of an equal pay claim for women bag makers. Recognising that this was 'regarded as a test case' in Victoria, the board agreed that 'Mrs Norris should accede to this request'.[62] The *Canberra Times* reported the extraordinary event: 'the wife of a Victorian County Court judge gave evidence in support of equal pay for women before a wages board in Melbourne today'.[63]

The success of this exercise encouraged the board to consider a full-scale intervention in a federal test case, a claim by the Meat Industry Employees Union. The national law convenor, Philippa Hallenstein, prepared a document showing the options for intervention, and the state councils were asked to nominate their preferred way of proceeding. The options were three:

---

61   Report on 'Women at Work', *NCWA News*, May 1966.
62   NCWA Board Minutes, 23 November 1967, Box 14, MS7583, NCWA Papers, NLA.
63   *Canberra Times*, 5 December 1967, p. 7.

1. by placing a Statement of Opinion on the Bar table,

2. the method ... adopted by Industrial Trade Unions wishing to associate themselves with a case brought by the Australian Council of Trade Unions ...

3. an independent intervention in support of the principle included in a dispute between parties.[64]

Victoria and NCWACT—perhaps the two most politically experienced councils—favoured option 2, to make an intervention in association with the Australian Council of Trade Unions (ACTU). All the other councils opted for an independent intervention, and this was the approach adopted.

Five women's organisations requested and were granted leave to intervene in the 1969 case for equal pay bought before the Commonwealth Arbitration Commission by the Meat Industry Employees Union and the Clerical Officers' Association of the Commonwealth Public Service: the Federation of Business and Professional Women, the Nursing Federation Employees, the Union of Australian Women, the Australian Federation of Women Voters, and the National Council of Women of Australia. In March 1969, the board minutes reported the unaccustomed activities of the 'NCWA equal pay "team" (Mesdames Norris, Hall and Horne)'.

> [They] have attended the sittings so far, have studied material and gathered facts in readiness for making submissions; have engaged in "field work", e.g. Talks with key people and a visit to a meat works in Altona in search of equal work (and did not find very much of it).[65]

It was to prove difficult to find much 'equal work' in court.

---

64   NCWA Board Minutes, 28 November 1968, Box 14, MS7583, NCWA Papers, NLA.
65   NCWA Board Minutes, 12 March 1969, Box 14, MS7583, NCWA Papers, NLA.

Employer advocates argued that the cost to the economy of the wholesale removal of the 25 per cent differential between male and female wages would be prohibitive, and that 'the needs basis of wages was still fundamental in relation to family responsibility or "social responsibility" and that such responsibility devolved on the male'.[66] Norris opened the NCWA's case with a 'battle-cry':

> My Council would submit that the fundamental argument in support of the principle of equal pay for equal work is simply that of justice. If two people do the same paid work, whether two men, two women or a woman and a man, they should receive the same financial reward for that work.[67]

In response to the employers' case, Norris put to the court 'the element of economic partnership in marriage today and the contribution of the married woman not only to the workforce but to the home'; the 'unjust discrimination in wages' suffered by women who paid the same as men for goods and services; the poverty levels endured by female heads of households; and the possibility of dealing with family dependency by means of taxation rebates and family endowment—an analysis which as we have seen had been long developing within NCWA.

The outcome of the hearing was disappointing. The commission acknowledged the justice of the women's case, but failed to redress the problem, claiming that the court 'could not escape its own history': 'If there was no history of wage fixation in this country and we were starting afresh we might well not approach male and female rates as they were approached in the beginnings of the Federal arbitration system'.[68] Not starting afresh, the commission based its response on recent practice in the states, giving equal pay for 'work of the same or a like nature

---

66 Ada Norris, Report on Equal Pay Intervention, 10th June 1969, typescript, Box 33, MS90/190, Norris Papers, UMA.

67 Submission to the Australian Arbitration Commission, 1969, typescript, Box 33, MS90/190, Norris Papers, UMA.

68 Cited in Ryan and Conlon, *Gentle Invaders*, p. 150.

and equal value', but qualifying this with the provision from the New South Wales act, that equal pay was 'not applicable where the work is essentially or usually performed by females'. Again, the bulk of women workers were excluded.

Nothing daunted, the Victorians pressed on. In 1972, under the presidency of Jessie Scotford, Shirley Horne took yet another case to the Arbitration Commission on behalf of NCWA. It was based in large part on Norris's research.[69] In that year, the council pointed out, 'it was estimated that only 18.24 per cent of the women in the work force now receive equal pay'. Horne called on international precedent and example to show that the 1969 limited decision was 'out of phase with the principles enunciated by the United Nations and its associated organisation, the International Labour Organization'. The NCWA case also pointed to recent legislation in New Zealand and to the fact that community attitudes to women's work, including that of married women, had changed—in part, they might have added, as a result of their own work amongst their affiliates and the wider community.[70]

All these arguments were used by Mr Justice Moore to justify the court's decision to support a full reading of the principle enunciated more than two decades earlier by the ILO of 'equal remuneration for work of equal value'. But the decision explicitly rejected the request of the NCWA and other women's groups to apply the male minimum wage to women workers and thus finally abandon the family basis of wage fixation.[71] As Norris had commented of the 1969 decision, Australia could not ratify the 1951 ILO Convention until its terms 'exist in law and practice throughout Australia',[72] and the 1972 decision still

---

69 Ada Norris, 'Equal Pay Review (Victoria & Commonwealth)', in Shirley Horne's equal pay file, NCWV Papers, SLV (accession pending).
70 'Statement Made on behalf of the National Council of Women of Australia in the Commonwealth Conciliation and Arbitration Commission in Intervening in the Equal Pay Case, 3rd November 1972', Horne file, NCWV, SLV (accession pending).
71 'National Wage and Equal Pay Cases 1972—Statement by Mr Justice Moore', Sydney, 15 December 1972, Horne file, NCWV Papers, SLV (accession pending).
72 Norris, 'Equal Pay Review', Horne file, NCWV Papers, SLV (accession pending).

left mandated equal pay incomplete. A single adult minimum wage was not conceded until 1974, when NCWA again intervened, along with the Union of Australian Women and the Women's Electoral Lobby. At last, in December of that year, Australia ratified ILO Convention 100.[73]

---

73 Ada Norris, *Champions of the Impossible: A History of the National Council of Women of Victoria*, Melbourne, Hawthorn Press, 1978, pp. 140–1, 145; Judith Smart, 'Ada Norris (1901–1989): Champion of the Impossible', in Fiona Davis, Nell Musgrove and Judith Smart (eds), *Founders, Firsts and Feminists: Women Leaders in Twentieth-century Australia*, Australian Women's Archives Project, 2011, http://www.womenaustralia.info/leaders/fff, p. 316.

Chapter 11

AUSTRALIA AND THE WORLD

We have seen how the NCWA conferences of the 1950s began by affirming a Christian fellowship with women from all nations: 'In fellowship with our sisters in the National Councils of Women of many generations and in many countries let us say together the Lord's Prayer'.[1] Here we will look more closely at the internationalism that flowed from that Christian commitment, and at the ethnocentric nationalism that cannot be separated from that international impulse. Just as the ideal of universal equality was based for many members of the councils in the equality of all people before the Christian God, so the social and political ideals offered to other nations were based in the assumed supremacy of the British race and its cultural achievements. And it was that supremacy that justified the exclusion from Australian citizenship of people believed to be of inferior race. These themes will be pursued across four areas of concern and action by the Australian councils: efforts to get Australian ratification of UN Conventions and Declarations; attempts to come to terms with the problems endured by Aboriginal people; attitudes towards the reform of the White Australia policy; and the promotion of Asia and the Pacific as a sphere of special interest, for association and nation both.

---

1   *NCWA Report 1949–1952*, Melbourne, p. 1.

Signing up to Equality

The chapter of NCWA's internationalism that is least shadowed by racism is the story of the leaders' persistent efforts to bring Australia into line with United Nations Conventions on human rights. The NCWA's struggles for equality within marriage and in the workplace might be understood as being fuelled to some degree by self-interest, for daughters and neighbours if not for the leaders themselves. Their concern to make Australia a signatory to Conventions on matters of no immediate concern to Australians, issues like refugees, slavery and genocide, reflects both their commitment to an international movement of women and their wish to make their nation a responsible member of the world community.

NCWA action on such Conventions was invariably prompted from abroad. Often the prompt came directly from ICW. Thus in 1949 the ICW president, Jeanne Eder, wrote to NCWA president Ivy Brookes relaying a message from an American activist working for the ratification of the UN Convention on Genocide who made a special plea for women's action on the issue:

> I wonder if you agree with me that the women of the world have a special stake in this convention. Genocide is primarily directed against women as the weaker members of the group and also in their capacity as mothers and wives responsible for the demographic and moral future of the group. Sterilization, stealing of children, breaking up of families are matters affecting women primarily. Their humanitarian sensitivities are very strong and they might use them now for the benefit of this cause so tragically connected with past and present history.[2]

The board wrote immediately to the prime minister, asking him ratify the Convention 'at the earliest possible moment', and Chifley replied

---

2   Jeanne Eder to Ivy Brookes, 27 April 1949, NCWA Correspondence, Box 8, MS5193, NCWA Papers, National Library of Australia (NLA).

equally promptly that 'a Bill to approve Australian ratification of this Convention has been introduced at the current Parliamentary session'.[3]

Governments responded more slowly in the 1950s. Short delays were due to the increasing complexity of the Canberra bureaucracy. By 1951 a request for ratification of the 1949 Convention on the Protection of Civilians in Time of War passed through the Ministries for Defence and the Interior before reaching its proper target in the Ministry of External Affairs, and that minister then referred it for 'the consideration of interested Commonwealth Departments' before a decision could be reached.[4] Much longer delays were caused by the existence within Australian state law of provisions that were incompatible with the terms of Conventions. When the minister for external affairs, R.G. Casey, responded in July 1952 to NCWA's call for ratification of the Convention on the Traffic in Persons and the Exploitation of Others, he assured them that 'certain technical difficulties' would be overcome 'in the near future'.[5] In this case, the problem was the presence in state law of legislation intended to control the spread of venereal disease by policing prostitution, legislation that contained provisions incompatible with the terms of the Convention. In the event, the process of persuading the states to repeal the offending clauses continued until 1963.[6] At that point the Department of External Affairs told the councils that while 'all States have agreed generally to introduce the necessary amendments to their laws to bring them into conformity with the Convention' and some anomalies had been repealed, it had now been discovered that

> the Convention does not distinguish between sexes, and laws will have to be passed for example making it an offence to

---

[3] Margaret Howard to J.B. Chifley, 27 May 1949, and the reply, 3 June 1949, NCWA Correspondence, Box 2, MS5193, NCWA Papers, NLA.

[4] Secretary of the Department of External Affairs to Honorary Secretary NCWA, 14 December 1951, NCWA Correspondence, Box 2, MS5193, NCWA Papers, NLA.

[5] R.G. Casey to Mrs P.A. Hall, 4 July 1952, NCWA Correspondence, Box 2, MS5193, NCWA Papers, NLA.

[6] External Affairs to NCWA, 23 November 1961, 4 July 1962, 29 March 1963, 26 August 1963, NCWA Correspondence, Box 2, MS5193, NCWA Papers, NLA.

procure a male person ... for prostitution with females and punishable in the same way as the procuring of a female.

The department suggested that these requirement could be why 'so many nations with advanced social legislation have not acceded to the Convention'.[7]

By 1963, the Department of External Affairs had a United Nations section with special responsibility for matters like the ratification of UN Conventions. NCWA queries generally drew a helpful response from these bureaucrats. Take for example the exchange of letters concerning the right of asylum. The 1963 ICW conference in Washington resolved that all member councils should press their governments to support the adoption of the draft Declaration on the Right of Asylum by the UN General Assembly, and the Australian board wrote in those terms to the minister for external affairs, now Sir Garfield Barwick. The bureaucrat who prepared the minister's reply provided a brief history of the Declaration, perhaps as much for the minister as for the board. The Australian delegation had generally supported the draft Declaration, though it had voted against amendments proposed in committee by Russia and Poland. The letter concluded:

> I am pleased to be able to inform you that the Australian Delegation has been instructed to vote for the adoption of this Declaration when it comes before the General Assembly at the current session provided no substantial amendments are proposed.[8]

This welcome information may not have been news to the Launceston board. By 1963, Ada Norris was into her third term as Australian delegate to the UN Commission on the Status of Women (CSW), and

---

[7] M.G.M. Bourchier to Mrs L.B. Hooper, 26 August 1963, NCWA Correspondence, Box 2, MS5193, NCWA Papers, NLA.

[8] Sir Garfield Barwick to Mrs L.B. Hooper, 12 November 1963, NCWA Correspondence, Box 2, MS5193, NCWA Papers, NLA.

she made it her business to keep her colleagues in the councils well informed about issues that concerned them.

The work of the councils in advocating and promoting UN Conventions and Declarations was an important factor in community acceptance and government ratification of these instruments of human rights. Across the 1950s and 1960s, the leaders of NCWA supported the adoption by Australia of Conventions or Declarations concerned with genocide, protection of civilians in time of war, recovery abroad of maintenance obligations, consent to marriage, nationality of married women, traffic in persons for the purpose of prostitution, abolition of slavery and the right of asylum. We must thank them for that.

Aboriginal and Torres Strait Islander peoples —'removing the stigma of neglect'

The internationalism that the leaders of NCWA espoused in their support of UN Conventions demonstrates their sense of themselves as citizens of the world. In this context, the ICW creed, 'Do unto others as you would have them do unto you', was applied equally to the people of all nations. But national, imperial and racial considerations continued to run alongside this internationalism. A move to remove the word 'British' from the title of the British Commonwealth of Nations—a move intended to accommodate newly independent nations in Asia and Africa—drew a horrified response from Australians whose loyalties were to a white empire and commonwealth. Ivy Brookes told a meeting of the national board that

> We should not sacrifice that Empire unity which was transformed into the British Commonwealth of Nations in order to endeavour to keep a non-British section within the group and sacrifice our Empire unity and allegiance to the British throne for such a tenuous objective as a so-called Commonwealth of Nations with no sense of kinship and common allegiance.[9]

---

9   NCWA Board Minutes, 3 December 1948, Box 13, MS7583, NCWA Papers, NLA.

Brookes had moved very little from the essentially racist understanding spelled out by the men who established the White Australia policy in the first years of the century: 'The crimson thread of kinship runs through us all'.[10] Her declaration went unchallenged by other board members.

Understandings of race shifted significantly within the national councils across the middle decades of the century. In 1950, most members of NCW held to a defence of white supremacy that saw the values of the 'coloured races' as incompatible with Australian values. By 1970, discussions of race relations within the councils tended to assume that Australian society could absorb individuals from other cultures, whatever the colour of their skin. This section of the chapter will trace this shift as it affected thinking about Aboriginal and Torres Strait Islander peoples.

In October 1952, Paul Hasluck, recently appointed minister for territories, gave an address to the NCWA biennial conference in Melbourne. The board invited him to speak on Aboriginal issues in the Northern Territory, an important part of his portfolio. He chose to speak around a broader topic, 'the transition from the idea of protection to the idea of welfare'.[11] Hasluck was a historian as well as a politician, in his youth an activist for bettering the conditions of Indigenous people and a member of the Australian delegation that helped set up the United Nations; a biographer has noted that this last experience 'intensified [in him] an existing awareness of the danger of racist thinking'.[12] He gave the conference an eloquent, even passionate, lesson on the history of Aboriginal–settler relations in Australia. In the past, Aboriginal people had been protected, alongside 'game and fisheries', and 'wildflowers'. They were protected because 'they were weak and ill-used', because

---

10 Henry Parkes calling for Australian federation at the 1890 Melbourne Premiers' Conference; cited in Douglas Cole, '"The crimson thread of kinship": Ethnic Ideas in Australia, 1870–1914', *Historical Studies*, 14 (56), 1971, p. 511.

11 Paul Hasluck, 'Native Welfare', *NCWA Biennial Conference*, Melbourne, 14 October 1952, pp. 1–7; typescript inserted into *NCWA Report 1949–1952*, Melbourne.

12 Sue Taffe, 'Paul Hasluck', *Collaborating for Indigenous Rights*, National Museum of Australia, http://indigenousrights.net.au/people/pagination/paul_hasluck.

they were 'anthropologically of some interest', and, in the case of some missionaries, because they were 'also God's children'. But 'by no means all missionaries, station owners or officials saw the future of the natives even with this limited measure of hope and affection'; rather 'missionary effort lost its original hope and often became only a work of kindness rather than one of faith'. Today

> any person who seriously addresses himself to the conditions of aborigines in Australia … is no longer satisfied by preventing cruelty to them, as to animals, or the restricted hope of smoothing the pillow of a dying race. He thinks of the advancement of their welfare.[13]

That advancement was to be achieved by a policy of assimilation: a recognition that 'the life of the coloured people is going to be lived as members of the Australian community and, that being so, they should live in the same manner as the whites'. Aboriginal 'social welfare' was necessary for pragmatic reasons: 'We do not want a submerged caste or any pariahs in our community but want a homogenous society'. More positively, 'With the growth of our national life, we are developing our own national ideals'. We valued 'the standard of living', 'equal opportunity', 'equal rights before the law and equal rights to share in the benefits of membership of our society'—and these ideals should apply to 'all our people'. The first step towards this was to improve native health, in the broadest sense: 'to cover detection and treatment of disease, infant welfare, hygiene, sanitation, better housing and better nutrition'; the second was

> to try to improve the standards of livelihood so that these people can build the houses in which they live and raise the better food they are to eat and gradually acquire the skills that will give them a useful and happy place, either on their own settlements or in the community at large.[14]

---

13   Hasluck, 'Native Welfare', p. 4.
14   Hasluck, 'Native Welfare', p. 5.

And, while assimilation into the white community was inevitably the fate of the Aboriginal people, from the point of view of individuals it was in a sense voluntary. Some in the cities had 'an immediate social hunger' for full citizenship; in the North many others 'will never in their lifetime be able to live after the manner of the white community and very few if any of them will have any interest in doing so'. To the reader in the twenty-first century, the most marked omission in Hasluck's presentation is the forced removal and assimilation suffered by so many Aboriginal children, a practice continued and augmented during his regime.

Hasluck concluded with a check list of actions that his audience could and should take to advance native welfare: 'as taxpayers and voters' to 'kick' the state governments into action; as church-goers to support the work of the missions; and to take on work in the local community to assist Aboriginal neighbours face to face. Most importantly, he told members of the councils to fully inform themselves about the issues, and to inform other Australians: 'We want goodwill. Even more than that we want understanding'.

It is hard to know what the women of NCWA made of this message. Women's organisations working with Jessie Street in the 1940s would have been familiar with the comprehensive program for Aboriginal reform developed in the 1946 Women's Charter, including a demand for Commonwealth control of Aboriginal welfare.[15] But, while most of the state councils had long been concerned about 'the plight' of the Aboriginal people and some had argued for Commonwealth control, as we have seen, understandings of what should be done varied considerably. In Western Australia, newspaper reports about the poor living conditions of Aboriginals on the fringes of country towns led NCWWA to pass a resolution calling for action 'by responsible authorities' to commit all 'Native Half-caste children who are deemed to be living in unsavoury

---

15 Marilyn Lake, *Getting Equal: The History of Australian Feminism*, Sydney, Allen & Unwin, 1999, pp. 194–6.

and undesirable conditions' to 'approved institutions'.[16] The South Australia council, in contrast, invited Aboriginal rights activist Dr Charles Duguid[17] to speak on the forced removal of half-caste children from Aboriginal mothers.[18] The Victorian state council responded to press criticism of the treatment of outback Aboriginal people by asking the national board to call for a royal commission 'to inquire into the whole position of Australian aborigines';[19] the board wrote promptly to all states asking their approval, but failed to get majority support. The Queensland executive's response to calls for protest against 'the alleged brutal treatment of Aboriginals in the Gulf Country' was to refuse to act 'on any matter merely on verbal or newspaper reports'.[20] The New South Wales and South Australian councils informed themselves by inviting speakers from the local Aboriginal Welfare Boards;[21] Thelma Metalfe reported that the meeting was particularly struck by the fact that 'the aboriginal woman who is not living in a reserve, but living as a civilised woman in a town, is not entitled to maternity benefits'. Again the NSW understanding of universal rights was a limited one.

Brookes's board was sympathetic to the problems of Aboriginal people but not well informed, at least initially. In June 1950, they responded indignantly to a letter from the secretary of the Department of the Interior—soon to be part of the Department of Territories. The bureaucrat wrote that Aboriginal policy was not a federal concern.

---

16 NCWWA Council Minutes, 27 September 1950, ACC7678 A/17, NCWWA Papers, State Library of Western Australian (SLWA).

17 W.H. Edwards, 'Duguid, Charles (1884–1986)', *Australian Dictionary of Biography* (*ADB*), http://adb.anu.edu.au/biography/duguid-charles-12440.

18 NCWSA Council Minutes, 14 August 1952, Box 4, SRG297, NCWSA Papers, State Library of South Australia (SLSA).

19 *NCWV Annual Report 1950*, Resolutions, May 1950, p. 8. The call for a royal commission came first in a letter to the *Age*, 26 April 1950, from local activist Mrs Anna Vroland.

20 NCWQ Executive Minutes, 19 June 1950, Box 16045, 7266 NCWQ Minute Books, NCWQ Papers, State Library of Queensland (SLQ).

21 Resolution on Aborigines, Open Session, *NCWA Biennial Conference*, Melbourne, 14–18 May 1951, pp. 24; NCWSA Council Minutes, 11 September 1952, Box 4, SRG297, SLSA.

The board was 'astonished that the Commonwealth has no overriding responsibility to the aborigines of Australia', and they wrote to all state premiers and the prime minister demanding 'a uniform national policy that could override that of the States, a national policy being necessary'.[22] Necessary perhaps, but not constitutionally achievable unless the states agreed to abrogate their powers. A year later, in May 1951, the board was on more secure ground in supporting a conference resolution put forward by the Launceston council,

> That all Councils make it an urgent matter to collect information on the social, educational, legal and political treatment of aborigines and halfcastes in their States so that they can present a recommendation to the Governments concerned and the Board make recommendations to the Federal Government.[23]

At the conference in the year following, in October 1952, delegates voted in favour of a South Australian resolution, which was put and carried before Hasluck spoke:

> That each State Council be asked to promote the interests of the aborigines within their respective States, with particular regard to:-
>
> 1. The prevention of mothers and children being separated
>
> 2. Proper feeding (and the use of child endowment for the purpose)
>
> 3. Education for all aboriginal children.

Perhaps this owed more to Charles Duguid's understanding of Aboriginal rights than to Hasluck's doctrine of assimilation.

---

22 NCWA Board Minutes, 4 June 1950, Box 13, M7583, NCWA Papers, NLA.
23 Resolution on Aborigines, Open Session, *NCWA Biennnial Conference*, Melbourne, 14–18 May 1951, pp. 24–5.

Copies of Hasluck's speech were widely distributed through the councils and their affiliates, and his ideas probably complicated thinking about Aboriginal problems, at least to the extent of persuading people that those problems would not go away. The only clear evidence of its impact comes from Western Australia. In January 1953 a special meeting of the Western Australian council heard a reading of Hasluck's paper, which was followed by a discussion of Aboriginal citizenship that endorsed 'the principle of citizenship rights in graded steps'. The meeting passed resolutions calling for government recognition of 'the principle of citizenship from birth for Australian Natives', and for 'immediate provision of housing, education, health and any other opportunities to ensure the fulfilment of the principle'.[24]

After the flurry of concern in the early fifties, media interest in Aboriginal issues died away and, with it, interest from most of the councils; only South Australia and Western Australia continued to seek reports from their local Aboriginal Welfare Boards and, later, Aboriginal Advancement Leagues. At a national level, there was no significant further discussion until the biennial conference in Canberra in 1960. South Australia proposed that the association should

> request the Federal and State Governments to bring in legislation to provide that, if profits be made from anything on or under Aboriginal Reserves, a fixed percentage of such profits—we recommend 20%—should be placed in a Trust Fund for the benefit of Aborigines.[25]

The South Australian delegates argued that the development of 'previously untouched' Aboriginal land reserves was becoming inevitable, particularly by the mining industry, and that Aboriginal people should be recompensed for the use of their land. 'Australia has said "this is your

---

24 NCWWA Council Minutes, 12 January 1953, ACC7678 A/17, NCWWA Papers, SLWA.
25 NCWSA Special Executive Minutes, 25 June 1960, Box 4, SRG297, NCWSA Papers, SLSA.

land", and we feel something beyond wages and amenities should be made available for their benefit.'²⁶

The resolution received general support from all states except Victoria. Ada Norris made an extraordinary intervention in the debate. Speaking from her experience as a member of the Commonwealth Immigration Advisory Committee, Norris took a line entirely congruent with Hasluck's principles and practice of assimilation. She opposed the resolution because 'it is making the Aborigines a class apart'. Rather than seeking special benefits for Aboriginal and Torres Strait Islander peoples, efforts should be directed towards including them within 'the overall financial responsibility that the Commonwealth Government takes for all citizens'. And the desert countrymen and women did not come within this area of responsibility: 'Money must be spent on education, vocational training etc. wherever the Aboriginal is not living in his original nomadic state'. Delegates did not accept her reasoning, that special benefits would 'lead to a type of segregation and would be a retrograde step'. The resolution was passed with Victoria abstaining. The South Australian executive celebrated in 1961 when the Commonwealth legislated to allow royalties from production on reserves to be paid into a fund for the use of the Aboriginal owners of those reserves.²⁷

Dorothy Edwards' board took up another strand of Hasluck's recommendations: the need to work with Aboriginal people face to face. Edwards successfully applied to the minister for territories for funding to bring two Aboriginal women from the Northern Territory to the Seminar on International Understanding she planned for Brisbane in 1964.²⁸ The delegates were selected by the administrator of the Northern Territory, and accompanied to Brisbane by a white welfare officer. Mrs Nagamara and Mrs Fourcroy were reported to be

---

26   *NCWA Biennial Conference*, 29 October – 4 November 1960, Canberra, p. 41.
27   NCWSA Executive Minutes, 31 October 1961, Box 4, SRG297, NCWSA Papers, SLSA.
28   C.E. Barnes to Mrs L.B. Hooper, 2 April 1964, Department of External Affairs: Status of Women, A1838/1, National Archives of Australia (NAA).

rather shy at the beginning, but by the end of the Seminar we felt that a lot of their reserve had broken down and we trust that much helpful information will be passed on to their own people through their contact with the National Council of Women of Australia.[29]

There is no indication that NCWA learnt anything from Mrs Nagamara and Mrs Fourcroy.

In the Shadow of White Australia

In the last years of the 1940s, Australia's restrictive immigration policy came under strong criticism, at home and abroad.[30] The Labor government's rigid application of the Immigration Act's ban on 'natives of Asia, Africa and the Pacific' led to strong reactions amongst Asian nationalists. Reports of a decision to expel a 'Siamese' nursemaid from Australia led to a press campaign in Bangkok to expel all Australian expatriates from Thailand, and the Malayan parliament debated a 'retaliatory' immigration bill to deny permanent residence to 'people whose countries did not permit the immigration of natives of Singapore, Malaya, British North Borneo, Sarawak or Brunei'.[31]

In Australia, the summary deportations ordered by the minister for immigration, Arthur Calwell, drew public criticism from clergymen from all the major denominations.[32] The Reverend Alan Walker called the White Australia policy 'a denial of the Christian estimate of man'.[33]

---

29 Mrs L.M. Hooper to the Minister for Territories, 13 October 1964, Department of External Affairs: Status of Women, A1838/1, NAA.
30 Gwenda Tavan, *The Long Slow Death of White Australia*, Melbourne, Scribe, 2006, chapter 3.
31 'Siamese Anger at Australia', *Advertiser*, 9 May 1949, p. 3; 'No Asian Protest on Migration', *Advertiser*, 20 October 1949, p. 3.
32 'Methodist View of Communism', *Advertiser*, 29 May 1948, p. 2; 'Immigration Policy', *West Australian*, 22 October 1948, p. 11; 'Immigration Quotas', *Sydney Morning Herald*, 29 May 1949, p. 2; 'Australia "Less Popular" in Ceylon', *Advertiser*, 9 June 1949, p. 11.
33 'Disgrace to Australia: Pastor Criticises Mr. Calwell', *Advertiser*, 28 February 1949, p. 3.

The national gatherings of the Methodists, the Churches of Christ and the Presbyterians all called for an end to the blatant racism of the White Australia policy—though not to the restriction of Asian immigration. The leader of the Presbyterian church, the Reverend J.R. Blanchard, declared that 'Australia must rid itself of the term "White Australia" if it was to fit into the pattern of world-community'. He argued that

> The peoples of Asia understand and appreciate the realities behind the policy ... but they do not commit the folly of confusing and embittering the issue between themselves by using a slogan that raises a color bar and insinuates racial superiority.[34]

Blanchard and other clerics suggested that immigration might be better restricted by a quota system similar to that operating in America, which allocated a limited number of places to emigrants from different countries according to a formula framed to 'maintain the composition of the American people'.[35] The minister responded by refusing to change either the content or the administration of the Immigration Act.[36] The issue became politicised in the run-up to the 1949 elections. Labor defended its deportation of 'aliens' as the only way possible to 'maintain the racial and cultural homogeneity of Australian society'.[37] In the weeks before the election, the Liberal Party ran newspaper advertisements promising to administer immigration policy humanely and with common sense in individual cases.[38]

NCW councils responded strongly to this debate. Members seem to have been moved both by cases of individual injustice and by larger issues of human rights. Thus the Western Australian executive was

---

34 'Church Hits at Color Bar', *Advertiser*, 9 September 1948, p. 3. See also 'Churchmen Oppose "Colour" Policy', *Argus*, 7 May 1949, p. 5.
35 C.E.W. Bean, 'U.S. Excludes Without Insulting", *Sydney Morning Herald*, 26 May 1949, p. 2.
36 'Quotas Would "Open Door To Asiatics"', *Sydney Morning Herald*, 13 July 1984, p. 2.
37 Tavan, *The Long Slow Death of White Australia*, p. 60.
38 Tavan, *The Long Slow Death of White Australia*, p. 64.

outraged by the government's decision to expel the Thai nursemaid who had been caring for the family of a Cottesloe clergyman.[39] In NSW, the council was concerned by 'the arrest and gaoling of Chinese with a view to their deportation'; given that Australia was a signatory to the Human Rights Convention, 'a grave injustice is being done to these men and their families'.[40] The 1948 NCWA conference resolved that 'White Australia' should be eliminated 'as a term of reference', though they did not advocate completely abandoning the racial basis of immigration policy.[41]

At a national level, the board responded both to the press controversy and to requests for information from the International Council of Women. In March 1949, the board wrote to Calwell asking him to explain the grounds on which a Ceylonese woman had been prohibited from landing in Australia. They explained their need to know in terms of the council's international standing:

> As the Australian National Council of Women is the link with the International Council of Women and the matter is sure to be raised in other countries, as a result of the publicity given the matter, we wish to be able to reply correctly to such queries.[42]

The national migration convenor, Ada Norris, undertook a study of the Migration Act and initially reported that the problem lay not with the exclusions laid down in the act, but with the government's discretionary powers.[43] The Canberra council suggested an 'All Party Conference' to debate the issues; the board felt that this would be unacceptable to the minister and prejudicial to 'any further request we might wish to

---

[39] NCWA Board Minutes, 27 April 1949, Box 13, MS7583, NCWA Papers, NLA.
[40] NCWNSW Executive Minutes, 25 August 1949, MLK03011, MS3783, NCWNSW Papers, State Library of New South Wales (SLNSW).
[41] NCWA Board Minutes, 28 February 1949, Box 13, MS7583, NCWA Papers, NLA.
[42] Letter to the Minister for Immigration, 28 March 1949, Board Correspondence, Box 11, MS7583, NCWA Papers, NLA.
[43] NCWA Board Minutes, 27 April 1949, Box 13, MS7583, NCWA Papers, NLA.

make'.[44] In June Norris suggested a solution that moved away from absolute exclusion on racial grounds.

> If the migration policy were to be one of tolerance to our neighbour countries, of humanity and of a desire for peace, the only thing the Council could suggest to any Government was, that it should accord with our present policy, but should be administered to cause offence to no country.

This might be achieved by 'a comprehensive quota system, to be published openly, so that all nations could easily ascertain their quota numbers, even if that were only one person per year'.[45]

Norris had arrived at an assimilationist position congruent with the message Paul Hasluck would present to the NCWA conference in 1952; in the words of historian Gwenda Tavan, it was a position 'still demand[ing] social and cultural homogeneity' while 'conced[ing] that racial characteristics need not prevent a person from becoming a valuable member of Australian society'.[46]

The election victory of the Liberal Party and the appointment of Harold Holt as minister for immigration brought to power a politician already committed to assimilation. Holt wrote warmly to 'My dear Mrs. Brookes', explaining that he had decided to reconstitute the Immigration Advisory Council to make it 'fully representative, on the Federal level, of all important organisations in the community which are most directly interested', and inviting NCWA to nominate a representative.[47] The committee was to advise the minister on all matters pertaining to immigration, including 'European restricted immigration', 'Non-European immigration', and 'methods of facilitating the assimilation of foreign migrants into the Australian community'.

---

44 NCWA Board Minutes, 11 May 1949, Box 13, MS7583, NCWA Papers, NLA.
45 NCWA Board Minutes, 27 June 1949 Box 13, MS7583, NCWA Papers, NLA.
46 Tavan, *The Long Slow Death of White Australia*, p. 68.
47 H.E. Holt to Mrs H. Brookes, 21 April 1950, NCWA Correspondence, MS5193, NCWA Papers, NLA.

Brookes nominated Ada Norris, who found herself the only woman on the committee. Within a few months she was requesting the committee to set up a critical survey of the education available for migrant children, and NCWA was supporting her initiative by asking all state councils to bring the matter to the attention of their local minister and director of education.[48] This mode of working both inside and outside of the committee continued, with the board writing to the minister requesting that at least one woman should be appointed to the new Migrant Hostel Board, while Norris wrote privately to both Holt and his ministerial secretary.[49] It was a technique that Norris and the officers of NCWA perfected across the 1950s and 1960s.

Holt also initiated the annual Citizenship Conventions, held from 1950 in January each year and bringing together representatives from voluntary associations across Australia to work towards 'the assimilation of foreign migrants into the Australian community'. Ivy Brookes took on the task of representing NCWA at these gatherings, and Norris attended as the delegate of the Immigration Advisory Committee; both women soon found themselves chairing conference sessions.[50] The minutes of a NCWWA council meeting addressed by Brookes in April 1950 show her advocating a rather coercive model of assimilation.

> She stressed the fact that new immigrants must be assimilated into the country. For all concerned it would be better that migrants were not allowed to settle in groups—that they should speak English—and must mix. The children were no trouble as the second generation made good Australians. If possible all organisations of Council were asked to do "something" towards

---

48   NCWA Board Minute Books, 11 December 1950, Box 13, MS7583, NCWA Papers, NLA.
49   NCWA Board Minute Books, 28 August 1951, 23 October 1951, Box 13, MS7583, NCWA Papers, NLA.
50   NCWA Board Minute Books, 27 November 1950, 11 December 1950, 23 October 1951, Box 13, MS7583, NCWA Papers, NLA.

helping these migrants to settle here, as it would be years before we could assimilate them.[51]

Under Brookes's leadership 'assimilation' became a popular topic for discussion at state and national conferences of NCW, and state councils co-operated with the Good Neighbour Councils that were formed to co-ordinate voluntary activity in towns and localities. Brookes passed on the mantle of community leadership to Thelma Metcalfe, national president from 1957 to 1960, and then national convenor for migration from 1962 to 1964; Metcalfe was a founding member of the Good Neighbour Council of New South Wales and its vice-president and then president for many years.

Anne Hamilton, the Queenslander who became NCWA president in 1964, has left us interesting accounts in the *NCWA Newsletter* of the Citizenship Conventions of 1965 and 1966. She spoke from an assimilationist position more open to the needs of immigrants than Brookes fifteen years earlier. In 1965, she reported that 'Discussion ranged round integration, naturalisation and the sensitivity of new settlers to the implications of difference in the word "migrant"'. She was particularly interested in the problems of migrant women, feeling that the male-dominated gathering 'showed a disturbing lack of concern for the emotional insecurity of adult women entering this country with scant knowledge of our customs and standards'. These women 'have come to this country to make a better life' but they 'do not know how to help themselves … Please go more than halfway to meet those who wish to join us in being Australians'.[52] The 1966 convention was marked by discussion of migrant claims for 'special privileges',[53] and Hamilton found it necessary to stress the other side of the equation: that 'for

---

51 NCWWA Council Minutes, 24 April 1950, ACC7678A, NCWWA Papers, SLWA.
52 *NCWA Newsletter*, February 1965.
53 'New Settler Welfare to be Topic', *Canberra Times*, 6 January 1966, p. 8; 'Rights and Duties: Letters to the Editor', *Canberra Times*, 23 January 1966, p. 2.

orderly and peaceful development' Australia had to attract migrants 'with the potential capacity to integrate successfully'.

> We don't expect slavish conformity to our existing customs from new settlers, do we? We know that the influx since 1945 has changed our social habits considerably, though perhaps superficially. We do expect to maintain certain values and standards. We must insist on this.

Reform to Australia's racially restrictive immigration policy and practice took place against these slowly evolving attitudes to the assimilation of migrants from Europe. Ada Norris was deeply involved in this process. She served on the Immigration Advisory Committee for more than twenty years, at the same time working within NCWA as national migration convenor and within ICW as vice-convenor and convenor of the International Committee on Migration. She was also a leading member of the Good Neighbour Council of Victoria. Her biographer notes that 'She had perhaps more expertise on local, national and international migration issues than any Australian of her generation'.[54]

The Immigration Advisory Committee oversaw the gradual process of liberalisation of the White Australia policy. Tavan's study suggests that proposals for reform came mainly from bureaucrats from the Department of Immigration, with committee members acting to authorise the reforms, sometimes persuading reluctant politicians to act. The changes were gradual, even minimal, preserving the practice of racial discrimination and exclusion. From 1950, Asian students were admitted to study in Australian universities. In 1957, non-Europeans with fifteen years of residence in Australia were allowed to apply for citizenship. From 1958, 'distinguished and highly qualified' Asians were welcomed as migrants, with the prospect of permanent settlement.

---

54 Judith Smart, 'Ada Norris (1901–1989): Champion of the Impossible', in Fiona Davis, Nell Musgrove and Judith Smart (eds), *Founders, Firsts and Feminists: Women Leaders in Twentieth-century Australia*, Australian Women's Archives Project, 2011, http://www.womenaustralia.info/leaders/fff, p. 311.

In 1959, Australian citizens were allowed to sponsor Asian spouses for citizenship.[55]

In 1960, Norris's report as NCWA convenor of migration welcomed these changes, while stressing that at base they changed nothing: 'it is a fundamental part of our immigration policy that those people who come to live here permanently should be capable of economic and social integration within a relatively short time'. She concluded that

> The right of every Sovereign State to determine the composition of its own population is freely exercised by all countries. Australia is endeavouring to create a homogeneous nation—and gives preference to migrants from countries in which the people are racially similar.[56]

Over the next few years such explicit endorsement of racial differentiation became less common in public discourse. Journalists, bureaucrats and politicians began using terms like 'social homogeneity' to describe the same assimilationist ideals.[57] Rejection of the White Australia policy in favour of a quota system became generally acceptable across Australian society. When in 1966 a new Migration Act formally—though not actually—took racial considerations out of immigrant selection, it provoked very little debate in the community.[58]

Within the national councils there was a complete lack of interest. By that time Ada Norris had resigned as NCWA migration convenor to take up the ICW migration convenorship, and in her conference report the new convenor failed to even register the passage of the Act.[59]

---

55 Tavan, *Long Slow Death of White Australia*, pp. 89–90.
56 Ada Norris, 'Migration Report', *NCWA Biennial Conference*, Canberra, 29 October – 4 November 1960, pp. 99–100.
57 Tavan, *The Long Slow Death of White Australia*, p. 132.
58 The only significant organisations to publicly oppose the deracialisation of immigration were the Returned Services League and the Australian Natives Association.
59 O. Watson, 'Migration', *NCWA Conference Report*, 1964–1967, Melbourne, 1967, p. 23.

Looking to Asia and the Pacific

In June 1963 NCWA President Dorothy Edwards attended the ICW triennial conference in Washington, and returned invigorated in her mission. In July she wrote briskly to the secretary of the Department of External Affairs:

> Dear Mr. Truscott,
>
> I propose to visit Canberra on the afternoon of Wednesday 21st August and would appreciate an opportunity of speaking to you or some member of your Department. There are various aspects of our recent International Conference in Washington and a projected Conference for the National Councils of Women of South East Asia and the Western Pacific in Brisbane in September 1964 which I would like to discuss with you.[60]

Her note provoked anxious marginalia amongst the bureaucrats in External Affairs: 'would this be one of yours'; 'you might please talk with the lady'. The United Nations section accepted responsibility for women's affairs and wrote asking Edwards for 'more specific advice as to "the various issues" she intends to raise'.[61] She responded by adding to her list a range of topics including the UN 'Convention on Prostitution', the 'Work of US women's organisation in liaison with the US State Department', 'What can be done to help gain women's sympathies in South East Asia', the 'Attitude of Australia to frequency of meetings of Status of Women Commission', and 'Representation at U.N. Conferences where women's interests are particularly concerned'.[62] Clerks in External Affairs busied themselves preparing briefing notes for

---

60 Dorothy Edwards to Mr Neil Truscott, 29 July 1962, Department of External Affairs: Status of Women, A1838/1, NAA.
61 Memo, United Nations Branch, 14 August 1963, Department of External Affairs: Status of Women, A1838/1, NAA.
62 Dorothy Edwards to Mr M.G.M. Bourchier, 12 August 1963, and memo, United Nations Branch, 21 August 1963, Department of External Affairs: Status of Women, A1838/1, NAA.

the officer detailed to meet with Mrs Edwards, courteous but cautious notes. Thus, on the issue of the work of US women's organisations in liaison with the US State Department, 'I don't think we should give her the impression that this Department is willing to take on the same responsibilities'. The department was, however, willing to channel aid to Asian countries if 'Women's organisations in Australia could initiate their own voluntary aid schemes'.[63] But, in the event, Dorothy Edwards was probably more concerned with the issues that she raised in her first letter, and especially with finding government sponsorship for the international gathering of women for the National Councils of Women of the Pacific and Southeast Asia that she was planning to hold in Brisbane in September 1964.

Feeling perhaps that her case needed strengthening, on her return to Launceston Edwards approached a powerful friend, Senator Denham Henty, recently appointed minister for customs and excise. She asked the senator to pass on to the minister for external affairs, Sir Garfield Barwick, a letter she had written reflecting on her American visit. It was an engaging missive, touching on the high regard in which the Australian embassy was held in Washington, the strong resentment of England (as 'decadent monarchy') that was 'still being taught in America', the energy with which the USA was trying to extend its influence in Africa, Asia and South America, and the need for Australia to be 'doing similar but smaller work in South East Asia'—starting perhaps amongst the women of the region.[64] Barwick minuted on Henty's covering letter: 'An interesting letter. We do need to *actively* cultivate the ladies. Pls dft reply accordingly' [sic, emphasis in original]. The reply to Henty assured him that the interesting letter would be circulated to officers of the department, and that Mrs Edwards' 'request for assistance in

---

63 Memo, United Nations Branch, 21 August 1963, Department of External Affairs: Status of Women, A1838/1, NAA.

64 Dorothy Edwards to Senator Henty, attached to Denham Henty to Garfield Barwick, 3 September 1963, Department of External Affairs: Status of Women, A1838/1, NAA.

bringing delegates from Pakistan, India, Thailand, Indonesia, Korea and West Samoa to the International Council of Women in Brisbane next September' would be kindly received.[65]

Dorothy Edwards gave new energy to NCWA's engagement with Asia, but she was working in an established tradition. As we have seen, Elsie Byth's 'Pacific Assembly' in Brisbane in 1948 brought together politicians, academics, and bureaucrats to speak on topics ranging from democratising Japan to the status of women in the Pacific, and resolutions were passed suggesting 'that the Governments and peoples of the Commonwealth take a greater interest in Pacific affairs and problems'.[66] The heightening of Cold War tensions in the early 1950s did not temper NCW interest in the region. The Brookes board included a session on the Pacific in the 1952 biennial conference,[67] and they worked hard to send a suitable delegate to the 1952 meeting of the Pan Pacific Women's Conference, securing a fare from the Prime Minister's Department for their chosen representative, Elsie Byth.[68]

The next president, Ruth Gibson, began her tenure in 1953 by visiting London to represent NCWA at the Coronation of Elizabeth II; on her return she told her board members that 'While in England ... it became obvious to her that we must take an increasing interest in international affairs'. She suggested that all state councils should be given the rather limited choice of nominating 'whether the Pacific should become our main sphere of interest, our only sphere of interest, or chief among wider international affairs'.[69] The following year Gibson attended the

---

[65] Garfield Barwick to Senator W.H.D. Henty, 9 September 1961, Department of External Affairs: Status of Women, A1838/1, NAA.
[66] Program, *Pacific Assembly, September 6th, 7th and 8th*, Brisbane Telegraph Typ. Item in A9108, ROLL 10/18, NAA.
[67] NCWA Board Minutes, 27 February 1951, Box 13, MS7583, NCWA Papers, NLA.
[68] NCWA Board Minutes, 29 May 1951, 13 September 1951, Box 13, MS7583, NCWA Papers, NLA.
[69] NCWA Board Minutes, 12 August 1953, Box 13, MS7583, NCWA Papers, NLA.

inaugural meeting of a revived Pan Pacific Women's Organisation of Australia, chaired by Senator Agnes Robertson.[70]

At the end of the decade, Thelma Metcalfe represented the International Council of Women at a conference of the UN Economic Commission for Asia and the Far East. The experience convinced her of the importance of regional activism in the interests of improving the lives of women in the Asia–Pacific area. She particularly urged the national councils to focus on education in Papua New Guinea. The last conference of her presidency in 1960 saw discussion of the possibility of an annual conference of ICW being held in Australia, or perhaps a gathering of National Councils of Women from the Asia–Pacific region. Metcalfe favoured the idea of a regional conference, believing that it would attract government support as a way of cementing good relations with our neighbours.[71]

Dorothy Edwards took up Metcalfe's suggestion and ran with it. On her return from the ICW Washington conference, she told the association that the work of the next decade should focus on the National Councils of Asia and the Pacific. These councils were

> anxious to participate fully in ICW, have fields of work which ... are no longer necessary in our country, and can profit by our experience of organisation and of social legislation and its implementation ... The future of millions of people may depend on the relations we establish now.[72]

She reported that she had taken the opportunity of the ICW conference to issue an invitation to the councils of South East Asia and the Western Pacific to attend a regional conference in Brisbane in 1964. And, as

---

70 NCWA Board Minutes, 25 September 1954, Box 13, MS7583, NCWA Papers, NLA.
71 'Dorothy Edwards', *Stirrers with Style! Presidents of the National Council of Women of Australia and Its Predecessors*, http://www.womenaustralia.info/exhib/ncwa/presidents-10.html.
72 *NCWA Newsletter*, July 1963.

we have seen, Edwards was already booking her flight to Canberra to secure funding for her conference.

The Regional Seminar in International Understanding was a triumph for Edwards and also for the incoming president, Anne Hamilton, who took on most of the organisation. ICW was persuaded to bless the occasion as an official regional conference—the first in the Pacific region—and delegates attended from the national councils of India, Pakistan, Thailand, South Korea, Hong Kong, the Philippines, New Zealand and the United States of America, in addition to 118 delegates representing the Australian councils. The theme of the seminar was 'The Challenge to Women in the Decade of Development', with sessions around the sub-themes: 'The Responsibilities of a Woman to 1. Herself; 2. Her Home and Family; 3. Her Community; 4. Mankind'.[73] This morally loaded approach did not preclude detailed discussion of matters such as the technicalities of equal pay and the legal intricacies of domicile and residence. Ada Norris took the delegates through a close study of thirteen UN Conventions concerning human rights that were still to be ratified, explaining the obstacles to ratification and the position of nations represented at the seminar.

Edwards closed proceedings by evoking the things that participants shared—'friendship', 'the countries and homes and families belonging to us'. She called for prayer, with a form of words more open than Brookes's call for Christian fellowship in 1952: 'We think, too, of the peace of the world and pray in our own way for the continued peace of the whole of the world, thinking particularly of South East Asia'.[74]

The years after 1964 did not bring peace to South East Asia. By 1965 Australian troops were already involved in what the Vietnamese

---

73   NCWA, 'The Challenge to Women in the Decade of Development', ICW Regional Seminar in International Understanding, preliminary notice, Department of Territories A452 (A452/1), NAA.

74   NCWA, 'The Challenge to Women in the Decade of Development', ICW Regional Seminar in International Understanding, Brisbane, p. 17, Department of Territories, A452 (A452/1), NAA.

Anne Hamilton
NCWA President 1964–1967

Anne Hamilton was the second Queensland president of the Australian National Council of Women. She held office from 1964 to 1967, having served as the NCW Queensland president from 1961 to 1964. She was born in 1910 in Kerang, Victoria, and was educated at Esperance Girls' School before embarking on a business course. She married in 1936.

Hamilton's first public activism occurred in the post-war period when, wishing to abolish wartime rationing, she joined other women in campaigning to elect the first Liberal Party member for the Victorian federal seat of Balaclava in 1946. The following year, the family moved to Brisbane where her husband was appointed deputy city architect to the Brisbane City Council. Keen to become involved in her new community, she joined Forum, a group encouraging women in public speaking. It was as their delegate that she was introduced to the National Council of Women.

Hamilton's energetic leadership was focused first on finding solutions to the critical state of the state council's finances, and second, on shifting its headquarters from 'the squalid rooms in Celtic Chambers'. Her creative skills were responsible for beginning NCWQ's newssheet and inaugurating the Children's Film and Television Council and the Consumers' Association of Queensland. She successfully hosted the International Council of Women's regional seminar on international understanding in 1964, in conjunction with Australia's own triennial conference. Keen to extend the influence of NCW, she established a branch of NCW in Townsville, Far North Queensland.

On policy matters, Hamilton successfully used her national presidency to lobby the federal government to lift the marriage bar on the employment of women in the Commonwealth public service (achieved in 1967). She also encouraged state NCWs to include the welfare of Aboriginal people in their deliberations, persuaded the federal government to include the portrait of an outstanding Australian woman on the new $5 note, and agitated to liberalise the means test for pensions with the aim of its eventual abolition.

Extending her interest and energies into the International Council of Women, Hamilton oversaw the 'twinning' relationship between Australia and Thailand. A fund was set up to educate Thai children from remote areas with agricultural skills to take back to their communities. After attending the ICW Conference in Tehran in 1966, she said, 'the true development of nations depends on the state of advancement of the women'. Like her predecessors, she believed that support for the work of the UN was crucial for women everywhere. She died in Brisbane in 2002.

Explore further resources about Anne Hamilton in the Australian Women's Register.

call 'the American War', young men were being conscripted, and the mothers of the Save Our Sons Movement were protesting on the lawns and in the corridors of Parliament House.[75]

1965 was named International Co-operation Year to honour the twentieth anniversary of the United Nations. In Australia the major event of the year was the International Co-operation Year Convention held in Canberra in May 1965. Delegates were invited from voluntary organisations with consultative status with the Economic and Social Council of the United Nations, and NCWA was well represented.[76] The senior bureaucrats who addressed the convention were quick to condemn the United Nations as weak and inefficient,[77] and President Anne Hamilton's report on the convention suggested that delegates from NCWA found the experience uncomfortable.[78]

> N.C.W. Delegates attending the Convention were pre-disposed towards international co-operation since the International Council of Women is international co-operation and we are already working on that basis. However, from the plain speaking of the Convention emerged a feeling of urgency that present methods are insufficient to counter the spreading evil and disruption which brings about destruction.

The last years of the 1960s were indeed marked by disruption at home and abroad, but the national councils were not deterred from their old methods of fostering internationalism. State councils held local seminars on 'International Co-operation' and attracted audiences by staging international fashion parades and serving international afternoon tea. During her presidency, Edwards established a special relationship between the Thai National Council of Women and NCWA; state councils supported this 'Twinship' by raising funds for

---

75   See, for example, 'Vietnam Protest in Canberra', *Canberra Times*, 9 September 1965, p. 3.
76   'Minister to Open ICY', *Canberra Times*, 17 May 1965, p. 3.
77   'Criticism Can Aid World Body', *Canberra Times*, 19 May 1965, p. 12.
78   'ICY Convention', *NCWA Newsletter*, June 1965.

development projects in Thailand, and hosting study tours by Thai women. The *NCWA Quarterly Bulletin* reported in 1967 the satisfaction of the Launceston and Tasmanian councils in hosting a student interested in learning about the education of physically handicapped children; in Victoria members of the country branches enjoyed meeting a student of education for the deaf—'everywhere she went she joined in the life of the family'.[79]

The *Quarterly Bulletin* was the initiative of the Norris board, a printed magazine replacing the roneoed monthly newsletter put out by Edwards and Hamilton. The international activities of NCWA were a prominent, even dominant, part of the contents of the *Bulletin*. Glossy photographs showed visiting Asian women being welcomed by NCW officers,[80] and in-depth articles explained the workings of the UN and its agencies.[81] The year 1968 was named by the UN 'Human Rights Year', and every issue of the *Bulletin* carried articles on this theme: 'What is a United Nations Convention?'; 'The UN Convention on the Recovery Abroad of Maintenance'; 'Slavery ... Who, in this Human Rights Year, works for it abolition?'.[82]

Our nearest neighbours to the north featured strongly in the *Bulletin*. The doings of KOWANI—the Kongres Wanita Indonesia—were regularly reported,[83] and events in Papua–New Guinea made news in most issues.[84] Dorothy Edwards made the initial NCWA contact with women in Port Moresby in 1962, but her attempt to promote the establishment of a Papua–New Guinea National Council of Women was blocked at that time by lack of co-operation between settler and

---

79 'Twinning with Thailand', *NCW Quarterly Bulletin*, 1 (2), February 1968.
80 See for example 'Mrs Indira Ghandi visits Australia', *NCW Quarterly Bulletin*, 1 (3), June 1968.
81 See for example Ruth Gibson, 'UNESCO Panel: Representative of Australian Women's Organisations', *NCW Quarterly Bulletin*, 1 (3), June 1968.
82 *NCW Quarterly Bulletin*, 1 (3), June 1968; 1 (4), August 1968; 1 (5), November 1968.
83 For example see 'Kongres Wanita Indonesia', *NCW Quarterly Bulletin*, 1 (6), February 1968.
84 For example, see 'New Councils', *NCW Quarterly Bulletin*, (1 (7), May 1969.

indigenous women.⁸⁵ In 1969, an all-indigenous Papua and New Guinea women's organisation was formed with the assistance of the wife of the administrator, Mrs David Hay, and, in 1970, 'after a lot of hard work', Ada Norris established a Provisional Committee of NCW.⁸⁶ Hay and Norris also worked together to help found a women's hall of residence at the fledgeling University of Papua New Guinea. Norris brought together all the Australian women's organisations with international representation and the women's groups associated with all the major churches to form a powerful appeal committee, and persuaded Lady Hasluck, wife of Governor-General Sir Paul Hasluck, to launch the appeal in November 1969.⁸⁷

All this international news appeared in the *Bulletin* alongside snippets about the doings of local councils and the travels of local leaders. A reader of the *Bulletin* could readily imagine herself as a citizen of the world—a more peaceful world than the one on her television screen.

The proceedings of the triennial conference held in Melbourne in August 1970 can be read as a point of transition for the national councils—looking back to projects accomplished, and forward to issues that would shape the future. The attitudes and beliefs of members of the councils in 1970 make interesting comparison with those twenty years earlier—evolving in some ways, barely changed in others. Ada Norris, the outgoing president, sensed the historical significance of the

---

85 Correspondence between Dorothy Edwards, the Minister for Territories and the Administrator of Papua New Guinea, October–December 1962, especially J.T. Gunther to Secretary, Department of Territories, 27 November 1962, Department of Territories A452 (A452/1), NAA.
86 Mrs D.O. Hay, 'Opening Address', *NCWA Triennial Conference*, Melbourne, 12–19 August 1970, pp. 4–5. See also 'A New NCW', *NCW Quarterly Bulletin*, 1 (12), September 1970.
87 'Lady Hasluck to Open Appeal …', *NCW Quarterly Bulletin*, 1 (9), November 1969.

occasion. She appended to the conference report an extract from the 'First Annual Report' presented to the first truly national council in 1932, an extract that outlined the history of the councils to that date, together with a list of all the national presidents to 1970. She also seized the moment to note that while 'In 1950 it was decided to change the name [of the association] to Australian National Council of Women', it would 'now revert to N.C.W. of Australia'.[88]

Ivy Brookes told the 1952 conference that 'women have had to battle for their political, legal and social rights and they are still battling'.[89] Ada Norris took up the same theme, shaping her presidential address around the long battles that NCWA had fought over the years. She described the national councils as 'champions of the impossible', 'an instrument of social change, concerned not only with advancing the status of women, but with the broad stream of national and social development'.[90] Attempts to safeguard the nationality of women who married aliens were first made in 1916 and formally achieved in 1955. The struggle for federal marriage and divorce law began in 1928 and was won in 1959. The battle for equal pay had been even longer and was still to be won. She suggested that instead of the Golden Rule, the council's motto should be 'Baffled [only] to Fight Better!'

The opening address was given by Mrs David Hay on 'the women of Papua and New Guinea'.[91] She told delegates that when she first went to Port Moresby, three years before, 'there was a great deal of talk about the paternalism of the past and how the people must now learn to stand on their own feet'.

---

88 Appendix, *NCWA Triennial Conference*, Melbourne, 12-19 August 1970, pp. 59–60.
89 *NCWA Report 1949–1952*, Melbourne, Victoria, pp. 5–8.
90 Ada Norris, 'President's Address', *NCWA Triennial Conference*, Melbourne 12–19 August 1970, p. 5. Norris cited in full a quotation from Baroness Barbara Wootton, the first woman member of the House of Lords: 'It is from the champions of the impossible rather than the slaves of the possible that evolution draws its creative force'.
91 Mrs D.O. Hay, 'Opening Address', *NCWA Triennial Conference*, Melbourne 12–19 August 1970, p. 4.

But she soon realised that paternalism was not the only problem: 'there was a great deal of maternalism, and the local women had not only been told repeatedly how to do things, but when to do them—and so most understandably they were lacking in confidence'. Maternalism in the way Mrs Hay used it would have been a new idea to her audience. Those women who had taken part in ICW or United Nations conferences or seminars—and by this date there were scores of them—would have understood the need for cultural sensitivity across the ethnic divide. But the critical and more abstract reading we give to the word today—as the valuing of motherhood above other human attributes, and the exercise of maternal authority in relationships beyond childhood—would have made no sense to an audience that was thoroughly if unconsciously maternalist. Motherhood remained the essence of womanhood for most of these women, the bond they shared with the other women of the world.

For all that, there is evidence in the conference record of changing attitudes towards motherhood. The problem is no longer the mother who works; even the conservative members of the Child and Family Standing Committee 'concluded that the real problem is the quality of the mother—her personality, her concern for her children—and not whether she is working'.[92] A self-confessed 'career woman' told the conference that 'the dangers are not great [if we] provide adequate facilities for the care of the child'.[93] The conference passed a resolution calling for the extension of child-care facilities across Australia, with 'All-Day Care' provided for children under six years of age and after-school care for older children.

Proceedings were generally more secular than in the 1950s. The conference no longer opened with a prayer. Anne Hamilton was an agnostic who objected to leading meetings in the Lord's Prayer; the

---

92   Mrs T. Thatcher, 'Child and Family', *NCWA Triennial Conference*, Melbourne 12–19 August 1970, p. 37.
93   Mrs Zena Harman, 'Women's Role in an Era of Rapid Change', *NCWA Triennial Conference*, Melbourne 12–19 August 1970, p. 30.

international council had already dropped the practice in deference to its non-Christian members.[94] Members were no longer asked to stand for the loyal resolution; a version was printed in the conference program and taken as read. The language of the conference was generally less enthusiastic and more scientific, though the earnest moralism remained. A speaker on 'Food' concluded that

> The homemaker must be educated to the full realization of the sociological and psychological, as well as the physical, importance of food to all members of her family, and in the management of all the resources of her home. She must be prepared to meet the changes in values, as well as physical resources, and know how to evaluate these, so that she may make new scientific and technological developments her servants, and not allow them to become her masters.[95]

The conference theme, 'The Effects of Science and Technology on the Lives of Women', prompted consideration of the future. The writer charged with summing up the 'Conference Conclusions' found them to be mostly optimistic. Women's role in the contemporary world was 'less feminine', more merged 'into the broad stream of social and economic development', and the outcomes were for the better. New technologies required new training for women at work; domestic drudgery had been largely eliminated; pregnancy and childbirth had been made safe and avoidable. Women had gained new freedom.[96]

Voices questioning this freedom would be heard in the councils in the decade to come.

---

94   Interview with Laurel Macintosh, Brisbane, 26 June 2009, NCWA History Project Interviews.
95   Mrs Winifred Williams, 'Food', *NCWA Triennial Conference*, Melbourne 12–19 August 1970, p. 24.
96   'Conference Conclusions', *NCWA Triennial Conference*, Melbourne 12–19 August 1970, p. 31.

PART FOUR

REMAKING THE NATIONAL COUNCILS 1970–2006

Late in May 1973 the president of NCWA, Jessie Scotford, flew to Melbourne to attend a meeting called by the United Nations Association of Australia (UNAA). She made the journey even though to do so she had to cancel an important executive meeting in Sydney, and overcome a violent bout of illness. In her lengthy, handwritten report of the meeting, she explained that because

> Mrs Freda Brown, President of UAW [was] to be present at the meeting, also in view of the fact that Miss Eliz. Reid was likely to be present, I considered that it would be wise to go to the meeting if it were at all possible.[1]

The meeting was called to establish a national committee to oversee preparations for International Women's Year in 1975. The initiative came from the UNAA Status of Women Committee, chaired by Ada Norris, who recommended a short list of the national organisations that should be represented. In addition to the National Council of Women and the Union of Australian Women, this included Women's Electoral

---

1   Jessie Scotford, Report of Meeting of UNAA on 30 May 1973 at 134 Flinders Street Melbourne, Folder 'International Women's Year', Box 7, MS7583, NCWA Papers, National Library of Australia (NLA).

Jessie Scotford
NCWA President 1970–1973

Jessie Scotford was born in 1917 in Casino in country NSW, where her father, the historical novelist E.V. Timms, was a soldier settler. She remembers her country upbringing as a time 'when we put down a lot of very good Australian roots'. Educated at Gosford High School, Scotford earned a BA from Sydney University in 1942 while working in several day jobs, including journalism. In 1955, research for a Diploma of Education at the University of New England introduced her to the new discipline of family history. This background instilled in her the importance of history and literature.

Scotford joined the Women Graduates Association and became their delegate to the National Council of Women NSW, then the convenor of Arts & Letters in 1965 and president from 1967. This led to her chairing the Women's Committee of the Captain Cook Bicentenary in 1970. The experience of visiting folk museums in England encouraged her to campaign through the National Trust to retain not only historic buildings but the contents of those buildings, in order to preserve Australian heritage. She was a dynamic council member of the National Trust of Australia (NSW) from 1974 to 1981.

Scotford was president of NCWA from 1970 to 1973. She continued the work of her predecessor, Ada Norris, in the struggle for equal pay, she initiated new programs to obtain equal treatment for women in relation to pensions and taxation, and she worked to improve the standard of child-care centres. In 1972, she called for reports from affiliates on the local treatment of Aboriginal people.

In retrospect, Scotford considered that the major achievement of her presidency was the staging of the 1973 ICW Regional Conference in Sydney, obtaining United Nations funding to invite women from the world to attend. Scotford was made a life member and vice-president of the International Council of Women in 1979, in recognition of her skills and achievements in organising this and several later ICW events. She represented ICW at United Nations conferences in Copenhagen, Nairobi, Paris and Port Moresby.

In her later years, Scotford published a historical novel, *The Distaff Side*, following her ancestral female line back to her great-grandmothers.

Scotford was active in her church for many years and became an elder in the Uniting Church in 1977. She died in Sydney in 2003.

Explore further resources about Jessie Scotford in the Australian Women's Register.

Lobby (WEL), the Australian Council of Employers' Federations, and the Australian Council of Trade Unions (ACTU).[2]

In the event, Elizabeth Reid sent her apologies but Scotford found the meeting worthwhile nevertheless. She reported that the ACTU had 'flatly refused to come as it was an NGO meeting', and that in their absence much of the discussion focused on how the 'large women's unions' might be involved. The committee seemed confident of getting a grant from the government, despite the fact that 'No one seemed to have any idea what to do or who to send it to'. Norris tended to dominate the discussion; Scotford reported that 'Ada was rattier than ever, non-stop talker, driving [the chairman] quietly MAD but SHE WAS ALWAYS RIGHT!!!'[3]

Scotford reserved her most detailed comments for the woman whose presence had drawn her to Melbourne—Freda Brown.[4] Brown was president of the Union of Australian Women and shortly to become president of the Women's International Democratic Federation, both closely associated with Russian communism. NCWA and its state councils had long been wary of associating with the Union of Australian Women. In Victoria incoming state presidents were advised to respond to UAW requests to affiliate with no more than a letter of acknowledgement. Scotford kept an observant eye on Freda Brown. She deduced that 'UAW is in close touch with Women's Bureau and UNAA secretariat'; she knew those bureaucrats 'very well'. Scotford observed that, although 'her thinking is exactly the opposite of ours' on international issues like Cuba, Freda Brown was no firebrand: 'She

---

2 Julie Dahlitz, UNAA Federal Executive Officer, to Mrs H.E. Scotford, NCWA President, May 1972, Folder 'International Women's Year', Box 7, MS7583, NCWA Papers, NLA.

3 Jessie Scotford, Report of Meeting of UNAA on 30 May 1973 at 134 Flinders Street Melbourne, Folder 'International Women's Year', Box 7, MS7583, NCWA Papers, NLA. Emphases in the original.

4 For a detailed biography see Tony Stephens, 'Rebel with Plenty of Causes: Freda Brown, 1919–2009', http://www.smh.com.au/comment/obituaries/rebel-with-plenty-of-causes-20090526-bm0i.html.

presents as a gentle and sincere person. She is no fool, but very quiet in her manner in conference'. Scotford recommended closer relations with Brown and the UAW:

> In view of the fact that WIDF is always invited to ICW Conferences (a fact we both recognised) she will have to be invited as an observer to our Reg. Conf.
>
> In fact, perhaps we should be claiming <u>them</u>, not they us. This is of course impossible, but we should not be afraid of them.[5]

This account is fascinating for what it tells about an issue that fundamentally shaped the political understanding of NCWA at this period, in terms of both national and international polity, and yet is barely visible in their records. Fear of communism coloured the world view of these women as strongly as Empire loyalty had done for their predecessors in the first half of the century, and, like that Empire loyalty, it went without question. The place of communism within Australia was more controversial and, for that very reason, was banned from discussion within the councils as 'party political'. But most of the leading women in the councils would have endorsed Scotford's assumptions about 'our' thinking and Freda Brown's. Many—but by no means all—would have agreed with her that 'we' should no longer be afraid of 'them'. Closer relations with the Union of Australian Women did follow, if slowly. An incoming Victorian state president quietly tore up the 'Pink List' of organisations not to be accepted as affiliates.[6] But construction of communists as a threat continued as an essential thread in the thinking of the generation of women who had joined the councils in the 1950s and 1960s.

---

5 Jessie Scotford, Report of Meeting of UNAA on 30 May 1973 at 134 Flinders Street Melbourne, Folder 'International Women's Year', Box 7, MS7583, NCWA Papers, NLA. Emphases in the original.
6 Interview with Diane Alley, 16 September 2009, Melbourne, NCWA History Project Interviews.

Scotford's account is also interesting for its omissions. If the presence of young Katy Richmond from the Women's Electoral Lobby made any impression on Scotford, she did not record it. The lingering Cold War fears that made Freda Brown a rival to be watched were fast becoming irrelevant to internal Australian politics. In the years to come, the major force reshaping the women's movement and its relations with government would be neither the Union of Australian Women nor the National Council of Women of Australia, but the Women's Electoral Lobby.

The last three decades of the twentieth century saw a transformation of Australian society in all its aspects: political, economic, social, cultural and sexual. In the 1960s Australia was still an inward-looking nation, largely protected against the world. Immigration barriers kept out the peoples and cultures of Asia, the Pacific and Africa. Tariff barriers protected domestic industry, and the arbitration system protected the wages of the mostly male workforce. For all their differences, the major political parties shared a social-liberal view of the state: that its role was to maintain these protections and especially to preserve full employment, whilst providing a safety net of social services for those who could not work.

These settled public understandings were paralleled by a fixed certainty about private familial roles. Despite increasing numbers of women in the workforce, a man was expected to become breadwinner to a family, and, despite decreasing fertility rates, a woman was expected to be a homemaker. Despite increasing levels of sexual activity before marriage, the only socially approved love-making was between married couples, and homosexuality was taboo. As we have seen in section 3, divorce became easier in the 1960s but remained a matter for shame in many families, especially church-going ones—as did pre-marital pregnancy.

By the 1990s these certainties, institutional and social, had largely melted away. Australia had become a multicultural nation taking in immigrants from all over the world. Australians who could remember the shock of first hearing a language other than English spoken in public now regularly heard five or six languages on the train into the city. The end of tariff protection meant the decline of the large-scale industries where most urban Australians had worked. Full employment was a thing of the past, and with the end of arbitration wages declined, especially for lower paid workers, and job security was measured in months rather than decades. Neo-liberal economic theory and declining revenues persuaded governments of all political persuasions to remove market controls, deregulate financial systems, privatise public enterprises and shrink social services. Conservative commentators declared that it was the end of the 'nanny state'.[7]

The period also saw great changes in the areas of sexuality, marriage and family. One thing became more certain; a young woman coming of age in the 1980s could control her fertility with an ease that her mother could only envy, thanks to the contraceptive pill. In case of accidents, abortion was readily available and covered by Medicare. Single mothers were no longer shamed into giving up their babies for adoption; the state provided a supporting mother's benefit and all-day childcare for those who preferred to work. The freedom of choice provided by reliable contraception fundamentally undermined the old patterns of marriage and family. Women looked to delay decisions about marriage and children until secure in a career job, and many did not marry at all. Couples increasingly chose to live together for years before committing to marriage. Marriages often ended in divorce, generally followed by remarriage, and many children grew up with a wide array of parents

---

7   Gerard Henderson borrowed the term from American commentators for an address to the Institute for Public Policy in 1988; he was probably not the first Australian to do so. Gerard Henderson, *Address to Australian Institute for Public Policy Seminar on the Nanny State: Government's Threat to Civil Liberties and Free Enterprise*, Sydney, Institute of Public Affairs, NSW, 1988.

and grandparents. By the 1990s the increasing social acceptance of homosexuality made this mix even more eclectic.[8]

This demographic shift fuelled and was fuelled by the demands of radical feminists for personal autonomy and sexual liberation—though the great majority of those who subsequently enjoyed the new freedom of choice had no time for a feminism that cast men as the enemy. Most were wary even of the more moderate liberal feminism long espoused by the leaders of NCWA, and written into government policy and practice by a new generation of femocrats in the 1980s.[9] The neo-liberal attack on the 'nanny state' that gained ground in the 1990s took strength from an anti-feminist group within what was by then a very fragmented women's movement. The point of division for these 'women who wanted to be women' was—and is—precisely that bodily freedom provided by the pill: the freedom to reject motherhood.

Much of this last part of the book is about the struggle of NCWA to find a secure foothold within that fragmented women's movement. This insecurity was compounded by shifts within the policy and practice of government as it chose to relate to representative bodies like NCWA. Over these years, policy moved from offering general funding to 'peak' groups as a way of channelling information to and from the community to a system of limited grants tied to specific projects determined by government, all within an increasingly corporate framework of managerial efficiency. The leaders of NCWA struggled to transform the organisation to meet the changing expectations of government, ultimately and perhaps thankfully without success.

This story of an organisation struggling to adjust is a difficult tale to tell. Where other sections of the book could be shaped around particular campaigns, like the push for divorce reform or equal pay, here there are few clear lines of action to shape the story, no long-term aim in

---

8   This and the following paragraph draw on Frank Bongiorno, *The Sex Lives of Australians: A History*, Melbourne, Black Inc., 2012.
9   Marian Sawer, 'Reclaiming Social Liberalism: The Women's Movement and the State', *Journal of Australian Studies*, 17 (37), 1993, pp. 1–21.

which to succeed or fail—bar perhaps survival. The major themes of the earlier sections are present: women at home and in the workplace, issues of equality and citizenship, women and the world. But the councils moved in reaction to the social and political changes around them, and these changes structure the narrative. So the three chapters in this section are ordered chronologically. The first covers the years 1970 to 1975: from the arrival in Australia of the radical feminist movement to the celebration of International Women's Year—and the end of the Whitlam government. The second spans the period 1976 to 1985: the UN 'Decade for Women', and the development of a national framework of women's organisations in part in response to that UN initiative. The third chapter, 1986 to 2006, tells how a succession of presidents tried to transform NCWA to meet the demands of governments above and constituents below—an impossible task.

Chapter 12

THE YEARS OF RAPID CHANGE 1970–1975

Women's issues were more prominent in the 1972 election than ever before, and possibly since. At the first press conference of the campaign given by Prime Minister William McMahon, the first question put to him was: 'How do you see some of the issues which a Royal Commission on women ... What sort of issues could it investigate? For instance, would it investigate the question of abortion law reform?'[1] McMahon's election policies did include a promise to hold a royal commission into the status of Australian women; but there was nothing in them about abortion law reform, and this was not a subject he wished to discuss. The prime minister fumbled for a safe answer.

> Would you like me to go back into the history of this a little? It's been consistently urged upon ... eh, put it a little differently. The Australian National Council of Women has persistently asked me if I would have an investigation, a Royal Commission into the status of women.

Undeterred and well informed, the reporters continued to press the prime minister, citing the Women's Electoral Lobby's concerns 'about such things as contraception, abortion and child care, as well as ... questions of equality'. McMahon gratefully seized upon child care—'We've already made provision in the Budget for child-care

---

1   'Federal Election: Text of P.M's Conference on Monday', *Canberra Times*, 22 November 1972, p. 14.

centres'—only to be asked how he reconciled 'this interest in equality for women with your Government's attitude to equal pay, which I don't think has been enthusiastic, has it?' Another ten minutes of the press conference were concerned with such issues as the shortage of women judges, the possibility of a non-party vote in parliament on abortion law reform, and—given the prime minister's support for women's equal citizenship—should women be conscripted to fight in Vietnam?

The unusual prominence of women's issues in the media coverage of the 1972 federal election was undoubtedly due to the enthusiastic electioneering of the newly formed Women's Electoral Lobby. WEL activists interviewed every electoral candidate, recording their responses to a battery of questions and publicising their 'report cards' as widely as possible. In Victoria 'the *Age* printed the form guide for Victorian candidates as a particularly successful lift-out Green Guide'.[2] The particular issue of abortion law reform enjoyed a high media profile even before the election, thanks to the noisy street marches and graphic demonstrations of the Women's Abortion Action Campaign.[3] The fluid groups of women's liberationists who took to the streets over abortion were, in the words of historian Marilyn Lake, in 'revolt against domesticity', demanding full control of all aspects of reproduction.[4] Members of WEL agreed with the substance of these demands, while phrasing them more politely.

But whilst WEL and Women's Liberation got most of the media attention, some credit should go to the National Council of Women of Australia for putting women's issues on the policy agenda—or more precisely on the government's policy agenda. McMahon's policy speech

---

2 Marian Sawer, *Making Women Count: A History of the Women's Electoral Lobby in Australia*, Sydney, UNSW Press, 2008, pp. 10–13.

3 Rebecca M. Albury, 'Reproductive Rights and Technologies', in Barbara Caine (ed.), *Australian Feminism: A Companion*, Melbourne, Oxford University Press, 1998, p. 275.

4 Marilyn Lake, 'Women's Liberation', in Caine (ed.), *Australian Feminism*, p. 141.

included a section on women;[5] the opposition went to the election without a women's policy as such.[6] The national board of NCWA had been lobbying the government for the establishment of a consultative committee on women's affairs since the 1960s—first in the area of women's employment,[7] and from 1968 for a National Commission on the Status of Women, to be established with the purpose of eliminating all forms of discrimination against women.[8] This was the 'consistent urging' that McMahon referred to in his press conference in Perth. But the commission imagined by NCWA was a more permanent and a more representative body than the 'investigation' envisaged by the prime minister.

Representing Women to Government and the Media

The national councils enjoyed good relations with government during the last years of the Liberal regime. Ministers responded sympathetically (and sometimes effectively) to a range of policy requests: pensions for the aged and chronically ill;[9] taxation relief for students and widows;[10] a contributory scheme of national superannuation.[11] The Department of

---

5   'Liberal Policy: Constructive Changes for the Better', *Canberra Times*, 15 November 1972, p. 16.
6   'Labor Policy: ALP to Promote Equality', *Canberra Times*, 14 November 1972, p. 10; Sawer, *Making Women Count*, p. 13.
7   Correspondence between Mrs R.J. Reader, Honorary Secretary NCWA, and Leslie Bury, Minister for Labour and National Service, 1967–69, Folder 'Women's Bureau', Box 5, MS7583, NCWA Papers, NLA.
8   Ada Norris, President NCWA, to J.G. Gorton, Prime Minister, 18 August 1968, Folder 'Prime Minister's Department', Box 5, MS7583, NCWA Papers, NLA; Ada Norris, President NCWA, to J.G. Gorton, Prime Minister, 14 May 1970, in Box 10, MS90/190, Papers of Mrs J.G. Norris (Norris Papers), University of Melbourne Archives (UMA).
9   Honorary Secretary NCWA to Wm McMahon, Treasurer, 5 October 1968, Folder 'Department of Social Security', Box 5, MS7583, NCWA Papers, NLA.
10 'Correspondence with Federal Ministers and Departments', Box 4, MS7583, NCWA Papers, NLA.
11 Wm Wentworth, Minister for Social Services, to Honorary Secretary NCWA, 27 November 1968, Folder 'Department of Social Security', Box 5, MS7583, NCWA Papers, NLA.

Foreign Affairs continued to support NCWA's international activities, with consular aid abroad and funding for fares and conferences at home.[12] Government committees and agencies asked the council to research and report on matters of concern.[13] And, most significantly for the future, in October 1972 the McMahon government granted the council's request for $5,500 for administrative costs and travel expenses, in recognition of NCWA's 'important work of expressing to the Government of the day the considered opinion of a great cross-section of the women of Australia on matters that concern the welfare of the community and the status of women'.[14]

The election of the Whitlam government in December 1972 opened Australian society and politics to a period of profound and rapid change. Gough Whitlam signalled the new order with a barrage of radical executive decisions, announced by press release—forty in his first fourteen days—including the abolition of conscription, the withdrawal of troops from Vietnam and the release of gaoled draft resisters, a ban on racially selected sporting teams, the diplomatic recognition of China and the scrapping of the Imperial honours system. Of special interest to women were the decisions to reopen the equal pay for women case, with strong government support; to abolish the sales tax on contraceptives and remove the ban on advertising contraceptives in the ACT; and to appoint a woman judge to the Conciliation and Arbitration Commission. Then in early 1973 Whitlam announced his intention to appoint an adviser on women's affairs working within the prime minister's office, with direct access to the Department of Prime Minister and Cabinet.

NCWA president Jessie Scotford wrote immediately to congratulate the new prime minister, assuring him of the association's loyalty to

---

12   See, for example, Jessie Scotford to Nigel Bowen, 24 January 1972, Folder 'Foreign Affairs', Box 4, MS7583, NCWA Papers, NLA.
13   The Case for a Commonwealth Government Grant to the National Council of Women of Australia, NCWA Board Minutes, 14 December 1972, Box 14, MS7583, NCWA Papers, NLA.
14   The Case for a Commonwealth Government Grant.

the nation and all who served it.[15] In March 1973 she wrote again, welcoming the government's concern 'to ascertain from the community the areas wherein women are at a disadvantage', and establishing NCWA's long-term interest in an inquiry into the status of women. She suggested that Whitlam should also appoint a Women's Advisory Council, 'composed of women who not only represent the various segments of women's interests, but can be said to have the confidence of the women they represent'. Scotford did not claim this 'confidence' exclusively for the National Council of Women, but her inference is clear. Such a council 'would enable your women's adviser to keep her finger on the pulse of women's opinion and needs in the warm atmosphere of friendly discussion not so readily found in statistical research or activist lobbying'.[16]

Whitlam's private secretary replied in neutral but not unfriendly terms; Whitlam was 'conscious of the work done by the Council in the past on women's issues'. Scotford's letter had been passed on to the newly appointed Elizabeth Reid, 'with a request that she look at the suggestions you have put forward'.[17] There was no immediate action on this front from Elizabeth Reid's 'Office for Women'; the over-worked staff were too busy answering the many hundreds of letters they received from women all over Australia.[18]

The media was fascinated by Whitlam's 'Supergirl' and intrigued by the very public performances of the 'women's libbers'. Papers and magazines carried a steady flow of articles about the 'new women's

---

15 Mrs H.E. Scotford, President NCWA, to the Hon. Gough Whitlam, Prime Minister, 13 December 1972, Folder 'Prime Minister's Department', Box 5, MS7583, NCWA Papers, NLA.
16 Mrs H.E. Scotford, President NCWA, to the Hon. Gough Whitlam, Prime Minister, 26 March 1973, Folder 'Prime Minister's Department', Box 5, MS7583, NCWA Papers, NLA.
17 Peter Wilenski to Mrs H.E. Scotford, 10 May 1973, Folder 'Prime Minister's Department', Box 5, MS7583, NCWA Papers, NLA.
18 Sara Dowse, 'The Prime Ministers' Women', *Australian Feminist Studies*, 29 (82), 2014, pp. 391–402.

movement' in which NCWA featured briefly if at all.[19] Scotford's board seemed unconcerned by this, and it was left to NCW Victoria, led by Scotford's vice-president, Gladys Brown, to defend the association's image. Brown had already written to the papers during the 1972 election campaign when Scotford was absent overseas; she reported to the president that after McMahon's policy speech announcing a Status of Women Royal Commission:

> We felt that all sorts of organisations would jump on the band wagon but that the public should know who had been plugging this for years. So I wrote to the "Age" a letter stating that the NCWA had been asking the Govt. for this since 1963, and outlining what should be done and its terms of reference.[20]

In June 1973, again in Scotford's absence, Brown wrote to the *Australian* in response to an article that described the work done by NCWA as confined to 'Church work, welfare and work amongst the young'. Brown made it very clear 'that this was ludicrous': 'NCW was in the forefront of organisations working for the removal of all disabilities of women as well as being interested in the many aspects of community life and had made many invaluable submissions to the Government'.[21]

NCWV was probably also responsible for the preparation of a five-page document received by the national board in mid-1973, 'Some Activities of the National Council of Women of Australia with Regard to Raising the Status of Women in Australia'.[22] This bears quoting at some length, both as an example of the strategic thinking engendered by

---

19 See, for example, Suzannne Baker, 'Ideas from the Female Think-tank: Dear Miss Reid, Please Tell Mr. Whitlam ...', *Sydney Morning Herald*, 12 April 1973, 'Look' section, pp. 1, 6.
20 Gladys Brown to Jessie Scotford, 30 October 1972, Folder 'Status of Women', Box 8, MS7583, NCWA Papers, NLA.
21 NCWV Council Minutes, 14 June 1973, NCWV Papers, State Library of Victoria (SLV) (classification pending).
22 'Some Activities of the National Council of Women of Australia with Regard to Raising the Status of Women in Australia', annotated 'B/M 16/5, 1973', Folder 'Status of Women', Box 8, MS7583, NCWA Papers, NLA.

the rise of the new women's movement, and as evidence of the council's real claims as an agent of reform representing the women of Australia. It opens by defining all NCW activities in terms a defence of the status of women, understood as a social issue.

> Many problems affecting the welfare and full development of women and children are brought to the attention of State and Territory Councils throughout Australia. Such problems almost always affect women's status, or are derived from their unequal status with men or from discrimination against them. On these social or discriminatory problems, N.C.W.A. has raised its voice, sometimes years ahead of alerted public opinion.

There followed a very long list of issues that the association had taken to government.

> These include (inter alia) the plight of civilian widows and their pension allowances, social service benefits for unmarried mothers, training and retraining of married women wishing to re-enter the work force, the tax on contraceptives, working conditions and salaries of the nursing profession, abolition of the means test, national superannuation, equal pay for work of equal value, hire purchase discrimination, housing loan discrimination, the infant mortality rate of Aboriginal children, war service home loans for women in the services, apprenticeships for girls, subsidies for nursing homes and children's homes, Commonwealth Public Service superannuation anomalies, people on the poverty line, pre-school education, housing for the elderly, deserted wives, family planning, equal opportunities for education for boys and girls, taxation deductions for child care or house-keeping, problems of country women …

This was followed by summary accounts of the council's recent campaigns: 'for a national enquiry or commission on the status of women'; 'Equal Pay Cases'; 'Jury Service'; 'Local Government', and more. The great bulk of these issues had been raised, and their solutions formulated, by the standing committees of NCWV.

There is nothing to suggest that the national board made any use of this document in its dealings with government and the media. It seems likely that some of the campaigns it celebrated were too radical for members of the board. We discuss below the gathering opposition in several state councils to much of the Whitlam government's reform agenda in what can be called body politics: issues relating to family and sexuality.

A Changing World

Jessie Scotford became national president of the National Council of Women of Australia in late 1970. The November issue of the *NCWA Quarterly Bulletin* gave her the opportunity to put before the membership a kind of 'policy speech on assuming office'. Scotford reminded her readers of the 'constantly recurring theme' of the recent conference: 'CHANGE, CHANGE, CHANGE'. The audience had been 'frightened, warned, reassured and stimulated by the word and its implications'. Now she wanted to propose an area of stimulating change, for the councils and for Australia. She asked readers to imagine before them a map of Australia and its region.

> If you put your thumb on Tasmania and take a span in a half circle across the globe from W. Pakistan to the South Pacific Ocean, you include India, Nepal, Thailand, Cambodia, Laos, Vietnam, Malaysia, Singapore, Hong Kong, the Philippines, Indonesia, Papua-New Guinea, Fiji, New Zealand and the islands of the South Pacific. Under the palm of your hand is Australia.

This region Scotford christened 'Indralasia'. She identified it as an area with 'an enormous potential for womanly co-operation', peopled by women who are 'by race gracious, kindly and compassionate', and as yet 'comparatively untouched by the weary sophistication of the Western world, the blighting animosities of the African continent, the bewildering negation of the Americas, the spiritual deprivation of the Marxist-Lenin-Peking ideologies'. And it was where Australians lived.

> The future of 'Indralasia' is your future and mine—and I am convinced it is the future of the National Council of Australian Women. This is where our work lies ... Whatever our ethnic origins, "Indralasia" is our future homeland, and its peoples members of an "extended" family of neighbours of whom we are a member.

Scotford proposed as the major work of her board the holding of an ICW regional conference in Australia, as a step 'towards mutual understanding and the pursuit of peace' in Indralasia.[23]

Jessie Scotford's life to this point does not mark her immediately as a citizen of the world.[24] Unlike her successor, Joyce McConnell, she had not lived outside Australia before taking up the national presidency, and her travel overseas had been limited to Britain and Europe. Scotford had a deep attachment to Australia's past. Her father was the historical novelist E.V. Timms, and Scotford remembered her country upbringing as a time when 'we put down a lot of very good Australian roots'. In the 1950s she became involved in the popular movement to establish folk museums for the preservation of, in her own words, 'our Australian heritage'. While president of NCW New South Wales, Scotford involved the council in the Captain Cook bicentenary celebrations of 1970. Scotford chaired the bicentenary women's committee and effectively managed a range of events including a women's 'Pageant of Endeavour'—an exhibition in the Sydney Town Hall demonstrating women's contribution to the development of New South Wales. But this

---

23 Jessie Scotford, 'Indralasia', *NCWA Quarterly Bulletin*, 2 (1), November 1970, p. 1.
24 'Jessie Scotford', *Stirrers with Style! Presidents of the National Council of Women of Australia and its Predecessors*, http://www.womenaustralia.info/exhib/ncwa/presidents-25.html. The direct quotations from Scotford in the following paragraphs are taken from 'Jessie Scotford Interviewed by Hazel de Berg for the Hazel de Berg Collection' [sound recording], 7 July 1977, ORAL TRC 1/1010, National Library of Australia Oral History Collection.

focus on the nation and its heritage did not preclude an interest in the international.

This period in Australia has been characterised as the time of the 'new nationalism'.[25] Britain was turning towards Europe and away from her colonial ties; Japanese markets were opening to replace those lost in Britain; and historians, novelists, painters and film-makers were challenging Australians to reimagine their national identity. The dominant note in the new nationalism was optimistic and outward looking, imagining a future in which an independent Australia found security and prosperity in a post-imperial Asia/Pacific—Scotford's Indralasia. Within this understanding an active Australian citizenship was entirely congruent with an active internationalism.

Readers of the *Bulletin* were encouraged to see themselves as members of an international movement of women. There were frequent news items about the doings of women's organisations in the region and what Australia could do to help them.[26] Scotford kept up the Indralasia theme. Her presidential letter in August 1971 developed the theme of duty. Taking as her text the Christian injunction 'To love your neighbour as yourself', she asked her readers to consider who were their neighbours? Not the 'remote' British with whom we shared 'ethnic and cultural origins', but rather

> peoples so different in appearance, religion, dress, history, language and faith that at first we feel wary—then curious—then interested—then fascinated—and finally at ease as we discover that the things we have in common are many, that some of the problems that face us also face them ...[27]

---

25   Douglas Cole, 'The Problem of "Nationalism" and "Imperialism" in British Settlement Colonies', *Journal of British Studies*, 10 (2), May 1971, pp. 160–82.

26   See, for example, Edang Sulbi Suska, 'WHAT IS KOWANI', *NCWA Quarterly Bulletin*, 2 (1), November 1970, p. 3.

27   Jessie M. Scotford, 'From the President: 'Who is My Neighbour?', *NCWA Quarterly Bulletin*, 2 (4), August 1971, p. 1.

THE YEARS OF RAPID CHANGE 1970–1975

She argued that Australian women were uniquely equipped to lead the women of Indralasia to solve these problems: 'short on history, long on pioneering hard work', with 'vitality and purpose' and 'useful areas of technical and scientific expertise that we can share'. And being 'non-Asian' we could stand aside from existing tensions in the area. This last claim is astonishing, given Australia's continuing part in the war in Vietnam.

Scotford's plan to stage an ICW regional conference in Sydney was achieved in October 1973. In retrospect Scotford remembered this as the major achievement of her presidency. She had to overcome reluctance within ICW to commit to the project, then to persuade the United Nations Development Program to fund it—'about the hardest thing I ever did in my life'.[28] On the suggestion of the UNDP, the theme chosen for the conference was 'Population—Poverty, Development and the Role of Women'.[29] Potential participants from 22 neighbouring countries were offered half-fares and accommodation expenses in the hope that their governments would pay the rest. In the event, women from eighteen countries of the ECAFE[30] region attended the conference, together with experts and advisers from ICW and a number of UN agencies, and several hundred women from Australia. For Scotford the conference was distinguished by a 'rich diversity of culture and traditional concepts of relationship in life'. 'Discussion of responsible parenthood and family planning led the conference into broad consideration of the family', and the acceptance of 'family life as the essential basis for human society'.[31] There is a suggestion in her account that these traditional values were imperilled by western development.

---

28 'Jessie Scotford Interviewed by Hazel de Berg'.
29 NCWA Board Minutes, 6 December 1972, 5 May 1973, 16 June 1973, 29 July 1973, Box 14, MS7583, NCWA Papers, NLA.
30 Economic Commission for Asia and the Far East, soon to become ESCAP, the Economic and Social Commission for Asia and the Pacific.
31 'International Council of Women Regional Conference, "Population, Development and the Role of Women", Conclusions of the Conference', *NCWA Quarterly Bulletin*, 2 (10, 11, 12), 1973.

Much of the change in the Western world was not to be welcomed. Scotford wrote often in the *Bulletin* about what she called 'The nine-letter word—pollution'. Her targets were many: tasteless packaged food, soul-less supermarkets, 'mammoth' department stores; noise pollution from home appliances and thunderous semitrailers; garbage tips that burn 'into sky-darkening fragments, seeping through the subsoil, frothing into rivers and cradling the fringes of the sea, as man seeks to hide from himself the sad results of a technical advance that has got out of hand'.[32] This was a concern widely shared in the women's movement. The International Council of Women conference held in Bangkok in 1970 declared itself

> Alarmed at the accelerating deterioration of the human environment and the consequent undesirable effects on man's physical, mental and social wellbeing, [and]
>
> Aware of the general inadequacies of measures taken to combat the deteriorating process of biosphere such as air, water pollution and noise, the depletion of natural resources, and the destruction of beauty and wild life.[33]

The Australian councils were quick to register concern about pollution. The Northern Territory council worried about pollution of Darwin Harbour, the Tasmanian council about residue in Montrose Bay. In Victoria the country branches were particularly concerned with the issue.[34] A speaker told NCWSA that 'Most people today are alarmed at the general decay and fouling up of our living conditions and environment—destroyed beaches, infestation by service wires and

---

32 Jessie Scotford, 'The Nine-letter Word: Pollution', *NCWA Quarterly Bulletin*, 2 (2), February/March 1971.
33 Bangkok 1970, 'ICW Resolutions', hhttp://www.ncwcanada.com/ncwc2/wp-content/uploads/2014/02/ICW-CIF_Resolutions1.pdf
34 NCWV Council Minutes, 8 October 1970, 12 November 1970, NCWV Records, SLV (classification pending).

equipment, polluted water, etc.'.[35] The ever-increasing pace of modern civilisation could leave one, in the words of South Australian president Kathleen Rumbold, 'dizzy and confused as it whirls us around in its grip'.[36]

Towards the end of her national presidency, Scotford wrote an angry article called 'Now—An Eight-letter Word: Progress!' In pursuing 'profit-seeking innovation', Western society had lost sight of the values of a family life and a healthy body and mind. Abortion distressed Scotford:

> I find it hard to understand the attitude of a society that will happily condone the aborting of healthy fetuses and spend agonising thousands of dollars fighting to keep alive a full term baby born with irreversible and incurable physical defects.

And 'the most sinister cult of progress' was 'the emergence of the "permissive" society, gently and persistently eating away at standards of taste, morals, obedience, authority, clean speech, purity of thought and action'. In taking this stand, Scotford consciously distanced herself from, in her words, the 'newly emergent banner-waving groups' that called themselves 'progressive'.[37]

The Politics of International Women's Year

The United Nations Association of Australia was founded in 1946 to promote the aims and ideals of the United Nations amongst the Australian people. It worked for the adoption and implementation of UN Conventions on Human Rights, and from 1960 for the observation of UN International Years. Among the more significant of these were

---

35 NCWSA Report of Standing Committee for Housing, *NCWSA Annual Report 1970*, p. 16 (published as May 1970 issue of *NCWSA Newsletter*).
36 President's Report, NCWSA, 52nd Annual Report, May 1972 (published as *NCWSA Newsletter*, 3 (10)).
37 Jessie Scotford, 'Now—An Eight-letter Word, Progress!', *NCWA Quarterly Bulletin*, 2 (6), March/April 1972.

World Refugee Year in 1960, the International Year for Human Rights in 1968, and the International Year for Action to Combat Racism and Racial Prejudice in 1974.[38] At the urging of the UN Commission on the Status of Women (and with the strong support of the International Council of Women), 1975 was chosen as International Women's Year (IWY), and the Melbourne meeting that Jessie Scotford made such efforts to attend in May 1973 was called by UNAA to establish a national committee to oversee preparations for IWY in 1975.[39]

As Scotford reported to her board, the UNAA National Committee for International Women's Year seemed confident of getting a grant from government to fund the year's activities, which were envisaged as rather more extensive than those planned for previous years. NCWA proposed two projects, neither of which involved any expenditure—the issuing of a series of stamps 'to commemorate women's contribution to national development', and an approach to government 'to set up a Commission on the Status of Women'.[40] Both were endorsed by the UNAA National Committee, together with a number of major projects, including a national conference of delegates from voluntary organisations 'along the lines of former Citizenship Conventions', on the theme 'The Rights and Responsibilities of Women as Citizens of Australia'.[41] In the event the government refused the UNAA National Committee's application for funding. Meeting in Canberra in February 1974, the committee resolved to apply again, and asked all the organisations it represented to write to the government supporting the application.[42] Julie Dahlitz, UNAA executive officer, feared that these private representations would

---

38   'United Nations Observances: International Years', http://www.un.org/en/events/observances/years.shtml.
39   Scotford, Report of Meeting of UNAA on 30 May 1973.
40   Jessie Scotford to Julie Dahlitz, Executive Officer UNAA, 14 September 1973, Folder 'International Women's Year', Box 7, MS7583, NCWA Papers, NLA.
41   UNAA National Committee for International Women's Year Minutes, 11 February 1974, Folder 'International Women's Year', Box 7, MS7583, NCWA Papers, NLA.
42   UNAANC for IWY Minutes, 11 February 1974, Folder 'International Women's Year', MS7583, Box 7, NCWA Papers, NLA.

not be effective. After the meeting she took it upon herself to circulate a draft 'letter to the Editor' for members to sign:

> If we can quickly demonstrate our common purpose and determination, we will no doubt have a much better chance of receiving the financial support and practical assistance which is indispensable if our ambitious programme is to be put into effect.[43]

Dahlitz presented this proposal as the suggestion of the 'President of the National Council of Women of Australia, Joan McConnell'—a mistake on several fronts.

In late 1973, the NCWA presidency had passed from Scotford to Joyce McConnell of the National Council of Women of the Australian Capital Territory. In her speech accepting office, McConnell declared herself 'humble' before the achievements of 'those women whose selfless work ... has made NCWA the organisation that it is'.[44] She noted that this was 'the first time the Board has been in ACT', that she and her board 'were inexperienced but ... very determined to do nothing but our best': 'Our strength may well be in the very nature of Canberra—in the relative accessibility of those who sit in the seats of power and who are the architects of our national policy'.

This was undue modesty. The council of NCWACT was far from inexperienced politically. Under McConnell, its standing committees pioneered the technique of surveying opinion as a way of politicising particular issues and bringing them to government: in the first instance government housing and consumer prices. McConnell's academic training was in economics with a strong strand of political science, and as a student at Sydney University she was active in student politics. By

---

43 Julie Dahlitz to members of UNAANC for IWY, 15 February 1974, Folder 'International Women's Year', Box 7, MS7583, NCWA Papers, NLA.
44 'Triennial Conference of the National Council of Women of Australia', *NCWA Quarterly Bulletin*, 2 (10, 11, 12), 1973.

the 1970s she held senior office in the Australian Liberal Party and was very familiar with the Canberra corridors of power.[45]

Joyce McConnell responded immediately to Dahlitz, dissociating herself from the proposal to write to the press: 'From the point of view of obtaining help from the Australian Government, I think it would be most ill-advised at this stage for such a letter to be published'.[46] She continued to work with National Committee for International Women's Year, becoming vice-president to Ada Norris, but she quickly established networks independent of the UNAA committee. In March 1974 she discussed with the minister for immigration, Al Grassby, the possibility 'of all Australian Councils making contact with the women's groups of the various ethnic organisations, with a view to those groups affiliating with their State National Councils of Women'. She told the state councils that: 'The Minister is enthusiastic about the proposal and assured me of all possible help from his Department, both in the way of practical work and publicity'.[47] In mid-year she discussed with Elizabeth Reid the establishment of a women's resources centre and rape referral centres, both projects of interest to a broad range of women's organisations. McConnell proposed a resources centre offering 'reasonable office equipment for the use of women's organisations' to get 'submissions and similar work done'. In the case of the rape referral centres, McConnell claimed particular expertise on the part of NCWA, thanks to its international links, and proposed that NCWA

---

45   'Joyce Marion McConnell', *Stirrers with Style! Presidents of the National Council of Women of Australia and its Predecessors*, http://www.womenaustralia.info/exhib/ncwa/presidents-16.html.

46   Mrs H.G. McConnell to Mrs J. Dahlitz, 19 February 1974, Folder 'International Women's Year', Box 7, MS7583, NCWA Papers, NLA.

47   Mrs H.G. McConnell to Mrs R. Reader, 15 March 1974, Folder 'International Women's Year', Box 7, MS7583, NCWA Papers, NLA. See also letter from McConnell to Mrs J.M. Keays, President NCWQ, 15 March 1973, Folder 'Housing', Box 5, MS7583, NCWA Papers, NLA.

representatives could form the basis of an expert subcommittee to advise government.[48]

Later in the year McConnell sought an appointment with the leader of the opposition, Billy Snedden, 'to discuss some of the matters of concern to women associated with the National Council of Women'. This assignment was probably also taken on behalf of the UNAA National Committee for Women's Year; the first matter raised by McConnell was this body's need for funding. Other matters were of concern to particular state councils. A general concern was 'The importance of emphasising that no social stigma need be attached to the role of women in the home'. Snedden promised his full attention and that of his colleagues to these matters.[49]

In September 1974 Whitlam announced the appointment of a new body, the National Advisory Committee for International Women's Year (NAC IYW), and provided $2 million to fund its activities.[50] The letter of appointment received by those chosen to be members gave as the committee's aims:

> improving the status of all women by achieving equality between men and women, ensuring the integration of women in society by emphasising women's responsibility and role in economic, social, and cultural developments, and the removal of discrimination against women.[51]

The press release accompanying the inaugural meeting of the committee announced more practically that: 'The committee will advise the Government in the development of themes for International Women's

---

[48] Joyce McConnell to Elizabeth Reid, 19 August 1974, Folder 'International Women's Year', Box 7, MS7583, NCWA Papers, NLA.

[49] B.M. Snedden to Mrs H.G. McConnell, 3 November 1974, Folder 'Prime Minister and Minister Assisting the Prime Minister', Box 5, MS7583, NCWA Papers, NLA.

[50] 'Australian National Advisory Committee on International Women's Year', *NCWA Quarterly Bulletin*, 3 (2, 3), 1974.

[51] Nan Musgrove, 'New Fields for 2 TV Women', *Australian Women's Weekly*, 28 August 1974, p. 10.

Year and in the formulation of a national program'.[52] Elizabeth Reid was the convenor of the NAC IWY, and Margaret Whitlam was one of the twelve members. Whilst members were not selected as representing particular organisations, several had connections with the Women's Electoral Lobby; none were associated with either the National Council of Women or the UNAA National Committee for International Women's Year.

Nothing daunted, Joyce McConnell directed her attentions to the secretariat established to service the new National Advisory Committee. In mid-September Margaret Davey, president of NCW South Australia, wrote asking McConnell's advice about obtaining funding for a film about Australian pioneer women. McConnell wrote in reply that she had 'just returned from a long conference with the Executive Officer of the Secretariat which has been set up for I.W.Y.'. She gently discouraged Davey's film proposal, advising that the members of the National Advisory Council were likely to commission a similar film themselves, and added archly: 'I do happen to know that applications are in for two other such projects (please regard this last sentence as confidential)'. McConnell enclosed a draft copy of an information sheet on how to apply for IWY funding which the secretariat was intending to send to all women's organisations the following week; she was mailing this to all the state national council presidents 'for their early information, as I imagine everyone will be writing in and applying for funds for all sorts of projects, so the earlier the better'.[53]

In the event, five NCW state councils applied for funding for projects ranging from festivals and exhibitions to the establishment of a women's refuge; four were successful. The unsuccessful project was Margaret Davey's film about pioneer women. At the national level, NCWA did not undertake any activities requiring direct government funding other

---

52   'PM on Equality of Women', *Canberra Times*, 12 September 1974, p. 11.
53   Joyce McConnell to Margaret Davey, 18 September 1974, Folder 'International Women's Year', Box 7, MS7583, NCWA Papers, NLA.

than sending a delegate to the UN Conference for Women in Mexico. Rather, the council recommended government action in a number of areas, all strategically aligned with concerns expressed by the UNAA National Committee and/or Elizabeth Reid's National Advisory Committee: support for women's refuges; research on rape crisis centres; research on attitudes in trade unions and employer organisations towards women workers; and the provision of 'a permanently staffed office in Canberra which could be used by all women's organisations for the preparation of submissions to the Australian Government and for reference and research'. In his report at the end of International Women's Year, the co-ordinator of the National Advisory Committee reported progress on all of these except the last; the committee had recognised the need for a central women's resource centre but found the expense too great.[54]

One other matter remained to be tackled: the establishment of a women's advisory council. In September 1975, the *Canberra Times* reported that the government was considering the establishment of a branch within the Prime Minister's Department to deal with women's affairs. McConnell responded by forwarding a motion from the annual executive meeting of NCWA, requesting the government to establish in conjunction with this branch a women's advisory committee representing national women's organisations, and 'areas of special need'. Her letter listed six ways in which such a council could be of assistance to government:

a) to identify areas of concern affecting women and to make recommendations to the Australian Government in relation to those areas

---

54 NCWA Report of International Women's Year Activities [to the UNAANC for IWY], 21 February 1976; P.J. Galvin, Co-ordinator of the Australian National Advisory Committee for IWY to Mrs H.G. McConnell, 24 February 1976, Folder 'International Women's Year', Box 7, MS7583, NCWA Papers, NLA.

b) to establish a list of priorities of areas of concern to women, both as individuals and in the context of the family

c) to call for submissions from, and liaise with, interested groups, including voluntary organisations and individuals on these matters

d) to submit recommendations to the Prime Minister for appropriate action by Australian Government Departments

e) to act as a consultative group to the Australian Government on any legislative or administrative proposals affecting women

f) to liaise closely and co-operatively with authorities in the Australian States on matters of mutual concern.[55]

It is likely that Elizabeth Reid would have been in almost full agreement with this proposal. But the initiative was to be overtaken by the tumultuous events of the Whitlam dismissal.

The Politics of Motherhood and Family

The Whitlam government's reform agenda generated opposition from almost every vested interest group in Australia, and women were no exception. As we have seen, the leaders of NCWA worked to maintain good relations with government, but some state councils became increasingly hostile to elements of government policy. The fundamental point at issue that moved such women into active opposition concerned their self-understanding as mothers and members of families.

In April 1973 the honorary secretary of Scotfield's board, Pat Bernard, forwarded to the federal government a letter from NCW Queensland protesting at the recent introduction of maternity leave and pensions for

---

55 Mrs H.G. McConnell to the Hon. E.G. Whitlam, 1 October 1975, Folder 'Prime Minister', Box 5, MS7583, NCWA Papers, NLA.

Joyce McConnell
NCWA President 1973–1976

Joyce Marion McConnell was born in 1916 at Wollstonecraft, NSW. She was educated at North Sydney High School and Sydney University. She met her future husband when they were studying economics as evening students and both were active student politicians. Joyce served as director of the Women's Union and vice-president of the Student Representative Council.

Moving to Canberra, she joined the Canberra Association of University Women and became their delegate to the National Council of Women in the ACT. As convenor for housing and civic affairs she was responsible for the first two surveys carried out by the council in Canberra seeking information regarding government housing and consumer pricing. McConnell served as honorary secretary from 1957 until 1958 when she resigned to accompany her husband overseas. From 1964 to 1969, they lived in Argentina and McConnell joined the local University Women's Club and became a committee member of the Mission to Seamen in Buenos Aires.

McConnell was president of NCWA from 1973 to 1976, the first to be resident in Canberra. She quickly established good working relationships with the emerging women's bureaucracy appointed by the Whitlam Labor Government and, despite her active membership of the Liberal Party, communicated effectively with politicians on both sides of parliament. In 1975, McConnell on behalf of NCWA proposed that a representative National Women's Advisory Council be formed, but it was not until 1978 that Prime Minister Fraser formed such a body and appointed her to it. When Prime Minister Hawke abolished NatWAC in 1984 and replaced it with the National Women's Consultative Council, McConnell was again appointed, the only woman to serve both governments in this capacity. That she successfully negotiated the extreme opposition from right-wing radical women during this period is a tribute to her tact and communication skills. She continued to work with NCWA, becoming an honorary vice-president in 1979 and being the convenor of the economics standing committee in 1980. She also returned to the Australian Federation of University Women, organising their 1981 national conference.

McConnell was made an officer of the Order of the British Empire (OBE) in 1976 for service to the community, and awarded the Queen's Jubilee Medal in 1978. She died in 1991 a few days before her 75th birthday.

Explore further resources about Joyce McConnell in the Australian Women's Register.

unmarried mothers. The Queensland council feared that 'the provision of a pension would influence a girl to keep her baby'. Bernard approved of these sentiments. She told the Queensland secretary about a recent luncheon to launch Child Care Week in New South Wales: 'The Guest Speaker was our own Dr Claire Isbister who spoke out on just these questions—her address was excellent and of world standard'.[56]

Claire Isbister was a consultant paediatrician at the Royal North Shore Hospital in Sydney, and convenor of the Child and Family Committee for NCWNSW. She told guests at the Child Care Week luncheon that the Australian family was threatened by great social problems, 'and some of these problems are being permitted and even created by academic experts, governments and fanatical selfish minorities'. Unmarried mothers were paid to keep their babies, de facto couples lived off government support, married couples struggled to find child care when preference was given to working women, and teenagers contemplated 'trial marriage'. 'So who is getting the best deal at present, the responsible committed parents or the irresponsible?'[57]

Dr Isbister's views found a sympathetic hearing in several state councils, especially among the delegates of affiliated organisations based in the churches. Their influence was probably strongest in the South Australian council, where President Margaret Davey was a prominent member of the Young Women's Christian Association. In late 1973 the British campaigner for family values, Mary Whitehouse, made her first Australian tour, and Davey's board publicly supported her position, rallying and marching with her Festival of Light.[58] After a visit from Isbister, NCWSA put forward as a discussion topic at the NCWA executive meeting in August 1974 the proposal that the federal government should set up a 'Ministry of the Family' in order to defend

---

56   Mrs P.B. Bernard to the Hon. William G. Hayden, 7 April 1973, Folder 'Department of Social Security', Box 5, MS7583, NCWA Papers, NLA.

57   Claire Isbister, 'The Rights of the Child', *NCWA Quarterly Bulletin*, 2 (9), March/April 1973.

58   NCWSA Annual Report 1973–74, published as *NCWSA Newsletter*, 5 (9), p. 9.

THE YEARS OF RAPID CHANGE 1970–1975

'the integrity of the family unit as the basis of a sound society. We feel that present processes undermine the importance of the family unit'. At the same meeting NCW Queensland proposed as a topic for discussion 'Principle 10 of the UNICEF Rights of the Child, wherein it is stated … "He shall be brought up in full consciousness that his energy and talents should be devoted to the service of his fellow man"'. 'We feel that some of the permissiveness of our society is due to the fact that a sense of responsibility to their fellow man is not instilled into our children'.[59]

In May 1975, Isbister visited Brisbane at the invitation of the Presbyterian Women's Association and the National Council of Women.[60] Her address to the council was nothing short of a call to arms. She 'emphasised the role NCW must play in fighting for the maintenance of the family unit, and fighting against all those things which are corrosive forces in today's world'.

> The force singled out for special attention was the Women's Liberation Movement insofar as its credo would lead people, and young men and women especially, to abandon certain moral principles which are vital not only for the social but the physical well-being of the community.

The outcomes of unrestrained sexuality were venereal diseases, abortions, and mental illness for women on the pill, whom she described as 'hormonally castrated'.

> If we believe that the "advanced" women's groups are undermining what we stand for, NCW ought to state where it stands on the rights, the needs and the responsibilities of a woman … and parallel the interpretation of the Women's Libbers of "Live, Work and Love" with one of our own.[61]

---

59 NCWQ Executive Minutes, 15 July 1974, Box 16045, 7266 NCWQ Minute Books, NCWQ Papers, State Library of Queensland (SLQ).
60 NCWQ Executive Minutes, 11 November 1974, Box 16045, 7266 NCWQ Minute Books, NCWQ Papers, SLQ.
61 NCWQ Council Minutes, 15 May 1975, Box 16045, 7266 NCWQ Minute Books, NCWQ Papers, SLQ.

The Queensland executive was moved by this 'stimulating talk' to call a special meeting to consider how 'to make the voice of NCW more clearly and widely heard in the land'.[62] The meeting embraced for NCW the role of 'spokesman for women who do not subscribe to the theories and principles of Women's Lib', with the central belief that 'family life is the keystone, with both parents having equality in their roles, but carrying out their functions as wife and mother, husband and father, as a woman and a man'.[63] A 'Declaration' was prepared and circulated to affiliates, but the enthusiasm generated by Isbister's visit seems to have faded fast; the Methodist Church of Australia was the only affiliate to respond.[64]

The impact of these conservative opinions can be seen in the councils' reception of two measures bearing on family and private life introduced to parliament by Whitlam's attorney general, Lionel Murphy—bills concerning family law and human rights. In both cases, the force of the conservative reaction was moderated by the national councils' traditional commitment to equality and equal rights, preserved especially by the lawyers who dominated NCW legal committees.

Murphy was a passionate rationalist who believed that the law should reflect (or even anticipate) the increasing secularism of Australian society and values.[65] His Family Law Bill completely overhauled Australian divorce law, making no-fault divorce the norm and giving men and women complete equality before the courts. Joyce McConnell's board circulated a draft of this bill for comment from the state councils in mid-1974, with little response. The South Australian laws and suffrage committee was clearly divided, reporting that the

---

62 NCWQ Executive Minutes, 19 May 1975, Box 16045, 7266 NCWQ Minute Books, NCWQ Papers, SLQ.

63 NCWQ Executive Minutes, 9 June 1975, Box 16045, 7266 NCWQ Minute Books, NCWQ Papers, SLQ.

64 NCWQ Executive Minutes, 20 October 1975, Box 16045, 7266 NCWQ Minute Books, NCWQ Papers, SLQ.

65 Jenny Hocking, *Lionel Murphy: A Political Biography*, Melbourne, Cambridge University Press, 2000.

bill met the association's requests for reform but 'also includes many provisions which would be disadvantageous to women'.[66] Queensland took no action on the bill until asked to do so by affiliates with church connections; a special meeting was called 'with a lawyer and a theologian to speak about the implications'.[67]

In October 1974 McConnell sent Murphy a detailed critique of the bill. On the advice of the national convenor for laws, NCWA expressed no argument with the central provision of the bill; McConnell wrote that 'the National Council of Women of Australia supported the concept of "irretrievable breakdown" as a general ground for divorce'. But 'certain sections of the proposed Family Law Bill 1974 give us concern on behalf of those women in the community who are likely to be disadvantaged by this legislation'. Those women were the same imagined women whose interests the councils had defended in their response to Barwick's divorce reforms: the middle-aged, stay-at-home wives deserted by their husbands for no fault of their own. NCWA wrote: 'We submit that evidence of guilt should still be considered relevant in relation to maintenance and costs'. The arguments supporting this proposition were socially and morally based, pleading special needs.

> Under the conditions which prevail in Australia generally, husband and wife cannot be considered to be on an equal footing in the ability to maintain themselves and family. Women who have been out of the workforce for a number of years while rearing children are most disadvantaged by these provisions. The wording of the proposed Bill places the wife in the degrading position of having to prove inability to maintain herself.[68]

---

66   NCWSA Annual Report 1973–74, published as *NCWSA Newsletter*, 5 (9), p. 19.
67   NCWQ Council Minutes, 25 September 1974, Box 16045, 7266 NCWQ Minute Books, NCWQ Papers, SLQ.
68   Mrs H.G. McConnell to the Hon. Lionel Murphy, 24 October 1974, Folder 'Correspondence with Federal Ministers and Departments', Box 4, MS7583, NCWA Papers, NLA.

The council added to this the less emotional argument that: 'Contributions to superannuation, insurance etc. are a capital investment on the part of both, therefore irrespective of the fact that she could maintain herself after divorce she is justly entitled to her part of the investment'.

Women's Electoral Lobby made the same argument in their submission on the bill, basing it on 'women's contribution as homemakers' to the marriage's 'community of property';[69] the historian of WEL attributes the inclusion of this proposal in the amended bill to the Women's Electoral Lobby, but perhaps NCWA should share the credit. Murphy's response to the council acknowledged the economic aspects of NCWA's arguments, but gave no ground on the issue of guilt.

> I have noted the Council's views about the difficulty of women who have been out of the work force for a number of years while rearing children. But I think that the provisions of the Bill provide adequately for this matter to be taken into consideration when dealing with applications for maintenance.[70]

Early in 1975 the revised version of the Family Law Bill came before parliament. The board wrote in May to the attorney general restating their concerns but without a specific request for guilt to be taken into account in judgements about maintenance and costs.[71] The passage of the bill in the last months of the Whitlam government went unremarked within the National Councils of Women.

Murphy's Human Rights Bill

> sought to implement the International Covenant on Civil and Political Rights 1966 in Australia and would have protected a range of rights such as freedom of expression, freedom of

---

69 Marian Sawer, *Making Women Count: A History of the Women's Electoral Lobby in Australia*, Sydney, UNSW Press, 2008, p. 84.
70 Lionel Murphy to Mrs H.G. McConnell, 19 October 1974, Folder 'Correspondence with Federal Ministers and Departments', Box 4, MS7583, NCWA Papers, NLA.
71 Mrs H.G. McConnell to the Hon. Kep Enderby, 6 May 1975, Folder 'Correspondence with Federal Ministers and Departments', Box 4, MS7583, NCWA Papers, NLA.

movement, the right to marry and found a family and individual privacy.⁷²

It was generally accepted by the legal profession, but met with fierce opposition from the churches. NCWA's response to the bill was clearly marked by religious concerns. Councils objected to the possibility that any limitations might be placed on the 'freedom to manifest one's religion or beliefs'. The section of the bill on 'Marriage and the Family' followed the UN Convenant on Civil and Political Rights, but omitted the clause that read: 'The family is the natural and fundamental group unit of society and is entitled to protection by society and the State'; the councils questioned this omission, 'which is basic to our society'. And, finally, 'right to life' as defined in the bill was qualified with the proviso 'except according to law', a qualification they claimed, 'would allow legislation in Australia permitting or requiring euthanasia … [and] abortion on demand'.⁷³ In May Joyce McConnell wrote to Lionel Murphy applauding the work of the government in ratifying UN Conventions regarding women, but expressing 'grave concern' about these aspects of the Human Rights Bill.⁷⁴

In June 1974, NCWNSW forwarded to the board a lengthy document prepared from reports on the bill submitted by affiliates including the Salvation Army, the Presbyterian Women's Association, St Joan's Alliance, the Anglican Press Service, the Catholic Women's League, the Methodist Women's Federation, the Lutheran Women of NSW and the WCTU. These groups endorsed the objections already made, and added more. Several wanted more protection of the rights of parents to determine their children's education and religion. The

---

72 George Williams, 'The Federal Parliament and the Protection of Human Rights', Research Paper 20, 1988–89, *My Parliament*, http://www.aph.gov.au/About_Parliament/Parliamentary_Departments/Parliamentary_Library/pubs/rp/rp9899/99rp20, accessed 6 January 2015.
73 NCWA, 'Human Rights Bill, March 1974', Folder 'Attorney General and Human Rights Commission', Box 4, MS7583, NCWA Papers, NLA.
74 Mrs H.G. McConnell to the Hon. Lionel Murphy, 24 May 1974, Folder 'Attorney General and Human Rights Commission', Box 4, MS7583, NCWA Papers, NLA.

Salvation Army noted that 'Freedom of Expression' should be qualified for the protection of national morals. The Catholic Women's League feared that the bill's qualification of 'the right to life' would open the door to 'free abortion', and observed that the bill 'departed from the Covenant on Civil and Political Rights in being more restrictive in some ways and more liberal in others—liberation from moral restraint'.[75] The file copy of the letter from New South Wales is minuted 'no action'. In August the Attorney General's Department wrote to NCWA acknowledging its criticisms of the bill and indicating that a number of these would be met by intended amendments.[76] But the bill was not re-introduced into parliament before the untimely end of the Labor government in late 1975.

The play of body politics in the state councils is also evident in submissions made to the Royal Commission on Human Relationships, established in 1974 to enquire into 'the family, social, educational and legal aspects of sexual relationships', with special reference to the causes and effects of abortion.[77] The national councils generally avoided the issue of abortion as being too controversial for direct discussion. Thus NCW Queensland decided in preparing its submission to the royal commission, 'on the question of Abortion, so contentious a matter could be left to individual members to submit their private views if they so desired'.[78] The issue tended to emerge only as a sub-text in NCWA publications, as in Jessie Scotford's comment about 'healthy fetuses'

---

75 Gwenda Welsh to the Hon. Secretary, NCWA, 26 June 1974, Folder 'Attorney General and Human Rights Commission', Box 4, MS7583, NCWA Papers, NLA.
76 A.T. Watson for the Secretary of the Attorney General's Department to Mrs H.G. McConnell, 15 August 1975, Folder 'Attorney General and Human Rights Commission', Box 4, MS7583, NCWA Papers, NLA.
77 Michelle Arrow, 'Public Intimacies: Revisiting the Royal Commission on Human Relationships', in Lisa Featherstone, Rebecca Jennings and Robert Reynolds (eds), *Acts of Love and Lust: Sexuality in Australia from 1945–2010*, Newcastle upon Tyne, Cambridge Scholars Publishing, 2014.
78 NCWQ Executive Minutes, 21 May 1975, Box 16045, 7266 NCWQ Minute Books, NCWQ Papers, SLQ.

already noted.⁷⁹ In the same vein, Claire Isbister concluded an address with a rhetorical flourish: 'I am thoroughly tired of hearing those who have failed at marriage and killed their unborn children trying to throw out the good with the bad'.⁸⁰

But even without direct discussion of abortion, the royal commission provided a platform for views that were increasingly conservative in the context of current debates, aligning the councils with groups on the right axis of body politics. In reporting the view of the ACT council that 'The family is of prime importance in the preparation of children for adolescence and adulthood', the royal commission noted that similar views were expressed by the Catholic Social Welfare Commission and the Baptist Union of NSW.⁸¹ The opinion of the NSW council that 'Children are being exploited in advertising and by exposure to the sensational and even abnormal in sex and violence' was linked in the commission's report with the condemnation of the media by the Festival of Light.⁸² The NSW council went so far as to raise the abortion issue, endorsing adoption as a solution to abortion in terms similar to those used by the National Right to Life Association.⁸³

In the second half of 1975 the conservatives on the NSW council became even more vocal. In July, the ABC's 'Lateline' program carried a light-hearted look by Richard Neville at deviant sexual practices, described by the NSW minute-taker as 'sodomy and pederasty'. The NSW executive sent a telegram of protest to the ABC, and took to the August federal executive meeting of NCWA a motion asking for

---

79   Jessie Scotford, 'Now—An Eight-letter Word, Progress!', *NCWA Quarterly Bulletin*, 2 (6), March/April 1972.
80   Claire Isbister, 'The Rights of the Child', *NCWA Quarterly Bulletin*, 2 (9), March/April 1973.
81   Elizabeth Evatt, Felix Arnott, Anne Deveson, *Royal Commission on Human Relationships* (*RCHR*), vol. 2, Canberra, Australian Government Publishing Service, 1977, p. 8, http://apo.org.au/node/34438, accessed 7 January 2015.
82   Evatt et al., *RCHR*, vol. 2, p. 15.
83   Evatt et al., *RCHR*, vol. 3, p. 143.

stronger government control of the national broadcaster.[84] That motion lapsed, as did a proposal that the government be asked to explain a large grant made to Germaine Greer by the Arts Council.[85]

In September NCWNSW moved into activity that can only be described as political. Nadia Haxton, the convenor for laws and suffrage, was a lawyer who had recently transferred from NCW Queensland. In her convenor's report she raised three issues, all reflecting hostile criticism of the Whitlam government in parliament and the press: the funding of International Women's Year, the position of Elizabeth Reid, and the scope and funding of the Royal Commission into Human Relationships. Claire Isbister spoke strongly in support of Haxton, and a motion was carried recommending to all affiliates that they write to their members of parliament expressing their concern about these issues.[86] In thus raising their voices, delegates to the NSW council added their small weight to the wave of conservative complaint that swept the Whitlam government out of office in December 1975.

---

84 NCWNSW Council Minutes, 31 July 1975, Box 4, MS3739 Add On 2061, NCWNSW Further Papers, State Library of NSW (SLNSW).
85 NCWNSW Council Minutes, 28 August 1975, Box 4, MS3739 Add On 2061, NCWNSW Further Papers, SLNSW.
86 NCWNSW Council Minutes, 5 September 1975, Box 4, MS3739 Add On 2061, NCWNSW Further Papers, SLNSW.

Chapter 13

A DECADE FOR WOMEN?
1976–1985

International Women's Year, 1975, was full of tumult at home and abroad. Women seeking equality with men achieved more publicity than ever before, much of it about their public disagreements. In Australia the giant Women and Politics Conference, held in Canberra and funded as a major element in the government's program for IWY, was presented by mostly male journalists as 'a right old rort', 'a monumental waste of money', and a pack of 'brawling women'.[1] The United Nations International Women's Year Conference in Mexico was reported by the world's press under headlines like 'Women Find Unity Elusive at World Parley' and 'Division Emerges at Women's Year Meet'.[2]

Joyce McConnell attended the Mexico gathering as one of the ten representatives of non-government organisations funded by the Australian government. She reported that 'hopes that this United Nations Conference would be free from the usual political infighting … were not realised'. Nevertheless the member nations present endorsed a World Plan of Action for the next decade, the Decade for Women, 'and this in itself is a tremendous achievement'. And while the open sessions were marked by 'a certain amount of tumult and shouting', the

---

1 Kay Keavney, 'Women and Politics Conference: Was It Worthwhile?', *Australian Women's Weekly*, 1 October 1975, pp. 18–19.
2 Philippa Day Benson, 'Looking to Australia for a Lead in Women's Policies', *Australian Women's Weekly*, 30 July 1975, pp. 4–5.

gatherings achieved 'a world-wide exchange of experiences and feelings' and a swell of popular support for the plan of action.[3]

In her report as chair of the UNAA International Women's Year Committee, Ada Norris also remarked on the tumult of the year. While she believed it was too soon to assess the impact of 'the IWY campaign' on 'the imperceptible tide of social change', the year's debates had brought 'the concept of equality between men and women into clearer focus'. She identified as 'the ultimate dilemma of equality' the problem of 'life itself': the fact that society had not yet come to terms with women's new ability to avoid pregnancy and childbirth. Looking across the clamour of 1975, Norrris saw as 'the most urgent message of the Year for Australia' 'the dangers of denying equality of opportunity and equality of achievement to women in such a way as to make the gift of life unacceptable'.[4] Norris's insight speaks directly to the dilemma of women like Jessie Scotford, liberals who believed passionately in women's equality with men but found it painfully difficult to align this with their equally passionate belief in the value of motherhood.

Norris's immediate aim was equality of opportunity. She wrote in early January 1976 to the newly elected prime minister, Malcolm Fraser, notifying him that her UNAA International Women's Year Committee would 'conclude its special I.W.Y role in February', but would 'continue as a National Committee on the Status of Women in practically the same form'. She put before the prime minister recommendations for measures towards 'the elimination of sex discrimination at Federal level' that might be achieved during the coming Decade for Women. These included 'co-ordinated national machinery ... [such as] a National Advisory Council', 'equitable representation of women on public Boards, Commissions, Committees etc.', and, especially, federal antidiscrimination legislation. She reminded him of actions 'with regard

---

3   Joyce McConnell, 'The Conference and the Tribune: Mexico 75', *NCWA Quarterly Bulletin*, 4 (1, 2).

4   Ada Norris, 'Equality is the Goal', Box 23/58, MS90/190, Papers of Mrs J.G. Norris (Norris Papers), University of Melbourne Archives (UMA).

to legislation' at a state level: recent sex discrimination acts in South Australia and Queensland, preparatory drafts in Victoria and Tasmania, and a Women's Advisory Council in New South Wales, 'which is concerning itself with the need for legislation changes'. It was the hope of her committee that the federal government would follow Britain's example and 'give some priority to the matter of legislation to eliminate sex discrimination'.[5]

One strand in this chapter follows the efforts of Norris to achieve this formal equality for Australian women. Another strand follows the changing play of tensions within the councils and the wider women's movement over Norris's 'dilemma', with some rejecting equality in the name of motherhood, and others working to make the gift of giving life acceptable to women by changing Australian government and society. A third strand follows the programs and styles of the presidents across the decade.

Joyce McConnell's presidency continued until August 1976, when she was succeeded by Margaret Davey from the South Australian council. Davey's style was very different from McConnell's. As we have seen, McConnell was a skilled political operator and at the same time a true liberal; her connections with the Liberal Party in no way limited her commitment to reform. She readily established good relationships with Elizabeth Reid and her staff, co-operated closely with NCWV on equality and welfare issues, and did her best to ignore the flurry of motions from NCWNSW in late 1975 demanding action against women's health centres and radical programs on the ABC.[6] After her retirement from the presidency, her ties with the Canberra bureaucracy would give her a continuing role in the shaping of national women's policy.

---

5   Ada Norris, Chairman of the UNAAC for IWY to the Prime Minister, 5 January 1976, Box 23/58, MS90/109, Norris Papers, UMA.
6   Folder 'Action Clinics', Box 4, MS7583, NCWA Papers, NLA.

Margaret Davey
NCWA President 1976–1979

Margaret Davey was born in 1915 in South Australia, a fourth-generation South Australian with ancestral and cultural links to England and Ireland. Both of her parents were excellent role models involved in the community. Davey was educated at Girton School and majored in zoology at the University of Adelaide. She taught biology for 21 years and, in 2005, she was made a life member of the Adelaide University alumni.

Davey's early community activity centred on the Young Women's Christian Association (YWCA), and she became its president from 1956 to 1961. She helped establish the YWCA in New Guinea, and was a world council member from 1961 to 1969 and on the national executive from 1970 to 1974. It was through this link, together with the fact that her grandmother had been a member of NCW, that she became involved in the National Council of Women. Davey was president of NCW SA from 1972 to 1975 and, during this time, established a committee involving police and the community to counteract pornography. She was president of NCWA from 1976 to 1979, leading Australian delegations to ICW meetings in Kenya, Vienna and London. She was made an ICW life member in 1976. She also convened the International Relations and Peace Standing Committee of NCWA from 1979 to 1982 and was acting convenor for ageing. The proudest achievement of her presidency, she said, was gaining government-funded accommodation and equipment for the NCWA headquarters to be strategically placed in Canberra. Before this, the current national president and her board ran the NCWA from the city in Australia in which they lived.

In the early 1990s Davey, with a generous personal donation of $5,000, established a travel fund to assist members in attending major conferences and international symposia, lifting the profile of NCWA as a representative of mainstream Australian women. She also held a number of positions in the Liberal Party of SA including membership of the State Council from 1971 to 1980, the Women's Council and the Women's Policy Committee.

Davey was first recognised for her work in women's affairs in 1963 with appointment as a Member of the Order of the British Empire (MBE) and, 20 years later, was promoted to Commander in the Order of the British Empire (CBE). She was awarded the Queen's Silver Jubilee Medal in 1977. She was the Adelaide Rotary Award winner in 1973 for community service, only the fourth woman to achieve this, and also one of the women who received the NCWA Centenary Award in 2001. She died in Adelaide in 2010.

Explore further resources about Margaret Davey in the Australian Women's Register.

A DECADE FOR WOMEN? 1976–1985

Margaret Davey's professional career resembled those of her two South Australian predecessors, Ruth Gibson and Adelaide Miethke, in that she never married and taught for many years; unlike them her degree was in science. She came to the National Council of Women, and national politics, through the Young Women's Christian Association. She understood her professional role, and that of the council, very much in terms of service to the community, and she understood this service in terms of social benevolence and defence of traditional community standards. Like McConnell, she was an active member of the Liberal Party; unlike McConnell, her links within the Liberal Party were with its most conservative faction.[7]

In 1979 Davey was followed as president by Laurel Macintosh from the Queensland council. Dr Macintosh served for almost forty years as an ophthalmic surgeon in Brisbane's hospitals. She was rare amongst NCWA presidents in maintaining a full-time professional career alongside her voluntary activity. Her presidency of the Queensland state council led to her taking the chair of the Queensland International Women's Year Committee, and serving on Ada Norris's national committee. She remembered the year as 'traumatic', in part because the local committee found itself with a representative from the Communist Party. She consulted the UNAA president about this 'and he said "Of course you must keep them—the United Nations Association is for everyone". It was an unbelievable year'. Macintosh agreed to take on the NCWA presidency because after 1975 she believed she could cope with anything.[8]

Diane Alley's presidency ran from 1982 to 1985, the concluding year of the UN Decade for Women. Alley was a member of the Victorian

---

7   'Margaret Davey', *Stirrers with Style! Presidents of the National Council of Women of Australia and its Predecessors*, http://www.womenaustralia.info/exhib/ncwa/presidents-08.html

8   Interview with Dr Laurel Macintosh, 26 June 2009, Brisbane, NCWA History Project; 'Laurel Macintosh', *Stirrers with Style! Presidents of the National Council of Women of Australia and its Predecessors*, http://www.womenaustralia.info/exhib/ncwa/presidents-15.html.

council, trained in the liberal rights tradition of Norris and Brookes, and fully committed to implementing all aspects of human rights. Children's rights and welfare were matters of particular concern but equally so were the rights of women workers. Unlike conservatives such as Claire Isbister, Alley did not see a necessary contradiction between family and work. She was heavily involved in the equal pay struggles of the 1960s and a supporter of the Melbourne Working Women's Centre from its inception in 1975. Like Laurel Macintosh in Queensland, Alley chaired the state International Women's Year Committee, and graduated to the National Status of Women Committee in 1976. And there, Alley remembered in an interview, Ada Norris—now Dame Ada—'wanted me to follow her as Convenor'.[9]

The story of how Norris, McConnell, Macintosh and Alley worked for equality across the Decade for Women must be told with an eye to events and structures outside the National Councils of Women as well as within.

A New Field for Women's Action

The return of Malcolm Fraser as prime minister in the 1975 election was not the disaster for women and women's policy predicted by many on the left. Like McMahon before him, Fraser decided late in the campaign to make a policy statement with respect to the special needs of women. He pledged three things: to retain within the Prime Minister's Department the Office of Women's Affairs established by Labor; to work for a 'more equitable representation' of women on public boards, committees and commissions; and 'to seek means to obtain from women in non-governmental areas of the community ... recommendations on ways to improve the position of women, eliminate

---

9   Interview with Diane Alley, 20 July 2010, Melbourne, NCWA History Project; 'Diane Alley', *Stirrers with Style! Presidents of the National Council of Women of Australia and its Predecessors*, http://www.womenaustralia.info/exhib/ncwa/presidents-01.html.

discrimination and promote equal opportunity'.[10] In formulating the statement he took the advice of Beryl Beaurepaire, chair of the Women's Sections of the Liberal Party, and a close colleague. Beaurepaire told her biographer that it was she who suggested the wording of the third of these pledges. The whole statement echoes recommendations made to Whitlam by Ada Norris's International Women's Year Committee, and copied to Fraser; Beaurepaire was an active member of this committee, representing Liberal women.[11]

Fraser was as good as his word. He retained the Office of Women and accepted as his women's adviser its executive officer, Sara Dowse, despite her reputation as a 'socialist'.[12] At Dowse's suggestion he included both Women's Electoral Lobby and the National Council of Women of Australia within the 'key national bodies' invited to pre-budget consultations. The NCWA records contain an interesting account of these consultations. The WEL and NCWA representatives caucused beforehand and divided between them 'the matters to be raised', with WEL pushing amongst other things for federally funded child care and a women's advisory committee, and NCWA for welfare issues: domiciliary care of the aged, probate, tertiary allowances, maternity leave, and—again—child care.[13]

In July 1976 Fraser invited representatives from national women's organisations, including NCWA, to meet to consider the formation of a women's advisory committee.[14] In August 1976 Margaret Davey took over the presidency of NCWA, and early in September she wrote to the

---

10   Michael McKernan, *Beryl Beaurepaire*, Brisbane, University of Queensland Press, 1999, p. 139.

11   UNAAC for IWY 1975, Members, Box 23/58, MS90/109, Norris Papers, UMA.

12   Sara Dowse, 'The Prime Minister's Women', *Australian Feminist Studies*, 29 (82), 2014, pp. 391–402.

13   Margaret Finnis to Mrs H.G. McConnell, Pre-Budget (n.d. but early July 1976), Folder 'Correspondence to and from Ministers', Box 4, MS7583, NCWA Papers, NLA.

14   National Status of Women Committee of UNAA Minutes, 6 August 1976, Box 4, MS7583, NCWA Papers, NLA.

prime minister proposing two new topics for the agenda—censorship of hard-core pornography, and defence of the family as 'the basic unit in our society'.[15] Following the consultations, a small working group was appointed to decide the composition and agenda of the advisory council. Davey was not selected to join the working group. Beryl Beaurepaire from the Women's Sections of the Liberal Party was chosen, together with representatives of the Business and Professional Women, the Council for the Single Mother and her Child, and the Country Women's Association (CWA).[16]

Margaret Davey was slow to appreciate the changed position NCWA now held in relation to other women's organisations and to government. Joyce McConnell had worked closely with Ada Norris and her committee for International Women's Year, taking NCWA concerns to government through the UNAA committee, and writing directly to government in support of Norris's recommendations. Davey initially refused an invitation to join the UNAA National Status of Women Committee, holding to the old understanding that NCWA could not join any committee at national level because the organisation was itself the national representative of Australian women.[17] After lengthy correspondence she was persuaded to appoint a Melbourne member to represent the association.[18] Davey seems also to have assumed that NCWA's appointment to Fraser's advisory committee would be automatic. Norris wrote to her in late January 1977, urging her to put forward to the working party the names of possible representatives 'as

---

15 Margaret Davey to the Rt Hon. Malcolm Fraser, 1 September 1976, Pre-Budget, Folder 'Correspondence to and from Ministers', Box 4, MS7583, NCWA Papers, NLA.
16 Malcolm Fraser to Margaret Davey, 10 December 1976, Folder 'Prime Minister', Box 5, MS7583, NCWA Papers, NLA.
17 Margaret Davey to Ada Norris, 30 September 1976, Folder 'United Nations and Status of Women', Box 8, MS7583, NCWA Papers, NLA.
18 Ada Norris to Margaret Davey, 26 September 1976; Margaret Davey to Ada Norris, 30 September 1976; Questionnaire from Davey to Norris and responses, n.d. Folder 'United Nations and Status of Women', Box 8, MS7583, NCWA Papers, NLA.

we have done from the S. of W. Committee'.[19] Davey wrote to her representative on the committee: '[T]rust Ada to get in first'.[20] In the event neither Norris nor Davey were to be members of the Women's Advisory Council.

Under Beaurepaire's leadership the working party undertook a lengthy process of consultation, visiting towns and cities all over Australia to hold 'open house' meetings where local women set the agendas. Beaurepaire's biographer comments that while 'radical women from the Left' ignored the consultations, 'radicals on the right' were all too active, interrupting meetings to insist that 'home-caring was the only true role for women'.[21] In July the working party reported to cabinet, recommending the establishment of a permanent advisory committee of twelve members selected by the prime minister not to represent particular organisations but 'to reflect the diversity of backgrounds and interests among women'.[22] When Ada Norris received a copy of the working party's report she was outraged. The working party had ignored the recommendations of her National Status of Women Committee, and women's organisations in general 'have been very badly treated'.[23] She responded with a lengthy critique that took particular issue with the non-representational composition of the council.[24] Davey's NCWA board made a submission to government in much the same terms.[25] Neither submission had any effect.

---

19 Ada Norris to Margaret Davey, 28 January 1976 [should be 1977], Folder 'United Nations and Status of Women', Box 8, MS7583, NCWA Papers, NLA.

20 Margaret Davey to Gladys Brown, 4 February 1977, Folder 'United Nations and Status of Women', Box 8, MS7583, NCWA Papers, NLA.

21 McKernan, *Beryl Beaurepaire*, pp. 151–9; quotes from p. 153.

22 McKernan, *Beryl Beaurepaire*, p. 159.

23 Ada Norris to Margaret Davey, 14 October 1977, Folder 'United Nations and Status of Women', Box 8, MS7583, NCWA Papers, NLA.

24 Comments of UNAA National Status of Women Committee on the Report of the Women's Advisory Body Working Party, n.d. but c.14 October 1977, Folder 'United Nations and Status of Women', Box 8, MS7583, NCWA Papers, NLA.

25 Margaret Davey to Ada Norris, 4 November 1977, Folder 'United Nations and Status of Women', Box 8, MS7583, NCWA Papers, NLA.

By the time the formation of the National Women's Advisory Council (NWAC) was announced in July 1978, Fraser had downgraded its status by moving the Office of Women out of the Department of Prime Minister and Cabinet and making a junior minister responsible for women's affairs. Of the twelve women appointed to NWAC, four were involved with the Liberal Party at federal or state levels, including Beryl Beaurepaire as convenor. Two had connections with the Labor Party, one with the CWA, and one with WEL. Joyce McConnell was the only member associated with the National Councils of Women.[26] Ada Norris wrote to Davey in sympathy: 'I think it is scandalous that you were not put on the NWAC'.[27]

Letters between Davey and Norris became warmer across this period. Davey bowed to Norris's experience, asking her advice on matters like the current status of the UN Convention on the Elimination of All Forms of Discrimination Against Women (CEDAW). But Davey still resented the ambitious reach of Norris's committee, feeling 'that it is in many ways a duplication of so much of the work we do at N.C.W.A level'.[28] And Davey was right. The committee's brief was very broad: 'To examine and where necessary to take action with regard to all factors—political, educational, economic legal and social, which affect the equality of status between men and women'.[29] Norris was constantly in touch with ministers and bureaucrats from every government department, and women's organisations increasingly used the committee to channel requests and protests to government where previously they might have gone through NCWA.

---

26 News Release: Appointments to National Women's Advisory Council: Minister for Home Affairs, Folder 'United Nations and Status of Women', Box 8, MS7583, NCWA Papers, NLA; McKernan, *Beryl Beaurepaire*, p. 172.

27 Ada Norris to Margaret Davey, 25 August 1978, Folder 'United Nations and Status of Women', Box 8, MS7583, NCWA Papers, NLA.

28 Margaret Davey to Gladys Brown, 28 October 1977, Folder 'United Nations and Status of Women', Box 8, MS7583, NCWA Papers, NLA.

29 Draft letter reconstituting the National IWY Committee as the National Status of Women Committee, n.d., Folder 'United Nations and Status of Women', Box 8, MS7583, NCWA Papers, NLA.

For her part, Ada Norris also had some concerns about the relationship between her committee and NCWA. Some time in mid-1977 she seems to have had a mild stroke.[30] In August she told Davey: 'I won't be around much longer!!' and that she felt 'the NCWA should be the body bringing all the national women's bodies together ... and perhaps gradually working towards real national unity'.[31] She revived a proposal she had originally made in 1974, to restore to the NCWA constitution a clause that allowed the Australian presidents of women's organisations with international affiliation to become members of the national council. Davey took the proposal to the September board meeting, but it fell on barren ground. Norris's succession worries were eased when Diane Alley came onto the National Status of Women Committee as the NCWA representative and was promptly appointed deputy-convenor, with a large share of the convenor's responsibilities.[32]

Resisting Equality

In late August 1977 Margaret Davey sent a letter to Ian Macphee, minister assisting the prime minister in women's affairs, attacking the new 'femocrats' who were being appointed as women's advisers at state and federal levels. The letter claimed that 'numbers of the women who hold these public service positions are women who have been closely connected with radical and minority groups', and so are unable 'to understand that the vast majority of women in Australia are fairly conservative, do no want radical change and should have a right

---

30 Interview with Diane Alley, 20 July 2010, Melbourne, NCWA History Project; 'Diane Alley', *Stirrers with Style! Presidents of the National Council of Women of Australia and its Predecessors*, http://www.womenaustralia.info/exhib/ncwa/presidents-01.html.

31 Ada Norris to Margaret Davey, 24 August 1977, Folder 'United Nations and Status of Women', Box 8, MS7583, NCWA Papers, NLA.

32 Margaret Davey to Ada Norris, 22 September 1978, Folder 'United Nations and Status of Women', Box 8, MS7583, NCWA Papers, NLA; Interview with Diane Alley; 'Diane Alley', *Stirrers with Style!* The clause referred to had been included in the original NCWA constitution in 1931.

of choice'. 'There seems to be no thought given to the many women who do not wish to enter the work force, but prefer to make a success of being home makers and being responsible for their own child care.' The letter concluded with the hope that the government 'would ensure that new recruits appointed to the Women's Affairs Branch of the Public Service are trained women without any previous affiliation with minority and radical groups'.[33] Macphee responded in placatory terms, agreeing 'women in the home … are often not accorded the status and recognition they deserve'.[34] In March 1978 a letter to the new minister for home affairs, Robert Ellicott, made the same points in even stronger language.

> Our past experience … of women appointed to advisory positions on women's affairs both at State and Federal level, is that they appear to be the more radical academic, career-seeking women who come from a broken home situation and see themselves as a general pattern for all women.[35]

The letters were probably drafted by Claire Isbister and forwarded by the New South Wales council. It is difficult to know the strength of the Adelaide board's endorsement of their contents. Margaret Davey herself was committed to a defence of the traditional family as this was understood within the more conservative protestant churches. As we have seen, in 1973 under her leadership, the Adelaide council endorsed the evangelical campaign of Mary Whitehouse's Festival of Light; and Davey's national board was unusual in containing a majority of women with strong religious concerns. The honorary secretary was active in the Methodist Home Mission Association, and the international secretary was an elder of the Presbyterian Church. A committee member was an

---

33 Margaret Davey to the Hon. Ian Macphee, 19August 1977, Folder 'Correspondence with Federal Ministers and Departments', Box 4, MS7583, NCWA Papers, NLA.
34 Ian Macphee to Margaret Davey, 10 November 1977, Folder 'Correspondence with Federal Ministers and Departments', Box 4, MS7583, NCWA Papers, NLA.
35 Margaret Davey to Robert Ellicott, 31 March 1978, Folder 'Correspondence with Federal Ministers and Departments', Box 4, MS7583, NCWA Papers, NLA.

associate of the Australian College of Theology and the first woman to be appointed to the General Synod of the Church of England in Australia.[36] But none of these connections necessarily involved a conservative approach to social change. The international secretary, Heather Southcott, described herself as a Presbyterian brought up in the liberal tradition of the Scots Free Church, 'a church full of dissenters', which 'did not discriminate against women in the ways other denominations have done'.[37]

The New South Wales council continued to monitor the bureaucracy. In February 1978, Claire Isbister—now the Australian convenor for Health, Child and Family—brought the attention of the national board to the fact that the federal Department of Social Security was giving $2,250,000 to fund a 'pilot scheme to foster innovative family support services'. The word 'innovative' rang alarm bells. Isbister pointed out that the Royal Commission into Human Relationships had defined family as 'a varying range of people living together in relationships of commitment'—which could include 'homosexuals and communes'. A family support scheme following this definition would take no account of 'blood relationship, legal adoption, or any legal commitment'.[38] Davey responded by writing to the minister of social security, Margaret Guilfoyle, asking what kind of family would be supported by this funding. She feared lest it 'end up supporting alternative lifestyles very different from the traditional family, which NCWA has always been very keen to support'.[39] Guilfoyle's response made it clear that her department would not differentiate between married and unmarried

---

36 'Board of Officers 1976–1979', *NCWA Quarterly Bulletin*, 5 (1), n.d. but *c.* August 1977.
37 Nikki Henningham, 'Heather Southcott (1928–2014)', in Judith Smart and Shurlee Swain (eds), *The Encyclopedia of Women and Leadership in Twentieth Century Australia*, http://www.womenaustralia.info/leaders/biogs/WLE0711b.htm.
38 Margaret Davey to Margaret Guilfoyle, 23 March 1978, Folder 'Correspondence with Federal Ministers and Departments', Box 4, MS7583, NCWA Papers, NLA.
39 Margaret Davey to Margaret Guilfoyle, 23 March 1978, Folder 'Correspondence with Federal Ministers and Departments', Box 4, MS7583, NCWA Papers, NLA.

couples, but she assured Davey that 'I do agree that the Family Support Services Program should be used to strengthen the traditional family in every way possible'.[40]

The United Nations designated 1979 the International Year of the Child, offering an opportunity for conservatives to moderate the radical implications of the Decade for Women. NCWNSW seized the moment, bringing to the NCWA executive in August 1978 a lengthy resolution that effectively spelled out a complete program for federal activity in the International Year of the Child. From the basic premise that the year should emphasise 'Strengthening the basic family unit by providing assistance of all kinds to men and women who have accepted the responsibility of marriage, home-making and child rearing as a long-term contract', the resolution developed a typology of problem 'families under stress', and an exhaustive list of essential research topics. It concluded with a note that 'the size of the task' necessitated the establishment of a 'Children's Bureau', which 'could carry out the immediate tasks of I.Y.C. and provide the ongoing action emphasised by United Nations General Assembly in the resolutions declaring I.Y.C. 1979'.[41] Davey recommended the proposal to Senator Guilfoyle, who referred the matter to the newly established International Year of the Child National Committee of Non-Government Organisations.[42]

Here a difficulty arose. The March meeting of the New South Wales council had 'unanimously resolved' that Dr Isbister should be nominated to the IYC National Committee, 'as her interest in children made her ideally suitable to fill this position'. But to the 'extreme disappointment' of the council, Davey's board chose to nominate its international secretary, Heather Southcott, to the committee. The state

---

40 Margaret Guilfoyle to Margaret Davey, 31 May 1978, Folder 'Correspondence with Federal Ministers and Departments', Box 4, MS7583, NCWA Papers, NLA.
41 NCWNSW Executive Minutes, 18 April 1978, Box 3, MS3739, Add On 2061, NCWNSW Further Papers, SLNSW.
42 Margaret Davey to Senator Margaret Guilfoyle, 31 August 1977; Margaret Guilfoyle to Margaret Davey, 11 July 1978. Folder 'Correspondence with Federal Ministers and Departments', Box 4, MS7583, NCWA Papers, NLA.

council protested, informing the board that as 'a co-ordinating body' it might be acting 'too independently',[43] but the board refused to reverse its decision. In the end Isbister was appointed to the IYC committee as a representative of the Royal Australasian College of Physicians.[44]

Davey's board did in fact act as 'a co-ordinating body' for much of its tenure, taking the opinion of the state councils on issues as they arose, and bringing these to relevant ministers. Motions from state councils that may have been unwelcome to board members were nevertheless forwarded to the appropriate minister; thus a query from the South Australian council on the possible loss of Medibank funding for abortions was sent on to the minister for health.[45] Davey also supported programs initiated by the International Council of Women, including some with radical potential. She pressed persistently for government action on UN Conventions and Covenants: for the Suppression of Traffic in Persons and the Exploitation of the Prostitution of Others, for the Suppression of Circulation of and Traffic in Obscene Publications, on Discrimination against Minorities, on Civil and Political Rights, and for the Elimination of All Forms of Discrimination Against Women.[46] And, as noted above, after a hesitant start Davey's board generally co-operated with the National Status of Women Committee on the program for the Decade for Women.

Davey achieved significant gains for NCWA as an organisation. She understood that its role as advocate required supporting infrastructure, and set about persuading her contacts in the Liberal government to provide this. In the end her major ally was the conservative senator

---

43 NCWNSW Executive Minutes, 18 May 1978, Box 3, MS3739, Add On 2061, NCWNSW Further Papers, SLNSW.
44 NCWNSW Executive Minutes, 20 June 1978, Box 3, MS3739, Add On 2061, NCWNSW Further Papers, SLNSW.
45 Davey to the Hon. R.J. Hunt, 17 February 1978, Folder 'Correspondence with Federal Ministers and Departments', Box 4, MS7583, NCWA Papers, NLA.
46 See, for example, Margaret Davey to Peter Durack, 1 July 1977; 30 September 1977; Margaret Davey to Minister for External Affairs Andrew Peacock, 17 February 1978; 15 December 1978. Folder 'Correspondence with Federal Ministers and Departments', Box 4, MS7583, NCWA Papers, NLA.

and minister for administrative affairs, Reg Withers. In February 1979 Davey presided over the official opening of 'NCW Headquarters', an office suite in Kurrajong House, Canberra, provided by the government 'to facilitate the work of women's voluntary organisations with national and international status'; NCWA was to share the facility with the Girl Guides and the YWCA.[47] And late in 1979—at the very end of Davey's presidency—another minister for administrative affairs agreed to raise NCWA's grant-in-aid from $5,500 to $8,000 a year.

Negotiating the Decade

Equality was the first objective of the Decade for Women but by no means the only one. The 'full theme' was threefold: 'Equality, Development and Peace', and political jockeying in the UN planning committees produced a 'subtheme', again threefold: 'Employment, Health and Education'.[48] Norris's National Status of Women and Decade for Women Committee chose targets for Australia that were 'precise, limited and attainable', and included 'women on advisory bodies, anti-discrimination legislation, adequate social support services to enable parents to combine employment and home care, and greater emphasis on the value of technological and vocational training for women'.[49] The UNAA committee was high powered, bringing representatives of all the major women's organisations together with state and federal women's advisors and their support staff. It was effective, closely monitoring the work of government departments for instances of discrimination,

---

47 'The Official Opening of the Office Suite in Canberra, A.C.T.', *NCWA Quarterly Bulletin*, 6 (5), May 1979; Margaret Davey to the Hon. John McLeay, 5 October 1979, Folder 'Correspondence with Federal Ministers and Departments', Box 4, MS7583, NCWA Papers, NLA.

48 Kath Taperell, 'Report of the Australian Delegation to the Preparatory Committee of the World Conference of the United Nations Decade for Women, 1980: First Session Vienna 16–30 June 1978', Folder 'United Nations and Status of Women', Box 8, MS7583 NCWA Papers, NLA.

49 UNAANC Status of Women and Decade for Women Minutes, 2 February 1979, Folder 'United Nations and Status of Women', Box 8, MS7583, NCWA Papers, NLA.

and pressing vigorously for the appointment of women to advisory and planning committees on everything from employment to the future of technology.[50] And relations between the UNAA National Committee and the government's National Women's Advisory Committee were close and productive; Beryl Beaurepaire's biographer notes that the agenda adopted by NWAC 'borrowed somewhat'[51] from the UNAA committee. The most constructive activity of the Mid-Decade was possibly a national seminar in 1979, which Norris initiated and Beaurepaire funded, on the working of the equal opportunity and sex discrimination acts already promulgated in several states and territories.[52] The gathering confirmed and strengthened the commitment of the Attorney General's Department to a federal anti-discrimination act, though the full outcome would not be achieved within the tenure of the Fraser government.

In October 1978, Beaurepaire brought representatives of the UNAA National Committee and NWAC together with the state women's advisers to plan Australian activities for the Mid-Decade Year, 1980. The National Council of Women was not directly represented at this meeting, but the planning group's decisions had implications for the councils. Diane Alley wrote to Margaret Davey in November with a list of tasks 'for N.C.W.A to undertake'—primarily the establishment of Decade for Women committees in those states where they did not already exist: 'The N.C.W.s could initiate a move to call all the main State women's organisations together to plan the setting up of a Decade for Women Committee'. Davey was not impressed; a note on the letter in her handwriting reads: 'Attention Presidents of NCWs to deal with as

---

50   UNAANC Status of Women and Decade for Women Committee Minutes, 2 February 1979, 25 May 1979, 7 September 1979, Folder 'United Nations and Status of Women', Box 8, MS7583, NCWA Papers, NLA.
51   McKernan, *Beryl Beaurepaire*, p. 181.
52   UNAANC Status of Women and Decade for Women Minutes, 4 August 1979, Folder 'United Nations and Status of Women', Box 8, MS7583, NCWA Papers, NLA.

they think fit'.⁵³ It may be a measure of their waning influence amongst women's organisations that none of the state councils initiated or organised these planning committees.⁵⁴ Some women prominent in the NCWs took leadership in their local Decade for Women committees, notably Joyce McConnell in the ACT, Laurel Macintosh in Queensland and Diane Alley in Victoria. But they did so as representatives of NWAC and UNAA Status of Women Committees rather than the National Councils of Women.⁵⁵

If 1975, International Women's Year, had been 'tumultuous' for the women's movement, the Mid-Decade years were still more contested, and the debates were much more bitter. The pattern was set early in 1979 when a conservative backbencher introduced a private member's bill intended to remove abortion from the medical procedures funded by Medibank. Beaurepaire and NWAC took a prominent part in a campaign by women's organisations that saw the bill decisively defeated.⁵⁶ But victory came at the cost of alienating the large and influential Australian Catholic Women's Association and infuriating the much smaller and much more strident anti-abortion groups, Women's Action Alliance and Women Who Want to be Women. Members of these groups set out to disrupt the planning process for the Decade for Women, unsettling local committees and sabotaging state conferences. The Melbourne conference had to be abandoned when a move to stack the meeting produced 4,000 largely hostile registrations. At the Canberra conference, Joyce McConnell had to deal with a walk-out by a contingent of Mormon women, and passionate attacks on abortion by

---

53   Diane Alley to Margaret Davey, 8 November 1978, Folder 'United Nations and Status of Women', Box 8, MS7583 NCWA Papers, NLA.
54   UNAANC Status of Women and Decade for Women Minutes, 7 September 1979, Folder 'United Nations and Status of Women', Box 8, MS7583 NCWA Papers, NLA.
55   Interviews with Dr Laurel Macintosh, 26 July 2009, Brisbane; Diane Alley, 20 July 2010, Melbourne. NCWA History Project; Agenda ACT Conference for UN Decade for Women 1976–85, 6 October 1979, Box 9, MS8260, McConnell Papers, NLA.
56   McKernan, *Beryl Beaurepaire*, pp. 185–90.

mothers 'very obviously displaying their babies'.[57] Federal members of parliament were flooded with letters from their constituents calling for the abolition of NWAC because it did not represent Australian women.

This attack from the right brought moderate groups around to support the embattled NWAC. In Queensland the Women's Electoral Lobby was unhappy with Laurel Macintosh's chairing of the UNAA's committee for the Decade for Women, but took no public action for fear of destabilising NWAC.[58] The 1979 triennial conference of the National Council of Women of Australia placed itself solidly behind Beaurepaire and her council, expressing 'its appreciation of and support for the work of the National Women's Advisory Council. The N.C.W.A. is particularly conscious of the N.W.A.C.'s awareness of and concern for women in all sections of Australian society'.[59]

The 1979 NCWA conference also appointed Laurel Macintosh as president. Macintosh's work for the National Status of Women Committee kept her profile high with government, and she was one of the 'five prominent Australian women' included in the official Australian delegation to the 1980 World Conference for the United Nations Decade for Women in Copenhagen. The government also partially funded the attendance of some 22 representatives of voluntary associations at the 'Forum', the 'alternative conference' held in conjunction with the official one; only one of these chosen representatives represented the national councils.[60]

Laurel Macintosh remembered the World Conference, in retrospect, as something of a disappointment. As an official government representative she could speak publicly only with the government's voice: 'you

---

57 McKernan, *Beryl Beaurepaire*, p. 195.
58 McKernan, *Beryl Beaurepaire*, p. 193.
59 Report of the NCWA Triennial Conference, Adelaide, October 1979, *NCWA Quarterly Bulletin*, 7 (1), March 1980.
60 Laurel Macintosh, 'The World Conference of the United Nations Decade for Women, Copenhagen, 14–30 July 1980', and 'Report on the Forum: The Alternative Conference in Copenhagen', *NCWA Quarterly Bulletin*, 7 (3, 4), October 1980.

Laurel Macintosh
NCWA President 1979–1982

Dr Laurel Macintosh served for nearly 40 years as an ophthalmic surgeon in Brisbane hospitals, working all the while for women's rights as a community activist. In her professional life, she chaired the Queensland Branch of the Royal Australian College of Ophthalmologists. Her community work took her to two terms as president of the NCW in Queensland (1977–1979, 1994–1996) and a term as president of the National Council of Women of Australia 1979–1982.

Macintosh is justly proud of winning the case for late-night shopping for Brisbane and Ipswich in the Queensland industrial court in 1978 against the opposition of unions and shop-owners alike. This successful extension of trading hours created many part-time jobs for women and girls within the economy and was eventually adopted Australia-wide.

Born in 1924 in country New South Wales, Mackintosh was educated at Sydney Girls' High School and the University of Sydney, choosing ophthalmology and then training as a surgeon at the Royal Eye Hospital in London. Returning to Brisbane, she worked at the Royal Children's Hospital, the Repatriation Department, the Princess Alexandra Hospital and the Narbethong School for the Visually Handicapped.

She joined National Council of Women of Queensland via the Quota Club and rapidly took on several leadership roles. She was rare among NCWA presidents in holding down a full-time job during her presidency, and only survived the workload by taking months of long service leave to allow her to travel within and beyond Australia. A significant achievement of her presidency was the close relations developed by 'twinning' with the National Councils of Fiji and Thailand.

In July 1980 Mackintosh was one of 4 women from voluntary organisations funded federally to represent Australia at the World Conference of the United Nations Decade for Women in Copenhagen. Macintosh enjoyed good relations with politicians, state and federal, and with the federal Office of the Status of Women. She chaired the United Nations Association of Australia's Status of Women Committee in Queensland in the run-up to International Women's Year 1975, and when the Queensland government established an Advisory Council of Queensland Women in 1975 she was a founding member.

Mackintosh was awarded a Queen's Silver Jubilee Medal in 1977, an Order of the British Empire in 1980, became a life member of NCWQ in 1984 and an honorary life-president of NCWA in 1988. She was appointed a dame in the Knights Hospitaller of St Lazarus in 1988 and awarded an Australian Centenary Medal for service to the community in 2001.

Explore further resources about Laurel Macintosh in the Australian Women's Register

had to read every word exactly from a script, you couldn't dare vary by one syllable'.⁶¹ Australia voted against ratification of the 'Programme of Action' adopted by the conference, objecting to 'certain political references' that condemned Zionism and supported the Palestine Liberation Organisation. Beryl Beaurepaire told the conference that 'Australia's vote on the Programme should not be construed as negating the very many valuable and constructive objectives it contains',⁶² but the experience left a bitter taste in the mouth. The best moment for the Australians came when R.J. Ellicott on behalf of the government signed the Convention on the Elimination of All Forms of Discrimination Against Women, and even this was spoiled by a small group of protesters from Women Who Want to be Women. Ellicot and Beaurepaire had to push their way through, with the group 'waving banners and chanting that the minister should not betray Australian women'.⁶³

Economic Talk

The Fraser government gave more than token attention to the needs of women citizens, at least in its early years. In addition to maintaining the Office of Women's Affairs and establishing the National Women's Advisory Committee, the government created new infrastructure and new avenues for consultation with women. By 1978 Women's Policy Units had been established in most of the major departments in Canberra. Senator Margaret Guilfoyle set up a Women's Welfare Consultative Committee in her Department of Social Security; Margaret Davey represented NCWA.⁶⁴ And the prime minister continued the practice begun by Gough Whitlam of pre-budget consultations with a range of community organisations, including a session with representatives of

---

61 Interview with Dr Laurel Macintosh.
62 Laurel Macintosh, 'The World Conference of the United Nations Decade for Women, Copenhagen, 14–30 July 1980', *NCWA Quarterly Bulletin*, 7 (3, 4), October 1980.
63 McKernan, *Beryl Beaurepaire*, p. 202.
64 *NCWA Quarterly Bulletin*, 6 (1, 2), 1978.

women's groups. At first WEL and NCWA were invited to attend; later the session was extended to include the CWA and Women Who Want to be Women.

After a hesitant start the Adelaide board became quite skilled at this form of lobbying. The hour-long session with the prime minister and treasurer (and other ministers as relevant) offered an opportunity to raise a range of issues, some with specific budgetary implications and others more general. While it was doubtful that there would be much immediate impact on the budget for the year in hand, participants felt that 'the things we asked for that year, we often got the next year in the budget'.[65] As we have noted, the representatives of WEL and NCWA always caucused before the meeting, agreeing on the issues to be brought forward jointly from the longer list in each organisation's written submission. Thus in 1977 both groups spoke to the problems of unemployment, the need for more funding for geriatric services, also for children's services, for better and less discriminatory benefits for sole parents, and for measures 'to strengthen the family unit'. This last formulation was drawn from the position argued by Isbister and the New South Wales council, but there is a clear movement away from this in later years. In 1978 NCWA argued against the payment of joint pensions and social security benefits to married couples (and thus to the husband): 'We believe that such payments should be made on an individual basis, and should not be dependent on marital status; need rather than a marriage certificate should be the criteria for payment of benefits'.[66] The following year, the NCWA submission criticised the proposal for 'split income tax' by which the income of married couples

---

65   Interview with Dr Laurel Macintosh.
66   National Council of Women of Australia: Pre-Budget Talks: Submissions for the 1978 Budget, Presented by Mrs H.J. Southcott, NCWA Correspondence with Federal Ministers and Departments, Box 4, MS7583, NCWA Papers NLA.

was treated as a unit for tax purposes: 'The decision to marry or not to marry should not be tied to a fiduciary relationship'.[67]

The Macintosh board reflected the higher levels of education that women were achieving by 1980, with five of the seven members holding tertiary degrees, and three with experience of teaching at that level. In their hands the pre-budget submissions were more strongly argued, better evidenced, and more focused on economic outcomes. Thus the 1980 submission put a well-considered case for 'regular permanent part-time work'. It cited statistical evidence for the increasing numbers of part-time employees in the workforce, and for women's preference for part-time work. This was put in the context of the impact of technological change on the patterns of employment; the advent of silicone chips meant that 'there will never again in the foreseeable future be enough work for a 40-hour working week for everyone who wants employment'. The submission recommended that: 'The Commonwealth Government should take the lead and greatly expand part-time opportunities within the Commonwealth Public Service at all levels of seniority'.[68]

The 1980 submission continued NCWA's opposition to split income tax as unfairly advantaging married couples on a single income, and offering 'no help to the most disadvantaged in our community'. Rather, an increase in family allowances was the best avenue 'for increased benefit to families'. The 1981 submission restated this case: family allowances were both 'the most equitable means of family support and a means of ensuring that the money is used for that purpose since it is usually paid to the mother'. The same case was argued more fully by WEL's Meredith Edwards in a report published by the National Women's Advisory

---

67 National Council of Women of Australia: Pre-Budget Talks, May 30th, 1979, Submissions for 1979 Budget, Presented by Miss Margaret Davey, NCWA Correspondence with Federal Ministers and Departments, Box 4, MS7583, NCWA Papers NLA.

68 National Council of Women of Australia: Pre-Budget Talks: Submissions for 1980 Budget, 30th April 1980, Presented by Dr Laurel Macintosh, Folder 'Pre-Budget Talks', Box 8, MS7583, NCWA Papers NLA.

Committee, also in 1981.[69] And, in the same year, NCWA suggested an even more radical intervention in national economic policy, a proposal originating from the Copenhagen Decade for Women Conference concerning women's 'contribution to the economy through their unpaid work in the domestic sphere': 'we ask that the Federal Government take measures to assess this contribution with a view to including it in the Gross Domestic Product'.[70]

Laurel Macintosh remembered the pre-budget talks as 'a real circus'. WEL and NCWA continued to caucus before the meetings and, in Macintosh's words, 'we always had a cordial discussion and our minds met on most things'.[71] Certainly their minds met on benefits and taxation policy. But the CWA and Women Who Want to be Women were not interested in co-operation. Babette Francis of WWWW interrupted the 1982 consultation to present a pink-iced fruit cake to the prime minister with the inscription 'To the men in the House from the women in the home'.[72]

NCWA Abroad

In hindsight Laurel Macintosh nominated as the most important work of her presidency 'our relationship with our two twinning Councils', Thailand and Fiji. Macintosh understood this as carrying forward work begun by earlier presidents, and especially by Dorothy Edwards who 'was really the source of everything'. The twinning arrangement brought real benefits to Thailand and Fiji in the form of aid for specific projects and assistance with travel overseas. But the international work of the

---

69 Meredith Edwards, *Financial Arrangements within Families: A Research Report for the National Women's Advisory Council*, Canberra, NWAC, 1981. Cited in Sawyer, *Making Women Count*, p. 193.

70 The National Council of Women of Australia, Pre-Budget Talks, Submissions for 1981 Budget, 27th May 1981, Presented by Dr Laurel Macintosh, Folder 'Pre-Budget Talks', Box 8, MS7583, NCWA Papers NLA.

71 Interview with Dr Laurel Macintosh.

72 Sawyer, *Making Women Count*, p. 192.

councils was not appreciated in Australia: 'sometimes it's really hard to work up much interest'.[73]

In 1980 the national councils remained largely untouched by the ethnic changes that were transforming Australia's population. In 1973, in her role as NCWA representative on the Commonwealth Immigration Advisory Committee, Audrey Matheson had queried the Australian councils' attitude towards 'Australia becoming a multicultural society (or as it is often termed, cultural pluralism)'. Matheson personally was not in favour: 'We want a united community and not undigested minorities. I don't know how multi-culturalism would fit in with our long held policy of a homogeneous population'.[74] The following year Joyce McConnell in Canberra was more receptive to the idea of multiculturalism. She sought the support of the 'Minister for Multi-Culturalism', Al Grassby, for a proposal that, as part of NCWA's activities for International Women's Year, each state council should invite ethnic women's organisations to affiliate.[75] Several state presidents contacted local ethnic groups in the hope of boosting their declining numbers, but the response was minimal.[76] So the membership of NCWA continued to be overwhelmingly of British descent, English speaking, and insular, the long-standing affiliation of Jewish women's organisations notwithstanding. Interest in the international was mostly limited to leading members of the council, inspired by attendance at conferences and seminars organised by ICW.

Across the decade, Australians came to take more prominent roles within the international council. Dorothy Edwards took a term as ICW treasurer, radically reorganising the funds, and acting as returning

---

73 Interview with Dr Laurel Macintosh.
74 Audrey Matheson to Jessie Scotford, 2 April 1973, Folder 'Immigration Policy', Box 7, MS7583, NCWA Papers NLA.
75 Joyce McConnell to Al Grassby, 21 February 1974, Folder 'Immigration Policy', Box 7, MS7583, NCWA Papers NLA.
76 See, for example, 'President's Report', NCWSA 53rd Annual Report 1973–74, published as *NCWSA Newsletter*, 5 (9), p. 1.

officer for every election because 'everyone trusted her'. Jessie Scotford and Ada Norris were convenors of ICW standing committees (arts and migration respectively), and a number of other Australians took on official positions and chaired committees. Jessie Scotford worked closely with Dame Miriam Dell of the National Council of Women of New Zealand to organise several ICW conferences and seminars. In addition the Australian government became a significant benefactor of the international council. NCWA's close relationship with the Australian Development Assistance Bureau (ADAB) opened the door for funding NCWA projects in Asia and Africa that were co-sponsored by the national council of the country concerned. And Macintosh rates as one of her main achievements the large cheque for ICW delivered to her in a Brisbane restaurant by an ADAB official: a particularly useful cheque because it was not tied to a specific project.[77] Macintosh also put in place an arrangement that allowed Australian affiliates of NCWA to approach ADAB through NCWA for assistance with approved overseas development projects, especially small projects aimed at women. The announcement of this arrangement in the November 1981 *NCWA Quarterly Bulletin* reflected the new understanding of women's role in development that was emerging within the United Nations: 'There is a need for more women's projects as not all large aid programmes have proved advantageous to them and a few have been detrimental to their economic and social well-being'.[78]

It is a measure of the importance Dr Macintosh placed on NCWA's international aid program that she chose as the lead speaker at the triennial conference in Brisbane in November 1982—her last as president—the bureaucrat in charge of the Non-Government Section of ADAB, Neville Ross. Ross told the gathering that women's role was central to development. Women were 'the income earners, the workers, the producers and family organisers, yet programmes for the Third

---

77 Interview with Dr Laurel Macintosh.
78 *NCWA Quarterly Bulletin*, 7 (7, 8), November 1981.

World were designed and delivered by men'. Ross identified NCWA and ICW as 'important linkage organisations' in the delivery of aid—and he presented a second large cheque from the Australian government to Dame Miriam Dell, now the president of ICW.[79]

Removing the Obstacles to Equality

In April 1983 the recently elected prime minister of Australia, R.J. Hawke, invited representatives of industrial and community organisations to an Economic Summit in the chambers of federal parliament. The aims of the summit have been characterised by public policy researchers as 'corporatist':[80] to foster constructive co-operation, especially between employers and unions; to tailor community expectations to the capacities of the economy; and to reduce unemployment and restore economic growth.

In her account of the conference, NCWA President Diane Alley suggested that the meeting might also be described as masculinist. In his opening address, the prime minister declared that 'this Conference is master of its own destiny'—a very apt statement, she thought, given that 'women were barely visible in the Chamber of Representatives'. The only woman to speak was Senator Susan Ryan, the new minister assisting the prime minister for the status of women. Of the twenty community observers present, only three were women: Alley herself, representing NCWA, and representatives from WEL and the Australian Council of Churches. She became very aware of the language used at the summit. She noted that Hawke referred to the conference 'as an event of **genuine and seminal** importance in the life and history of our country'. The problems before them called for 'the application of all those qualities of innovation, initiative, independence, tolerance—and need I say—

---

79   Diane Alley, 'Brisbane 1982—Conference of N.C.W.A.', *NCWA Quarterly Bulletin*, 8 (1), March 1983.
80   Frank G. Castles et al. (eds), *The Great Experiment: Labour Parties and Public Policy Transformation in Australia and New Zealand*, Sydney, Allen & Unwin, 1999, p. 11.

Diane Alley
NCWA President 1982–1985

Diane Alley worked consistently for more than five decades to promote the principles set out in the *Universal Declaration of Human Rights*. Equally committed to the status of women and to social justice in the community, Alley was a force for change within the National Council of Women of Australia. She served as Victorian state president from 1977 to 1980 and national president from 1982 to 1985. Both periods saw new challenges to the National Councils of Women from second-wave feminist organisations and the conservative reactions that these provoked. She was particularly focused on the portfolio of child and family and became its convenor at state, national and international levels, representing Australia at many ICW conferences.

Diane Alley was born in 1927 in Ballarat, Victoria. She attended PLC in Ballarat, MLC in Melbourne and Girton in Bendigo, and gained a BA (Honours) from the University of Melbourne. Marriage in 1949 to law student and future judge Stephen Alley led her later to complete a Diploma of Criminology. Alley served on the Fairlea Women's Prison Council 1979–1983 and was also an official prison visitor. Other community service included positions of leadership in the Free Kindergarten Union, the Lady Gowrie Child Centre, the Adult Deaf Society, the La Trobe University Brain-Behaviour Research Institute, the University of Melbourne Social Biology Research Unit, the Friends of the Victorian College of the Arts and the Winston Churchill Memorial Trust (Victoria).

Alley played a positive role in times of great change in the women's movement, working hard to maintain existing networks and create new ones. Both state and federal governments appointed her to advisory bodies such as the National Women's Consultative Council, and Dame Ada Norris chose Alley as her successor as chair of the National Status of Women Committee, United Nations Association of Australia (UNAA).

In 1981, she was appointed an officer in the Order of the British Empire. In 1993 she received a testimonial from the United Nations Co-ordinator for the International Year of the Family designating her an IYF patron for exemplary support for the UN program for IYF. On her retirement from the Children's Protection Society in 1999, she was made a life vice-president. She also received the NCWA Centenary Award in 1998 and was one of the first women admitted to the Victorian Women's Honour Roll in 2001.

Explore further resources about Diane Alley in the Australian Women's Register

mateship, the qualities which we like to think are distinctively Australian'. Several speakers went on to evoke mateship.[81]

Alley's sensitivity to the exclusionary power of language reflects the high profile of feminist analysis in popular and academic writing in the early 1980s—and, of course, Alley's intelligent reading of these sources. Two feminist academics were present as advisers at the summit: sociologist Bettina Cass advising NCWA and jurist Jocelynne Scutt advising WEL. NCWA and WEL jointly produced a daily comment sheet for participants called *Observant Women*. They dealt with their exclusion from the matey camaraderie of workers and employers by caucusing with a group of socially minded community organisations led by the Australian Council of Social Service. Their joint efforts succeeded in adding to the final communiqué issued by the summit a statement recognising women's need for 'equal access to job creation programmes, to employment training, retraining, and [for] educational measures designed to break down occupational segregation and discrimination'.[82]

Diane Alley was accustomed to co-operating with the Women's Electoral Lobby. WEL became an affiliate of the Victorian council in April 1973; the minutes recorded:

> WEL expresses pleasure in being affiliated with NCW. They are an interesting vital group not political, nonaligned, not religious or non-religious, not women's lib, not academic trendies. WEL aims to create more awareness of women's power to vote and to reform.[83]

Alley remembered that she invited them to join.[84] Members of NCWV seem to have needed some reassurance about the new organisation; the following month Alley reported to council that she had attended

---

81 Diane Alley, 'NCWA at Economic Summit', *NCWA Quarterly Bulletin*, 8 (2), July 1983 p. 1. Emphasis in the original.
82 Alley, 'NCWA at Economic Summit', pp. 1, 3.
83 NCWV Council Minutes, 12 April 1973, NCWV Papers, State Library of Victoria (SLV) (classification pending).
84 Interview with Diane Alley.

a meeting of WEL, and 'The President was feminine, charming and completely in command. Matters taken up were family planning, women and work'.[85] WEL and NCWV generally understood the causes of women's inequality and the means of remedying this in very similar ways. The Victorian council did have some very conservative affiliates; Babette Francis from Women Who Want to be Women and Margaret Tighe from Right to Life both joined in the mid-1970s. But, under the leadership of social liberals like Philippa Hallenstein, Audrey Matheson and Alley herself, conservative voices were never as loud in Victoria as in the New South Wales council.

Alley's co-operation with WEL extended to the UNAA Status of Women Committee, which she chaired from 1980. Anne Jackson from WEL was an active member of this committee, and WEL members were involved in the activities that it organised. By the early 1980s it was clear that the struggle to end global discrimination against women would need to continue long after the close of the Decade for Women in 1985. In 1983 the Australian committee organised a conference on the theme, 'Women and the Year 2000'. One session dealt with Australian preparations for 1985, but the main concern was the possible effects of technological and social change by the end of the century, and the difficulties of already disadvantaged groups in dealing with these changes: older women, Aboriginal women, young women, migrant women and disabled women. WEL members were prominent amongst the speakers.[86]

For all the unconscious masculinism of the prime minister, the Hawke government was quick to act in the interests of women. In its first statement of policy at the opening of parliament in March 1983, the government announced two important initiatives:

---

85   NCWV Council Minutes, 10 June 1973, NCWV Papers, SLV (classification pending).
86   'Women and the Year 2000', *NCWA Quarterly Bulletin*, 8 (4), January 1984.

Legislation will be introduced dealing with discrimination on the basis of sex or marital status, and

Australia will ratify the United Nations Convention on the Elimination of All Forms of Discrimination Against Women.[87]

The Sex Discrimination Act was amongst the first laws passed by the Hawke government, receiving assent on 21 March 1983, and the ratification of CEDAW was achieved by the end of July. Under the guidance of Senator Susan Ryan, the Office of the Status of Women (OSW) was upgraded to a division, and returned from the Department of Home Affairs to the Department of the Prime Minister and Cabinet. And Dr Anne Summers was appointed as first assistant secretary of OSW.

These innovations were announced in speeches by Hawke and Ryan delivered to the National Labour Women's Conference in January 1984—another of Ryan's initiatives. One can perhaps detect a slight note of pique in Alley's article in the *Quarterly Bulletin* informing members of the national councils about the government's activities; she tells them that NCWA has been recommending 'uniform complementary Federal and State non-discrimination legislation' since 1975, and that CEDAW 'contains principles that were enunciated by the International Council of Women since 1888'.[88] But any failure to recognise NCWA's pioneer status was soon remedied by the cordial relationship that grew between Anne Summers and Diane Alley. In February 1984 Summers made time on a trip to Melbourne to meet with Dame Miriam Dell, the president of ICW, and the members of the NCWA board. And she became a frequent speaker at conferences and workshops organised by the national councils.[89]

---

87 Ada Norris, 'UN Convention Protects Status of all Women', *NCWA Quarterly Bulletin*, 8 (2), July 1983.
88 Diane Alley, 'Commonwealth Sex Discrimination Legislation', *NCWA Quarterly Bulletin*, 8 (5), April 1984.
89 'ICW President Visits Australia', *NCWA Quarterly Bulletin*, 8 (5), April 1984.

In June Hawke replaced the five-person National Women's Advisory Council with a National Women's Consultative Council (NWCC) of twenty members, all representing women's organisations; Diane Alley was invited to represent NCWA, and Joyce McConnell the Australian Federation of University Women.[90] Subcommittees were established to attend to the particular interests of members and their organisations; Alley joined the subcommittees for the End of the UN Decade for Women, social security, and child care.

Hawke presented a report to the November meeting of NWCC on the progress already made towards equality. This included the establishment of an Affirmative Action Pilot Program intended to promote women's employment, training and promotion in selected business enterprises, and eventually to formulate legislation 'to ensure that women are given equal job opportunities with men in our society'. It also involved a serious effort by government to increase the number of women involved in decision-making, which had seen 'more than 100 women appointed to Government Boards and Authorities since we took office'. Within the Commonwealth Public Service the number of women in the highest divisions had been increased from 32 to 68, with 4 women at the most senior rank.[91] Ada Norris had by this time stepped out of public life, but she could be well pleased; a start at least had been made on all the aims that she had formulated in 1976 for Australia's Decade for Women.

Hawke announced one further innovation to the November meeting of the NWCC: 'a program of grants totalling $472,000 to assist women'. About a quarter of this would be distributed amongst 'national women's organisations' to improve their capacity to 'take part in community decision-making', and to undertake research, consultation and debate 'on issues of particular concern to women'; it could also support services like 'mailing and newsletter production'. Another part of the funding

---

90 'The National Women's Consultative Council', *NCWA Quarterly Bulletin*, 8 (9), January 1985.

91 'The National Women's Consultative Council', *NCWA Quarterly Bulletin*, 8 (9), January 1985.

would go directly to organisations with representatives on the NWCC, to cover the costs of consulting their membership on the issues brought to the consultative council by government—some $10,000 a year. Diane Alley had already approached Summers and OSW about the possibility of boosting the $8,000 per annum that NCWA had received since 1979. Now she called a special meeting of her board 'to discuss the most efficient and productive use' of the $10,000 they had been granted. 'We will need to set our priorities and define our basic philosophy in order to achieve the maximum benefit of this grant.'[92]

Alley's time as national president was enormously productive. Like its predecessor, her board was highly qualified. Five of the members were graduates and three also held diplomas: Shirley Horne had added a diploma of public policy to her bachelor of commerce.[93] Shirley Horne and lawyer Jan Pannam had long years of experience in working with government committees and tribunals. Alley's skill at networking attracted other expert women to serve on the most active standing committees, creating a powerhouse of feminist energy.

In the first year of Alley's presidency, the board produced four substantial submissions in response to government reviews and planning documents. One commented on the 'broad economic strategies evolved by the Economic Planning Advisory Committee', focusing on employment, taxation and social security. Another commented on plans for equal opportunity provisions in the Commonwealth Public Service; while fully supporting these, NCWA stressed the need 'to recognise the requirements of family commitments alongside employment duties and the need for more flexible working conditions and community services like child care'. A submission to the Commonwealth Inquiry Reviewing Labour Market Programs suggested 'new initiatives' like 'greater opportunities for women in management roles' and 'locum positions

---

92   NCWA Board Minutes, 13 November 1984, Box 27, MSAcc07/96, NCWA Papers, NLA.
93   'Board of NCWA Office-Bearers', *NCWA Quarterly Bulletin*, 8 (1), April 1983.

with staff with experience taking over those positions temporarily vacant through maternity, long service, study leave etc.'. And, in response to an invitation from the minister for employment and industrial relations, NCWA commented on a research report on the Community Youth Support Scheme, supporting its recommendation for more women staff in CYSS offices and the extension of the help available from CYSS to young rural women, migrant women, married women and single mothers.[94]

In 1984–85 submissions were made to the Review of the Taxation System, to a Human Rights Commission inquiry into 'discrimination in relation to occupational superannuation', and to a Senate Select Committee on Video Material.[95] The submission on 'Women, Taxation and Tax Reform' is particularly striking for its grasp of complex issues and its assured moral tone. It notes as a special difficulty the operation of the dependent spouse rebate, by which a non-working wife with or without children could be claimed as a deduction on her husband's income tax. While acknowledging that any move to abolish this rebate would be interpreted 'in some quarters' as 'a threat to the family as a social institution', the submission saw it as 'a discouragement to employment', and 'a taxation advantage to middle and upper income earners'. The submission recommended 'the replacement of the present rebate with an actual payment, especially if this were subject to a means test'. Citing the work of the Victorian Consultative Committee on Social Development, NCWA advocated the integration of the income tax and social security systems to avoid the situation in which 'women who have no access to the income of their husbands will be penalized because of that income, in obtaining a pension or benefit for themselves'.[96]

These same points were central to the submission made by NCWA to the Australian Taxation Summit, a gathering of community, business

---

94 'Submissions', *NCWA Quarterly Bulletin*, 8 (6), July 1984.
95 *NCWA Quarterly Bulletin*, 8 (10, 11), April 1985.
96 'Submission to the Review of the Taxation System: Women, Taxation and Tax Reform', *NCWA Quarterly Bulletin*, 8 (10, 11), April 1985.

and union representatives called by the government in July 1985 to debate proposals to reform the taxation system. NCWA represented the women's movement, alongside WEL and the Australian Federation of Business and Professional Women. NCWA representatives also attended a National Women's Tax Summit organised by WEL, which met in Canberra immediately before the government-sponsored gathering. The two hundred women attending agreed in opposing a broadly based consumption tax and income-splitting between spouses for taxation purposes, and in support for a capital gains tax, taxation of employee fringe benefits, and efforts to stamp out tax evasion; these points were taken forward by the women's representatives to the Australian Taxation Summit.[97]

In her report on the women's summit, Shirley Horne stressed that NCWA's participation had been 'on the basis of the ideas and views expressed by its member Councils in response to a questionnaire and circulation of preparatory material'.[98] It is not clear how far state council members shared the board's understanding of women as disadvantaged by the tax system. In Brisbane, at an executive meeting called to consider a draft of NCWA's submission, some members queried the assumptions that women paid less tax than men, and were less likely to be tax evaders than men. They did not share the board's enthusiasm for tax as a redistributive mechanism, wanting a reduction in income tax and an increase in sales tax.[99] But there is no reflection of this in the documents produced by the board.

Diane Alley remembered opposition from state councils on some of the issues that she promoted as president. When the National Women's Consultative Committee took up the Affirmative Action Project in

---

97 Shirley Horne, 'The Australian Taxation Summit', *NCWA Quarterly Bulletin*, 8 (12), October 1985.
98 NCWA Board Minutes, 5 December 1984, Box 27, MSAcc07/96, NCWA Papers, NLA.
99 NCWQ Executive Minutes, 15 April 1985, Box 16045, 7266 NCWQ Minute Books, NCWQ Papers, SLQ.

1984, NCWA had no established policy in this area. Alley circulated a statement of principle from the National Council of Women of the United States endorsing 'Affirmative Action and Equal Opportunity', and suggested its endorsement by the state councils. The answer came back from NCWWA, 'If we did that we wouldn't have any members!' NCWA's promotion of CEDAW also roused opposition in some councils. In Adelaide a council meeting was swayed by a representative of Women Who Want to be Women—'an attractive young woman with a baby'—to declare that CEDAW was a threat to the family unit. At the next meeting of the South Australian council Alley 'read the riot act': 'Look, we belong to the International Council of Women and that's been their main thrust—we don't ask do we or don't we—we do!'[100]

Alley usually seems to have carried the doubters with her. All the state councils were represented at the NCWA executive meeting in Darwin in September 1984, and the debates give some sense of the readiness of delegates to embrace the new status of women. Child care was still a contentious issue. The Tasmanian council proposed a resolution urging NCWA to request the federal government to make payment for child care an income tax deduction. Several delegations spoke in opposition, but the issue was not the principle of child care as an entitlement, rather the best means of making it available. Some states argued for state-subsidised child care, others for special provision for 'very low income earners'. The resolution was carried 35 for to 20 against.[101]

This debate was immediately followed by one on family policy. NCW Victoria urged NCWA 'to seek the establishment of a Federal Family Commission as a matter of high priority in order to promote family stability and co-ordinate government activity in relation to the family'.[102] This resolution came not from the Victorian executive but directly from

---

[100] Interview with Diane Alley.
[101] NCWA Executive Minutes, 16–18 September 1984, Box 27, MSAcc07/96, NCWA Papers, NLA.
[102] NCWA Executive Minutes, 16–18 September 1984, Box 27, MSAcc07/96, NCWA Papers, NLA.

the state council, where it was proposed by an affiliate, the Loreto Past Pupils' Association. In a council meeting in which new delegates were introduced from the Christian Women's Fellowship of the Churches of Christ, the Right to Choose Coalition, and the Catholic Women's League of the Melbourne Diocese, the resolution was carried with very little opposition.[103] Things went less smoothly at the NCWA executive meeting. The resolution was lost with only 8 votes in favour and 34 against, but 20 votes were abstentions, suggesting that several councils identified with the problem, if not the solution.[104]

The Darwin executive meeting in 1984 was particularly well attended because it followed immediately on a Pacific and Asia Regional Seminar of the International Council of Women. Alley was keen to follow the example set by Dorothy Edwards and Jessie Scotford, to bring women from the Asia–Pacific area to meet to discuss matters of mutual concern. When the Northern Territory council offered to hold the executive meeting in Darwin—the first time the Territory had hosted a national gathering—Alley suggested to Dame Miriam Bell, president of ICW, that 'this could be developed into a regional meeting for Councils of the Pacific and South East Asia', to promote the international council's 'growing involvement in assisting grassroots development in developing countries'.[105] The seminar was planned as part of ICW's preparation for the End of the Decade for Women meetings in Nairobi in 1985. It focused not on the major theme of the decade, 'Equality', but on the sub-themes more relevant to the needs of the women of the region: 'Health, Education and Employment'. More than twenty councils in the Asia–Pacific region were invited to attend, and assistance with fares was offered to six representative women with skills in community development, courtesy of the Australian Development Assistance

---

103 NCWV Council Minutes, 10 June 1984, NCWV Papers, SLV (classification pending).
104 NCWA Executive Minutes, 16–18 September 1984, Box 27, MSAcc07/96, NCWA Papers, NLA.
105 'ICW President visits Australia', *NCWA Quarterly Bulletin*, 8 (5), April 1984.

Bureau. Twelve delegates from the region were able to attend, from Papua, the Philippines, Thailand, Fiji, Malaysia, Indonesia and New Zealand.[106]

Alley's report of the meeting stresses the cultural relativism of the event. The first day was devoted to 'Primary Health Care', with respectful attention paid to medicine both old and new, provoking 'an interesting and lively exchange of views between the women of different cultures on their traditions and practices'. Women spoke frankly about their common problems: domestic violence, alcoholism and prostitution. A visit to the islands off Darwin offered the opportunity for an interesting exchange between delegates and local Tiwi Aboriginal women, with the two groups taping the songs each other sang. The seminar concluded with 'a simple service of worship' in the Botanic Gardens, with Aboriginal women from a local college forming a choir. 'As we took part in the service, an Asian bridal party and wedding procession filed past us along the nearby path—a true reflection of the multicultural atmosphere of Darwin.'[107]

Reading Alley's report today, one must observe that the multiculturalism of the seminar did not extend to religion. The unremarked Christianity of the ceremony in the Botanic Gardens reminds us that members of NCWA still brought a sense of Christian mission to their concern for the women of the Asia–Pacific, mission to assist those less fortunate than themselves. Fund-raising remained an important part of council activity at a state level, and an important marker of personal commitment. International secretary Kathleen Rumbold had worked as a missionary and teacher in Bangladesh.[108] She told the Darwin executive committee that it was proving difficult to raise funds amongst

---

106 Diane Alley, 'Pacific and Asia Regional Seminar Darwin September 11 to 16 1984', *NCWA Quarterly Bulletin*, 8 (7 and 8), October 1984.
107 Diane Alley, 'Pacific and Asia Regional Seminar Darwin September 11 to 16 1984', *NCWA Quarterly Bulletin*, 8 (7 and 8), October 1984.
108 'Board of NCWA Office-Bearers, 1982–1985', *NCWA Quarterly Bulletin*, 8 (1), April 1983.

A DECADE FOR WOMEN? 1976–1985

affiliates and members, but stressed the need to show 'NCWA's practical involvement' in overseas projects: 'Councils, the affiliates, the individual women should be challenged to raise moderate funds to assist women in other countries'. Diane Alley, however, was more interested in carrying forward the close relationship that Laurel Macintosh had developed with the Australian Development Assistance Bureau. She told the executive meeting that ADAB-funded projects were being planned in Papua New Guinea and Thailand in a three-way co-operation between ADAB, the local National Councils of Women and NCWA.[109]

To young Janet Galley, the secretary of NCW Victoria, the meeting in Darwin was something of a revelation. She had been involved with the council for some years, but this experience showed her another aspect of NCWA—'how the board could work with another organisation, a world-wide organisation, and also how they could work with the countries outside Australia that were part of our environment'. Galley told us that Diane Alley made a particularly good president because

> She always seemed to have her finger on the pulse of things, and maybe that was something to do with her work with the United Nations ... and the International Council of Women, that gave a further aspect to her viewing the world and being able to come back to us and tell us what was happening.[110]

The story of Diane Alley's presidency is almost entirely a positive one, an account of energetic action rewarded with achievement. In remembering those years, Alley expressed only one regret. She expected to end her presidency at the ICW meeting planned for the End of the Decade Year in November 1985, and wrote her three-year report for presentation there. But the conference was postponed until the following year. 'So

---

109 NCWA Executive Minutes, 16–18 September 1984, Box 27, MSAcc07/96, NCWA Papers, NLA.
110 Interview with Janet Galley, 9 December 2010, Melbourne, NCWA History Project.

my Committee had had enough, they didn't want to go on and I didn't want to go on without my Committee, so we withdrew.' So the incoming president of NCWA, Necia Mocatta, 'stands up at the International Council of Women and reads out my report as hers. And I never gave a report'.[111]

---

[111] Interview with Diane Alley.

Chapter 14

THE NEW FACE OF THE NATIONAL COUNCIL 1986–2006

In a much-discussed article in 1995, American scholar Robert Putnam used the evidence of declining membership in voluntary organisations to argue that the social bonds underpinning democracy were wearing thin. The problem was particularly evident in the mainstream women's movement, where membership in 'traditional women's groups' had declined by more than half since the 1960s. Putnam posited that the major reason for this was the movement of women into the labour force, but this was not a sufficient explanation; given the corresponding decline from the 1980s in associations traditionally joined by men, 'something besides the women's revolution seems to lie behind the erosion of social capital'. He suggested as causal factors changes in family patterns, in commerce and industry, and particularly in 'the technological transformation of leisure': 'television has made our communities ... wider and shallower'.[1] Putnam's argument was fiercely contested in academia and the media, and the conclusions he drew from his evidence were coloured by the place and time from which he was writing. But the organisational decline that he documented in traditional voluntary groups was real and, in some cases, terminal.

---

1   Robert D. Putnam, 'Bowling Alone; America's Declining Social Capital', *Journal of Democracy*, 6 (1), 1995, pp. 65–78.

The experience of Australian voluntary associations at the end of the twentieth century might be seen as confirming Putnam's analysis. Long-established groups like political parties, unions, religious congregations and service organisations have lost the bulk of their membership. National organisations can no longer maintain a base in every state, and often survive in only one or two. New movements rise and fall with the popularity of the single social issues that sustain them, with a transient membership and little or no face-to-face interaction.

With a membership largely located within the affiliated societies of its constituent councils, the National Council of Women of Australia is particularly vulnerable to organisational decline. The total number of associations affiliated with the constituent councils has fallen away since its peak in the early 1970s: from more than 600 to about 250 in the early years of the new century, with the steepest fall between 1995 and 2005. The experience of membership loss has varied across the councils. Most seem to have reached peak membership in the early 1970s, but the ACT and Queensland councils both continued to grow through the 1970s, and NCWNSW peaked in the late 1980s. NCWSA has a pattern all its own, peaking at more than 100 affiliates in the early 1950s and declining thereafter. The small councils in Perth and Hobart seem to have maintained their memberships, beginning and ending the period with about 30 affiliates. The Launceston council fell away from 60 to only 13 members by 2003. Victoria was by far the largest council in 1981, with more than 140 members, but declined to fewer than 40 by the new century, while Queensland declined from about 100 members to about 60 across the same period. New South Wales claimed about 90 members in the late 1980s and about 70 by the new century.[2] Clearly local factors play a large part in these changing patterns; the continuing growth of NCWACT in the 1980s, for example, reflects

---

2   These figures have been gathered from a variety of sources: national and state council reports, applications for government funding, introductory puffs to submissions on various subjects. Their reliability is variable.

both the demographic growth of Canberra and the effect of strong local leadership. But the pattern overall is a steady loss of affiliate members to the mid-1990s, and a spectacular fall away in the following decade.

Perhaps it is survival that needs explaining here. Voluntary groups in Australia and the United States have very different relationships with government. Where voluntary groups in America pride themselves on their independence from government, and celebrate the often-corporate sponsorship that keeps them in existence, Australian voluntary associations over the last forty years have received significant funding from governments, both state and federal. This phenomenon can be understood as reflecting a commitment on the part of both Labor and Liberal governments to notions of active, participatory citizenship, together with a pragmatic acceptance of the value of unpaid voluntary labour in achieving useful social outcomes. And with the decline in the traditional, grass-roots membership of the major political parties and the rise of special-interest political groups, governments have looked to their relationships with community organisations as a way of generating electoral support. At the same time, and in contradiction to ideas of participatory democracy, bureaucrats have worked to manage those relationships with the economy, efficiency and accountability required by government. The inevitable result has been the at least partial reshaping of the voluntary sector into a vehicle for government policy.

The National Councils of Women received significant funding from federal and state governments from the 1980s, and, with the decline of fee income from affiliates, they became heavily dependent on that funding. The women who led NCWA across this period all felt the burden of representing their councils and affiliates to a bureaucracy that kept changing the rules about funding and representation. The first section of this chapter follows the presidents' efforts to find a workable place for the councils as they related to other women's organisations and the Australian government.

Necia Mocatta
NCWA President 1985–1988

Necia Mocatta devoted most of her life, energy and enthusiasm to the betterment and dignity of the lives of women and children. She believed that the family unit was the foundation on which a caring, prosperous society was built and worked to strengthen this at local, national and international levels.

Mocatta was born in 1938 and educated in rural South Australia. She married George Mocatta and had four children. The family was active in the church and school community in Tintinara for many years, but moved to Adelaide for the children's education and there became involved in real estate. Necia worked in the business and became the first woman auctioneer in South Australia.

Mocatta came to NCW South Australia as a delegate from the Soroptimists. With her passion for organisation she willingly took on executive roles, becoming president from 1980 to 1983 and again in 1996. She served as president of the National Council of Women of Australia from 1985 to 1988. As national president, she followed business practices, like organising Qantas to sponsor Board members to attend conferences. Mocatta represented NCWA on the National Forum of Non-Government Welfare Co-ordinating Bodies, the National Keep Australia Beautiful Council, the Parliamentary Disarmament Forum and the committee that established the Telecom Consumers' Council.

From 1988 to 1991 Mocatta was a voting member of the International Council of Women board, becoming a vice-president in 1991. She represented Australia in Kiel, Lucerne, Malta, Auckland, Kenya, Korea and Bangkok, and managed ICW projects for women and girls in developing countries. On the home front, she was on the Board of the St Lawrence Home for the Aged and the parish council of All Souls Anglican Church.

Mocatta was a long-time member of the Liberal Party, serving on the SA State Executive and Council and as vice-president of the Women's Council. She became mayoress of St Peters and a member of the Metropolitan Mayoress's Charity Committee.

Mocatta responded enthusiastically to the needs of all women and families, not just in Australia, but throughout the world. In 1990 she was made a member of the Order of Australia for her services to the community, and was awarded the Ruth Gibson Memorial Award in 1992. Rostrum honoured her twice in 1993 and 1995 with the Adrian Stock Award. She died in Adelaide in 2000.

Explore further resources about Necia Mocatta in the Australian Women's Register.

The second section looks at the growing importance of NCWA and its representatives within the international women's movement.

The Vagaries of Government

In November 1985 Prime Minister Bob Hawke announced his 'National Agenda for Women', a draft plan of action to improve the status of women in Australia.[3] In the months that followed, the Office of the Status of Women (OSW) undertook a long process of consultation with women across the country intended, it was said, to ensure that the 'National Agenda' was 'owned' by Australian women. Organisations represented on the National Women's Consultative Council (NWCC) were urged to organise meetings to discuss the agenda. Women's Electoral Lobby (WEL) was funded by OSW to stage a national forum in Canberra in April 1986, bringing in representatives of women's organisations from across the country. Three members of the NCWA board attended,[4] not including the national president, Necia Mocatta, who was in London for an International Council of Women (ICW) conference.

Mocatta's background was in small business, and neither she nor her board had much experience of working with politicians and bureaucrats.[5] Relations with OSW had begun awkwardly for Mocatta. When she inquired about applying for a grant in December 1985, the office responded by asking for copies of the association's certificate of incorporation. Mocatta rang members of the previous board, and discovered that NCWA was not an incorporated body. Arrangements were made for an officer of NCWACT to organise incorporation for the council in Canberra, which was finally achieved in July 1986. The annual grant was increased to $15,000 for 1986/87.[6]

---

3   'National Agenda for Women', *NCWA Quarterly Bulletin*, 9 (1), April 1986.
4   'Meeting on National Agenda for Women Held for Older Women in Adelaide', *NCWA Quarterly Bulletin*, 9 (2), July 1986.
5   'Board of NCWA Office-Bearers', *NCWA Quarterly Bulletin*, 9 (1), April 1986.
6   NCWA Board Minutes, 21 January 1986, 15 May 1986, 17 July 1986, Box 27, MSAcc07/96, NCWA Papers, NLA.

In June 1986 Senator Ryan called for nominations for the National Women's Consultative Council, and the board put forward the names of Mocatta and two others. Mocatta's absence from the Canberra gathering may have influenced Ryan's decision to choose Joan Brewer, the board's assistant secretary, as NCWA representative on the advisory committee; Brewer seems to have made a good impression at the WEL forum.[7]

Consultations about the National Agenda for Women continued, but all was not well at the Office of the Status of Women. Anne Summers left OSW in 1986, and Susan Ryan became increasingly alienated from her cabinet colleagues over their enthusiasm for the 'user-pays' principle, in education and elsewhere. Late in 1987, the Office of the Status of Women announced that 'as a result of budgetary constraints' there would be no further funding to cover administrative costs. OSW wrote that only project funding would be available, for 'small scale programs of activities or theoretical or practical research which reflect the priorities of the National Agenda for Women. Future assistance will be targeted to respond directly to the concerns of women expressed in this document'.[8]

Ryan resigned from the Senate and her parliamentary career in December 1987. In January 1988, OSW was relocated from the central Barton Building to the fringes of the administrative complex. In February, Hawke launched the final version of the National Agenda for Women in a Bondi shopping centre, claiming it as 'the most comprehensive series of commitments to women and of strategies on women's issues ever produced by an Australian Government'.[9] But the truth was that an agenda originally intended to write the needs of Australian women into the heart of government policy had become an instrument for grant assessment.

---

7   NCWA Board Minutes, 19 June 1986, Box 27, MSAcc07/96, NCWA Papers, NLA.
8   'Government Grant', *NCWA Quarterly Bulletin*, 9 (8), December 1987.
9   'President's Report', *NCWA Quarterly Bulletin*, 9 (9), March 1988.

NCWA protested vigorously against the decision to end the general funding, arguing that the council was 'concerned mainly with long-term aims concerning the welfare of women and children and supporting the health of the family'—in itself an interesting contraction of previous statements of policy—and that 'small scale programs of a one-off nature will in no way fulfil our long term goals'.[10] The Federation of Business and Professional Women organised an unlikely alliance of the Union of Australian Women (UAW), the Young Women's Christian Association (YWCA), WEL and NCWA to co-ordinate their lobbying in opposition to the funding cuts.[11] It seems that the new minister for women, Margaret Reynolds, found funds to support all the organisations represented on the National Women's Co-ordinating Council, though not at the level they had previous enjoyed.

The NCWA board was frankly resentful when offered a once-only grant of $8,000 over twelve months to 'implement the objects of the National Agenda for Women with special emphasis on women at home, women as carers and women in isolation'. They protested that:

> We represent the largest number of women in this country who need a voice with Government and all authorities touching their lives. Voluntary organisations such as the ones united under our umbrella make a very large contribution to the economy and the social well-being of the country both in terms of human effort as well as financially and need greater Government support to fulfil their task in the most cost-effective way possible, rather than being rendered ineffective.[12]

---

10 'Government Grant', *NCWA Quarterly Bulletin*, 9 (8), December 1987.
11 'President's Report', *NCWA Quarterly Bulletin*, 9 (9), March 1988.
12 'Government Grant to NCWA', *NCWA Quarterly Bulletin*, 9 (10), June 1988.

Maureen Giddings
NCWA President 1988–1991

Maureen Giddings worked with a wide range of community organisations, many connected with the National Council of Women. She served as president of NCWNSW 1970–1974 and became president of the National Council of Women of Australia from 1988–1991. She was educated at PLC in Melbourne, the Melbourne Conservatorium of Music and the University of Melbourne. Her studies were interrupted by enlistment in the Women's Auxiliary Air Force, and at the end of the war she married Major Niels Giddings, whom she had known since Sunday School.

Inspired by the voluntary and philanthropic work of her parents, she joined the National Council of Women of Victoria and on moving to Sydney transferred her membership to NSW. In 1970 she took on the NSW presidency and became vice-president of the National Council of Women of Australia when Jessie Scotford formed her NCWA Board that same year.

The political awareness learned from her mother also led Giddings into long-term membership of the Liberal Party. She was president of the Women's Council of the Liberal Party of Australia (NSW division) and chaired the Federal Women's Committee from 1977–1980.

Giddings' work in NCWA took her into leadership roles in other organisations, She was deputy chairman of the NSW International Women's Year committee 1973–1975. In 1978 she became chairman of the Status of Women Committee, United Nations Association of Australia (NSW) then president of UNAA (NSW) and vice-president of the national UNAA. In 1980 she was chosen by the federal government to attend the forum at the NGO UN Decade of Women conference in Copenhagen.

In addition to these responsibilities, Giddings contributed to other community activities such as the Captain Cook Bicentenary Women's Committee, the Festival Women's Committee for the opening of the Sydney Opera House, the Royal Flying Doctor Service of NSW. She was a Life Governor at the Rachel Foster Hospital and was active in the Heart Campaign, the Asthma Appeal and the Churchill Appeal. She wrote in the NCWNSW *News* in 1971 about the past, present and future of NCWA: 'Australian women, while enjoying a formal equality, do not as yet possess a complete practical equality…Confidently we look to the future, proud of our past achievements but remembering one of the objects of the National Council is that we must promote the interests of women and secure their proper recognition in the community.'

She died in September 2013.

Explore further resources about Maureen Giddings in the Australian Women's Register

In October 1988 the board moved to Sydney, under the presidency of Maureen Giddings. Giddings came from a family with a tradition of public service in voluntary and political organisations. Her mother advised her to join the National Council of Women: 'It gives people the opportunity to put their point of view. And the government will listen to you'. By 1988 she had a record of leadership at state and national levels within NCWA, the United Nation's Association of Australia (UNAA) and the Liberal Party of Australia. In 1985 she was one of 22 Australian women chosen by the federal government to attend the Nairobi 'End of the Decade' conference.[13] Giddings' board members were also women with experience of leading voluntary organisations and interacting with bureaucrats.[14]

Understanding the contingency of government funding, the board moved immediately to economise, closing the NCWA office in Canberra and producing a cheaper version of the *Quarterly Bulletin*. Joan Brewer, now deputy chair of the National Women's Advisory Committee (NWAC), helped with air fares to Canberra.[15] A reference from Brewer was probably influential in Margaret Reynolds' decision in March 1989 to provide another once-off grant of $12,000 to NCWA.[16]

The board was also diligent in accounting to government for grants expended. Two projects for which funding had been received remained unfinished when the Mocatta board ended its term in October 1988: an investigation of smoking habits amongst young women and girls, and a survey of the voluntary caring work done by members of state councils. The methodology of the smoking project was not rigorous—each state

---

13 'Maureen Giddings', *Stirrers with Style! Presidents of the National Council of Women of Australia and its Predecessors*, http://www.womenaustralia.info/exhib/ncwa/presidents-12.html.
14 'Curriculum Vitae of Office Bearers', *NCWA Quarterly Bulletin*, 10 (1), April 1989.
15 NCWA Board Minutes, 6 February 1989, 6 March 1989, 3 April 1989, Box 27, MSAcc07/96, NCWA Papers, NLA.
16 'President's Message', *NCWA Quarterly Bulletin*, 10 (4), December 1989.

council had been sent $500 and asked to proceed as they saw fit[17]—and auditing to the satisfaction of OSW proved something of a nightmare. The Giddings board learnt from this experience, taking into a redesign of the carers project 'the need for using a common questionnaire throughout Australia and for phrasing questions in a careful and simple manner'.[18] Auditing problems were eased by distributing to state councils 'a simple pro-forma for accountability'. Problems remained; the first version of the carers survey results was apparently lost in the mail between Adelaide and Sydney.[19] But the final report was scientifically sound, providing the first quantified information gathered in Australia 'about the time spent on household chores and the care of the family',[20] and the next president, Yvonne Bain, would make good use of this in her campaign to have unpaid labour included in accounts of Australian productivity.

In December 1991 Paul Keating replaced Bob Hawke as prime minister of Australia. Like Hawke, Keating began his conduct of women's affairs on a high note, appointing Anne Summers to a reinvigorated Office for the Status of Women. Unfinished business from the mid-1980s was taken up again. Women's issues were increasingly brought to bear on the federal budget process. Treasury's Economic Planning Advisory Committee (EPAC) regularly consulted with national women's organisations during the shaping of the budget, and women's voices were heard to good effect; NCWA reported in July 1992 that its submission to EPAC was accepted and included in the budget submission to the treasurer.[21]

---

17 '"Smoking Habits of Young Women and Girls": Assessment Value of Project', *NCWA Quarterly Bulletin*, 10 (4), December 1989.
18 Secretary's Report, Carers Project, Mid-Term Executive Meeting, 17–19 May 1990, Hobart, Box 30, MSAcc07/096, NCWA Papers, NLA.
19 NCWA Board Minutes, 2 October 1989, 5 February 1990, Box 27, MSAcc07/96, NCWA Papers, NLA.
20 Secretary's Report, Carers Project, Mid-Term Executive Meeting, 17–19 May 1990, Hobart, Box 30, MSAcc07/096, NCWA Papers, NLA.
21 NCWA Board Minutes, 28 July 1992, Box 28, MSAcc07/96, NCWA Papers, NLA.

Yvonne Bain
NCWA President 1991–1994

During her presidency, Yvonne Bain persuaded the Australian Bureau of Statistics to include the categories of work in the home and volunteer work in the national census data, allowing the value of unpaid work to be incorporated into calculations of national productivity. This is perhaps her most lasting, but by no means her only, contribution to the Australian women's movement.

Born in Brisbane, she was dux of her Rainworth primary school and at Brisbane Girls' Grammar was dux of the state in history. Forced to leave without completing her final year, she started work in the Postmaster General's Department, but enrolled in night classes and gained a Diploma in Civil Engineering. She completed a Bachelor of Administration in 1983 and a Master of Philosophy in Administration 1988. Her continuing interest in Griffith University led to appointment to the Queensland Planning and Finance Committee of the Commonwealth Schools Commission in 1979. Passionate about education, she was still actively involved with the Brisbane Grammar Old Girls and, in 1968, she was appointed to the school's Board of Trustees, serving till 1990. It was as their delegate she became involved with NCW Queensland.

Bain rapidly rose to vice-president and then president from 1986 to 1990 and, in 1991, she became the president of the National Council of Women of Australia. It was during this time that the NCWA constitution was rewritten to conform with new federal legislation and resulted in the omission from the articles of membership of the clause providing for only one constituent council for each state or territory. This compounded the 'Tasmanian problem', which had been festering since 1946. In the international sphere, Bain strengthened NCWA's international profile with ICW, and in 1994 the ICW Paris conference adopted Australia's resolution that rape should be recognised as a war crime and included in the UN *Convention on the Elimination of All Forms of Discrimination against Women* (CEDAW). She also served as the ICW Convenor in Economics, enabling her to extend her campaign for the recognition of women's unpaid work globally.

Bain contributed to a wide range of other community activities. She worked as president and chairman of the Queensland Arts Council and director of the Arts Council of Australia. In April 1999, Griffith University conferred on her an honorary doctorate for her services to education. She was appointed a Member of the Order of Australia for service to women's affairs, particularly through the National Council of Women. She died in Brisbane in May 2004.

Explore further resources about Yvonne Bain in the Australian Women's Register.

Within government the preparation of a Women's Budget Statement required government departments to assess the impact of their budget proposals on women and families.[22] The same concern for economic outcomes shaped government action on issues of equality, and NCWA's response. In mid-1992, the House of Representatives Committee on Legal and Constitutional Affairs released *Half Way to Equal*, its report on how far equal opportunity measures had improved the status of women in Australia.[23] The summary of the report printed in the *NCWA Quarterly Bulletin* focused on the committee's recommendations about women-friendly superannuation and the value of unpaid work.[24]

Yvonne Bain became president of NCWA in October 1991. The economic turn in policy and practice suited Bain's style of leadership. Bain was the first and perhaps the last national president to really understand statistics. Her first professional qualification was a diploma of civil engineering. Like several other presidents she took the opportunity provided by Whitlam's removal of university fees to return to tertiary study, but her choice of discipline was unique; Bain completed a bachelor of administration in 1983 and a master of philosophy in administration in 1988. In 1980 she was appointed to the Statistics Advisory Committee of the Australian Bureau of Statistics, and in 1983 she gave a talk to NCW Queensland on the topic 'Statistics as a Means of Communication between Individuals and Public Authorities'.[25] It was a means of communication in which she excelled, and she set about

---

22   'President's Report', *NCWA Quarterly Bulletin*, 12 (3), September 1992.
23   Sawer, *Making Women Count*, p. 188.
24   '*Half Way to Equal*', *NCWA Quarterly Bulletin*, 12 (2), June 1992.
25   'Yvonne Bain', *Stirrers with Style! Presidents of the National Council of Women of Australia and Its Predecessors*, http://www.womenaustralia.info/exhib/ncwa/presidents-02.html.

persuading the advisory committee and the ABS that unpaid work could and should be measured.

Board member Noela L'Estrange remembered that Bain recognised 'fairly early on' that the bureau already collected data relevant to unpaid work in the national census, and that 'joining those dots and then starting to get questions in there ... would yield data that would then support further analysis'.[26] In March 1992, Bain could report to NCWA that the Office of the Status of Women and the bureau were planning a joint publication, *Women in Australia*, a social report based on the census returns.[27] By 1993, material from time-use surveys made it possible for the ABS to produce 'satellite accounts' that 'enlarged the boundary of economic production',[28] allowing the calculation of the value of unpaid and voluntary work within national productivity. The National Women's Consultative Council took the results to the Department of Prime Minister and Cabinet, and the national accounts were never the same again.[29]

Bain brought to the presidency years of experience on government advisory committees, 'a very good strategic mind', and a good deal of charm.[30] Connections with Brisbane's Anglican ascendancy did not hinder her ability to relate well to Labor politicians; state premier Wayne Goss found a rent-free room for the NCWA board in government offices,[31] and Wendy Fatin, the federal minister for the status of women, found $15,000 for NCWA's administration under the National Agenda

---

26 Interview with Noela L'Estrange, Brisbane, 29 June 2009, NCWA History Project.
27 'Proposed Australian Bureau of Statistics: Social Report on Women in Australia', *NCWA Quarterly Bulletin*, 12 (1), March 1992.
28 'Australian Social Trends, 1994: Unpaid Work', *Australian Bureau of Statistics*, http://www.abs.gov.au/AUSSTATS/abs@.nsf/2f762f95845417aeca25706c00834efa/F5F60386CA7E5CFBCA2569FF0017F146?opendocument.
29 'Voluntary and Unpaid Work', *NCWA Quarterly Bulletin*, 12 (6), June 1993.
30 Interviews with Noela L'Estrange, Brisbane, 29 June 2009, and Georgina Pickers, Brisbane, 29 June 2009, NCWA History Project.
31 'President's Report', *NCWA Quarterly Bulletin*, 12 (1), March 1992.

for Women Grants program.³² Bain also reached out to other women's organisations, looking to co-operate on matters of mutual interest; in the first six months of her presidency, she held useful consultations with organisations including the Country Women's Association (CWA), the Australian Federation of University Women (AFUW) and the UNAA National Status of Women Committee.³³ But negotiations with a newly formed peak body for women proved more difficult.

CAPOW—Coalition of Participating Organisations of Women—grew out of a WEL conference in January 1992. Its first aims were 'closer co-operation in lobbying government and providing a unified and powerful voice for women'. CAPOW attracted significant funding from OSW: a seed grant of $21,000 and $60,000 in operational funds for 1993.³⁴ In July 1992 NCWA responded cautiously to an invitation to join CAPOW; the board did not wish to affiliate but was willing to co-operate. Noela L'Estrange remembered that: 'There was a strong view out of CAPOW that the NCWA was just this bunch of grey-headed, ex-Liberals who had afternoon teas and really didn't do anything'. Bain believed, in L'Estrange's words, that this was nothing but 'political gamesmanship'.³⁵ But she persevered, attending CAPOW business meetings in Canberra, and leading a workshop session on 'Unpaid Work' at the national conference that CAPOW organised for women's non-government organisations in preparation for the 1995 UN Conference on Women in Beijing. In December 1993 Bain had the satisfaction of reporting that CAPOW had unconditionally endorsed NCWA's position on 'Unpaid Work', and that a resolution on the

---

32 NCWA Board Minutes, 28 January 1993, Box 28, MSAcc07/96, NCWA Papers, NLA.
33 'President's Report', *NCWA Quarterly Bulletin*, 12 (2), June 1992.
34 Marian Sawer and Abigail Groves, '"The Women's Lobby": Networks, Coalition Building and the Women of Middle Australia', *Australian Journal of Political Science*, 29 (3), 1994, pp. 435–59; quotes from pp. 443–4.
35 Interview with Noela L'Estrange.

subject would go forward as an official Australian contribution to the Beijing conference.[36]

The members of this Queensland board were not as highly qualified in a formal sense as some previous boards had been; only Yvonne Bain and vice-president Noela L'Estrange had university degrees. But the group's informal qualifications were impressive; all had taken leading roles in community and women's organisations, and several had worked on government advisory committees.[37] As Janet Galley told us, it was 'a smooth-running board',[38] and they put their funding to good use, producing a series of research reports and seminars that influenced public and government opinion in Queensland and Canberra both. Three were particularly significant. The seminar, 'Women and Ecologically Sustainable Development', held in February 1993, presented the results of two major research projects carried out in conjunction with the National Women's Consultative Council.[39] In February 1994, a seminar on 'Future Strategies for the Care of Carers' looked back to earlier research on unpaid work and forward to federal policy changes that were not achieved until the new century. And in October 1994 a seminar on 'Women and the Economy' showed how readily the concept of the economic value of unpaid work was coming to be accepted within government and non-government agencies.[40] The relationship with government did not please everyone; an editor of the *Bulletin* resigned in protest against what she saw as government exploitation of the councils. 'As far as the Federal and State Governments are concerned, to my mind

---

36 NCWA Board Minutes, 2 December 1993, Box 28, MSAcc07/96, NCWA Papers, NLA.
37 'The Board', *NCWA Quarterly Bulletin*, 12 (3), September 1992.
38 Interview with Janet Galley, Melbourne, 9 December 2010, NCWA History Project.
39 'Women and Ecologically Sustainable Development', 27 February 1993, Gold Coast Arts Centre, Box 1, MSAcc07/96, NCWA Papers, NLA.
40 'Women and Ecologically Sustainable Development', 27 February 1993, Gold Coast Arts Centre; 'NCW Australia—Future Strategies for the Care of the Carers', 26 February 1994, Queensland Parliament House; 'Women and the Economy', 15 October 1994, Brisbane. Box 1, MSAcc07/96, NCWA Papers, NLA.

they are using NCWA to meet their own ends i.e. calling it "community consultation with women's organisations"'.[41]

In mid-1993 Prime Minister Keating established an inquiry 'to review the mechanisms which provide advice to the government on women's affairs'.[42] The NCWA board suspected the hand of CAPOW. Their submission to the review urged

> the retention of the National Women's Consultative Council as a mechanism for major voluntary women's organisations to identify the needs of women through consultation throughout Australia, to pro-actively initiate research and to permit the voluntary section to offer recommendations in policies affecting women.[43]

Note that this submission implicitly accepts NCWA's role as *one* of the 'major voluntary women's organisations' in Australia, working with other major groups through a consultative process set by government. This was perhaps an inevitable reading of the state of the women's movement in the early 1990s. An academic study of 'The Women's Lobby' carried out in 1992–93 found a fragmented network of relationships between women's organisations, with two 'distinct clusters': one revolving around Women's Electoral Lobby and the other around the National Councils of Women. The study asked organisations to identify others with whom they often co-operated; the groups still linking to the national councils included AFUW, CWA, the Soroptomists and the Pan Pacific and Southeast Asia Women's Association, while old allies like the Business and Professional Women and the Young Women's Christian Association now prioritised their links to WEL.[44]

---

41   Letter from Susan Thomson, included in NCWA Board Minutes, 18 March 1993, Box 28, MSAcc07/96, NCWA Papers, NLA.
42   'President's Report', *NCWA Quarterly Bulletin*, 12 (7), September 1993.
43   'President's Report', *NCWA Quarterly Bulletin*, 12 (7), September 1993.
44   Sawer and Groves, '"The Women's Lobby"', p. 453.

In the event, Keating's review recommended the replacement of the National Women's Consultative Committee with a new body, the Australian Council for Women. It was 'back to the future'; members were chosen not as representatives of specific organisations but 'for their particular expertise and knowledge on specific issues concerning women'. Noela L'Estrange was one of the eleven chosen women. The review also recommended that: 'Operational grants for national women's organisations under the National Agenda for Women's Grants Program be increased to underpin the ongoing activities of women's organisations and to increase their capacity to input into government decision making'. NCWA was granted $25,000 to continue its research and, in the words of the editor of the *Quarterly Bulletin*, to 'utilise the expertise in the enormous network of women's organisations which are affiliated with NCWA through the State and Territory Councils'.[45] Less favourably, the government also announced the end of project grants initiated by non-government organisations; rather, the government's needs would be met by projects it put out to tender.[46]

Carmen Lawrence was appointed minister assisting the prime minister for the status of women in March 1994. Her energy injected new life into the Office for the Status of Women and sent the members of the Australian Council for Women into a prolonged process of consultation with women across Australia intended to identify 'major, persistent obstacles to advancing the status of women'. Lawrence also announced that the federal budget would provide funding to 'maintain the momentum of reform in areas of greatest concern to Australian women'.[47] But in August Bain returned from a round table meeting with Lawrence with the news that OSW was looking at the US model

---

45 'The Australian Council of Women', *NCWA Quarterly Bulletin*, 12 (3), December 1993.
46 NCWA Board Minutes, 2 December 1993, Box 28, MSAcc07/96, NCWA Papers, NLA.
47 Noela L'Estrange, 'Report To NCWA on the Activities of the Australian Council for Women'; 'Women's Budget Statements'. *NCWA Quarterly Bulletin*, 12 (10), June 1994.

Gwen Roderick
NCWA President 1994–1997

Gwen Roderick was the first Western Australian woman to be elected president of the National Council of Women of Australia. She brought to the presidency a concern for efficient management that served the association well during a difficult period in terms of its relations with government.

She was born Gwendoline Blanche Pearce in Toowoomba in Queensland and educated there at Fairholme Presbyterian Ladies College. She trained as a secretary, and held several administrative positions including that of personal assistant for public relations to the Queensland manager of the ANZ Bank. She then travelled overseas, working in London and Canada, and became an assistant producer for Canadian Television. She married a Canadian geologist, Stanley Roderick, and had two children. The family spent 6 years in Brazil, then 5 years in Queensland, finally settling in Perth WA where she was a producer in community radio.

Roderick joined the National Council of Women of Western Australia as a delegate from the State Women's Council of the Liberal Party and served as president of NCW WA from 1991 to 1994. Relations with the Liberal state government were excellent during this period, with the government supplying an office and equipment for NCWA to counteract the tyranny of distance between Perth and Canberra. The federal Labor government was more of a challenge. Roderick was obliged to work with a new coalition of women's organisations, CAPOW, towards the creation of a 'peak body' which would speak to government on behalf of Australian women. Roderick responded by developing promotional material which publicised the fact that NCWA represented over 470 affiliated organisations and 700 associated members, 'reaching nearly a million women throughout Australia'. Roderick also initiated a corporate image with a national logo, badges and stationery. When the Howard government took office after the 1996 election, Roderick was funded to run a business strategy workshop for the state presidents and the board of NCWA, training them in the principles of business management.

Roderick represented NCWA at international meetings in New York, Beijing and Ottawa. She acknowledged the importance of putting Australia's views to ICW but emphasised that her major concerns were always national, 'that Australian women were my priority.'

In 1998 Roderick received the NCWA Centenary Award and in 1999 she was made a member of the Order of Australia for 'service to women, particularly through the National Council of Women.'

Explore further resources about Gwen Roderick in the Australian Women's Register

of women's organisations funded by private donors. In this model 'no organisation has the automatic right to funding'.⁴⁸

Western Australia's Gwen Roderick succeeded Yvonne Bain in late 1994. She told us that Bain was 'an absolutely fabulous role model', though 'the joke at the time' was that 'following in her heels was going to be a bit hard' because 'she wore very high heels'! Bain's act was indeed hard to follow, but the difficulties that challenged the balance of the new president lay largely beyond her control, in the changing demands of government. Roderick was politically experienced; she had come to NCW Western Australia as a delegate of the State Women's Council of the Liberal Party and, when she became NCWA president, state premier Richard Court was quick to provide an office for the board. But the Canberra scene could be 'a nightmare'.⁴⁹

From the first months of her presidency Roderick felt that the status of NCWA was under serious challenge. In December 1994 she was summoned to Canberra by the Office of the Status of Women to a meeting to evaluate the operational grants component of the Agenda for Women's Grants Program. Roderick and other recipients of grants were asked to provide objectives and desired outcomes, reporting against program objectives and using quantifiable data.⁵⁰ Roderick's work experience was in business management, and she was impressed by this approach. In February 1995, it was announced that CAPOW had won the tender to conduct a feasibility study into the establishment of a new 'peak body' for women's non-government organisations. Roderick

---

48   NCWA Board Minutes, 23 August 1994, Box 28, MSAcc07/96, NCWA Papers, NLA.
49   Interview with Gwen Roderick, 22 February 2012, Perth, NCWA History Project.
50   'President's Report', *NCWA Quarterly Bulletin*, 13 (1), December 1994.

reluctantly nominated for this study's steering committee, believing that 'it is important for NCWA and its vast network of member organisations to be represented'.[51] The committee met by teleconference, and Roderick found the meetings both exasperatingly inefficient and confronting. At one point a special meeting was called to discuss a 'conflict of interest' on Roderick's part, because she insisted that she spoke and acted on behalf of her affiliated societies.[52]

Roderick remained convinced that NCWA was *the* peak body representing women in Australia. She acted both to strengthen the council's claims and to restate them. She alerted state presidents to the challenge and asked them to send her regularly updated lists of affiliates and associates. These proved useful both in confrontations with other women's organisations and in lobbying politicians: 'I found that was a huge step toward influencing government'.[53] At the same time she slightly qualified her claim to representivity; NCWA represented the views of its affiliated societies but not necessarily of their members. From June 1995 the banner of the *Quarterly Bulletin* carried a new description of the association's role as an advocate: 'The National Council of Women of Australia is an umbrella organisation which ... represents over 470 affiliated organisations and 700 associated members, thus reaching more than 3 million women throughout Australia'.[54]

In August 1995 OSW announced the grants for 1995–96. NCWA—together with 'other worthy and hard-working women's NGOs'[55]—found their funding reduced; NCWA received $20,000. Roderick told NCWA's annual general meeting that the board would seek

---

51 NCWA Board Minutes, 13 February 1995, Box 28, MSAcc07/96, NCWA Papers, NLA.
52 NCWA Board Minutes, 3 April 1995, 12 June 1995, Box 28, MSAcc07/96, NCWA Papers, NLA.
53 Interview with Gwen Roderick.
54 'NCWA: Working for Women and the Welfare of Society', *NCWA Quarterly Bulletin*, 13 (3), June 1995.
55 NCWA Board Minutes, 14 August 1995, Box 28, MSAcc07/96, NCWA Papers, NLA.

corporate funding;⁵⁶ she was also talking with a marketing consultant about rebadging the *Bulletin* as a glossy women's magazine carrying advertising.⁵⁷ Meanwhile OSW continued its protracted 'feasibility study' into the making of a new 'peak body'. A firm of consultants, Roadmap, was employed to carry out 'an Australian wide process of interviews with about 60 national women's NGOs'.⁵⁸ The report from Roadmap was to go to Carmen Lawrence in February 1996, then back to the organisations represented on the CAPOW steering committee for final consideration at a round table meeting with the minister in April.⁵⁹ But by April Labor had lost the election and John Howard was prime minister of Australia.

Under Roderick NCWA took a proactive role in the 1996 election. The state councils were invited to submit a list of topics of concern; these were then consolidated by the board and sent to the three major political parties, requesting details of their policies. The topics ranged from the very general, such as the environment and the economy, to issues presented as specific to women like ageing and violence. Interest was also expressed in politicians' attitudes to National Women's Agenda grants and the Office of the Status of Women.⁶⁰ There is no indication in the records of any response to this initiative, and it probably made little impression on an election in which women's issues were not prominent.

The appointment of Tasmanian Senator Jocelyn Newman as minister advising the prime minister for the status of women was welcome to the national councils. Newman had long been a member of the Launceston council. Roderick wrote immediately to the new minister putting NCWA's case against the establishment of a new peak body, and in late

---

56 NCWA Board Minutes, Annual General Meeting by Teleconference 20 August 1995, Box 28, MSAcc07/96, NCWA Papers, NLA.
57 NCWA Board Minutes, 24 July 1995, Box 28, MSAcc07/96, NCWA Papers, NLA.
58 NCWA Board Minutes, 24 July 1995, Box 28, MSAcc07/96, NCWA Papers, NLA.
59 NCWA Board Minutes, 12 February 1996, Box 28, MSAcc07/96, NCWA Papers, NLA.
60 NCWA Board Minutes, 12 February 1996, Box 28, MSAcc07/96, NCWA Papers, NLA.

May she met with Newman to present to her a professionally prepared report spelling out the councils' response.⁶¹ In June the senator was a key speaker at 'The Decision Is Yours', a seminar organised by NCWA at Parliament House, Sydney, with the aim of encouraging women 'to take greater control over their lives'. Newman spoke on the difficulties of getting women into parliament: 'Even physically speaking Parliament House seems to have been designed for men'.⁶²

Newman moved to promote a more corporate culture amongst selected leading women's NGOs. She offered five of these groups a weekend conference with a management consultant 'to formulate a business and planning strategy for the future'. For NCWA the offer included airfares and accommodation in Perth for the board and all the state presidents.⁶³ Those who attended the 'Business Strategy Workshop' were put through a rigorous analysis of the association's strengths, weaknesses, opportunities and strengths, and guided into the formulation of a five-year plan.⁶⁴

Newman delayed the announcement of further funding. The administration grants made under Labor ended in June 1996, and Newman promised funding only until the end of the year.⁶⁵ At the same time, rumours spread about cuts to other NGOs and the imminent end of all NGO funding. At the 1996 NCWA annual general meeting, held in early September by teleconference, speakers from almost every state expressed alarm about the situation. Chris Lidgard from the ACT was 'puzzled at the appointment of further office staff and the purchase of a

---

61   NCWA Board Minutes, 11 March 1996, 19 May 1996, Box 28, MSAcc07/96, NCWA Papers, NLA.
62   'The Decision is Yours', Parliament House, Sydney, 28 June 1996, Box 1, MSAcc07/96, NCWA Papers, NLA.
63   *NCWA Mid-Term Conference*, Sydney, June 25–29 1996, published in *NCWA Quarterly Bulletin*, 13 (8), September 1996; NCWA Board Minutes, 9 July 1996, 2 September 1996, Box 28, Acc07/96, NCWA Papers, NLA; interview with Gwen Roderick.
64   'President's Report', *NCWA Quarterly Bulletin*, 13 (9), December 1996.
65   *NCWA Mid-Term Conference*, Sydney, June 25–29 1996, published in *NCWA Quarterly Bulletin*, 13 (8), September 1996.

THE NEW FACE OF THE NATIONAL COUNCIL 1986–2006

computer ... when the financial situation is parlous'. Necia Mocatta and Janet Galley asked about contingency plans if the government funding failed, and did not get an answer.[66] The presidents, meeting in Perth three weeks later for the business strategy workshop, may have received private assurances from Roderick that she could not give in public; they concluded a discussion of financial issues by unanimously confirming 'their complete confidence in the NCWA Board'.[67]

In the event, NCWA received a further short-term grant in January 1997 and, in June, an annual grant of $50,000. The board planned the purchase of a computer system and the employment of an executive officer, and investigated the possibility of establishing an office in Canberra.[68] Roderick was happy to report to the national councils in September 1997 that the government required approaches that were 'effective, well researched and professionally presented', and that NCWA was achieving this. She had met with the prime minister to discuss 'current areas of concern' and had found Mr Howard 'most receptive'. Nevertheless she warned the incoming board that

> Although the Federal Government Operation Grant to NCWA was substantially increased this year, there is no guarantee that this will continue into the future and this no doubt will depend on our maintaining an acceptable level of contribution to the women of Australia.[69]

---

66 Minutes of the Annual Conference of the NCWA Inc. Ltd (held by teleconference), 2 September 1996, Box 28, MSAcc07/96, NCWA Papers, NLA.

67 NCWA Committee of Presidents' Meeting Notes, 21 September 1996, Perth, Box 28, MSAcc07/96, NCWA Papers, NLA.

68 NCWA Board Minutes, 21 July 1997, Box 28, MSAcc07/96, NCWA Papers, NLA.

69 'President's Report', *NCWA Quarterly Bulletin*, 13 (12), September 1997.

Gracia Baylor
NCWA President 1997–2000

Gracia Baylor is the first woman to have been president of the Shire of Healesville (1977) and one of the first two women to be elected to the Victorian Legislative Council (1979). She held the seat of Boronia for the Liberal Party for 6 years. Her public career started when, as a mother of four children, she stood for her local Council on the issue of the need for kindergartens in the district. There are now two, and one is named after her. In 1973 she became president of the Victorian Local Government Women's Association and actively supported women to stand for local government positions. Later, her parliamentary intervention helped preserve part of the Queen Victoria Hospital building in Melbourne as the Queen Victoria Centre, specifically for women. During her parliamentary term she initiated a program ensuring that free car safety baby capsules were available to all parents.

Baylor joined the National Council of Women in 1984, serving as Victorian president from 1989 to 1992, and national president from 1997 to 2000. She introduced a program of reform intended to bring the image of NCWA into the 21st century. Structural reforms included a reorganisation of the national Board to include in its membership state presidents, with monthly meetings by teleconference. She also redressed the longstanding problem of the two independent Tasmanian councils, overcoming strong opposition to create the NCW Coalition of Tasmania. Relations with the federal government were also an issue during her presidency; in 1999 she took the association into the government-backed Australian Women's Coalition with the aim of ensuring a continuing leadership role within the women's movement. Fluent in French, Baylor was also active at the international level, attending the International Council of Women (ICW) Executive and Triennial meetings worldwide. Under her leadership, NCWA successfully moved a motion calling for a review of ICW's assets and financial operations. She also attended the 1999 United Nations Commission on the Status of Women and took part in the drafting of the Optional Protocol to the *Convention to Eliminate all Formed of Discrimination Against Women* (CEDAW).

Baylor was educated at Anglican schools in Brisbane, Ballarat and Hobart and subsequently trained as a secondary school teacher and, during her NCW Victorian presidency, gained a Bachelor Arts degree (1993). She was made a Member of the Order of Australia in 1999 in recognition of her services to parliament and women's affairs. In 2003 she was admitted to the Victorian Honour Roll of Women.

Explore further resources about Gracia Baylor in the Australian Women's Register

THE NEW FACE OF THE NATIONAL COUNCIL 1986–2006

Shortly before he became prime minister, John Howard gave a lecture on 'The Role of Government: A Modern Liberal Approach'. He argued that, under Labor, the policy process had become dominated by 'noisy vested interest groups', disempowering 'mainstream' Australians. He promised that under his government 'particular interests' would be assessed 'against the sentiments of mainstream Australia'.[70] As the incoming national president in October 1997, Gracia Baylor had good reason to expect the support of the Howard government for the undeniably mainstream National Council of Women of Australia.

Baylor was already an insider in Liberal circles. She was a member of the state executive in the 1970s, and served as a member of Victoria's Legislative Council from 1979 to 1985—one of the first two women to do so. Under her presidency NCW Victoria enjoyed close relations with the Liberal Party, sharing its office space and meeting rooms.[71] This is not to suggest that the national council was in any way influenced by Liberal Party policies during Baylor's presidency. Baylor came to parliament from a background of working with women's groups and community associations, and she told us that as 'a small "l" Liberal person' she 'had some problems toeing my own party line'; 'one of the great liberating things when I left parliament was the right to vote as I wished and the freedom to take up issues and judge them on their merits'.[72] But Baylor's Liberal connections certainly influenced her expectations of the Canberra bureaucracy.

Baylor reported to the March meeting of the board[73] that the prime minister had invited her to Canberra to meet with him to discuss

---

[70] John Howard, 'The Role of Government: A Modern Liberal Approach', The Menzies Research Centre 1995 National Lecture Series, 6 June 1995, cited in Marian Sawer, 'Governing for the Mainstream: Implications for Community Representation', *Australian Journal of Public Administration*, 61 (1), March 2002, pp. 39–49.

[71] Interviews with Elizabeth Steeper-Sampson, Melbourne, 2 September 2007, and Sheila Byard, Melbourne, 3 June 2013, NCWA History Project.

[72] Interview with Gracia Baylor, Melbourne, 30 April 2008, NCWA History Project.

[73] From February 1998, meetings of the Melbourne-based office bearers of NCWA became meetings of the Operations Committee, because changes to the Articles of

women's issues, and that she hoped to extend her visit to include the Office of the Status of Women, 'to see whether a "liaison officer" could be co-opted to look out for our interests in Canberra'. Mollie Campbell-Smith of the Launceston state council, newly appointed to the board as vice-president, offered to approach Minister Jocelyn Newman 'to see if she can recommend someone'.[74] In the event Baylor's hopes were dashed; she was referred to a private 'executive centre' whose services proved to be too expensive.[75]

In August 1998 a more formal Women's Round Table conference was held in Canberra involving all 52 national women's groups,[76] but there is nothing to suggest that the reports presented there had any influence on developing policy. Decisions on funding were increasingly made on political grounds; OSW grants for the year 1998–99 were restricted to some dozen organisations, and groups like Women's Electoral Lobby and CAPOW, which had been publicly critical of government decisions, were excluded.[77]

In February and March 1999 a series of meetings was held in Canberra, Sydney and Melbourne with all the national women's organisations registered with OSW, the purpose being to discuss 'the future development of the National Women's NGO Funding Program'.

    Association defined the Executive Group as including the presidents and honorary secretaries of the state councils.

74 NCWA Operations Committee Minutes no. 7, 20 March 1998, Box 30, MSAcc07/96, NCWA Papers, NLA.

75 NCWA Operations Committee Minutes no. 10, 11 June 1998, Box 30, MSAcc07/96, NCWA Papers, NLA.

76 'President's Message', *NCWA Quarterly Bulletin*, 13 (15), September 1998.

77 A list of organisations funded by OSW in 1998–99 was included in an email from Judy Harrison of the National Women's Justice Coalition and inserted in the bundle of papers sent to NCWA executive members in June–July 1999 concerning the OSW NGO Funding Program. Folder '1998–99, Correspondence', Box 6, MSAcc07/96, NCWA Papers, NLA. Those funded included: @$50,000—BPW, Guides Australia, NCWA, the National Council for Single Mothers and Their Children, Older Women's Network, YWCA; @$25,000—Catholic Women's League, Muslim Women's National Network, National Council of Jewish Women, National Women's Justice Coalition, National Women's Media Centre, Women's Action Alliance.

THE NEW FACE OF THE NATIONAL COUNCIL 1986-2006

In essence the government offered to fund women's organisations to a top limit of $500,000 a year—the current allocation—and asked the meetings how this should be distributed. The government offered three options: funding 'just one big organisation'; splitting the money equally; and, in the efficiency-speak of the day, 'A funding program which utilised a service purchasing approach for a smaller number of broadly representative national organisations funded at viable levels, known as "roof" organisations and capable of doing good policy work'. The Melbourne meeting proposed an additional strand of project funding 'aimed at supporting smaller organisations to provide services to members, do small projects, encourage women to contribute and participate in community organisations'.[78] NCWA supported this 'two-strand' option but suggested that the project funding should be increased, lest some smaller organisations 'go to the wall'.[79]

Finally, in June 1999, OSW proposed a 'restructuring' involving four 'roof organisations', each funded for three years to run a national secretariat. Total funding remained at $500,000, $100,000 for each peak body and another $100,000 for project funding. Tenders were called for organisations willing to host one of these secretariats and NCWA prepared to put in a bid.[80] Marian Sawer's account of the defunding of WEL and CAPOW presents the award of secretariat funding to NCWA as predetermined by OSW and Minister Newman, but this was not the understanding of the executive at the time. Baylor wrote to board members in August reminding them that 'only four organisations will receive major funding grants' and that even if NCWA's tender was

---

78 Elizabeth Morgan, 'Review of the National Women's Non-Government Organisations Funding Program', Office of the Status of Women, Department of Prime Minister and Cabinet, 17 June 1999, Box 6, MSAcc07/96, NCWA Papers, NLA.

79 Questionnaire for responding to the discussion paper on the future of the National Women's Funding (NG) Program, n.d., Box 6, MSAcc07/96, NCWA Papers, NLA.

80 NCWA Executive Minutes no. 16, 5 July 1999, Box 30, MSAcc07/96, NCWA Papers, NLA.

successful it might not receive funding in the future; she called for 'a willingness to move toward being self-funding' by setting 'realistic membership fees'.[81]

In the event, three rather than four organisations were initially funded to establish secretariats: BPW Australia, YWCA and NCWA—all long-established, respectable, and 'mainstream'. While Sawer's dismissal of NCWA as not 'policy-active' is less than accurate, she is right to suggest that the organisation did not see its role as criticising government. The executive apparently made no objection to the insertion of novel provisions in the contract it signed with government to receive 'secretariat' funding, provisions that prohibited the public release of any material produced as part of its funded secretariat services without the prior approval of the Commonwealth, and that also required prior notice to the Commonwealth before the public release of any other announcement, statement, publication or information.[82]

The executive seems to have understood the process of becoming a 'secretariat' in two ways: as an extension of the existing organisation; and as the means of creating of a new facility in Canberra for the use both of NCWA and of other women's organisations. In March 2000, the *NCWA Quarterly Bulletin* announced plans to establish 'the NCWA National Secretariat … in Canberra', and invited applications from organisations or individuals interested in joining NCWA in doing so.[83] In October the *Bulletin* declared that

> As one of the three peak bodies to achieve major funding contracts with the Office of the Status of Women last year we are now setting in place a range of services and facilities which will be available to other women's groups (both large and small) from our Canberra office.[84]

---

81   Board Meeting Agenda Item, 27 August 1999, Box 6, MSAcc07/96, NCWA Papers, NLA.
82   Cited in Sawer, 'Governing for the Mainstream', p. 46.
83   President's Message', *NCWA Quarterly Bulletin*, 15 (1), March 2000.
84   President's Message', *NCWA Quarterly Bulletin*, 15 (3), October 2000.

The office was established and staffed in good time to be handed over in November 2000 to the new executive headed by Judith Parker.

The major problem troubling the Baylor board was not of its own making. The 'Tasmanian problem' had vexed the association from its earliest years. The issue was the existence in Launceston of a semi-autonomous council, claiming and achieving separate identity and jurisdiction, and eventually complete autonomy, from the original council established in Hobart in 1899. This created a constitutional problem of representation on the board of NCWA. By the late 1990s this could no longer be ignored or dealt with by compromise owing to the mutual hostility of the two councils, with the Hobart council insisting on its rights as the mother council and Launceston demanding independence. From 1994 the Launceston council ceased to consult with NCW Tasmania before sending off letters and submissions, and NCWT decided to break off all communications with NCWL in 1996.[85] The 1997 triennial conference in Perth agreed to the principle of one constituent state council representing each state (or region), and the state presidents meeting after the conference reported 'some positive movement' towards 'Tasmania electing a state executive and maintaining two autonomous councils in Hobart and Launceston'.[86]

It was left to Baylor and her board to attempt to achieve this. A long sequence of meetings and working parties was organised between the warring councils, mediated at first by members of the board and then by the anti-discrimination commissioner in Tasmania, Jocelynne Scutt.[87] The outcome—the creation of the 'Tasmanian Coalition of National Council of Women Inc.' as 'the Constituent Council of

---

85   Judith Smart and Marian Quartly, 'Identity Politics: The NCWA as Subject and Audience', Australian Historical Association 2007 Regional Conference, University of New England, Armidale, 23–26 September 2007.

86   NCWA Presidents' Meeting Minutes, 1–2 October 1997, Box 28, MSAcc07/96, NCWA Papers, NLA.

87   See, for example, NCWA Executive Minutes no.14, 1 March 1999; no.17, 13 September 1999; no.19, 6 March 2000. Box 30, MSAcc07/96, NCWA Papers, NLA.

Tasmania'[88]—was effectively forced on NCW Tasmania. Leading members of NCWT responded with a lawsuit alleging unconstitutional practice by the national board. The matter was only resolved by further mediation—and the capitulation of NCWT—after Judith Parker took over the national presidency in late 2000. But the establishment of the coalition failed to arrest the decline of the Tasmanian councils.[89]

Gracia Baylor's major success as national president was the development and promotion of a set of guidelines for industry on 'Balancing Work and Life'. Baylor initially planned a series of seminars to achieve 'better parenting, greater job satisfaction and better quality of life'.[90] When sponsorship for this approach proved difficult, she refocused the project towards the production of a brochure counselling employees and employers on how to establish a 'family friendly workplace'.[91] The result was an attractive booklet advising employees how to negotiate 'flexible work options', and persuading employers that these practices increased productivity. In her introduction to the booklet, Baylor urged that 'workplaces can give more positive messages regarding life-styles and family matters. For instance, pregnancy ought to be celebrated as an enhancing experience—a plus, instead of a minus, in a woman's career path'.[92]

As Baylor describes it, the project addressed the problem identified twenty years earlier by Ada Norris: the need to change social practices to make motherhood compatible with equality. But 'Balancing Work and Life' was set in a political frame that limited its applicability across class. Baylor's booklet was intended to assist employees to negotiate an individual workplace agreement with their employer: 'Your

---

88 NCWA Extraordinary Executive Committee Minutes no. 21, 11 September 2000, Box 30, MSAcc07/96, NCWA Papers, NLA.
89 Quartly and Smart, 'Identity Politics'.
90 'President's Message', *NCWA Quarterly Bulletin*, 13 (13) March 1998.
91 NCWA Executive Minutes no. 13, 7/12/1998; no. 15, 3 May1999; no. 16, 5 July 1999; NCWA Box 30, MSAcc07/96, NCWA Papers, NLA.
92 *Balancing Life and Work: How to Achieve Change in the Workplace: A Guide for Employers and Employees*, National Council of Women of Australia, November 1999.

work package can be designed to help you work the hours needed to accommodate your personal responsibilities, whilst also meeting your organisation's needs'.[93] But the Howard government's introduction of workplace agreements did nothing to mitigate the power differential between employer and employee in such negotiations, nor did it benefit women labouring in unskilled and temporary work.

Judith Parker came to the national presidency with great plans for NCWA, some already well in hand. Under a new constitutional arrangement, the new president was elected twelve months before taking office, and 'shadowed' her predecessor for that period; Parker told us that Gracia Baylor 'was very generous to me and she really taught me the ropes'. Three candidates contested this election, and Parker's supporters from Perth were pessimistic about the outcome; they told her: 'They're not going to accept you, you're too young. You're too radical. Half of them think you're Labor'. As Parker tells the story, she decided that 'I'm just going to have to be me, and I was really hard hitting'. She told them 'You've got to change this organisation if you are going to have any clout with government ... Everyone's done their best but we have to be more professional, we are in the big league now'.[94]

Parker used her time as president elect to prepare the ground for what was undoubtedly her greatest achievement: the staging of the Triennial General Assembly of the International Council of Women in Perth in 2003. This story is told later in this chapter. She also established an office for the national executive in Perth, thanks to the largesse of the Liberal state premier, Richard Court. The Canberra 'Secretariat' was officially opened by Jocelyn Newman in November 2000, one of her last official

---

93   *Balancing Life and Work*, p. 5.
94   Interview with Judith Parker, Perth, 24 February 2012, NCWA History Project.

Judith Parker
NCWA President 2000–2003

Judith Parker was born in 1941 in Geelong, Victoria, the youngest of eight daughters of Amelia and Thomas Sinclair. She completed her education at the Canberra Church of England Girls Grammar School and won a scholarship to study at the Melbourne Kindergarten Training College.

On graduating, she began her career of 32 years in the ACT education system. When a supervisor refused to endorse her decision to enrol a blind student, she took her issue to the parents and the press and eventually won her case. This inspired her to work in the field of education for the disabled. She held executive office in the National Council of Women of ACT, the Canberra Preschool Society, the Mothercraft Society, the ACT Teachers' Federation, SPELD ACT, the National Association for Loss and Grief, the ACT Women's Health Centre and Anglican Women ACT.

In 1993 her husband, George Parker, retired from the Customs Department and the family moved to Western Australia, where Parker joined the National Council of Women of Western Australia, serving as the convenor of child and family and then as its vice-president. She became president of the National Council of Women of Australia in 2000. She lists amongst the achievements of her term the formation, in 2002, of the Australian Women's Coalition, one of the three federally funded coalitions of women with direct representation to government. Parker is also proud of the NCWA Young Women's Consultative Group, which enabled young women across the country to comment by email on issues of concern, and present those concerns to government.

In 2003 Parker brought the International Council of Women (ICW) to Perth, Western Australia for its Triennial General Assembly. This was the first time ICW had held a general assembly in the Southern Hemisphere. Parker persuaded the WA Lotteries Commission to make a very large grant that added to the global success of the conference. During the assembly Parker was elected to the executive of ICW with the portfolio of managing 34 international projects to better the lives of women and girls over the next six years.

Parker was made a Member of the Order of Australia in 2004, and in 2009 she was invested as Dame Commander in the Sovereign Order of St John of Jerusalem Knights Hospitaller, honouring her for services to women and human rights.

Explore further resources about Judith Parker in the Australian Women's Register.

duties before passing the women's affairs ministry to Amanda Vanstone. Parker understood the Canberra office as 'the hub of NCWA',[95] and planned to be there at least twice a month.

Relations with Minister Vanstone and the Office for the Status of Women began well. NCWA participated in the 'Capacity Building Workshops' organised by OSW, and took on a mentoring role with organisations less accustomed to interacting with bureaucracy, like the Country Women's Association.[96] But the new 'peak body' role sat less well with some of the association's affiliates, especially those accustomed to direct access to Canberra. Babette Francis complained on behalf of Endeavour Forum that 'we are quite capable of communicating our views to governments and don't need the bottleneck of the NCWA Secretariat'.[97] Resentment was also expressed at OSW's organisation of the 2001 national women's conference in Canberra in 2001, where the session allocated to reports from non-government organisations was limited to thirty minutes and reports had to be delivered through the presidents of the three secretariats; Sawyer comments that these women 'were clearly uncomfortable in this "management" role'.[98]

The funding contracts signed with the three secretariats in 2001 clarified this management role. The hosting associations were to understand themselves as agents, funded to bring into being new coalitions of women's organisations. In mid-2001, OSW moved to support NCWA with an additional grant of $50,000 to hire a project officer to negotiate with potential partners.[99] In February 2002 ten organisations (including NCWA) came together in a workshop in

---

95 Sawer, 'Governing for the Mainstream', p. 47.
96 NCWA Executive Minutes, 3 August 2001, Box 30, MSAcc07/96, NCWA Papers, NLA.
97 Babette Francis to Judith Parker, 4 December 2001, Box 6, MSAcc07/96, NCWA Papers, NLA.
98 Sawer, 'Governing for the Mainstream', p. 47.
99 Jeff Whalan, Social Policy Group, Department of Prime Minister and Cabinet, to Judith Parker, 13 March 2002, Folder 'OSW Grant Contracts', Box 7, MSAcc07/96, NCWA Papers, NLA.

Canberra 'to look at ways of working collaboratively in the future'. All were organisations affiliated with NCWA at a state level, and all except the CWA agreed to come together in a new consortium, the Australian Women's Coalition (AWC).[100] A steering group with representatives from NCWA, AFUW, Zonta and the Guides was formed 'to facilitate the establishment and initial work of the AWC'. The 'key objectives' of the AWC were to:

> Increase communication within the women's sector
>
> Clearly identify the needs of women represented by the consortium partners, and
>
> Initiate policies, programs and partnerships to address these needs.[101]

In March 2002 Parker reported to her board that it was intended 'that NCWA will remain the Australian Women's Coalition agent until June 30th 2003'.[102] But trouble was brewing. A new structure for AWC replaced the steering group with a committee representing all member organisations, in which 'all members have equal rights in formulating the objectives of the Coalition and all have equal voting rights'.[103] At the first meeting of this committee in August 2002, members challenged NCWA's control of the coalition, arguing that 'the Secretariat no longer

---

100 Judith Parker, 'National President's Report 2001–2002', *NCWA Annual Report 2002*, Perth, p. 3.
101 'Introducing the Australian Women's Coalition', *NCWA Forward Together*, 5 February 2002. From February 2001 the *NCWA Quarterly Bulletin* was rebadged, renamed and renumbered as *NCWA Forward Together: The Quarterly Bulletin of the National Council of Women of Australia*; from September 2002, this became the *Quarterly Bulletin of the National Council of Women of Australia including the Australian Women's Coalition*.
102 President's Report, NCWA Executive Minutes, 28 March 2002, Box 30, MSAcc07/96, NCWA Papers, NLA.
103 'The Australian Women's Coalition (AWC) Update', *NCWA Forward Together*, 7 September 2002.

exists and the $150,000 is to be controlled by AWC'.[104] A teleconference late in August between the AWC executive and Rosemary Calder, chief of OSW, did little to calm the situation. Parker reported to the NCWA conference that the 'change of role and direction' had been 'extremely stressful', and that 'it has been disappointing to realize that the Government has disregarded two years of work establishing the Secretariat and building up its credibility'.[105]

In September OSW hosted a 'capacity-building' workshop for the four national secretariats (now including Rural Women, hosted by the CWA). AWC performed well in the session on 'policy issues', with Rosemary Everett from NCWACT proposing the prominence of 'gender specific language' in the Australian Constitution as an issue for action by all women's groups. But, at other sessions, especially that directed towards 'Evaluation of the Secretariats', tensions between members of AWC were barely concealed.[106] Worse was to come. Late in October, an officer from the Department of Prime Minister and Cabinet emailed the NCWA executive officer in Canberra warning her that a more formal letter was in train expressing concern because 'we have not yet received AWC's strategic plan', due at the end of July. Given that the quarterly report was due at the end of October, and should be 'written against the strategic plan', 'we are concerned that the AWC is already slipping behind other Secretariats'.[107] NCWA submitted the strategic plan within days, but the damage was done in terms of lost confidence.

By December 2002 the leadership of AWC had been reorganised, with each member of the executive taking the chair for four months in turn; the position went first to the Soroptomists and then to the Federation of

---

104 Email, Judith Parker to NCWA Executive, 7 August 2002, Folder 'OSW/GEN', Box 7, MSAcc07/96, NCWA Papers, NLA.
105 Judith Parker, 'National President's Report 2001–2002', *NCWA Annual Report 2002*, Perth, p. 3.
106 National Network of Women—National Secretariat's Workshop, 18/19 September 2002, Folder 'OSW—Policy', Box 7, MSAcc07/96, NCWA Papers, NLA.
107 Email, Sandra Parker to NCW Secretariat, 22 October 2002, Folder 'OSW/GEN', Box 7, MSAcc07/96, NCWA Papers, NLA.

Medical Women.[108] A formal evaluation of the implementation of the secretariats prepared for OSW at the end of 2002 found that, while it was too early to fully assess the success of the secretariats, members of some groups reported a lack of consultation and a lack of clear direction from leadership.[109] By March 2003 relations between NCWA and other members of AWC were noticeably strained; Judith Parker told the AWC executive that NCWA would not remain a member of the group unless they were assured that 'whoever had won the funding was going to handle the finances and the staff in a competent way', and further that she was consulting with a lawyer about the mutual responsibilities of NCWA and AWC.[110]

In retrospect it seems clear that the task presented to the coalition 'agents' was an impossible one for the National Council of Women. The commitment of OSW to strengthening volunteer capacity was sincere, but hardly relevant to NCWA's core concerns. The effect of OSW's demand for businesslike efficiency was to set standards of performance that could only be met by hiring consultants and office managers whose services could only be afforded through government funding. And the government's agenda, constant through changes of party and minister, was at base to channel community voices into a manageable stream whose content was directed more by government policy than by community needs as understood in the community. The old-style National Council of Women of the 1950s and 1960s was elitist and hierarchical and only rarely democratic in its functioning, but it was shaped by the needs and wants of its members, and delivered their messages to government.

---

108 'AWC Chairperson's Comments', *NCWA Forward Together*, 8 December 2002, 9 March 2003.
109 'A Research Report on Evaluation of the Implementation of the Four National Women's Non-Government Organisation Secretariats', prepared for the Office of the Status of Women, December 2002, Folder 'OSW Grant Contracts', Box 7, MSAcc07/96, NCWA Papers, NLA.
110 NCWA Executive Minutes, 27 March 2003, Box 30, MSAcc07/96, NCWA Papers, NLA.

Leonie Christopherson
NCWA President 2003–2006

Leonie Christopherson was born in Sydney in November 1939. Her father's career meant frequent relocation and 3 different Anglican schools in 3 states. On completing her education at St Peter's Collegiate Girls' School in Adelaide, she became an advertising copywriter for David Jones' Stores. She married in 1960 and Christopherson believes 'there is no finer training for public life than being an army wife'. Living in 5 different countries and 5 different States within Australia has given her a global perspective. When free tertiary education was introduced in the 70s, she took out a BA in Language and Literature at Swinburne University. She first encountered the National Council of Women in 1997 as a delegate from the Central Council of Women's Sections of the Liberal Party in Victoria, of which she was vice-chairman. Attracted by NCWA's apolitical, non-sectarian philosophy, she joined the NCWA Board in 1998 as editor in charge of publications. In 2000, at the ICW General Assembly in Helsinki, she was appointed as world editor of their quarterly *Bulletin,* producing it here in Australia in three languages, English, French and Spanish. She is currently ICW Advisor for Arts & Letters.

Christopherson's time as president of NCWA was one of great change, and her consensual style of leadership provided a secure basis for it to move forward. The lack of direct government funding was met by seeking corporate funding, by sharing funding for specific projects, and by rigorous economies. Making the most of her communication skills, Christopherson produced booklets for NCWA that proved to have a strong and lasting impact. *Breathtaking Women: Asthma Awareness and You* was produced in English, Greek and Italian with the Commonwealth Department of Health and Ageing and the Asthma Foundation of Western Australia. Thirty-thousand booklets *What now in Contraceptives?* were published and distributed under the imprimatur of NCWA Australia-wide. As Christopherson has said, 'If its educational information only prevents one teenage pregnancy—it's a success'.

Christopherson became a Member of the Order of Australia in 2006, and, in 2013, she was invested as a Dame of Honour in the Order of St John of Jerusalem Knights Hospitaller, honouring her services to the community. She is quoted in *Who's Who of Australian Women* as saying 'One can only complain about things in this country if you are prepared to stick the stamps and stuff the envelopes to bring about change. Whingeing on the sidelines is not an option'.

Explore further resources about Leonie Christopherson in the Australian Women's Register

When Leonie Christopherson thought about standing for the national presidency in 2002, the task looked challenging but manageable. Government funding was guaranteed at $150,000 a year, the Canberra secretariat was in place and the efficient office manager, Pat Dart, was handling all the council's correspondence and general administration. By the time she took over the job in late 2003, having spent a year as president elect 'shadowing' Judith Parker, the funds were under the control of the newly independent and incorporated Australian Women's Coalition and the future of the Canberra office and its manager was in doubt.[111]

Christopherson was not dismayed. She reported to her executive in November that a meeting in Canberra with representatives of AWC and OSW had been 'inspiring and heartening'. She told them that though 'the days of NCWA being funded solely to stand alone are gone', 'we have to accept that this is the new regime and find ways and means how best to work with this structure'. She warned against haste: 'Be aware that there will be no Instant Solution. It will and should take time to consult'.[112]

Relations with the state councils needed mending. There was widespread disillusionment with the path the national body had taken; some believed that 'NCWA should cease being a company', and that the board should be restructured so that it did not 'dictate but [rather should] execute the will of the members'.[113] Christopherson made it her business to visit every state council within a few months of taking up the presidency. She reorganised the agenda of board teleconferences so that each state had time to report on its activities, and to raise members' concerns. Technology was redirected towards the 'grass roots'; efforts

---

111 Interview with Leonie Christopherson, 26 November 2014, NCWA History Project; Leonie Christopherson, 'National President's Report 2004', *The Ringing Grooves of Change ... NCWA Annual Report 2004*, Melbourne, p. 1.
112 NCWA Executive Minutes no. 3, 28 November 2003, Box 30, MSAcc07/96, NCWA Papers, NLA.
113 NCWA Executive Minutes no. 3, 28 November 2003, Box 30, MSAcc07/96, NCWA Papers, NLA.

were made to get all office bearers onto email, and the website was redesigned to include a 'tell us what you think' facility. Some councils were slow to respond; Christopherson sometimes found it hard to shift a 'states rights' frame of mind. But most responded well to her ministrations.[114]

There was continuing discomfort with NCWA's membership of the Australian Women's Coalition. Christopherson told the 2004 conference that

> working in partnership with the Coalition will be how we can best function in the future. There is no compulsion to sign on to any strategy they put forward ... so we are not losing our voice as some members have feared.[115]

Not everyone was convinced; an anonymous note on a 'comments please' whiteboard at the 2005 conference read: 'Secretariat system makes double work for NCWA—and blurs our impact'.[116] In retrospect Christopherson said ruefully: 'I would agree with that'.

The loss of funds to AWC created a huge challenge. The dependence on government funding had been so absolute that the fees from state councils—the only other regular fund source—did not even cover the costs of the directors' liability insurance. Christopherson cut expenses 'to the bone' and sought grants and/or sponsorship wherever they might be found, initially without success. The breakthrough was a $10,000 grant won in partnership and shared with the Asthma Foundation of Victoria to produce and distribute a booklet on asthma management for women aged over fifty; another $10,000 was later provided to translate the booklet into Italian and Greek, and promote it in the migrant communities. Another $5,000 came from Telstra to conduct a survey on

---

114 Interview with Leonie Christopherson.
115 Christopherson, 'National President's Report 2004', *The Ringing Grooves of Change ... NCWA Annual Report 2004*, Melbourne, p. 2.
116 'The Good, the Bad and the Not So Good About NCWA', Minutes of the Mid-term Conference, NCWA, 20/21/22 May 2005, Canberra.

women's use of mobile phones, and $5,000 more from a drug company to 'advise and assist' with the production and distribution of a promotional booklet, *45 Years On—What's New in Contraception*. By such means a large annual deficit was turned into a very modest annual profit.[117]

When we asked Leonie—as we asked all the presidents we interviewed—to nominate the greatest success of her presidency, she suggested 'Survival'.

The Larger Stage: NCWA, ICW and the United Nations

The period from 1986 is marked by high levels of Australian activity in the International Council of Women, and a corresponding rise in the importance of NCWA within the international organisation. This was partly the effect of the decline of other national councils, especially that of the United States. But it also reflects the calibre of the Australian women who have given so much of their time and energy to the International Council. And the experience of ICW changed the way that these women saw themselves, and Australia. Leonie Christopherson told us that 'I didn't realise how good we were at what we did until I went to Helsinki [in 2000]—we were the movers and shakers'.[118]

The visibility of NCWA as a major player within the international council is probably best dated from the late 1970s, when Dame Miriam Dell from the National Council of Women of New Zealand held the international presidency, and Laurel Macintosh secured support from the Australian Development Assistance Bureau (ADAB) for ICW's administrative expenses.[119] The grant was made within an understanding shared by government and the national councils that Australia

---

117 Interview with Leonie Christopherson; Christopherson, 'National President's Report 2004'; Leonie Christopherson, 'National President's Report 2006', *NCWA Annual Report 2006*, Melbourne.
118 Interview with Leonie Christopherson.
119 Interview with Laurel Macintosh.

needed to play a leading role in the Asia–Pacific area—Scotford's Indralasia—and that support for development projects in the region would strengthen that position of leadership.

During her presidency, Diane Alley secured ADAB funds for several women-centred projects in the Pacific, including one in Papua New Guinea investigating law reforms intended to prevent marital domestic violence. Much to Alley's distress, the Mocatta board decided to reject this project, ostensibly because 'It is a matter of principle that Overseas Aid is funded through the International Council of Women'.[120] It seems more likely that the board's concerns were with the aims of the project. Within a few months they were applying to ADAB for funds for a project with less radical, more charitable aims: a small community project in Thailand to provide basic machinery for weaving rattan products for the international market.[121] Similarly uncontroversial projects followed in the next few years, such as the application made to ADAB in co-operation with the Home Economics Association of Australia to supply women in Western Samoa with 'equipment used for training women in basic home economics, such as sewing machines and saucepans', after 'the loss of these items … from their recent cyclone'.[122]

In July 1988 the International Council of Women held a giant centennial conference in Washington to celebrate the council movement's first hundred years. Australia's role in the festivities was somewhat dimmed when half of the artefacts collected by Jessie Scotford failed to arrive in time for the conference's monster exhibition. Scotford played an important role in the organisation of this conference and other ICW events. She had been a vice-president of ICW since 1985, when she failed in a bid for the presidency. Three other Australians were appointed international convenors at the 1985 conference: Diane Alley for child

---

120 Interview with Diane Alley; NCWA Board Minutes, 19 September 1986, Box 27, MSAcc07/96, NCWA Papers, NLA.
121 NCWA Board Minutes, 16 February 1988, Box 27, MSAcc07/96, NCWA Papers, NLA.
122 'From the President', *NCWA Quarterly Bulletin*, 12 (1), March 1992.

and family, Daphne Buckley for economics and Laurel Macintosh for women and employment.[123] In 1991 Necia Mocatta joined them as a vice-president and chairman of the ICW Development Committee, organising programs for women in 'developing countries'.[124]

The 1988 ICW conference saw an unsuccessful attempt to form an 'Asian–Pacific region' of the international council. Mocatta explained to readers of the *Quarterly Bulletin* that 'these forums work very satisfactorily in Europe, Africa and the Americas'. The proposal seems to have foundered on the difficulty of drawing the boundaries of such a region: 'Some of the Pacific Island countries felt it would be better to have two separate regions, as the geographical area is so large'. This arrangement effectively decentred Australia, and the suggestion 'that countries such as Australia could belong to both regions' was not well received.[125] Discussions about regionalisation continued at successive ICW conferences, and new groupings formed; in 1994 it was reported that: 'The strong alliance between the French speaking National Councils and the European National Councils reinforced the need for a greater degree of co-operation between the Councils situated in the Asia–Pacific Region of the ICW'.[126]

The following year Mocatta reported that regional boundaries were being drawn up, and that 'Asia–Pacific agreed that it needs to be two regional areas'.[127] In 1996 Gwen Roderick reported from the ICW Mid-Term Executive meeting in Auckland that 'During discussions on Regionalisation, Fiji and Tonga stated that they thought Australia and New Zealand should have a leading role in the South Pacific'.[128] But

---

123 NCWA Board Minutes, 16 February 1988, Box 27, MSAcc07/96, NCWA Papers, NLA.
124 NCWA Board Minutes, 7 October 1991, Box 27, MSAcc07/96, NCWA Papers, NLA.
125 'From the President', *NCWA Quarterly Bulletin*, 9 (11), September 1988.
126 'From the President', *NCWA Quarterly Bulletin*, 1 (10), June 1994.
127 'Report from the ICW Board', *NCWA Quarterly Bulletin*, 13 (5), December 1995.
128 'From the President', *NCWA Quarterly Bulletin*, 13 (7), June 1996.

it was not until 2003 that the Pacific Regional Council of ICW was finally formed.¹²⁹

The willingness of the Pacific councils to concede a leading role to Australia reflected the ready assistance offered them by senior NCWA women. Jessie Scotford was particularly active in this role. When Maureen Giddings set up her Sydney-based board Scotford joined it as 'ICW Consultant', and her continuing role on the ICW executive allowed a ready flow of information and advice. Thus in February 1989 Scotford reported that the NCW of the Solomon Islands 'was experiencing difficulties', and suggested contacting the Australian consular representative there to see what help was needed.¹³⁰ The Giddings board proved to have little interest in international affairs and, in 1991, Scotford took matters into her own hands, organising a series of lunches to raise funds 'to cover the registrations for ... National Council representatives in the Pacific region'—initially Western Samoa, the Solomon Islands and Papua New Guinea.¹³¹

Scotford also regularly reminded the board of the need to work towards implementing ICW resolutions and UN Conventions. In November 1989 the board accepted her motion 'that NCWA send to the Prime Minister a copy of ICW Resolution no. 3 on the Rights of the Child and urge the Australian Government to ratify the agreement when adopted by the General Assembly of the United Nations'.¹³² It is a measure of the growing conservatism of the state councils that the motion was received with 'widespread disquiet ... [and] concern that this could lead to the erosion of the rights of parents'. This was the position adopted in the 1970s by conservatives within the councils,

---

129 NCWA Board Minutes, 17 September 2003, Box 30, MSAcc07/96, NCWA Papers, NLA.
130 NCWA Board Minutes, 6 February 1989, Box 28, MSAcc07/96, NCWA Papers, NLA.
131 NCWA Board Minutes, 5 August 1991, Box 28, MSAcc07/96, NCWA Papers, NLA.
132 NCWA Board Minutes, 6 November 1989, Box 28, MSAcc07/96, NCWA Papers, NLA.

who distrusted any state 'interference' with children, but they were over-ridden then by social liberals committed to the principle of human rights. Now the board again took a strong stance, reminding the state councils that 'ICW had been a member of the Working Party which drew up the Convention'.[133]

The period of Yvonne Bain's presidency coincided with the lead-up to the Beijing End of the Decade for Women conference, and participation in ICW events reached new peaks. Bain reported in 1994 that 23 Australians attended the triennial ICW conference in Paris, Australia was represented at all the convenorship sessions and she found it 'an honour to lead the delegation'.[134] The resolutions submitted by Australia were passed unanimously. Three NCWA motions also went forward to the Beijing conference as part of the official Australian submission: one seeking UN recognition of rape as a crime of war; one committing the UN to the elimination of violence against women and children; and Bain's personal contribution, a motion asking the UN and world governments to recognise the economic value of unpaid work.[135]

About 500 Australian women were amongst the more than 30,000 delegates, observers and participants who attended the Beijing conference and the NGO Forum that accompanied it, and most found the experience both exhausting and exhilarating. NCWA president Gwen Roderick 'noted an extraordinary and sincere intensity of interest, never casual, about the topics covered'. Noela L'Estrange, also a delegate for NCWA, remembered 'the almost infinite capacity and ability of women the world over to find better ways of achieving their goals'.[136] But the exhilaration faded. Roderick came to believe that efforts to solve the problems of women in 'underdeveloped' countries were achieving

---

133 NCWA Board Minutes, 5 February 1990, Box 28, MSAcc07/96, NCWA Papers, NLA.
134 'President's Report', *NCWA Quarterly Bulletin*, 13 (10), June 1994.
135 NCWA Executive Minutes (by teleconference), 24 April 1994, Box 28, MSAcc07/96, NCWA Papers, NLA.
136 'Report from Beijing', *NCWA Quarterly Bulletin*, 13 (4), September 1995.

THE NEW FACE OF THE NATIONAL COUNCIL 1986–2006

very little.[137] In her last report to NCWA in late 1997 she observed that while there were some global issues for which Australian women should continue to work, such as an international Convention banning anti-personnel land mines,

> I believe that organisations such as NCWA will need to consider to what degree they should be involved at the global level and whether there is a priority to concentrate on issues close to home. Obviously the prime responsibility of NCWA is to its affiliated organisations, their members and to the wider Australian community.[138]

The presidents who succeeded Roderick have not followed her isolationist turn. Gracia Baylor was active on the international front, attending the ICW executive meeting in Oxford in 1999 and the ICW triennial conference in Helsinki in July 2000, where NCWA successfully moved a motion calling for a review of ICW's assets and financial operations. Baylor also attended the 1999 United Nations Commission on the Status of Women as a member of the ICW delegation, and took part in drafting the Optional Protocol to the Convention to Eliminate All Forms of Discrimination Against Women (CEDAW).[139] This establishes a process by which citizens of states that become parties to the protocol can take cases of discrimination to the Committee on the Elimination of Discrimination Against Women.[140] Baylor wrote in the *NCWA Bulletin* that:

> The Convention is important to Australian women since it sets out protections against discrimination in all its forms, and whilst

---

137 Interview with Gwen Roderick, Perth, 22 February 2012, NCWA History Project.
138 'President's Report', *NCWA Quarterly Bulletin*, 13 (12), September 1997.
139 'Gracia Baylor', *Stirrers with Style! Presidents of the National Council of Women of Australia and Its Predecessors*, http://www.womenaustralia.info/exhib/ncwa/presidents-03.html.
140 'Convention on the Elimination of All Forms of Discrimination against Women: Text of the Optional Protocol', United Nations Entity for Gender Equality and the Empowerment of Women, http://www.un.org/womenwatch/daw/cedaw/protocol/text.htm.

we may not think we need this extra protection in our country, there are still many cases of discrimination heard every day in Australia which fully justifies support for the new protocol.[141]

A resolution was passed at the NCWA 2000 conference 'expressing deep concern' at the Commonwealth government's failure to sign the Optional Protocol to CEDAW, and the new president, Judith Parker, urged members of the association to 'send a clear message to the Government that the Optional Protocol must be signed' by making the question an issue in the coming federal election.[142]

Judith Parker confirmed the importance of NCWA within the International Council of Women by staging the Triennial General Assembly in Perth, the first time the international assembly had met in the southern hemisphere. To bring ICW to Australia had seemed an impossible dream; the international president told Parker: 'the women from Europe are not going to fly to Australia'.[143] Parker made the dream possible by winning a Western Australian award that financed the preparation of the proposal to hold the assembly, by a passionate presentation of the proposal at the 2000 general assembly in Helsinki, and finally by persuading the WA Lotteries Commission to make a very large grant towards the running of the assembly.[144]

At that 2003 assembly Parker was elected to the ICW executive, with the portfolio of managing ICW projects worldwide. These included building water tanks in villages along the Kokoda Trail in New Guinea; setting up computer classes for women in Macedonia; establishing a women's collective in Kenya to buy cows and sell their produce; starting a sewing centre in India for widows forced by poverty

---

141 'President's Report', *NCWA Quarterly Bulletin*, 14 (2), June 1999.
142 'NCWA in Action: Resolutions Passed at the National Council of Women of Australia 2000 Conference', *Forward Together*, May 2001.
143 Interview with Judith Parker.
144 'Judith Parker', *Stirrers with Style! Presidents of the National Council of Women of Australia and Its Predecessors*, http://www.womenaustralia.info/exhib/ncwa/presidents-23.html.

THE NEW FACE OF THE NATIONAL COUNCIL 1986–2006

to become prostitutes; again in India supplying artificial limbs for people damaged by war and leprosy; and in South Africa two projects: one working with girl prostitutes whose parents had died of AIDS, the other teaching women to turn recycled materials into hats and bags and brooches for the tourist trade.[145] Eleanor Sumner, the Australian who preceded Parker in this role, told us that 'the projects are a vital part of ICW's work. Of women standing together and helping each other. And in a non-judgemental fashion'.[146]

The mid-term national conference in May 2005 can serve to show the ongoing role of NCWA as a link to the international women's movement and the human rights regime. Among the resolutions passed were several based on ICW resolutions and UN Conventions. One was concerned with the prevention of 'Trafficking': the forced movement between nations of people, especially women and children, for the purpose of exploitation.[147] Australia had signed the relevant protocol in 2002; now the issue lay with the Immigration Department's treatment of the victims of such trafficking. The resolution—passed unanimously—urged the government

> to review the guidelines regulating the granting of visas to women entering the witness protection program from sex work. The present provision (denying the grant of special visas to such women unless they are deemed likely to provide evidence leading to the successful prosecution of the traffickers) fails to bring into account the claims which such women have to protection and assistance on purely humanitarian grounds.[148]

---

145 'Judith Parker', *Stirrers with Style!*
146 Interview with Eleanor Sumner, Melbourne, 18 April 2013, NCWA History Project.
147 UN Protocol to Prevent, Suppress and Punish Trafficking in Persons, Especially Women and Children, Supplementing the United Nations Convention Against Transnational Organised Crime, http://www.osce.org/odihr/19223.
148 Amended Resolution 6—Trafficking—Optional Protocol to Prevent Suppress and Punish Trafficking in Persons, especially Women and Children, Minutes of the Mid-term Conference, NCWA, 20/21/22 May 2005, Canberra. See also interview with Sheila Byard.

Hean Bee Wee
NCWA President 2006–2009

Hean Bee Wee was born in Penang in Malaysia on 23 March 1946. After completing her secondary education there, she came to Australia to study Economics at Adelaide University. After graduating as a Bachelor of Economics (Honours) in 1969, she then gained a Diploma of Education and an Advanced Diploma of Financial Services. She became a secondary school teacher, developing further expertise internationally by teaching and co-ordinating Baccalaureate programs and becoming an ambassador for South Australian schools in Southeast Asia. She married fellow teacher Victor Wee in 1970.

Having grown up in a society where girls were less valued than boys, she was passionately committed to the principle of social equality, in terms of both gender and ethnicity. Very active in the Penguin Club, Wee soon became their delegate to the National Council of Women of South Australia. She also set about recruiting other women from non-English speaking backgrounds to join the club to polish their public speaking skills, with considerable success. From 1995–1997 she was appointed a commissioner for the SA Multicultural and Ethnic Affairs Commission and, from 1999 to 2003, she served as president of the Asian Women's Consultative Council of South Australia. She also served as treasurer for the South Australian Women's Trust from 1999–2002 and treasurer of the National Council of Women of Australia from 2004.

Within the National Council of Women of South Australia, Wee soon took on executive roles as Advisor for Economics and as vice-president. Federally, she was elected president of the National Council of Women of Australia for the term 2006–2009 and was the first Asian-born woman to hold that position. Her proudest achievement as NCWA president was to obtain generous federal funding for two government projects directed towards the advancement of women. The first of these worked to promote the wellbeing of women in Oodnadatta, the second to provide a culturally and linguistically appropriate training course for non-English speaking women at TAFE. In 2012 she was elected a vice-president of the International Council of Women, with responsibility for supervising a project in Samoa to establish a financially viable marketing structure for handicrafts produced by local Samoan women—a project ideally suited to her financial expertise, managerial skills and commitment. Her work on behalf of Asian and non-English speaking women is ongoing. She became a Member of the Order of Australia in 2014 in recognition of her contribution to the community in Australia and internationally.

Explore further resources about Hean Bee Wee in the Australian Women's Register

THE NEW FACE OF THE NATIONAL COUNCIL 1986-2006

Another resolution—also passed unanimously—asked the government 'to conform with the International Convention on the Rights of the Child' by releasing from detention all children currently held in immigration detention centres.[149] Among the official speakers at the conference, Senator Kay Patterson reported how, as a representative of the Australian government, she had assured the 49th session of the UN Commission on the Status of Women that 'Australia places a high priority on combatting domestic violence and sexual assault and trafficking of women and children'. Professor Hilary Charlesworth told the delegates that Australia needed a bill of rights, because 'You've got to imagine better things'.[150]

The 2005 conference was also notable for the informal discussions that took place about the appointment of Hean Bee Wee, Leonie Christopherson's chosen successor as national president. Hean Bee Wee came to NCWA with a strong record of achievement in business and NGO activity. She had served on the executive of the South Australian Branch of the Asian Pacific Business Council for Women, as commissioner for the South Australian Multicultural and Ethnic Affairs Commission, and as president of the Asian Women's Consultative Council of South Australia. Christopherson recruited her as treasurer on her national board, and was impressed by her ability and her commitment to social and gender equity. Hean Bee was willing to serve as NCWA president, but it became apparent that her home council, NCW South Australia, was unwilling to nominate her. Christopherson put a strong case to the South Australians for Wee's appointment, but failed to change their minds. The problem was solved when the ACT council accepted Hean Bee as a member and nominated her for the presidency. Hean Bee Wee

---

149 Resolution 10, Minutes of the NCWA Mid-term Conference, 20/21/22 May 2005, NCWA, Canberra.

150 Minutes of the NCWA Mid-term Conference, 20/21/22 May 2005, NCWA, Canberra. Charlesworth was quoting Albie Sachs.

became president at the triennial conference in 2006, and served both NCWA and ICW with distinction.[151]

Looking back to her years in the early 1980s as NCWA president, Laurel Macintosh remarked that 'we were working all the time for our planned obsolescence'. She gave as an example the establishment of the Office for the Status of Women in Canberra: 'that was one of the things we'd worked for for years and years', but 'once that was set up, it did change the nature of national council's work a lot'.[152]

In retrospect it seems inevitable that the building of national machinery to improve the status of women—a dedicated bureaucracy, a national advisory committee—would make aspects of the work of the national councils redundant. This was not only because long-held aims were achieved, but also because the machinery displaced NCWA from its role of representing to government the voices of Australian women. And that machinery also worked to limit NCWA itself by making it the agent of government policy.

Another Queenslander, Noela L'Estrange, talked to us in her interview about the relationship between government and voluntary organisations at the international level. L'Estrange attended Beijing '95, the Fourth World Conference for Women, wearing two hats: as an official representative of the Australian government, and as a member of ICW. L'Estrange valued the formal contribution that the Australian delegation made to the official UN conference; she cited the significance of the international acceptance of the inclusion of the value of unpaid work in national productivity, something originally put to the Australian government by NCWA.[153] But what she chiefly remembered from Beijing was not the official conference but the NGO Forum running beside it, and the energy and 'wealth of shared experience' of the women

---

151 'Hean Bee Wee', *Stirrers with Style! Presidents of the National Council of Women of Australia and Its Predecessors*, http://www.womenaustralia.info/exhib/ncwa/presidents-14.html; Interview with Leonie Christopherson.
152 Interview with Laurel Macintosh.
153 Interview with Noela L'Estrange, 29 June 2009, Brisbane, NCWA History Project.

who gathered there 'to find better ways for the achievement of their goals'.[154] She believed that Beijing could show NGOs like NCWA the way forward into the twenty-first century.

Equality between men and women is still a distant goal: conceivable for Australian women, almost unimaginable for most of the women of the world. NCWA's support for women's rights is necessary within Australia and crucial at the global level, where most women lack the resources and political power to speak for themselves. Their needs will keep the women's movement from obsolescence for many years to come.

---

154   Noele Lestrange, 'Beijing 95: Report on the Fourth World Conference for Women and the NGO Forum', *NCWA Quarterly Bulletin*, 13 (4), September 1995.

AFTERWORD

The June 1999 issue of the *NCWA Bulletin* carried a message from Eleanor Sumner, ICW vice-president, announcing that the year 2000 had been proclaimed the 'International Year for the Culture of Peace' by the United Nations, and the period 2001–2010 the 'International Decade for a Culture of Peace and Non-violence for the Children of the World'. Sumner wrote: 'The year 2000 must be a new beginning for us all. Together we can transform the culture of war and violence into a culture of peace and non-violence'.[1] Fifteen years later Sumner's optimism seems cruelly impossible. But perhaps we need to take a longer perspective.

The Australian National Councils of Women began the twentieth century with an ideal that seemed at the time almost as impossible as a world without war: to bring to bear on public life the values that women exercised in private life, for the good of both family and nation. The founders of the Australian councils would not recognise the ideals they fought for in the programs of women's non-government organisations today. Their moral certainties have vanished and, with those certainties, their cultural exclusivity. But one can argue that much of what the founders dreamed has been achieved, and that the Australian councils have been significant players in that achievement. The movement of women into public life, into the workforce, into all levels of education and training, into the professions and legal system and the executive levels of business—none of this is fully achieved, but the achievements thus far owe much to the National Councils of Women. The equality of men and women before the law, the protection and support of children and families, the removal of discrimination in so many areas

---

1 'Manifesto 2000: For a Culture of Peace and Non-Violence', *NCWA Quarterly Bulletin*, 14 (2), June 1999.

AFTERWORD

of institutional life—again these are works in progress, and again much credit is owed to the councils.

The Australian state across the twentieth century has been effectively transformed from a site for men's voices and men's business to one in which women's voices and business previously understood as women's business—the business of home and family—are a central part of national life. Perhaps one hundred years from now the world will have seen a similar transformation.

APPENDIX

Our sincere thanks to the donors, large and small, who contributed to the production of this publication.

(in alphabetical order)

Diane Alley OBE
Mary Allinson
Anonymous of Bendigo Victoria
Anonymous of Burnley North Victoria
Attendees at the lunch hosted by Rabbi Aviva Kippen
Attendees at the Pioneer Women's Garden Ceremony, Victoria 2007
Merell Browne
Sheila Byard
Janet Calvert Jones AO (in honour of Ethleen King)
Geri Campbell
Jean Cheshire GCSJ OAM
Leonie Christopherson AM DSJ
Val Cocksedge OAM
Eunice Craythorn
Margaret Davey CBE
Gladys Dodson
Kath Donegan
Judith Douglas
Alice Engel (née Penketh)
Paddy Firstenberg MBE AM
Janet Galley OAM
Sylvia Gelman MBE AM
In Memory of Patricia Goble
Janni Goss
Rayleen Haig OAM
Betty Hayes
Margaret Heffernan OAM

APPENDIX

Lois Hoeper OAM
Glenys Jones OAM
Jan Kinloch DSJ
Ruth Mainsbridge OAM
Methodist Ladies' College (Kew) Old Collegians' Club
Naomi Milgrom AO
Dame Elisabeth Murdoch AC DBE
NCW Australian Capital Territory
NCW Devonport
NCW Goulburn Valley
NCW New South Wales
NCW Victoria
NCW Victoria Associates
NCW Victoria Central Gippsland Branch
NCW Victoria Geelong Branch
NCW Western Australia
Elisabeth Newman
Anne Parton DSJ
Rysia Rozen OAM
Jenny Rawther Russell AM
Elizabeth Steeper Sampson
Eris Smyth OAM
Heather Southcott AM
Coral Sundblom
Joy C. Tate
Elizabeth Taylor
The League of Women Voters
Yvonne Tully
Pattie Verco
Pamela Williams AM
Margaret Wilson (In Memory of Phyllis Wilson)

SELECT BIBLIOGRAPHY

Repositories Holding NCWA Sources

The women of Australia's National Councils of Women knew they were making history, and they kept good care of their records. Largely complete runs of council and executive minutes exist nationally and for every state and territory. The most relevant documentary holdings in state and national libraries and archives are listed below. The National Library of Australia is the richest source, holding the records of nearly all the national presidencies; in addition the NLA has a wealth of published material including an almost complete run of the *NCWA Quarterly Bulletin*, annual reports, and reports of conferences and research projects. It also holds the papers of a number of women of importance in NCWA's history. The National Archives of Australia hold the record of the NCWA's interaction with federal government. At state level the Mitchell Library in the State Library of New South Wales has the richest collection, including a run of the local *NCW News*, while the voluminous records of NCWV have only recently been transferred to the State Library of Victoria and still await accession.

LINC Tasmania
National Council of Women of Tasmania Records, 1899–1987, NS1035, NS325, NS579, NS1456, Tasmanian Archive and Heritage Office, LINC Tasmania

National Council of Women of Launceston records, LMSS99, Launceston LINC, LINC Tasmania

National Archives of Australia
Australian Security Intelligence Organisation, A9108 (A9108, ROLL 10/18) NAA

Department of External Affairs, Correspondence files, A1838 (A1838/1) NAA

SELECT BIBLIOGRAPHY

Department of Territories, Correspondence files, A452 (A452/1) NAA
Department of the Attorney General, Marriage and Divorce Bill 1947, A432, NAA

National Library of Australia
Records of the National Council of Women of Australia, 1936–1972, MS5193, NLA
Records of the National Council of Women of Australia, 1924–1985, MS7583, NLA
Records of the National Council of Women of Australia, 1924–1990, MSAcc07/96; MS Acc GB 1993/1502; MS7583, NLA.
Records of the Liaison Committee of Women's International Organisations, Australia Group, 1947–1963, MS1082, NLA
Records of the Australian Federation of Women Voters, 1920–1983, MS2818, NLA
Records of Joyce McConnell, 1960–1989, MS8260, NLA
Papers of Herbert and Ivy Brookes, 1869–1970, MS1924, NLA
Papers and Objects of Bessie Rischbieth, MS2004, NLA

Northern Territory Archives Service
National Council of Women in the Northern Territory Inc. Records, NTRS836, NTAS

State Library of New South Wales
National Council of Women of New South Wales Records, 1895–1976, MLMS3739 (MLK 3009–MLK 3012), SLNSW

State Library of Queensland
7266, National Council of Women of Queensland Minute Books, 1905–2004, John Oxley Library, SLQ

State Library of South Australia
Records of the National Council of Women of South Australia, 1920–1992, SRG 297, SLSA

State Library of Victoria
Records of the National Council of Women of Victoria, 1902–2006, Accession Pending, SLV

State Library of Western Australia
National Council of Women of Western Australia Records, 1911–2001, MN187, ACC 1389A, ACC 6604A, ACC 7678A, ACC 8450A, ACC 8646A, SLWA

University of Melbourne Archives
Norris, Dame Ada May, Papers, 1990.0109, University of Melbourne Archives

Interviews

National Library of Australia Oral History Collection
Jessie Scotford interviewed by Hazel de Berg, 7 July 1977, ORAL TRC 1/1010

NCWA History Project
Diane Alley, 20 July 2010, Melbourne
Gracia Baylor, 30 April 2008, Melbourne
Daphne Buckley, 26 June 2009, Brisbane
Pat Burgess, 17 August 2009, Brisbane
Elaine Bushby, 22 August 2008, Launceston
Sheila Byard, 3 June 2013, Melbourne
Leonie Christopherson, 26 November 2014, Melbourne
Ruth Clemente, 14 October 2011, Melbourne
Val Cocksedge, 26 June 2009, Brisbane
Betty Davy, 21 February 2010, Sydney
Gladys Dodson, 26 June 2007, Hobart
Joan Elliston, 22 February 2010, Sydney
Paddy Firstenberg, 26 September 2009, Adelaide
Janet Galley, 9 December 2010, Melbourne
Sylvia Gelman, 9 December 2010, Melbourne
Monica Glenn, 26 September 2009, Adelaide
Maureen Giddings, 22 February 2010, Sydney
Linley Grant, 28 June 2007, Hobart
Noela L'Estrange, 29 June 2009, Brisbane
Laurel Macintosh, 26 June 2009, Brisbane
Ruth Mainsbridge, 22 August 2008, Launceston
Elisabeth Newman, 16 January 2012, 4 September 2013, Melbourne
Judith Parker, 24 February 2012, Perth

SELECT BIBLIOGRAPHY

Georgina Pickers, 29 June 2009, Brisbane
Gwen Roderick, 22 February 2012, Perth
Margot Roe, 28 June 2007, Hobart
Zita Sidaway, 17 August 2009, Brisbane
Kaylin Simpson, 22 February 2010, Sydney
Evonne Sullivan, 25 March 2010, Canberra
Eleanor Sumner, 18 April 2013, Melbourne
Elizabeth Steeper-Sampson, 2 September 2007, Melbourne
Robin Toohey, 22 February 2010, Sydney

Secondary Sources

The First Fifty Years in the History of the National Council of Women of Queensland, Brisbane, NCWQ, 1959

From Vision to Reality: Histories of the Affiliates of the National Council of Women of Victoria, Melbourne, NCWV, 1987

'ICW Resolutions', http://www.ncwcanada.com/ncwc2/wp-content/uploads/2014/02/ICW-CIF_Resolutions1.pdf

Abeyasekere, Susan Blackburn, 'Blackburn, Maurice McCrae (1880–1944)', *Australian Dictionary of Biography*, http://adb.anu.edu.au/biography/blackburn-maurice-mccrae-5258/

Albury, Rebecca M. 'Reproductive Rights and Technologies', in Barbara Caine (ed.), *Australian Feminism: A Companion*, Melbourne, Oxford University Press, 1998

Allen, Judith, *Sex and Secrets: Crimes Involving Australian Women since 1880*, Melbourne, Oxford University Press, 1990

Allen, Judith, *Rose Scott: Vision and Revision in Feminism*, Melbourne, Oxford University Press, 1994

Allen, Judith, 'Rose Scott (1847–1925)', *Australian Dictionary of Biography*, http://adb.anu.edu.au/biography/scott-rose-8370/

Arrow, Michelle. 'Public Intimacies: Revisiting the Royal Commission on Human Relationships', in Lisa Featherstone et al. (eds), *Acts of Love and Lust: Sexuality in Australia from 1945–2010*, Newcastle upon Tyne, Cambridge Scholarly Publications, 2014

Baldwin, M. Page, 'Subject to Empire: Married Women and the British Nationality and Status of Aliens Act', *Journal of British Studies*, 40 (4), October 2001, pp. 522–56

Barbalet, Margaret, *Far from a Low Gutter Girl: The Forgotten World of State Wards: South Australia 1887–1940*, Melbourne, Oxford University Press, 1983

Bertrand, Ina, *Film Censorship in Australia*, Brisbane, University of Queensland Press, 1978

Birman, Wendy, 'Robertson, Agnes Robertson (1882–1968)', *Australian Dictionary of Biography*, http://adb.anu.edu.au/biography/robertson-agnes-robertson-11540

Bredbenner, Candice Lewis, *A Nationality of Her Own: Women, Marriage and the Law of Citizenship*, Berkeley and Los Angeles, University of California Press, 1998

Brignell, Lyn and Heather Radi, 'Matthews, Susan May (1877–1935)', *Australian Dictionary of Biography*, http://adb.anu.edu.au/biography/matthews-susan-may-7525/

Brown, Margaret, 'Cowan, Edith Dircksey (1861–1932)', *Australian Dictionary of Biography*, http://adb.anu.edu.au/biography/cowan-edith-dircksey-5791/

Bomford, Janette, *That Dangerous and Persuasive Woman: Vida Goldstein*, Melbourne, Melbourne University Press, 1993

Bongiorno, Frank, *The Sex Lives of Australians: A History*, Melbourne, Black Inc., 2012

Brown, Nicholas, *Governing Prosperity: Social Change and Social Analysis in Australia in the 1950s*, Melbourne, Cambridge University Press, 1995

Browne, Geoff, 'Herring, Sir Edmund Francis (Ned) (1892-1982)', *Australian Dictionary of Biography*, http://adb.anu.edu.au/biography/herring-sir-edmund-francis-ned-12626

Butler, A.G.H., *The Australian Army Services in the War of 1914–18*, vol. III, Canberra, Australian War Memorial, 1943

Campbell, Kate, 'Scantlebury Brown, Vera (1889–1946)', *Australian Dictionary of Biography*, http://adb.anu.edu.au/biography/scantlebury-brown-vera-8350/

Castles, Frank G. et al. (eds), *The Great Experiment: Labour Parties and Public Policy Transformation in Australia and New Zealand*, Sydney, Allen & Unwin, 1999

Cole, Douglas, '"The crimson thread of kinship runs through us all": Ethnic Ideas in Australia, 1870–1914', *Historical Studies*, 14 (56), 1971, pp. 511–25

SELECT BIBLIOGRAPHY

Cole, Douglas, 'The Problem of "Nationalism" and "Imperialism" in British Settlement Colonies', *Journal of British Studies*, 10 (2), 1971, pp. 160–82

Coltheart, Lenore, 'Citizens of the World: Jessie Street and International Feminism', *Hecate*, 31, 2005, pp. 182–9

Damousi, Joy, 'Aileen Fitzpatrick, UN, International Refugees', paper presented at Women and Leadership Conference, 2 December 2011, Museum of Australian Democracy, Canberra

Damousi, Joy, Kim Rubenstein and Mary Tomsic (eds), *Diversity in Leadership: Australian Women, Past and Present*, Canberra, ANU Press, 2014

Darian-Smith, Kate, *On the Home Front: Melbourne in Wartime 1939–1945*, Melbourne, Oxford University Press, 1990

Davis, Annette, 'Infant Mortality and Child-saving: The Campaign of Women's Organizations in Western Australia 1900–1922', in Penelope Hetherington (ed.), *Childhood and Society in Western Australia*, Perth, UWA Press with Centre for WA History, 1988, pp. 161–73

Dickey, Brian, *No Charity There: A Short History of Social Welfare in Australia*, Sydney, Allen & Unwin, 1987

Dowse, Sara, 'The Prime Ministers' Women', *Australian Feminist Studies*, 29 (82), 2014, pp. 391–402

Eather, Warwick, 'The Liberal Party of Australia and the Australian Women's Movement Against Socialisation 1947–54', *Australian Journal of Politics and History*, 44 (2), 1998, pp. 191–207

Edgar, Suzanne, 'Goode, Agnes Knight (1872–1947)', *Australian Dictionary of Biography*, http://adb.anu.edu.au/biography/goode-agnes-knight-6421

Edwards, W. H., 'Duguid, Charles (1884–1986)', *Australian Dictionary of Biography*, http://adb.anu.edu.au/biography/duguid-charles-12440

Falk, Barbara, 'Rosanove, Joan Mavis (1896–1974)', *Australian Dictionary of Biography*, http://adb.anu.edu.au/biography/rosanove-joan-mavis-11560/

Finlay, Henry, *To Have But Not To Hold: A History of Attitudes to Marriage and Divorce in Australia 1858–1975*, Sydney, Federation Press, 2005

Fitzherbert, Margaret, *So Many Firsts: Liberal Women from Enid Lyons to the Turnball Era*, Sydney, Federation Press, 2009

Foley, Meredith, 'Glencross, Eleanor (1876–1950)', *Australian Dictionary of Biography*, http://adb.anu.edu.au/biography/glencross-eleanor-6402/

Gillan, Helen, *A Brief History of the National Council of Women of Victoria 1902–1945*, Melbourne, Spectator, 1945

Gray, Kate, 'The Acceptable Face of Feminism: The National Council of Women of Victoria1902–18', MA thesis, University of Melbourne, 1988

Gregory, Robyn V., 'Corrupt Cops, Crooked Docs, Prevaricating Pollies and "Mad Radicals": A History of Abortion Law Reform in Victoria, 1959–1974', PhD, RMIT University, 2004

Gunson, Niel, 'Bevan, Louisa Jane (1844–1933)', *Australian Dictionary of Biography*, http://adb.anu.edu.au/biography/bevan-louisa-jane-5632

Henningham, Nikki, 'Heather Southcott (1928–2014)', in Judith Smart and Shurlee Swain (eds), *The Encyclopedia of Women and Leadership in Twentieth Century Australia*, http://www.womenaustralia.info/leaders/biogs/WLE0711b.htm

Heywood, Anne, 'Breen, Marie Freda (1902–1993)', *Australian Women's Register*, http://www.womenaustralia.info/biogs/IMP0013b.htm

Hicks, Neville, *'This Sin and Scandal': Australia's Population Debate, 1891–1911*, Canberra, ANU Press, 1978

Hilliard, David, 'God in the Suburbs: The Religious Culture of Australian Cities in the 1950s', *Australian Historical Studies*, 24 (97), 1991, pp. 399–419.

Hipgrave, Jan, Marian Quartly, and Judith Smart, *Stirrers with Style! Presidents of the National Council of Women of Australia and Its Predecessors*, http://www.womenaustralia.info/exhib/ncwa/

Hocking, Jenny, *Lionel Murphy: A Political Biography*, Melbourne, Cambridge University Press, 2000

Jacques, Catherine and Sylvie Lefebrve, 'From Philanthropy to Social Commitment', in Eliane Gubin and Leen Van Molle (eds), *Women Changing the World: A History of the International Council of Women*, Brussels, Édition Racine, 2005

Jaggs, Donella, *Neglected and Criminal: Foundations of Child Welfare Legislation in Victoria*, Melbourne, Phillip Institute of Technology, 1986

Johnson, Penelope, 'Gender, Class and Work: The Council of Action for Equal Pay Campaign in Australia during World War II', *Labour History*, 50, May 1986, pp. 132–46

Jones, Helen, *In Her Own Name: A History of Women in South Australia from 1836*, Adelaide, Wakefield Press, revised ed. 1994

Jones, Ross L., 'The Master Potter and the Rejected Pots: Eugenic Legislation in Victoria, 1918–1939', *Australian Historical Studies*, 30 (113), 1999, pp. 324–30

SELECT BIBLIOGRAPHY

Kelly, Farley, 'The Woman Question in Melbourne 1880–1914', PhD thesis, Monash University, 1982

Keep, Patricia, 'Allan, Stella May (1871–1962)', *Australian Dictionary of Biography*, http://adb.anu.edu.au/biography/allan-stella-may-4998/

Lake, Marilyn and Farley Kelly (eds), *Double Time: Women in Victoria—150 Years*, Melbourne, Penguin, 1985

Lake, Marilyn, 'Female Desires: The Meaning of World War II', *Australian Historical Studies*, 24 (95), 1990, pp. 267–84

Lake, Marilyn, 'The Independence of Women and the Brotherhood of Man: Debates in the Labour Movement over Equal Pay and Motherhoood Endowment in the 1920s', *Labour History*, 63, November 1992, pp. 1–24

Lake, Marilyn, 'Women's Liberation', in Barbara Caine (ed.), *Australian Feminism: A Companion*, Melbourne, Oxford University Press, 1998

Lake, Marilyn, *Getting Equal: The History of Australian Feminism*, Sydney, Allen & Unwin, 1999

Lake, Marilyn, 'State Socialism for Australian Mothers: Andrew Fisher's Radical Maternalism in its International and Local Contexts', *Labour History*, 102, May 1912, pp. 55–70

Langmore, Diane, 'Duncan, Ada Constance (1896–1970)', *Australian Dictionary of Biography*, http://adb.anu.edu.au/biography/duncan-ada-constance-10061/text17747

Leppännen, Katarina, 'The Conflicting Interest of Women's Organizations and the League of Nations on the Question of Married Women's Nationality in the 1930s', *Nora: Nordic Journal of Feminist and Gender Research*, 17 (4), 2009, pp. 240–55

McCarthy, Kathleen D., 'Parallel Power Structures: Women and the Voluntary Sphere', in Kathleen D. McCarthy (ed.), *Lady Bountiful Revisited: Women, Philanthropy and Power*, London, Rutgers University Press, 1990

McKernan, Michael, *All In! Australia during the Second World War*, Melbourne, Nelson, 1983

McKernan, Michael, *Beryl Beaurepaire*, Brisbane, University of Queensland Press, 1999

Marginson, Julie, 'à Beckett, Ada Mary (1872–1948)', *Australian Dictionary of Biography*, http://adb.anu.edu.au/biography/a-beckett-ada-mary-4963/text8235

Matthews, Jill Julius, *Dance Hall and Picture Palace: Sydney's Romance with Modernity*, Sydney, Currency Press, 2005

Moore, Andrew, 'Doyle, Alec Broughton (1888–1984)', *Australian Dictionary of Biography*, http://adb.anu.edu.au/biography/doyle-alec-broughton-12436

Murphy, John, *Imagining the Fifties: Private Sentiment and Political Culture in Menzies' Australia*, Sydney, UNSW Press, 2000

Murphy, John, *A Decent Provision: Australian Welfare Policy, 1870–1949*, Farnham, Ashgate, 2011

Musgrove, Nell, *The Scars Remain: A Long History of Forgotten Australians and Children's Institutions*, Melbourne, Australian Scholarly Publishing, 2013

Nicholls, Roberta, 'The Collapse of the Early Council of Women of New Zealand, 1896–1906', *New Zealand Journal of History*, 27 (2), 1993, pp. 157–72

Norris, Ada, *Champions of the Impossible: A History of the National Council of Women of Victoria*, Melbourne, Hawthorn Press, 1978

O'Brien, Joan M., 'Morrison, Sibyl Enid (1895–1961)', *Australian Dictionary of Biography*, http://adb.anu.edu.au/biography/morrison-sibyl-enid-7664/

Offen, Karen, 'Defining Feminism: A Comparative Historical Approach', *Signs*, 14 (Autumn), 1988, pp. 119–57

Offen, Karen, 'Overcoming Hierarchies through Internationalism—The Council Idea: May Wright Sewall's Objectives for the International Council of Women (1888–1904)', Paper presented at the IFRWH/CISH Conference, Amsterdam, August 2010

Oldfield, Audrey, *Woman Suffrage in Australia: A Gift or a Struggle*, Cambridge, Cambridge University Press, 1992

O'Neill, Cate, 'Victorian Family Council (1958–)', *Find and Connect*, http://www.findandconnect.gov.au/ref/vic/biogs/E000630b.htm

Oppenheimer, Melanie, '"The Best P.M. for the Empire in War"?: Lady Helen Munro Ferguson and the Australian Red Cross, 1914–1920', *Australian Historical Studies*, 33 (119), 2002, pp. 108–24

Page, Dorothy, *The National Council of Women: A Centennial History*, Auckland and Wellington, Auckland University Press and Bridget Williams Books, with the National Council of Women of New Zealand, 1996

Paisley, Fiona, 'A Geneva in the Pacific: Reflecting on the First Three Decades of the Pan-Pacific and Southeast Asia Women's Association (PPSEAWA)', in Kathryn Kish Sklar and Thomas Dublin (eds),

SELECT BIBLIOGRAPHY

Women and Social Movements International, 1840 to Present, http://wasi.alexanderstreet.com/help/view/a_geneva_in_the_pacific_reflecting_on_the_first_three_decades_of_the_panpacific_and_south_east_asia_womens_association_ppseawa

Patrick, Alison, 'Brookes, Ivy (1883–1970)', *Australian Dictionary of Biography*, http://adb.anu.edu.au/biography/brookes-ivy-5640

Pitt, Barbara J., 'The History of the National Council of Women in South Australia 1902–1980', typescript, Adelaide, NCWSA, 1986

Putnam, Robert D., 'Bowling Alone: America's Declining Social Capital', *Journal of Democracy*, 6 (1), 1995, pp. 65–78

Aveling [Quartly] Marian and Joy Damousi (eds), *Stepping out of History: Documents of Women at Work in Australia*, Sydney, Allen & Unwin, 1991

Quartly, Marian, 'Defending "the purity of home life" against Socialism: The Founding Years of the Australian Women's National League', *Australian Journal of Politics and History*, 50 (2), 2004, pp. 178–93

Quartly, Marian and Judith Smart, 'The Australian National Council of Women: Its Relations with Government to 1975, *Australian Feminist Studies*, 29 (82), 2014, pp. 352–65

Quartly, Marian, Shurlee Swain and Denise Cuthbert, *The Market in Babies: Stories of Australian Adoption*, Melbourne, Monash University Publishing, 2013

Radi, Heather, 'Whose Child? Custody of Children in NSW 1854–1934', in Judy Mackinolty and Heather Radi (eds), *In Pursuit of Justice: Australian Women and the Law 1788–1979*, Sydney, Hale & Iremonger, 1979, pp. 119–30

Radi, Heather, 'Street, Jessie Mary (1889–1970)', *Australian Dictionary of Biography*, http://adb.anu.edu.au/biography/street-jessie-mary-11789/

Rasmussen, Carolyn, *The Lesser Evil? Opposition to War and Fascism in Australia 1920–1941*, Melbourne, History Department, University of Melbourne, 1992

Reiger, Kerreen, *The Disenchantment of the Home: Modernizing the Australian Family 1880–1940*, Melbourne, Oxford University Press, 1985

Rendall, Jane, *The Origins of Modern Feminism: Women in Britain, France and the United States, 1780–1860*, Basingstoke, Macmillan, 1985

Roe, Michael, *Nine Australian Progressives: Vitalism in Bourgeois Social Thought 1890–1960*, Brisbane, University of Queensland Press Scholars' Library, 1984

Rupp, Leila, *Worlds of Women: The Making of an International Women's Movement*, Princeton, Princeton University Press, 1997

Ryan, Edna and Anne Conlon, *Gentle Invaders: Australian Women at Work*, Melbourne, Penguin, 1989

Sawer, Marian, 'Reclaiming Social Liberalism: The Women's Movement and the State', *Journal of Australian Studies*, 17 (37), 1993, pp. 1–21

Sawer, Marian and Abigail Groves, '"The women's lobby": Networks, Coalition Building and the Women of Middle Australia', *Australian Journal of Political Science*, 29 (3), 1994, pp. 435–59

Sawer, Marian, 'Governing for the Mainstream: Implications for Community Representation', *Australian Journal of Public Administration*, 61 (1), 2002, pp. 39–49

Sawer, Marian, *The Ethical State? Social Liberalism in Australia*, Melbourne, Melbourne University Press, 2003

Sawer, Marian, *Making Women Count: A History of the Women's Electoral Lobby in Australia*, Sydney, UNSW Press, 2008

Sear, Martha, *The National Council of Women of NSW: A Chronology 1896–1996*, Sydney, NCWNSW, 1996

Sher, Noreen, *'The Spirit Lives On': A History of the National Council of Women of Western Australia, 1911–1999*, Perth, NCWWA, 1999

Sheard, Heather, 'Victoria's Baby Health Centres: A History 1917–1950', MEd, University of Melbourne, 2005

Sheridan, Tom and Pat Stretton, 'Pragmatic Procrastination: Governments, Unions and Equal Pay, 1949–68', *Labour History*, 94, May 2008, pp. 133–56

Smart, Judith, 'Feminists, Labour Women and Venereal Disease in Early Twentieth Century Melbourne', *Australian Feminist Studies*, 15, 1992, pp. 25–40

Smart, Judith, 'A Mission to the Home: The Housewives' Association, the Woman's Christian Temperance Union and Protestant Christianity, 1920–40', *Australian Feminist Studies*, 13 (28), 1998, pp. 215–34

Smart, Judith, 'Sex, the State and the "Scarlet Scourge": Gender, Citizenship and Venereal Diseases Regulation in Australia during the Great War', *Women's History Review*, 7 (1), 1998, pp. 5–36

Smart, Judith, 'Modernity and Motherheartedness: Spirituality and Religious Meaning in Australian Women's Suffrage and Citizenship Movements, 1890s–1920s', in Ian Fletcher, L. Nym Mayhall and

Philippa Levine (eds), *Women's Suffrage in the British Empire: Citizenship, Nation and Race*, New York, Routledge, 2000, pp. 51–67

Smart, Judith, 'The Politics of Consumption: The Housewives' Associations in Southeastern Australia before 1950', *Journal of Women's History*, 18 (3), 2006, pp. 13–39

Smart, Judith, 'Ada Norris (1901–1989): Champion of the Impossible', in Fiona Davis, Nell Musgrove and Judith Smart (eds), *Founders, Firsts and Feminists: Women Leaders in Twentieth-century Australia*, Australian Women's Archives Project, 2011, at http://www.womenaustralia.info/leaders/fff

Smart, Judith, 'Women Waging War: The National Council of Women of Victoria 1914–1920', *Victorian Historical Journal*, 85 (1), 2015, pp. 61–82

Smart, Judith and Marian Quartly, 'Identity Politics: The NCWA as Subject and Audience', Australian Historical Association 2007 Regional Conference, University of New England, Armidale, 23–26 September 2007

Smart, Judith and Marian Quartly, 'Mainstream Women's Organisations in Australia: The Challenges of National and International Co-operation after the Great War', *Women's History Review*, 21 (1), 2012, pp. 61–79

Smart, Judith and Marian Quartly, 'Moderate and Mainstream: Leadership in the National Council of Women of Australia 1930s to 1970s', in Joy Damousi, Kim Rubenstein and Mary Tomsic (eds), *Diversity in Leadership: Australian Women, Past and Present*, Canberra, ANU Press, 2014, pp. 129–48

Spenceley, G.F.R., *A Bad Smash: Australia in the Depression of the 1930s*, Melbourne, McPhee Gribble, 1990

Spencer, Anna Garlin, *The Council Idea: A Chronicle of its Prophets and a Tribute to May Wright Sewall: Architect of its Form and Builder of its Method of Work*, New Brunswick NJ, Heidingsfeld Press, 1930

Stephens, Tony, 'Rebel with Plenty of Causes: Freda Brown, 1919–2009', http://www.smh.com.au/comment/obituaries/rebel-with-plenty-of-causes-20090526-bm0i.html

Stephenson, Freda, *Capital Women: A History of the Work of the National Council of Women (ACT) in Canberra 1939–1979*, Canberra, Highland Press for NCWACT, 1992

Sturma, Michael, 'Robertson, Jessie Marian (1909–1976)', *Australian Dictionary of Biography*, http://adb.anu.edu.au/biography/robertson-jessie-marian-11543

Summy, Hilary, 'From Hope ... To Hope: Story of the Australian League of Nations Union, Featuring the Victorian Branch, 1921–1945', PhD thesis, University of Queensland, 2007

Swain, Shurlee with Renate Howe, *Single Mothers and their Children: Disposal, Punishment and Survival in Australia*, Cambridge, Cambridge University Press, 1995

Swain, Shurlee, '"The Supervision of ... Babies Is Woman's Work, and Cannot Be Rightly Done by Men": Victorian Women's Organisations and Female Child Welfare Inspectors 1890–1915', *Victorian Historical Journal*, 79 (2), 2008, pp. 314–27

Swain, Shurlee, 'Social Work', in Judith Smart and Shurlee Swain (eds), *The Encyclopedia of Women and Leadership in Twentieth-Century Australia*, http://www.womenaustralia.info/leaders/biogs/WLE0636b.htm

Taffe, Sue, 'Paul Hasluck', *Collaborating for Indigenous Rights*, National Museum of Australia, http://indigenousrights.net.au/people/pagination/paul_hasluck

Tavan, Gwenda, *The Long Slow Death of White Australia*, Melbourne, Scribe, 2006

Townsend, Deborah, 'Kindergarten Teaching and Pre-school Education', in Judith Smart and Shurlee Swain (eds), *The Encyclopedia of Women and Leadership in Twentieth-century Australia*, http://www.womenaustralia.info/leaders/biogs/WLE0335b.htm

Van Molle, Leen and Eliane Gubin (eds), *Women Changing the World: A History of the International Council of Women*, Brussels, Éditions Racine, 2005

Walter, James, 'Designing Families and Solid Citizens: The Dialectic of Modernity and the Matrimonial Causes Bill of 1959', *Australian Historical Studies*, 32 (116), 2001, pp. 40–56

Watts, Rob, *The Foundations of the National Welfare State*, Sydney, Allen & Unwin, 1987

Williams, George, 'The Federal Parliament and the Protection of Human Rights', Research Paper 20, 1988–89, *My Parliament*, http://www.aph.gov.au/About_Parliament/Parliamentary_Departments/Parliamentary_Library/pubs/rp/rp9899/99rp20

Woollacott, Angela, *To Try Her Fortune in London: Australian Women, Colonialism and Modernity*, New York et al., Oxford University Press, 2001

SELECT BIBLIOGRAPHY

Zimmermann, Susan, 'The Challenge of Multinational Empire for the International Women's Movement: The Hapsburg Monarchy and the Development of Feminist Inter/national Politics', *Journal of Women's History*, 17 (2), 2005, pp. 87–117

INDEX

Page numbers in bold indicate NCWA biographies.

A

à Beckett, Ada 166
Aberdeen, Lady *see* Hamilton-Gordon
Aboriginal citizenship 317–19
Aboriginal policy 178–9, 309, 316–320
Aboriginal women and children 60–1, 171, 177–8, 316–8, 320–1, 416
abortion 174, 179–83, 346, 349, 350, 361, 375–7, 393, 396
adoption 66–8, 177, 270, 346, 377, 396
alcohol controls 80–2, 186–7, 269
Allan, Stella (Vesta) 92, 94, 129
Alley, Diane 383–4, 389, 395–6, 405–18, **406**, 459
Anderson, Louise 14
Anthony, Susan B. 1
Asia-Pacific engagement 147, 215, 224, 243, 331–3
    aid schemes/Twinning 330, 402, 404, 417, 459
    ICW Asia-Pacific Region 460–1
    ICW Regional Seminar/Conferences 330, 332–3, 359, 415
    Indralasia 356–8
    'Pacific Assembly' 226, 243, 331,
    Pan Pacific and Southeast Asia Women's Association 243, 434
    Pan Pacific Women's Conferences 47, 49, 126, 214, 224–5, 243, 263, 331–2
    Papua New Guinea 332, 336, 337, 338
Arbitration court interventions 207, 286–290, 297, 304–06
Archdale, Betty 218
assimilation 186, 315–16, 318, 320, 324, 325–8
Australian Catholic Women's Association 396
Australian Council of Employers' Federations 343
Australian Council of Salaried and Professional Associations 302
Australian Council of Social Service 407
Australian Council of Trade Unions 205, 294, 302, 343
Australian Development Assistance Bureau 404, 415–17, 458–9
Australian Federation of Business and Professional Women's Clubs 207, 218, 284, 289, 305, 386, 413, 425
Australian Federation of University Women 39, 127, 218, 286, 289, 410, 432,
Australian Federation of Women Voters 17, 47, 91, 160, 178, 218, 220, 261, 289, 305
Australian Federation of Women's Societies 39, 120
Australian Labor Party 38, 115, 126, 388
Australian Liaison Committee
    Australian Group of the Liaison Committee of Women's International Organisations 147, 215, 218–21, 261, 263, 289, 291
    Australian Women's Co-operating Committee of Federal Organisations 49–51, 209
    see also International Liaison Committee
Australian National Council for the United Nations 147, 215, 221, 260
Australian National Council of Women 40, 250, 257, 286, 323, 338, 349
    see also National Council of Women of Australia

Australian Nursing Federation 218, 305
Australian Women's Coalition 452, 456
Australian Women's National League 34, 35, 74, 84, 132

B
baby bonus 60, 69, 160–1
Bage, Freda 37
Bage, Mary 40
Bain, Yvonne 428, **429**, 430–7, 462
Barnard, Pat 368
Barrett, Edith 33
Barwick, Garfield 279–81, 312, 330–1
Baylor, Gracia **442**, 443–8, 463
Beaurepaire, Beryl 385–8, 395–9,
Bell, Catherine 16
Better Film League/Good Film League 87, 188, 189,
Bevan, Louisa 15, 92,
Birks, Rose 13–14
Blackburn, Maurice 73, 170,
Board, Ruby 37, 45–6, 137, 142, **143**, 144
Boël, Baroness Marthe 212
Braddon, Lady Alice 12, 27, 91
Breen, Marie 207, 252, 259, 270–2, 277
Brennan, Anna 114, 173, 198
Brewer, Joan 424, 427
Brimblecombe, Mrs 184–5
Brookes, Ivy 18, 137, 144, 158, 161, 166, 243, 245–9, **247**, 251–2, 257–9, 263–6, 276, 310, 313, 317, 324–56, 331, 338, 384
Brotherton, Hilda 184, 206
Brown, Freda 341, 343–4,
Brown, Gladys 354
Buckley, Daphne 460
Byth, Elsie 137, 145, **146**, 147–9, 185, 191, 207, 215, 218, 220–2, 224–6, 243, 263–4, 331

C
'Call to Australia' campaign 248–9
Calwell, Arthur 185–6, 321–3
Campbell-Smith, Mollie 444
Carvosso, Annie 16

Cass, Bettina 407
'Charter' conferences 144–5, 219
Chelmsford, Lady Frances 16, 32
Chifley, Joseph Benedict 158, 184, 220, 310
child and infant welfare 56–62, 66, 71–5, 79, 151, 153, 160–5, 184, 270–2
child care 164–6, 217, 303, 339, 346, 349, 355, 370, 385, 414
child endowment 70, 96, 160–2, 171–2, 180, 182–3, 204, 292, 318
Children's Cinema Council 88
children's rights 61, 371, 384, 461, 467
Chisholm, Rowena 153–4
Christopherson, Leonie **455**, 456–8, 467
Cilento, Dr Phyllis 182–3
citizenship 325–8, 348, 358, 421
Clarke, Lady Caroline 13, 27
Clarke, Lady Janet 12, 13
Coalition of Participating Organisations of Women 432–4, 437, 439, 444
Cockburn, Lady Sarah 13–14
Cocks, Joyce 67, 217, 288
Cold War attitudes 219, 223, 243, 249, 331, 345
  see also communism
Commonwealth Immigration Advisory Committee/Council 186, 265, 324, 327
Commonwealth Investigative Service/Australian Intelligence Service Organisation 243, 249
communism 223–4, 243, 249, 287, 343–4, 383
contraception 57, 174, 180, 182, 185, 346, 349, 458
Corrie, Christina 16
Couchman, Elizabeth (May) 18, 137, 175, 177, 209, 225
Country Women's Association 141, 218, 386, 400, 432
Cowan, Edith 17, 71, 93, 102, 133
Cumbrae-Stewart, Zina 19, 176, 181, 190
Curtin, John 70, 158, 171, 205

INDEX

D

Dale, Marguerite 121
Daly, Jean 223, 263–4, 285–6, 289, 290
Darian-Smith, Kate 206
Dart, Dr Ellice 176, 180
Dart, Pat 456
Davey, Margaret 366, 370, 381, **382**, 383, 385–95, 399
David, Caroline 81
delinquency 169, 250, 268–99, 271, 273
Dell, Dame Miriam 404–05, 409, 415, 458
Denman, Lady Gertrude 32–3, 38
disarmament 123–4, 126–7, 193, 208, 210
discrimination 73, 187, 193, 202, 265, 276, 287, 291, 306, 327, 351, 355, 365, 380–1, 385, 388, 394–5, 407–9, 412, 463–4, 470
divorce *see* marriage and divorce reform
Dobson, Emily **9**, 10–13, 28–31, 33, 36, 38, 40–1, 43–6, 76, 91, 129, 135, 148
Dodds, Lady Emily 11, 54
domestic science 75–8
domicile, local and international 63–5, 99, 104, 113, 151, 170–4, 276, 279, 333
    see also marriage and divorce reform
Downing, Cecilia 74, 181, 190
Duguid, Charles 317–18
Duncan, Constance 165

E

Eder, Jeanne 217
Edwards, Dorothy 253, 257, 299, **300**, 320, 329–33, 335–7, 402–4
Ellicott, Robert 390, 399
Emily McPherson College of Domestic Economy 75, 154
environmental pollution 360–1, 439
equal opportunity 207, 246, 288, 291, 294, 301–2, 385, 395, 411–4, 430
equal pay/equality in the workplace 73, 90, 94–7, 147, 159, 193, 200–7, 222–3, 250, 265, 283–99, 301–8, 333, 338, 350, 352, 355, 384
eugenics 167, 174–5, 179
Everett, Rosemary 453

F

family, concept of 4–5, 22, 52, 250, 267–8, 271, 391–2
Family Law Bill 372–4
family policy 250, 267–8, 271–2, 278, 370–1, 391–2, 414–15, 471
family wage 69, 70, 162, 200, 206, 223, 292–3
family welfare 104, 141, 147, 244, 271–2,
Fatin, Wendy 431
Federal Censorship Board 87, 88, 191–2
Federal Council of the National Councils of Women of Australia 41, 43–7, 49, 72, 79, 93, 97, 116, 124, 153, 224
feminism 3, 19, 56, 347, 407,
    anti-feminism 347, 371, 389–90
    liberal feminism 20, 347
    maternal feminism 53–4, 56
Festival of Light 370
film censorship and control 86–8, 188–92, 273
Fitzherbert, Margaret 301
Forster, Lady Rachel 38–41, 44, 123

Francis, Babette 402, 408, 451
Fraser, Malcolm 380, 384–6, 388, 395, 399
Frost, Phyllis 269–71, 273–4,
Fry, Edith 36
Furley, Eileen 264

G

Galley, Janet 417, 433, 441
gender equality 22, 55, 89–90, 93, 103, 104–05, 131–2, 159, 196, 214, 219, 246, 250
Gibson, Ruth 253, 261, **262**, 265, 278, 287, 289, 291–2, 294, 302, 331
Giddings, Maureen **426**, 427–8, 461
Glencross, Eleanor 39, 40, 49, 88
Goldstein, Vida 12, 27, 34, 59–60, 62, 72, 91, 92, 94, 108, 111
Goode, Agnes 76, 98, 101
Goodisson, Lillie 175, 180, 189

Gormanston, Lady 11
Gough, Evelyn 12, 53, 92
Greek children affair 223–4
Guilfoyle, Margaret 391–2, 399

H

Hague Peace Conferences 3, 5, 107–09
Hallenstein, Philippa 304, 408
Hamilton, Anne 253–4, 274, 326, 333, **334**, 335–6, 339
Hamilton-Gordon, Ishbel, Marchioness of Aberdeen and Temair 6, 10–12, 26–8, 32, 35, 43–4, 50–1, 54, 110, 112, 118, 122, 133–4, 209
Hampden, Lady 7, 10
Hasluck, Paul 314–16, 318–20, 324, 337
Hawke, R.J. 405, 408–10, 423–4, 428
Haxton, Nadia 378
Hay, Mrs David 337–9
Heagney, Muriel 202–03
Henderson, Jessie 119, 127
Henry, Alice 72
Hill, Edna 165–7, 169
Hogg, Dr Kate 74
Holder, Lady 14
Holmes, Phoebe 133
Holt, Harold 294, 301, 324–5
Hooton, Ettie 17
Horne, Shirley 303, 305, 307.411, 413
Housewives' Associations 39, 76, 155, 202, 258
Howard, John 439, 441, 443, 449
Hughes, Eva 84
Human Rights Bill 374–5

I

Industrial Arbitration (Female Rates) Amendment Act (NSW) 295–7
infant mortality 57, 60, 74, 355
Infant Protection Act NSW 63
International Council of Women 20, 35, 47, 58, 61, 64–5, 68, 77, 80, 86, 90, 92, 94, 96–7, 100, 102–03, 105–08, 115–16, 118–19, 126–7, 140–01, 145, 159, 167, 170, 172, 174–6, 190, 194–5, 199, 201–02, 204, 207, 211–12, 223, 269–75, 284, 292, 310, 333, 344, 357, 359, 403–05, 449, 458–60, 464–5, 468, 470
   the Australia problem 26–32
   creation of ICW Asia-Pacific Region 460–61
   formation 2, 6
   ideals and objectives 2–4, 17,
   standing committees 33, 34, 80, 96, 108, 217,
International Women's Year 360, 379–80
International Year of the Child 392–3
Isbister, Claire 370–2, 377–8, 392–3, 400–80

J

Jackson, Anne 408
Jacques, Catherine 269
James, Lady Gwenyfred 17, 133,
Joske, Percy 277, 279–81
Joyner, Ethel 17
Jull, Dr Roberta 84, 133–4,

K

Keating, Paul 428, 434–5
Keays, Helen 303–04
King, Ethleen 270, 286
Kingston, Molly 286–90
Kongres Wanita Indonesia 336
Kumm, Gertrude 251

L

Labor Party see Australian Labor Party
Labor Party women 17, 34, 60, 70, 76, 126, 155–6, 160, 162, 173, 259
Lady Teachers' Association (Vic) 95
Lake, Marilyn 56, 350
Latham, John 170, 197, 208
Lawrence, Carmen 435
League of Nations: 5, 21, 49, 105–06, 115–16, 118, 121, 123–7, 193, 197, 208–10, 214–15
   Australian delegates 47, 119, 120, 122, 129, 132–3, 210–11, 222, 290
   League of Nations Conference on the Codification of International Laws 116, 194

INDEX

League of Nations Union 119, 211
League of Nations Women's Consultative Committee on Nationality 117, 194, 196,
Lefebvre, Sylvie 269
L'Estrange, Noela 431–3, 435, 462, 468
Liberal Party of Australia 258–9, 264, 288, 301, 322, 324, 381–3, 385–6, 388, 427, 437, 443
Lidgard, Chris 440
Longman, Irene 70, 180
Lowe, Annie 92
Lyons, Dame Enid 154, 182–3, 260

M

MacDonald, Louisa 7
Macintosh, Laurel 253–4, 383–4, 396–7, **398**, 401–02, 404, 417, 458, 460, 468
McCarthy, Kathleen 5
McConnell, Joyce 357, 363–7, **369**, 372–5, 379, 381, 386, 388, 396, 403, 410
McCorkindale, Isabel 221–3, 285
McGuire, Mrs Paul 214
McIntyre, Margaret 149
McKernan, Michael 188
McLean, Margaret 12
McMahon, William 349–2, 354
Marks, Gladys 127
marriage and divorce reform 63–4, 68, 90, 98–104, 170–4, 275–81, 372–4
maternalism 3, 54, 56, 97, 105, 178, 245, 339
  see also family, concept of
masculinism 405, 408
Matheson, Audrey 403, 408
Matthews, Jill Julius 86
Matthews, May 126, 155–6, 189
Mayo, Helen 74
Melbourne Ladies' Benevolent Society 62, 154
Melbourne Peace Society 109
Menzies, Robert Gordon 158, 162, 204, 223, 257–9, 279, 298–9, 301
Metcalfe, Thelma 253, 261, 295, **296**, 298, 317, 326, 332

Michaelis, Alice 43–4, 119
Miethke, Adelaide 137, **138**, 139–42, 145, 157, 161–2, 171, 213, 225
migration 15, 34, 147, 184–6, 200, 222, 325, 326
  see also White Australia policy; Commonwealth Immigration Advisory Council
Mitchell, Roma 279, 281–2
Mocatta, Necia 418, **422**, 423–4, 427, 441, 459–60
moral standards/moral welfare 17, 19, 33, 52, 54, 61, 70–1, 80–6, 102, 156, 160, 163, 166, 174, 181, 187–8, 190–2, 248, 250, 267–70, 273–4, 340, 361, 376, 470
Morice, Mrs J.P. 15
Morrison, Sibyl 103
Moss, May 124, **125**, 126, 132, 134–7, 141, 159, 180, 182, 195–7, 210, 224
multiculturalism 345, 403, 416
Munro Ferguson, Lady Helen 36
Murphy, John 156, 162, 268
Murphy, Lionel 372–5
Muscio, Mildred 47, **48**, 50, 55, 69, 70, 86–7, 126–7, 153, 155, 157, 210–11

N

National Council of Women of Australia
  constitution 32–3, 50–1, 132–4, 148–9, 255, 389, 447–9,
  formation 18–19, 50–1, 127
  government grants to NCWA 352, 394, 411, 423, 425, 427, 431, 435, 438, 440, 445–6
  numbers of affiliates 135–6, 254–5, 420–1
  office in Canberra 394, 427, 446–7, 449–50
  Tasmanian problem 148–50, 447–8
National Council of Women of Canada 6, 27–8, 107, 216
National Council of Women of Greece 223
National Council of Women of Launceston 148–50, 254–55, 256–57, 318, 420

- 493 -

National Council of Women of New South Wales 1, 7, 29–30, 64–7, 74–7, 94–5, 100, 113–15, 122–4, 136, 254–6, 288–9, 295–6, 317, 370, 375–8, 391–2, 420
National Council of Women of New Zealand 8, 15
National Council of Women of Papua New Guinea, attempts to form 336–7
National Council of Women of Queensland 15–16, 36, 40, 94–5, 112, 114, 203, 254–6, 276–7, 291–2, 294, 317, 369–71, 413, 420
National Council of Women of South Australia 13–15, 154, 177, 204, 254–5, 291–3, 317–20, 370–1, 414, 420
National Council of Women of Tasmania 11, 29, 82, 91–2, 135, 147–50, 203, 254–5, 420
National Council of Women of Thailand 335
National Council of Women of the Australian Capital Territory 18–19, 136–7, 305, 363, 420–1
National Council of Women of the Netherlands 114
National Council of Women of the Northern Territory 18–19, 256, 415
National Council of Women of the Pacific, proposal for 243
National Council of Women of the Solomon Islands 461
National Council of Women of the United States 2, 27, 216, 414
National Council of Women of Victoria 12–13, 29–30, 35–6, 40–4, 72–8, 81–5, 92–6, 136–7, 203, 254–5, 286–7, 292, 303–05, 307–08, 408, 411, 420
National Council of Women of Western Australia 16, 35–6, 51, 112, 133–4, 203, 254–5, 295, 316–17, 319, 420
National Health and Medical Research Council 182–5
national insurance 151, 155–8
National Woman Suffrage Association (USA) 2

nationality of married women 106, 113–17, 127, 173, 193–9, 222
Newman, Joscelyn 439–40, 444–5
Nicholls, Elizabeth 13
Norris, Ada 167, **168**, 251–2, 333, 384, 410, 448,
  convenor of ICW standing committee on migration 404
  Equal Pay campaign 292, 294–5
  interventions in Arbitration Court 286, 297, 305–07
  migration and the Commonwealth Immigration Advisory Council 186, 224, 320, 323–5, 327–8
  president of NCWA 254, 266, 304,
  UN Commission for Status of Women 200, 265, 312,
  UNAA Status of Women Committee 341, 343, 389, 397
  UNAA National Committee for IWY 364, 380, 385–6,
  UNAA National Committee on the Status of Women/UNAA National Status of Women and Decade for Women Committee 380–1, 384, 386–9, 393–5
  Women's hall of residence, PNG 337–8

O

Offen, Karen 3
Office of Women's Affairs/Office of the Status of Women 384, 388, 409, 423–4, 428, 435, 439, 444–5, 468

P

Paisley, Fiona 225
Pankhurst, Adela 111
Pannam, Jan 411
Parker, Judith 447–9, **450**, 451–4, 464–5
peace and international arbitration [see also disarmament] 17, 106–09, 118–19, 122–7, 207–08, 210–11, 333, 470–1
Pennington, Frances 286

INDEX

philanthropy 54, 62, 73, 104, 122, 154, 251
postwar reconstruction 142–4, 151, 158, 166, 185, 215
population issues 73, 74, 174–9, 182–4
 see also eugenics; sterilisation of the unfit; White Australia policy
Pratt, Ruby 133, 220
pre-budget consultations/economic summits/Women's Budget Statement 385, 399–400, 405, 412–13, 430
professional women within National Councils 65, 74–5, 77–8, 84–5, 94, 102–03, 192, 252, 273
progressivism 19, 54, 68, 73, 80, 87, 104
prostitution 17, 34, 81, 269, 311–13, 393, 416
public health 17, 34, 80, 153, 186
Putnam, Robert D. 419
Pymm, Alison 33

R

Racial Hygiene Association of NSW 175, 179
Rankin, Annabelle 220, 299
Rawson, Alice 74
Red Cross [Australia] 35–6
Reid, Elizabeth 341–3, 353, 364, 366–7, 386
Reiger, Kerreen 55
Reynolds, Margaret 425
Rich, Ruby 219
Richmond, Katy 345
Right to Life Association 377, 408
Rischbieth, Bessie 17, 39, 47, 49, 84, 91, 112, 120–2, 129, 209, 220
Roberts, Leila 295
Robertson, Agnes 288, 299–300, 332
Roderick, Gwen **436**, 437–41, 460, 462–3
Rosanove, Joan 103
Royal Commission on Human Relationships 376–7, 391
Rumbold, Kathleen 416
Ryan, Susan 405, 409, 424

S

Sawer, Marian 374, 445–6
Scantlebury Brown, Vera 75
Scotford, Jessie 254, 307, 341, **342**, 343–5, 352–4, 356–63, 376, 380, 404, 459, 461
Scott, Rose 7, 15, 30, 34, 38, 56, 59, 64, 68–9, 91, 109–10, 112, 114, 119
Scutt, Jocelynne 407
Sewall, May Wright 1–3, 6, 12–13, 27, 107
Shaw, Anna Howard 92
Sheppard, Kate 8
Skene, Lillias 37, **42**, 43, 46, 61, 159, 170
Southcott, Heather 391–2
social reform 35, 52, 68, 78, 90
social welfare/social services 156, 271, 345, 355, 385, 400
 Aboriginal welfare 315
 family welfare 53, 104, 141, 147, 244, 271–2
 support for mothers 63–5, 70, 160, 169–71
Spence, Catherine 1, 13–14, 58–9, 61,
St Joan's International Social and Political Alliance 218, 223, 264, 277
sterilisation of the unfit 174–6
Stone, Dr Mary Page 53, 92
Stout, Anna 8
Street, Jessie 144, 147, 186, 215, 219, 220, 261, 316
Strickland, Lady Edeline 16–17
Strong, Jessie 109–11
Summers, Dr Anne 409, 411, 424, 428
Sumner, Eleanor 465, 470
Sweet, Georgina 126, 224

T

Tangney, Dorothy 198–9, 220, 280
Tavan, Gwenda 324, 327
Tenison Woods, Mary 285
Thompson, Catherine Hay 12
Thorp, Margaret 112
Tighe, Margaret 408
Tildesley, Beatrice 86
Tildesley, Evelyn 50, 80, 86, 190, 192,

– 495 –

U

unemployment 99, 151–2, 154–9, 163, 183, 201, 203, 400, 405
Union of Australian Women 305, 308, 341, 343–5, 425
United Nations 5, 147, 193, 198, 207, 214, 216, 218, 263, 314, 335
    United Nations Declaration of Human Rights 199, 215, 219, 245, 276, 323
    United Nations Economic and Social Council 21, 216
    United Nations Economic Commission for Asia and the Far East 332
United Nations Association of Australia 341, 343, 361–2, 383, 427
    UNAA National Committtee for IWY 362–7, 380, 383–4, 386
    UNAA National Committee on the Status of Women/UNAA National Status of Women and Decade for Women Committee 380, 384, 386–9, 394, 408, 432
    UNAA Status of Women Committee 341, 463
United Nations Commission on the Status of Women 194, 197, 207, 217, 219, 252, 261, 284, 329, 467
    Australian delegates to CSW 147, 186, 216, 219–22, 263, 265, 290–1, 312,
United Nations Conventions 200, 309, 310–13, 333, 336, 361, 393, 461, 465, 461, 465–7
    Convention on the Elimination of All Forms of Discrimination Against Women 388, 399, 409, 414, 463–4
United Nations Decade for Women 379–80, 383–4, 392–7, 402, 408, 410
    Decade for Women conferences 397–9, 415, 462

V

Vanstone, Amanda 451
venereal disease 80–5, 112, 151, 176, 187–8, 273, 311
Victorian Ladies Benevolent Society 154

W

war 35, 110, 127, 141–2, 211–13
Waterworth, Edith 183–4
Way, Lady Katharine 13
Webb, Jessie 122
Wedgwood, Ivy 260, 299
Wee, Hean Bee **466**, 467–8
Weekes, Clara 77, 84
White Australia policy 200, 309, 314, 321–2, 327–8
Whitlam, Gough 348, 352–3, 356, 365, 368, 372, 374, 378, 385, 39
Whitlam, Margaret 366
Willesee, Don 298
Williams, Agnes 16, 60
Williamson, Minnie 226, 243
Windeyer, Margaret 1–2, 6, 7, 10–11
Woman's Christian Temperance Union 3, 8, 12–16, 39, 58, 71–2, 80, 84, 92, 112, 178, 202, 218, 221, 375
women and the law: women Justices of the Peace, women on juries, women police 67, 71–3, 93, 269, 355
women and work 200–07, 283–308, 408
    affirmative action programs 410, 413–14
    flexible working hours and conditions 401, 411–12, 448–9
    working mothers 159, 164–5, 201–02, 268–71, 283–4, 291–3
    see also equal pay/equality in the workplace; equality of opportunity
Women Who Want To Be Women 396, 399–400, 402, 408, 414
Women's Action Alliance 396
women's advisory councils
    Australian Council for Women 435
    National Advisory Committee for IYW 365, 367,
    National Women's Advisory Council/ National Women's Consultative Council 387, 388, 395–7, 410, 423–4, 427
    Women's Advisory Council (proposed) 351, 353, 367–8, 380, 385

INDEX

Women's Electoral Lobby 308, 334, 345, 349–50, 366, 374, 385, 388, 397, 400–01, 405, 407–08, 413, 423, 425, 434, 444
Women's Employment Board 204–06, 284
Women's International Democratic Federation 216, 219, 261, 343–4
Women's International League for Peace and Freedom 20, 122, 208
Women's Liberation 350, 353, 371–2, 407
women's organisations, government relations with 347, 410, 421, 424, 433–4, 438, 440, 444–6, 451, 453–4
Women's Political Association (Vic) 34, 77, 85, 91–2, 95, 111
women's refuges/health centres 366, 367, 381
women's rights 2, 22, 54, 90, 104, 122–3, 132, 144, 275, 338, 371
Women's Service Guild (WA) 16–17, 34, 84
women, status of 93, 197, 226, 246, 248, 331, 338, 352–3, 355, 414, 430, 435, 468
women's suffrage 1, 8, 17, 33–4, 90–3, 217
women's unpaid work as contribution to GDP 402, 430–3, 462, 468
Wood, Madeline 123–4, 212
World's Congress of Representative Women 1

Y

Young Women's Christian Association 13, 39, 47, 79, 126, 218, 224, 277, 370, 383, 394, 425

Z

Zelling, Sesca 281
Zimmermann, Susan 25